Foundations for Multilingualism in Education

FROM PRINCIPLES TO PRACTICE

Caslon Publishing | Philadelphia

Caslon, Inc.
P.O. box 3248
Philadelphia, PA 19130

caslonpublishing.com

9 8 7 6 5 4 3 2

Library of Congress Cataloging-in-Publication Data

De Jong, Ester J.
    Foundations for multilingualism in education : from principles to
practice / Ester J. de Jong.
        p.   cm.
    Includes bibliographical references and index.
    ISBN 978-1-934000-06-9
    1. Bilingual education—United States.   2. Language and education—
United States.   3. Multilingualism—United States.   4. Multiculturalism—
United States.   I. Ttile.
    LC3731.D4   2011
    370.117'50973—dc22   2011008050

Figure 1.1, Figure 1.2, Table 1.2, Table 1.3
Used by permission, © 2009 by SIL International, Ethnologue: Languages of the
World, 16th Edition

Preface

Foundations for Multilingualism in Education: from Principles to Practice explores linguistic and cultural diversity in education policy, practice, and research. This foundational text is grounded in theoretical understandings about bi/multilingual individuals and their linguistic and cultural development. An important premise is that decisions about languages and language use shape the educational experiences afforded students in significant ways, especially for children who negotiate multilingual and multicultural realities. *Foundations* equips educators with the knowledge and skills they need to make principled decisions about language education in their schools. The book also explores multiple pathways for advocacy through classroom and school practices and policy-making and sets an agenda for research from a multilingual perspective.

Foundations for Multilingualism in Education is written for practicing teachers and administrators working in bilingual or multilingual school settings, for those preparing to work in these settings, and for those interested in conducting research on multilingual issues. The book takes a comprehensive, pluralistic approach to research, theory, policy, and practice, and introduces four core principles that are applicable across a wide range of educational contexts including bilingual, multilingual, and English-medium types of programs. *Foundations* is international in scope and includes examples of multilingual educational practices in the United States as well as in other countries around the world.

Pluralist Perspectives on Research, Theory, Policy, and Practice

Foundations for Multilingualism in Education: from Principles to Practice takes a holistic, context-sensitive approach to bi/multilingualism. It presents bi/multilingualism as a phenomenon to be understood and valued on its own terms, rather than in opposition to or derived from our understandings of monolingual realities. Research, policy, curriculum, pedagogy, and assessment, as well as other educational practices, are considered explicitly through this lens. The book examines what pluralistic discourses look and sound like and compares this pluralist perspective with assimilationist discourses that have dominated the education field. Students identify critical questions that teachers, administrators, researchers, and policy makers can ask from this perspective and learn to align practice (policy, program choices, instruction, assessment) with what we know about multilingual development and the role of students' linguistic and cultural experiences in their success at school.

A Principled Approach

In linking theory to policy, practice, and research, *Foundations for Multilingualism in Education* moves way from traditional dichotomies found in the field of bilingual education. The dichotomous choice between bilingual or English-only instruction, for instance, has led to a preoccupation with finding the one "best model" to work with linguistically and culturally diverse students. Sensitivity to specific local contexts and student populations is often not reflected in this debate.

Instead, this book focuses on four core principles that educators can use to make informed decisions about the schooling of multilingual children.

Principle 1: Striving for Educational Equity

Principle 2: Affirming Identities

Principle 3: Promoting Additive Bi/Multilingualism

Principle 4: Structuring for Integration

These four principles transcend traditional English-medium, bilingual, and multilingual models, and are applicable across a wide range of multilingual contexts.

PRINCIPLE 1: STRIVING FOR EDUCATIONAL EQUITY

The first principle is an overarching principle. Educators who apply the *Principle of Striving for Educational Equity* create school environments where each individual feels valued and respected. They work together to ensure that formal and informal language policies and practices at the school, program, and classroom level fairly represent the diversity in the school and do not discriminate systematically against certain groups of students.

PRINCIPLE 2: AFFIRMING IDENTITIES

The second principle, *Affirming Identities*, draws attention to how languages and cultural experiences are represented in schools. Educators who value this principle demonstrate respect for students' linguistic and cultural identities in school policies and classroom practices. These educators validate students' linguistic and cultural experiences and purposefully create spaces for diverse student voices.

PRINCIPLE 3: PROMOTING ADDITIVE BI/MULTILINGUALISM

The third principle, *Promoting Additive Bi/Multilingualism*, highlights languages as resources to draw on and nurture. Educators who promote additive bi/multilingualism understand the role that students' existing linguistic repertoires play in language and literacy development and in content learning. They create opportunities for using, developing, displaying, and engaging in multiple languages by building on and extending students' existing linguistic repertoires. They make knowing multiple languages an integral part of their curriculum and instructional decisions.

PRINCIPLE 4: STRUCTURING FOR INTEGRATION

The fourth principle, *Structuring for Integration*, recognizes schools as systems where diverse parts are interconnected and can work together to create an environment of mutual respect and equity. Educators who structure for integration promote representative involvement of constituents with diverse perspectives and expertise in decision making, including language policy, program structure, curriculum and materials, classroom structures, assessment practices, and extracurricular activities. These educators reject the notion that language minority groups (students, parents, teachers) must unilaterally assimilate to fit into the existing system. Instead, educators who structure for integration work to build a linguistically and culturally responsive system for all of their constituents.

SPECIAL FEATURES

Foundations for Multilingualism in Education: from Principles to Practice includes special features within the text to structure learning, teaching, and research.

Guiding Questions. Each chapter opens with a series of questions that preview the main ideas and concepts of the chapter. Guiding Questions encourage students to set a purpose for reading and to summarize and synthesize major concepts. Guiding Questions also prepare students to apply what they learn in the chapter to practice.

Key Terms. Key Terms are listed at the beginning of each chapter. Key Terms are highlighted and clearly defined in the text when first used. Key Terms can also be found in the Glossary for quick reference.

Critical Issues. Critical Issues questions at the end of each chapter invite students to review and critically analyze the main ideas discussed in the chapter. Critical Issues questions can be used to guide group discussion or responded to individually.

Application & Reflection Activities. Application and Reflection Activities help readers link what they have read to their own context. These activities also challenge readers to consider the implications of pluralist and assimilationist perspectives for research and scholarship. Students and professors can take these activities and develop them into more comprehensive research or application projects.

Recommended Readings. Each chapter concludes with a list of books and articles recommended by the author. The annotated list encourages readers to further explore key issues.

Glossary. The Glossary provides a quick reference to the vocabulary used in the field and to the Key Terms highlighted in the book.

Acknowledgements

This book is the result of ongoing interactions and conversations with many people, and I am grateful for all of the mentors and teachers that I have had the honor of meeting and who have helped with the writing of this book. María Estela Brisk and Susan McGilvray-Rivet deserve special mention as they planted the seeds for the book as I began working in the United States.

During my doctoral work at Boston University, María Estela Brisk introduced me to the notion that we must look at bilinguals 'as bilinguals' and not as deficient monolinguals. She pushed me to think about what a bilingual perspective entails. One important theme in this book is exactly this question—what research questions, what policies, and what instructional practices characterize a multilingual perspective? This book would not have been the same without her continued mentorship and on-going willingness to engage in many conversations about teaching, teachers, and multilingual children.

Working for the Framingham Public Schools with Susan McGilvray-Rivet (then Director for Bilingual Education) was an equally valuable learning experience. Sue helped me see the importance of guiding administrators and teachers to understand how theory translates into practice and how to approach implementation with integrity. She and the many bilingual and English as a Second Language teachers in the district that I had the honor of working with gave me the opportunity to engage in this translation process. Based on these experiences, this book considers specifically how the question of quality education plays out in different classroom and school contexts.

Finally, a special thanks is due to my editor, Rebecca Freeman Field. Her faith in the book, her expertise in this field, her enthusiasm, feedback, and

constant support were contagious and of tremendous help. Her encourage-
ment and patience allowed me to find my voice and this book to find its own
path. Publisher Charles Field's guidance and organization have also been a
great source of support. The final draft benefited greatly from copy editor
Debby Smith's eye for detail and consistency.

Contents

Educators as Language Decision Makers and Negotiators

1

GUIDING QUESTIONS

- *In what ways does the statement "Multilingualism is the norm around the world" need to be qualified?*
- *In what ways do educators advocate through their language decisions?*
- *What role do language ideologies play in influencing these decisions?*

KEY TERMS

advocacy

bilingual learners

emergent bilinguals

English language learner (ELL)

regional minority languages

official language

vernacular language

language ideology

pluralist discourses

assimilation

assimilationist discourses

native language

second language

societal or dominant language

minority or dominated language

Majula Datta grew up learning Bengali, Punjabi, Hindi, and English, which he used for different purposes: communication with his family and community and learning in school. He did not become aware of his multilingualism until he moved to England. He notes, "I must say I found it hard to relate to the term, because not only did I think multilingualism was the norm, but until then I had not thought of my languages as different or separate entities" (Datta, 2000, p. 1). He was also surprised to observe how many primary school students who spoke languages other than British English at home did not use these languages in school. Probing further, he found that the languages other than English were devalued in the classroom; these languages were invisible and not used as resources for teaching and learning. As a result, students were ashamed of their cultures and of speaking and using their native languages.

Datta's vignette introduces themes and lines of inquiry that are outlined in this chapter and repeated throughout the book as we examine the extent to which multilingualism is the norm around the world, the position of and response to linguistic and cultural diversity in society and particularly in schools, and the role that teachers play in making decisions about language in their own contexts.

Broadening Our View of Advocacy

Cohen, de la Vega, and Watson (2001, pp. 6–8) argue that **advocacy** is about visualizing change for a better society. They define advocacy as consisting of organized efforts and actions based on the reality of "what is" so that visions of "what should be" in a just, decent society become a reality. Advocacy efforts are directed at highlighting critical issues that have been ignored and submerged, at influencing public attitudes, and at enacting and implementing laws and public policies. For many educators, organized advocacy primarily involves working with politicians to design and pass or fight against bills. In this view, things that advocates do include writing letters to the editor and visiting the legislature or calling state or local representatives to let them know how they want them to vote.

While formal state- and national-level political advocacy is important (legislative bills, when passed, will affect many individuals), it is only one of many possible sites of advocacy (i.e., where advocacy takes place) and acts of advocacy (i.e., what counts as advocacy). Even though we tend not to label their actions as "advocacy," educators (including teachers, administrators, and teacher educators) are engaged in many different acts of advocacy at the classroom, program, school, and district levels.

For example, Helen was a middle school social studies teacher in the United States, working with primarily African American students in a largely urban district. She was told she had to use the district's adopted social studies textbook. When she analyzed the new social studies series, Helen saw that it did a poor job of representing the history and experiences of her students and preferred not to use it, knowing her students would have a difficult time connecting to the content. But she was under a mandate from the district. This is what Helen decided to do. Instead of teaching directly from the book, she engaged her students in a critical analysis of how the textbook (mis)represented minorities and provided supplementary materials that illustrated alternative interpretations of historical events. Helen's example illustrates that advocacy is more than what happens in the legislature and involves more than actions related to formal laws or bills. Helen's initial analysis of the text, her pedagogical approach, and her subsequent selection of supplemental material aimed at providing her students with access to instruction that was meaningful for them can be seen as acts of advocacy.

This broader definition of advocacy includes teachers' making decisions in their own classrooms, as well as educators' implementing policies and practices at the school and district levels. As Nieto (2002) observes, "As educators, all decisions we make, no matter how neutral they may seem, have an impact on the lives and experiences of our students" (Nieto, 2002, p. 43). Through their daily actions, administrators and teachers negotiate a myriad of choices related to teaching and learning, making decisions about programs, curriculum (what to teach), pedagogy (how to teach), and accountability and assessment practices.

The Centrality of Language in Schools

Language is an integral part of these processes as it shapes the ways in which teachers' decisions are put into practice. Language is the medium through which teachers directly and indirectly communicate to students what is valued by the school, that is, what is considered important and worthy of knowing and learning, and, by extension, also what is devalued. For Helen, including discussions about minority representation in history textbooks expressed her valuing of diversity. Teachers also make more specific linguistic decisions, that is, they make choices about which languages are permitted and where and how can they be used. In many schools, nonstandard varieties or languages other than the official, standard school languages are allowed for social purposes in the cafeteria or on the playground but not for academic learning or in the classroom.

Because of the centrality of language in school, formal and informal decisions about language choice and language use will have an important impact on the kind of learning environment that is created for students (Corson, 1999, 2001). A theme that runs through this book is that educators are language policy makers. Pennycook (2001), who has analyzed different postcolonial language policies, argues:

> For many of us, language policy seems to be something that other people do. . . . But actually, language policies and language politics are part of what each of us use every day. When we fight in support of a community-based language program, when we allow or disallow the use of one language or another in our classrooms, when we choose which language to use in Congress, conversations, conferences, or curricula, we are making language policy. (p. 215)

Taking into consideration all we know about multilingualism, biliteracy development, and high-quality schooling for multilingual learners, we ask throughout this book, What policies and practices support linguistically and culturally diverse students, students who speak languages other than the national language at home? This question is particularly important for those who enter school with little or no proficiency in the standard language of school and requires that we return to an examination of the centrality of language and language decisions at different policy levels (federal, state, district, school, and the classroom). But first we look at two examples that illustrate the implications of how educators label students and how their decisions affect student classroom participation.

LABELING STUDENTS

The field of second language teaching and bilingual education has generated many terms, acronyms, and abbreviations to refer to students and program types (more on this in Chapter 5). The choices we make, however, are never neutral. The terminology we use to describe **bilingual learners,** or children growing up in multilingual environments, reflects our thinking about the value of bilingualism and our expectations for students who speak languages other than the school language. García (2008), for example, has argued for the term **emergent bilinguals** to capture the bilingual potential of each child and the bilingual practices that will characterize a bilingual child's life. The term acknowledges that, regardless of what schools do, the children live in and daily negotiate bilingual environments. García's terminology aims to position multilingual learners and their experiences as a whole (i.e., within and across languages) and to validate and legitimate all their experiences. In the United Kingdom, *English as an additional language (EAL)* refers to a student who speaks a language other than English at home and who is limited in English proficiency. This term attempts to include the fact that students come to school with other language skills. These word choices focus our attention on both (or multiple) languages and keeps bilingualism at the forefront of our thinking as educators.

The terms **English language learner (ELL)** or, the older term *limited English proficient (LEP)* student, are used in the United States. These terms tend to shift the focus to one language, English (only). U.S. federal policy initially used *limited English speaker*, but it was subsequently replaced by *LEP* in recognition that literacy skills should also be considered for program planning. Although *LEP* has been severely criticized for its deficit orientation, it is still frequently used. The most recent label, *ELL*, also does not incorporate the bilingual experiences of the students it refers to. Some have reduced it even further to *English learner*, making bilingual learners virtually indistinguishable from any other learner in school.

As educators, it is important that we be aware of how we talk about linguistically and culturally diverse students. Teachers sometimes say that their bilingual learners are "nonspeakers" (meaning they do not yet speak English) or that their homes are places "where English is not spoken" (meaning the parents use the native language at home). When these phrases are used, the accompanying view focuses on English (or lack thereof) and what the child or parents do not know rather than what they do know. This orientation, in turn, leads to questions about how best to teach the students English and support achievement in English. These ways of framing the issue easily ignore the role of the child's native language in his or her life and in teaching and learning. They position multilingual learners as having a deficit compared with fluent English speakers and they tip the balance in favor of valuing those learners' experiences that are only in English. Stressing the bilingual and often multilingual experiences of linguistically and culturally diverse students at home, in the community, and at school through our labeling practices reminds educators to pay attention to what is occurring in and through those languages.

STRUCTURING CLASSROOM PARTICIPATION

Teachers establish classroom participation structures by defining how their students are expected to participate in the classroom and what constitutes appropriate interaction among students and between the teacher and the student. They also establish classroom norms that reflect who has the authority to initiate a topic or to change topics and who decides who is allowed to speak. In many North American classrooms, individualism is an important value and interaction patterns reflect this value. Teachers, for example, encourage the practice of having one person speak at a time by insisting that students raise their hands. They call on each student individually, highlighting his or her contribution, and they take charge of directing the flow of interaction. Teachers can also encourage overlapping conversations in which different students add to the development of a particular topic.

These classroom participation structures and expectations for interaction are culture specific, not universal (Peréz, 1998). Research with indigenous students has revealed important cultural differences in the expectations of classroom participation. In a well-known study by Philips (1972) with the Warm Springs Indian Reservation, Anglo teachers complained about their students' lack of participation and responsiveness to teachers' efforts to initiate conversations. They interpreted this behavior as indicative of laziness, lack of motivation, and low academic ability, and as a consequence, their expectations for the academic achievement of their students were low. Subsequent observations and interviews showed that in their homes and community, Native American students freely talked and communicated their ideas. An important difference was that in their homes the students were not expected to individually and publicly display their knowledge. Native American cultural norms emphasize cooperation and collective action. Once the teachers restructured their classrooms to incorporate more cooperative learning and to build a shared knowledge base, the students felt more comfortable participating in the classroom and responding to teachers' questions.

Philips's study stresses the importance of applying alternative cultural frames to help understand the behavior of linguistically and culturally diverse students. Her study also demonstrates the impact that teachers have on students' learning, for example, through their verbal and nonverbal feedback about what is linguistically and culturally accepted and not accepted and through the practices they implement in their classrooms. If classroom practices are consistently at odds with the linguistic and cultural experiences of minority students, these students can be systematically excluded from classroom activities that could be as meaningful to them as mainstream-oriented activities are to majority students. Without teacher mediation, this unequal access disadvantages minority students and privileges those students already familiar with the classroom practices that have become the (only) accepted norm in school (Cazden, 2001).

Linguistic Diversity Around the World

The view that educators can advocate for their students through the many linguistic decisions they make is particularly important because linguistic and cultural diversity is more likely to be the norm than the exception in schools. With more than 6,000 identified languages and around 200 nations officially recognized by the United Nations, few countries today can call themselves "monolingual" or "monocultural." International migration has contributed significantly to increased diversity in many societies (Table 1.1). Moreover, recent technological advances, including in the Internet and cable television, allow international migrants to remain connected with their families and communities across linguistic and cultural borders. These connections and communications encourage multilingual practices and result in the on-going engagement in multiple cultural practices. Even Japan, long considered a monolingual and monocultural country except for a very small indigenous group of Ainu speakers (Grosjean, 1982), is facing increased linguistic and cultural diversity through the arrival of workers and their families from Brazil and a growing Korean presence through international business and in higher education (Okano, 2006).

Counting languages, however, is a challenging exercise. Many languages have not yet been officially identified. Also, it is difficult to agree on the

TABLE 1.1

Migration Around the World.

Development group and major area	Number of international migrants (millions)					Percentage distribution of international migrants		International migrants as a percentage of the population	
	1990	1995	2000	2005	1990	2005	1990	2005
World	154.8	165.1	176.7	190.6	100.0	100.0	2.9	3.0
More developed regions	82.4	94.9	105.0	115.4	53.2	60.5	7.2	9.5
Less developed regions	72.6	70.2	71.7	75.2	46.8	39.5	1.8	1.4
Least developed countries	11.0	12.2	10.2	10.5	7.1	5.5	2.1	1.4
Africa	16.4	17.9	16.5	17.1	10.6	9.0	2.6	1.9
Asia	49.8	47.2	50.3	53.3	32.2	28.0	1.6	1.4
Latin America and the Caribbean	7.0	6.1	6.3	6.6	4.5	3.5	1.6	1.2
Northern America	27.6	33.6	40.4	44.5	17.8	23.3	9.7	13.5
Europe	49.4	55.3	58.2	64.1	31.9	33.6	6.8	8.8
Oceania	4.8	5.1	5.1	5.0	3.1	2.6	17.8	15.2

From International Migration Report: A Global Assessment, by Department of Social and Economic Affairs, Population Division, © 2006 United Nations. Reprinted with the permission of the United Nations.

criteria that identify a language as separate from all others. Speakers may perceive their language as being separate from the language spoken by another group even though linguistic criteria suggest that the two languages are the same. Finally, it is difficult to establish when a language is a separate language and not a dialect or variety of a language. While mutual intelligibility is a common criterion to distinguish languages, this distinction is not universally applicable. Danes and Norwegians can understand each other but would certainly claim they speak different languages. Many languages in China (despite a common script) are mutually unintelligible, yet are considered dialects of the same language spoken in China. New varieties of British English have emerged in postcolonial settings (such as India, Singapore, and Nigeria). Are these linguistic varieties to be considered separate languages or varieties of English, similar to dialects of English as spoken in the United Kingdom? These examples illustrate why it is difficult to count languages definitively, as well as why it is necessary to consider factors such as political boundaries and power, in addition to linguistic criteria, when identifying languages. The actual numbers reported can therefore differ widely, depending on the criteria used to distinguish different languages.

If we keep this caveat in mind, several patterns emerge when we take a global view of linguistic diversity. For example, the ratio of the estimated number of languages to the total number of nations makes clear that linguistic diversity is the global norm. There is, however, tremendous variation in how languages are distributed geographically, numerically, and politically in terms of the status they are given within and across nations.

Some countries house significantly more languages than others (Figure 1.1; Table 1.2). On one extreme are nations such as Papua New Guinea (820 living languages), Nigeria (516), and India (427). On the opposite extreme are South Korea (2 living languages), Madagascar (15), and New Zealand (21). Though western European countries are often thought of as monolingual, France houses 29 living languages and the United Kingdom 18. Even Denmark, a small northern European country, counts more than five languages. Looking at the five continents as a whole, Europe and the North America comprise only 7% of the total number of the world's identified languages. Asia and Africa, with about 64% of the world's languages, are the most linguistically and culturally enriched continents.

Some languages are numerically and geographically more dominant than others. Eleven languages are spoken as first languages by 70% of the world's population. The top ten languages spoken by the most first language speakers are (in numerical order): Chinese, Spanish, English, Arabic, Hindi, Bengali, Portuguese, Russian, Japanese, and (Standard) German (Table 1.3). The 100 most-used languages are spoken by 90% of the world's population, which leaves over 6,000 languages spoken by about 10% of the world's population

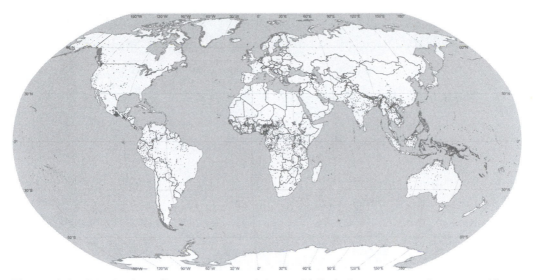

Figure 1.1   Distribution of languages around the world. Each dot represents the geographic center of the 6,909 living languages in the Ethnologue database. (used by permission, © 2009 by SIL International, Ethnologue: Languages of the World, 16th Edition)

(Nettle & Romaine, 2000). The geographical distribution of languages also varies widely. Thus, French is spoken in France and Canada, as well as in several North and West African countries as a result of French colonialism in the 19th century (e.g., Niger, Senegal, and Morocco). Occitan, in contrast, is spoken only in a small region in southern France. Such **regional minority languages** have a long history within a specific geographical region where the language is spoken. They encounter little recognition outside their geographical area, making it often difficult to advocate for their use.

Finally, languages have different functions within and across nations. Some languages enjoy a higher status than others as a result of sociopolitical

TABLE 1.2

Distribution of Languages by Area of Origin

Area	Living languages		Number of speakers			
	Count	**Percent**	**Count**	**Percent**	**Mean**	**Median**
Africa	2,110	30.5	726,453,403	12.2	344,291	25,200
Americas	993	14.4	50,496,321	0.8	50,852	2,300
Asia	2,322	33.6	3,622,771,264	60.8	1,560,194	11,100
Europe	234	3.4	1,553,360,941	26.1	6,638,295	201,500
Pacific	1,250	18.1	6,429,788	0.1	5,144	980
Totals	6,909	100.0	5,959,511,717	100.0	862,572	7,560

Source: used by permission, © 2009 by SIL International, Ethnologue: Languages of the World, 16th Edition

TABLE 1.3

Top 10 Languages in Number of First-Language Speakers

Rank	Language	Primary country	Total countries	Speakers (millions)
1	Chinese	China	31	1,213
2	Spanish	Spain	44	329
3	English	United Kingdom	112	328
4	Arabic	Saudi Arabia	57	221
5	Hindi	India	20	182
6	Bengali	Bangladesh	10	181
7	Portuguese	Portugal	37	178
8	Russian	Russian Federation	33	144
9	Japanese	Japan	25	122
10	German, Standard	Germany	43	90.3

Source: used by permission, © 2009 by SIL International, Ethnologue: Languages of the World, 16th Edition

and economic developments. Languages that have been declared, constitutionally, the **official language** of a particular country are formally supported in important societal institutions, such as schools, government agencies, and businesses. Proficiency in the standard variety of that language is seen as a precondition for access to schools and higher-paying jobs. International migrants fluent in the official language or languages of their country (e.g., Turkish speakers) often find that these languages have a low status with little formal recognition as an immigrant language in another country (e.g., Turkish speakers in the Netherlands). Many local languages in African nations are used only for daily interactions at home and in the community. A **vernacular language**, the language used informally at home and the community, is often not recognized in schools as a legitimate medium for learning.

Similar trends can be observed in the United States. Ethnologue, a database of living languages owned by SIL International, a faith-based nonprofit organization, reports 245 living languages for the United States (Figure 1.2). The 2007 American Community Survey reported 55.4 million individuals 5 years and older who speak a language other than English at home (20% of the total population and up from 8% in 1979). California, New Mexico, Texas (more than 30%), followed by Arizona, Florida, Hawai'i, Nevada, New York, and New Jersey (25–30%) continue to attract most multilinguals (García & Cuellar, 2006). The geographical settlement pattern has become more diverse, however, as immigrants have begun to move to new destinations, such as Nevada, North Carolina, and Georgia (Figure 1.3). No language has been declared the official language of the United States, although more than 20 states have declared English as their official state language. New Mexico

Figure 1.2   Living languages in the United States. (used by permission, © 2009 by SIL International, Ethnologue: Languages of the World, 16th Edition)

has two official languages, English and Spanish. The legal status of indigenous languages differs from that of other minority languages in the United States. Although the individual rights of speakers of all languages are protected through the Constitution and civil rights legislation, indigenous peoples also have a legal right to maintain and develop their native languages in their communities (including using their language as a medium of instruction).

- Of the 55.4 million individuals 5 years old and older who speak a language other than English at home, the majority are Spanish-speaking (62%). The fastest growing language group is Vietnamese, according to the 2007 American Community Survey.

- The following states have the largest percentages of residents who are multilingual: California (43%), New Mexico (36%), Texas (34%), New York (29%), Arizona (29%), Nevada (27%), Florida (26%), Hawai'i (26%), and New Jersey (26%).

- The following states saw the largest percentage increases in the number of speakers of languages other than English over the past decade: Nevada (193%), Georgia (164%), North Carolina (151%), Utah (110%), Arkansas (104%), and Oregon (103%).

- About 8% of emergent multilinguals over the age of 5 were reported as speaking no English in 2007 (up from 5% in 1980).

- Many ELLs are U.S. born (about 60% at the elementary level; about 30% at the secondary level).

Figure 1.3   Linguistic and cultural diversity in the United States

Discourses of Multilingualism

How societies respond to the challenges and opportunities of increased diversity resulting from globalization, technological advances, and continual migration (as well as the loss of human resources as people move away) has been a topic of conversation worldwide. Educators often find themselves at the center of these debates because of their role in the process of socializing students for (future) shared participation in society. The more diverse the student population (Figure 1.4), the more schools are challenged to respond more purposefully to a range of differences, including those of race, gender, language, ethnicity, and socioeconomic background. As schools try to meet these challenges, differences of opinion emerge about diversity in society and about the role of schooling, particularly with respect to students who speak a language other than the official school language at home and who have been socialized in different cultural practices than those assumed in school. This group includes children from indigenous language backgrounds, immigrant children, and children of immigrants. Their language expertise in their language(s) of their home and community will vary as will their proficiency in the standard language used in school. Those who come to school with limited or no proficiency in the school language are often identified (e.g., as ELL or EAL) and eligible for special language services. In addition to immigrant languages, linguistic diversity in classrooms around the world include speakers of local languages in post colonial settings where the European colonial language still dominates in schools (e.g., Touareq in French-language schools in Niger), regional language speakers (e.g., Frisian speakers in the Netherlands), and speakers of nonstandard varieties of the official school language (e.g., Appalachian speakers in the eastern United States).

This diverse group of students challenges educators to provide every student with access to high-quality schooling and equal educational opportunities. Nieto's qualifying phrase, "no matter how neutral they may seem," reminds us that our responses to this challenge and our policy decisions are not neutral but will be informed by certain values, beliefs, and convictions about how best to respond to linguistic and cultural diversity. A **language ideology** refers to the "shared bodies of commonsense notions" about lan-

---

- 44% of PreK–12 (aged 3–17) students were minority students (up from 24% in 1976).
- 22% of PreK–12 students were Hispanic.
- 5% of PreK–12 students were Asian.

Figure 1.4   Enrollment date of Linguistic and cultural diversity in U.S. schools in 2009. Source: http://www.census.gov/newsroom/releases/archives/education/cb11 -tps04.html

guages (Rumsey, 1990; cited in Woolard, 1998, p. 4). They reflect views on what is and is not acceptable language and language use and they play an important role in shaping educational practices.

Language ideologies are constructed and sustained by different constituents in all areas of society, including businesses, the media, and government. Our focus in this book is on language ideologies in schools and how these ideologies may influence which policies and practices are considered appropriate (legitimate) and which are valued within a particular context. For example, governments can officially declare and support more than one language as vehicles for learning in schools, thus expressing the value of multilingualism. If the standard language is considered the only "real" language of learning, schools can also elect to condone the use of the standard version of the school language and punish the use of nonstandard varieties (dialects) of the language. In their classrooms, teachers can encourage, tolerate, or prohibit the use of languages other than the official school language. These choices will depend on their beliefs about diversity in general and the role of the native language for bilingual learners in particular. Heath (1982, 1983) compared literacy practices in two different communities, one African American and one white, and noted distinctly different patterns in how language was used between parents and children, including language around books. She subsequently observed that the schools' response, however, was to uniformly value only those literacy practices that corresponded with middle class literate behaviors. This policy placed the African American students at a disadvantage in school because their practices and resources were not acknowledged.

Educational practices are shaped by personal beliefs and ideologies but do not occur in isolation from broader communal and societal notions about languages in society. Most nation-states have developed "grand narratives" about what it means to be a member of a particular community. Speaking a particular language has traditionally been an important part of the definition of such national identities. Since the early 1900s when large numbers of immigrants came to the United States, one of the most powerful narratives that has defined the country's national identity is that of the immigrant who, simply by learning English, working hard, and leaving his native language and culture behind, achieves educational and economic success (Olneck, 1989; Wodak, deCecilia, Reisigl, & Liebhart, 1999). This narrative of American identity is still visible in language policies in schools through the emphasis on teaching English and the invisibility of languages other than English. It also frequently emerges in the media, for example, when concerns are raised about recent arrivals' not wanting to learn English or not assimilating in the same manner as earlier immigrant groups. When Judge Samuel Kaiser in Texas ordered the mother of a 5-year-old girl to stop speaking Spanish at home so that the child would do well in school and not later be relegated to the job of a maid, his judgment reflected this long-standing language ideology about the relationship between native language use, second language learning, and economic success (Baron, n.d.).

Even though some discourses may be more dominant and visible than others at certain historical junctures, they are rarely uniform and universal. Individuals at different policy levels try to make sense of policies and practices for their own context, and this process of interpretation will be shaped by their personal ideologies as well as those portrayed by their institutions (such as a department of education, a school district, or a school). Being the actual implementers of educational policies, teachers often find themselves negotiating multiple discourses at the same time. For example, Massachusetts voters passed Question 2 in 2002, a law that mandates that all school districts in the state implement programs for students with limited proficiency in English that have English as the main instructional language and allow only limited use of the students' native language. The new law replaced a 20-year-old requirement that instruction be provided in the students' native language and English (bilingual education). For the bilingual teachers in the state who had to become English-only teachers, the change reflected a shift in discourse and practices: from thinking and acting bilingually to thinking and acting monolingually in English.

Teachers who believed that bilingualism is an asset and that bilingual education works found this shift to an English-only program troublesome. For them, a conflict arose between the official discourse (as represented by the law) and their personal discourse about the role of native language use for ELLs in school. In addition, they also had to take the school and district interpretations of the law into account. Districts with a strong pro-bilingual-education orientation and discourse tended to encourage the use of the native language whenever possible. Districts that had been more ambivalent about bilingual education or did not support it tended to interpret the law more strictly, telling teachers not to use the native language (unless absolutely needed). The district's discourse was another level that teachers had to negotiate as they made decisions about language in their classroom. Thus, the extent to which teachers felt safe to implement what they believed in was influenced by the districtwide response to the law and district administrators' interpretation of what limited use of the native language meant. Many teachers negotiated their belief in the importance of bilingualism and the English-only stricture by continuing to stress the use of the native language in their classrooms and explicitly communicating the value of bilingualism to their students and their parents (de Jong, 2008; Gort, de Jong, & Cobb, 2008; Sanchez, 2006). In other words, by maintaining a bilingual discourse within their classroom, they tried to counter the monolingual ideology of the law that devalued the students' native languages for learning.

Their actions remind us that decisions about language in school are based on "characteristic patterns of discourse, reflecting goals, values, and institutional or personal identities" and that these discourses are "never neutral" but are "always structured by ideologies" (Ricento & Hornberger, 1996, p. 409).

Although educational discourses are multiple and diverse, this book explores two broadly defined discourses related to the schooling of bilingual learners: pluralistic discourses and assimilationist discourses (Schmid, 2000), which we also refer to as multilingual and monolingual discourses, or diversifying and homogenizing discourses. These discourses are not simply each other's opposites, that is, we should not view a pluralist solution as the simple opposite of one that is assimilationist-driven. Instead, it is more useful to think of these discourses as two quite different societal conversations guided by distinct foci, values, and questions. Each perspective frames the schooling issues related to linguistic and cultural diversity differently and hence seeks different solutions in the form of policies and decision making about practices at the school, program, and classroom level. We return to the main tenants of these discourses throughout the book and illustrate their implications for bilingual learners. A brief description of the main premises of these discourses follows.

PLURALIST DISCOURSES

Within **pluralist discourses** diversity is accepted as a basic part of an increasingly mobile, global, and diverse world. Linguistic and cultural diversity is a force that, when capitalized on, can play a positive role in society. The pluralist perspective stresses the need to negotiate this diversity with respect and fairness to all. Though this process may be difficult, building on diversity can help to bridge differences, encouraging communication across group or national boundaries and leading to innovative solutions. In contrast, denying a rightful place and nondiscriminatory treatment to individuals and groups who speak different languages and come from different cultural backgrounds can lead to disunity or fragmentation.

In pluralist discourses, bilingualism and multilingualism are valued for the individual, the group, and society. According to this discourse, language is an important symbolic tool for making sense of the world around us; it is not merely a tool for communication or a linguistic system that consists of sounds and ways to put words together into grammatically correct sentences. We use language to express who we are, to describe and understand the world, and to develop and sustain relationships with one another. Through language, parents and community members socialize children into a group's values and norms and create in them a sense of belonging and identity. Thus, denying a child access to his or her native language devalues the experiences encoded in and through that particular language.

Educators who accept multilingualism as the norm and as a desirable outcome of schooling view the two or more languages of a multilingual student as interconnected (holistically) and consider them an integral part of the person. Their educational language policies treat proficiency in languages other than the school language as a resource that contributes to and enriches the learning experience.

An example of such a pluralist approach can be found in the *Guide for the Development of Language Education Policies in Europe* (Beacco & Byram, 2003). Arguing for the equal worth of speakers of different languages and linguistic varieties, the authors promote awareness of language varieties and multilingualism and the development of individuals' linguistic repertoires within and across languages. They advocate for a holistic approach that stresses the importance of coordinating efforts of teaching multiple languages to exploit the full range of linguistic and cultural resources that students have.

Within pluralist discourses we ask ourselves, "How can linguistic diversity be employed in solving social, environmental and technological problems?" (Martí, Ortega, Idiazabal, & others, 2005, p. 11). The issue is not whether bilingualism is good or bad but how multilingual competence can be maintained, sustained, and expanded for the well-being of individuals, groups, and societies.

ASSIMILATIONIST DISCOURSES

The notion of **assimilation** is associated with immigrants coming to a new country and becoming part of that new country in a way that makes them indistinguishable from those who were already living there. They have conformed to the cultural and linguistic norms in that particular society. Within **assimilationist discourses**, monolingualism is the ideal that groups or a particular nation should strive for. The existence of linguistic and cultural diversity is not denied but it is seen as a problem to be addressed because it interferes with certain desired outcomes, such as economic success or academic achievement. A core value is national unity, and a common language is considered an important condition for achieving such unity. The continued presence of multiple languages and cultural diversity will too readily lead to a divided society, inefficiency, chaos, and conflict.

In assimilationist discourses, restricting linguistic and cultural diversity is advocated for cultural, political, and economic reasons. Proponents of assimilationist discourses argue that social cohesion among diverse groups of people requires a shared language and common cultural norms (Silverstein, 1996; Wiley, 2000). Language standardization leads to the delineation of what is and what is not to be considered part of the "standard" or linguistic norm and hence what components of language (vocabulary, pronunciation, grammar) need to be mastered for efficient communication within and among groups.

Shaping decisions from a monolingual discourse perspective outcome has important implications for schools. Educational policies tend to promote competence in the societal language and cultural practices first; proficiency in another language is less important or may be something to be promoted only after competence in the standard language has been demonstrated. Assimilationist discourses take a more fractional view of bilinguals' language systems: students' native language systems are considered to be in competition with the language of school and to interfer with learning that language. Diverse linguistic practices (including signing, speaking more than one language, and speaking nonstandard varieties) that differ from the school norm are therefore problematic because they are seen as hindering educational, economic, and political progress. Emphasis is placed on socializing students from different backgrounds to the cultural norms of the mainstream.

Recent literacy reforms in Australia, the United Kingdom, and the United States exemplify such efforts to standardize literacy instruction with a focus on the official or national language. These countries have recently passed legislation that has resulted in prescribed, presequenced curricula that are expected to be implemented uniformly across widely different contexts. In the United States, this process of homogenization, or the streamlining of diversity into a common norm or structure, has taken the form of Reading First, implemented in the wake of the federal No Child Left Behind Act of 2001. Reading First divides reading instruction into five relatively autonomous components (phonics, phonemic awareness, fluency, vocabulary, and reading comprehensions) and scripts a sequence of activities for teachers to follow, often without modifications for specific populations, such as ELLs.

The assimilationist discourse asks, "How can we achieve greater efficiencies through the reduction and streamlining of diversity?" (Martí et al., 2005, p.11). Within these concerns with ensuring a certain level of homogeneity and shared cultural experiences, it becomes important that multilingual individuals measure up against the desired monolingual norm set by native speakers of the standard language.

A Note on Terminology

In this book, the terms *multilingual*, *multilingualism*, and *multilingual repertoires* are used to capture the complexity of multilingual settings and to acknowledge that languages and literacies are always influenced by the context in which they are used (Hall, Cheng, & Carlson, 2006; Martin Jones & Jones, 2000).

Most research has focused on two-language learners and bilingualism and hence bilingualism and multilingualism are used interchangeably to refer to competence in more than one language.

Bilingual learner is the term used to identify children who are growing up in multi-language environments, including school. This term will be the main term used in this book to refer to students developing multiple linguistic repertoires at home and at school. It is important to recognize that this term reflects a wide range of language skills across the two languages. The subgroup of bilingual learners who have limited skills in the school language and who are entitled to specialized support often have specific labels. In English-dominant societies, these terms include English language learner (ELL), English as additional language speakers or learners (EAL), and limited English proficient (LEP) students

Native language refers to the language the child has grown up speaking. A **second language** is a language learned at a later stage than the native language, often outside the home through school or the media. In multilingual environments this can be more than one language and may not always be the standard language taught in school. In these settings, the distinction between native language and second language is not very meaningful and sets up an artificial contrast between two languages that are intimately connected. *Heritage language* is the language used by a particular ethnic group.

The **societal or dominant language** is the language used for communication in the public domain (media, government, educational institutions). It often is formally declared the official language of the country and typically a high-status, standard language variety that is used and taught in schools. The **minority or dominated language** is that used by a language group that is politically and socially placed in a minority situation but may not necessarily be numerically in the minority. In many school districts in the United States, Spanish is a minority language even though Spanish-speaking students may constitute the largest student group. Majority language speakers are speakers of the dominant, or societal, language. They are increasingly a numerical minority, however, particularly in urban schools.

Outline of the Book

The book has three parts, and we use the assimilationist and pluralist discourses as critical lenses to examine linguistic diversity in schools throughout each part. Part I considers the causes of linguistic and cultural diversity and whether linguistic diversity is a global norm (Chapter 1). It goes on to define multilingual competence and present the main arguments for and against supporting bi- and multilingualism (Chapter 2). The discussion of multilingual repertoires continues in Chapter 3, which takes a closer look at bilingual language acquisition at home, biliteracy development in school, and the factors that affect bilingual or multilingual development. While most theoretical foundations are laid out in this part, these concepts are expanded and reinforced in subsequent chapters to make the link between theory and practice clear throughout the book.

Part II explores language in education policies, especially those involving elementary (primary) and secondary schools. Chapter 4 considers the role of globalization and diversity and the position of English in the world. Chapter 5 focuses on language, policy, and education and revisits the important role that teachers play in making language decisions in schools. It also presents program models that support multilingualism and those that emphasize monolingualism in the dominant language. Chapter 6 takes a more specific look at language policy in the United States, presenting the major legal and historical developments that have shaped how policies have defined the schooling of bilingual children in this country. Chapter 7 examines a long-standing debate about which model is "the best" and discusses the limits of this debate. It also illustrates the current shift toward the features that characterize effective schools for diverse learners.

Part III looks at how educators can arrive at informed policies and practices. It translates the foundational understandings of Parts I and II into four principles to guide decision making, with a particular focus on the school and classroom level. Chapter 8 lays out these four general principles, which involve educational equity, affirming identities, additive multilingualism, and integration. The three chapters that follow illustrate each of these principles, outlining the various language decisions that emerge from each one. Chapter 9 stresses affirming identities of linguisitically and culturally diverse students, in school, Chapter 10 focuses on creating additive bilingual learning environments for all students, and Chapter 11 examines the complex relationship between integration and equity. In the concluding chapter, we return to the dominant discourses that have framed the schooling of bilingual learners and highlight how we as educators can contribute to the reframing of our policies and practices.

CHAPTER 1
Discussion & Activities

Critical Issues

1. Crawford (2008) argues that individual activism for ELLs has little chance of being effective given the general public opinion and federal and state policies against bilingual education in United States. How does this view compare with the view of advocacy presented in this chapter? In what areas do teachers have more or less agency or control to shape their classroom practices?

2. Discuss the statement in the chapter that pluralist and assimilationist views of linguistic and cultural diversity are not simple opposites but different discourses. What does it mean? Can you think of some implications for how you might advocate in favor of policies within one discourse or the other?

3. A school board in District A approved a plan to teach Chinese as a foreign language to native English speakers but rejected a proposal for a program for its Russian-speaking ELLs in Russian and English. How might you explain the co-existence of these policies that, at the surface, appear contradictory, using the two discursive lenses discussed in this chapter?

Application and Reflection

4. Consider Nieto's observation that "all decisions [educators] make, no matter how neutral they may seem, have an impact on the lives and experiences of our students." Make a list of the different decisions teachers make about language in the classroom.

5. What are your beliefs about multilingualism? Which aspects of the pluralist discourse and of the assimilationist discourse do you agree with? Give one or two examples of decisions that are made that are reflective of each discourse.

6. Consider the following origin stories about linguistic diversity. The Tower of Babel is often referred to in the debate about linguistic diversity; it originates in the Old Testament story that is quoted from in the first passage. The other two stories are from Native American cultures. Identify the discourse on multilingualism that each one represents. Illustrate your response with examples from the text.
   - Now the whole world had one language and a common speech. . . . Then they said, "Come, let us build ourselves a city, with a tower

that reaches to the heavens, so that we may make a name for ourselves and not be scattered over the face of the whole earth." But the Lord came down to see the city and the tower, that the men were building. The Lord said, "If as one people speaking the same language they have begun to do this, then nothing they plan to do will be impossible for them. Come, let us go down, and confuse their language, so they will not understand each other." So the Lord scattered them from there over all the earth: and they stopped building the city. That is why it was called Babel; because there the Lord did confuse the language of the whole world. From there the Lord scattered them over the face of the whole earth. (Genesis 11:1, 4–9)

- [Iatiku,] the mother goddess of the Acoma tribe of New Mexico, . . . caused people to speak different languages so that it would not be so easy for them to quarrel. (Cited in Skutnabb-Kangas, 2000, p. 215).
- In the beginning . . . Elder Brother and Younger Brother were instructed through visions by the breath-giver to teach . . . the newly created people [how] to live. All the instructions were in the native language. The people lived happily for many years. . . . Something bad happened and there was a battle among the peaceful people. The head chief then commanded that there would be many languages. . . . The people migrated and divided into different language groups. . . . It is said that when the languages were created, language identified the people—who we are, where we came from, and where we are going." (From Lucille J. Watahomigie, *The Native Language Is a Gift* [1998]; cited in McCarty et al., 2006, p. 1.)

Recommended Readings

Cazden, C. B., John, V. P., & Hymes, D. (1972). *Functions of language in the classroom.* New York: Teachers College Press.

> *In this classic work, Cazden and colleagues, taking a multicultural perspective, explore the many roles that language plays in the classroom. The book illustrates how language use shapes teaching and learning and hence the important role that teachers play in making language decisions.*

Cohen, D., de la Vega, R., & Watson, G. (2001). *Advocacy for social justice: A global action and reflection guide.* West Hartford: Kumarian Press.

> *This book defines advocacy and lays out practical implications for organizations that want to engage in advocacy.*

Ricento, T., & Hornberger, N. H. (1996). Unpeeling the onion: Language planning and policy and the ELT professional. *TESOL Quarterly, 30,* 401–427.

> *This article illustrates the different layers of language policy from the international and national or state level to the institutional level and into the classroom, where teachers interpret policies and make decisions about language choices.*

Wodak, R., de Cillia, R., Reisigl, M., & Liebhart, K. (1999). *The discursive construction of national identity.* Edinburgh: Edinburgh University Press.

> *The authors have explored how national identities are constructed through text, oral and written. Here they illustrate how certain groups in society are positioned as belonging (and, by extension, other groups as not belonging), thus defining the boundaries of the community.*

Multilingualism as Norm and Desired Goal

GUIDING QUESTIONS

- *What are the origins of the need for multilingual proficiency development?*
- *What are some of the outcomes of language contact?*
- *What are the rationales used in pluralist discourses in support of linguistic and cultural diversity?*
- *What rationales are used in the assimilationist discourses to support more homogenizing practices?*

KEY TERMS

bilingalism	metalinguistic awareness
multilingualism	threshold hypothesis
diglossia	linguistic instrumentalism
language domains	imagined community
language shift	lingua franca
circumstantial bilingualism (also folk bilingualism)	moribund languages
	threatened languages
elective bilingualism (also elite bilingualism; voluntary bilingualism)	language revitalization
	linguistic ecology
	linguistic human rights movement
identity	

This chapter illustrates how patterns of language distribution and multilingualism are the result of a complex set of factors, including how contact between speakers of different languages has developed historically. It also presents various arguments that have been put forward, on one hand in support of maintaining the linguistic diversity (pluralist discourses) that has evolved within given areas, and on the other hand in support of encouraging a monolingual norm (assimilationist discourses).

Language Contact: Origins and Outcomes

Some people learn more than one language because they choose to and some do so because they must in order to survive in a new society. For others, learning more than one language is the natural outcome of living in a multilingual environment. This section considers some of the contexts that have promoted **bilingualism** (proficiency in two languages) or **multilingualism** (proficiency in more than two languages) and what happens when different languages come in contact (Figure 2.1).

CAUSES OF LINGUISTIC AND CULTURAL DIVERSITY

Widespread linguistic and cultural diversity is the result of migration, education, geography, and nationalism and political federalism. Nowadays, technology and the outsourcing of human resources also have led to increased contact among speakers of different languages and language varieties.

One of the most common reasons for diversity is the migration from one area to another by people from different language groups. This movement of people originates in push factors (negative factors in their home country that drive people to leave) and pull factors (positive factors of a country that encourage people to move and settle there). One extreme push factor is forced migration (slavery). In the 17th, 18th, and 19th centuries many West African people were forced from their home country to work as slaves in the Caribbean, South America, and the United States, contributing to the diversity in these countries today. Push factors are also responsible for relocation of refugees. The Refugee Act of 1980 defines refugees as individuals who are "unable or unwilling to return to their country of nationality because of a well-founded fear of persecution on account of race, religion, nationality, membership in a particular social group, or political opinion." Refugee populations tend to increase rapidly in certain areas in response to specific events. Cuban political exiles arrived in Miami in the early 1960s to escape Fidel Castro's communist regime. The Yugoslav civil war resulted in the resettlement of Croatian and Slavic refugees in Germany, Denmark, and other European nations. Natural disasters, such as hurricanes, draughts, and tsunamis, have also led to the involuntary movement of people.

Pull factors include the promise of political or religious freedom, employment, and better schools. A country's need for specific labor often draws immigrants. The United Nations (2009) reports that the number of international migrants increased from 155 million in 1990 to 191 million in 2005, with the flow going mostly from less developed regions (40% of all international migrants) to developed countries (60% of all international migrants). International migrants are the largest percentage of the population in North America (14%) and Australia/Oceania (15%). At times, countries actively

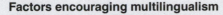

Factors encouraging multilingualism
- Migration: **push factors** force people to move; **pull factors** encourage migration to certain areas
- Military invasion and colonial expansion
- Geography: mountains, rivers, and border areas
- Education: languages taught in school

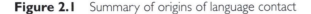

Figure 2.1   Summary of origins of language contact

recruit workers from other places. U.S. businesses made it very attractive and easy for Mexican laborers in the 1920s to come to the United States and work on the railroads and in construction. At the time, the economic situation in Mexico was depressed and migrating for the better pay offered in the United States was a survival strategy for many families. The governments of France, Germany, the Netherlands, and other western European countries made similar recruitment efforts among Turkish and Moroccan workers to help rebuild the economy after World War II. Countries may also recruit and admit individuals representing specific areas of skilled labor, such as computer experts.

Migration continues to be one of the main contributing factors to linguistic and cultural diversity around the world. Military invasion and colonial expansion, however, can also contribute to the creation (often forced) of multilingual settings. Some countries have individual pockets of regional minority languages that are historically related to a particular geographical area and incorporated into a new nation-state. Welsh and Gaelic in Great Britain, Basque in France and Spain, and Frisian in the Netherlands are examples. When the British and French began colonizing Africa and Southeast Asia, ethnic groups already existed there with their own languages and cultures in different kingdoms and territories. The artificial borders that the colonizers created around these pre-existing (and often antagonistic) groups and the subsequent imposition of the European language on the speakers of other languages led to complex multilingual and multicultural societies. In the Phillipines, the United States imposed English on an already diverse linguistic environment that included Filipino, Tagalog, and Spanish. Some political units with different languages are united into a federal system and are officially bilingual or multilingual. Flemish and French are the official languages of Belgium, and German, French, Italian, and Romansch are the official languages of Switzerland. Each language is linked to its own territory and governmental structures.

Mountains, rivers, and other geographical features can encourage the co-existence of many different languages in one area. The linguistic diversity in New Guinea, for example, is the result of a mountainous geography and many little islands. The relative isolation that results from these natural boundaries supports the maintenance of certain languages, yet the need to communicate with others promotes bi- or multilingualism (Nettle, 1998). Bilingualism is also natural in political border areas where individuals from different language groups belonging to different nations interact daily. Danish and German speakers understand and speak each other's language on the north Germany–south Denmark boundary. Dutch and German are both used in the northern part of Belgium and Dutch and French on the border with France.

Finally, education can also contribute to language contact, even if it is in some cases only minimally by learning a foreign language in school. Currently, the role of English as a language for international communication is greatly affecting educational practices world wide. It is estimated that there are about 750 million speakers of English, including first and second/foreign language speakers (Graddol, 2006). English is the official language of the traditionally English-speaking nations of Canada, Australia, New Zealand, the United States, and the United Kingdom, and it has also been maintained as the language of government and education in many nations previously colonized by the British in Southeast Asia (e.g., India, Pakistan, Singapore) and Africa (e.g., Nigeria, Kenya, Tanzania). Added to these two groups are those who are learning English as a foreign language in school. The status of English as the international language for business, technology, and science has made it a highly valued commodity around the world, and English instruction is being introduced in schools at an earlier age in more and more countries. Today English is by far the top foreign language learned in school in the European Union and used by adults (Pop, 2009).

The linguistic diversity of the United States is only partially the result of voluntary immigration. Other causes are the importation of slaves from Africa (the source of Gullah and the African American vernacular), colonization (which brought English, Dutch, French-Cajun, and Spanish), annexation and invasion (the sources of Spanish, Yup'ik, and Navajo), and the common borders with Mexico and Canada (the sources of Spanish and French). Also, some languages are taught as part of a foreign language curriculum (e.g., Russian, Chinese, French, and Spanish). If we add Puerto Rico, the Virgin Islands, and other territories, U.S. linguistic diversity becomes even more complex.

LINGUISTIC CONTACT AND UNEVEN PATTERNS OF MULTILINGUALISM

The presence of multiple languages within a political unit is clearly the norm around the world. A closer look within countries, however, illustrates that this global pattern does not necessarily mean that everyone learns more than one language or that bilingual proficiency is maintained across many generations. To help understand patterns of bilingual development as a result of intergroup contact, sociolinguists make a distinction between bilingualism as a societal or group phenomenon and as an individual phenomenon. **Diglossia** has traditionally been used to describe the relation between languages at the societal or group level (Ferguson, 2003), and bilingualism is reserved for an individual's ability to use two languages; some scholars use bilinguality for the same phenomenon (e.g., Hamers & Blanc, 2000). Beacco and Byram (2003) extend the distinction between diglossia and bilingualism to settings with more than two languages, using multilingualism for the presence of multiple languages within a certain geographical area and pluralism for an individual's proficiency in multiple languages.

Diglossia refers to the distribution of two languages or varieties of the same language within a particular community for different purposes or functions. As developed by Ferguson, the term focuses on two varieties of the same language that are used for distinctly different purposes with little overlap. One is used for formal purposes, such as church sermons, university lectures, news broadcasts, and newspaper editorials (the "high" variety) and the other for informal purposes, such as folk literature and conversations with family, friends, and colleagues (the "low" variety). Because the two varieties have these distinct functions and because they have different institutional support, they are maintained in a relatively stable relationship.

The functional distribution that characterizes diglossia was subsequently applied to situations with two different languages, not just varieties of the same language. Scholars have identified **language domains** to analyze where certain languages are used consistently (Fishman, 1972). Home (family), church, school, and work are commonly distinguished domains used for analyzing language distribution in society. Especially when communities are linguistically diverse, multiple languages are often used within and across domains. Although the home is seen as a stronghold for minority language use, the dominant language often trickles in through the media (newspapers, television) or when children go to school.

Different configurations of diglossia and bilingualism may emerge (Fishman, 2003). In diglossia with bilingualism, the parallel distribution matches at the societal and individual levels and occurs when the languages have a clear functional distribution that is relatively stable. In Paraguay, people are bilingual in Spanish and Guaraní. Spanish is used for written and other formal communication and Guaraní for informal communication. Diglossia without bilingualism is also quite common. This pattern occurs particularly in settings where groups are considered a political unit but tend to live side by side with little contact. While people who interact with both groups are bilingual, the majority of speakers are not. Switzerland, for example, is officially quadralingual. Since the different languages are regionally distributed (rather than competing within one geographical area), many people are monolingual in the language of their particular region.

One of the most common scenarios is bilingualism without diglossia. Language contact often results in the use of two languages in the same language domain. This pattern is typical for immigrant languages. Bilingualism in these contexts occurs where immigrant language speakers must learn the dominant language. Unaccompanied by a diglossic functional distribution, bilingualism in these cases tends to reflect a temporary stage between the use of one language and that of the other language. The direction of this **language shift,** the change from the use of one language to the use of another language, will depend on the functions that each language has in society: the language used in high-status domains (government, workplace, schools) will most likely be the language that takes over the one used in low-status domains (Fishman, 2001). First generation immigrants become bilingual as they acquire the dominant language of the host society in addition to their native language. Because of the high status of the dominant language and its use for different functions and in different domains, most immigrant groups increasingly use this language in more and more domains in their lives. When the dominant language takes over low-status domains central to socializing children into the language (such as the home, the community) and children no longer learn the immigrant language, the shift from minority to majority language use is complete. This three-generation pattern continues to be observed in many language groups. In some instances a four-generation shift has been observed, for example, among Greek-, Italian-, and Spanish-speaking immigrants, who place a high value on their language and cultural identities. Another factor that influences this pattern is whether new immigrants continue to arrive in the community, encouraging the continued use of the immigrant language.

Diglossia and its relation to bilingualism or bi-dialectalism (and extended to multilingualism/pluralism) draws our attention to the different functions that languages have in society. While the stable relations between languages that informed the original notion of diglossia are rarely observed in the realities of diverse communities today, the analysis of the distributions of languages within and across high and low status language domains is useful conceptually. For example, it helps us understand why it may be more difficult to maintain the use of some languages (restricted to lower status domains) than others, where efforts to maintain or revitalize minority languages could be focused (e.g., by protecting domains or by striving to increase the use of a language in high status domains) (Harris, 1994). Additionally, analyzing when, where, with whom, and for what purposes languages are used provides important insights about language proficiency development. Children's linguistic repertoires are likely to vary according to the domains in which the language or language they speak are used.

LINGUISTIC DIVERSITY AS A DESIRED OUTCOME

The presence of linguistic diversity also does not mean that the development of multilingual competence is valued as an educational goal for all individuals. The development and use of the standard language variety in schools is assumed and taken for granted. In contrast, institutional support for other languages, especially minority languages, is more controversial. Immigrants or speakers of nonstandard language varieties are expected to learn the standard variety used in school. The pressure put on these speakers is often to shift to the dominant societal language and to give up their native language. Maintaining their native language and developing competence in that language tend to be devalued by the wider society and support for bilingual skill development is often perceived by majority language speakers as a hindrance to the full integration of minority groups into the mainstream. Bilingualism achieved under these conditions has been referred as **circumstantial bilingualism** (another term is *folk bilingualism*): knowing a language other than the native language is not a choice but a necessity for survival (Valdés & Figueroa, 1996).

Elective bilingualism (also referred to as *elite bilingualism* or *voluntary bilingualism*), in contrast, is proficiency in another language attained by choice, usually through travel or in language classes or bilingual schools (De Mejia, 2002). Elective bilingualism is generally regarded with respect and is valued by the wider society. Typically, it involves majority language speakers learning another high-status language, for example, Japanese speakers learning English in Japan.

This double standard of valuing multilingual competence for one group (majority language speakers) while devaluing similar abilities in other groups (minority language speakers) emerges around the world. The combination of speaking a local language and the colonial language or an immigrant language and the official language is consistently considered of less value than the combination of having proficiency in a colonial or official language and another (international) language.

Common Arguments for Linguistic Diversity

The importance of building on linguistic diversity and multilingual skills (pluralist discourse) is argued from different angles. Cultural and educational arguments are put forward more frequently (though not exclusively) for minority language speakers in response to threats from the societal language

- Respect for and access to multiple languages is important for identity development (link between language, culture, and identity).
- Access to multiple languages, including one's native language, allows one to build on prior knowledge (educational benefits)
- Multilingualism leads to early metalinguistic awareness and mental flexibility (cognitive and linguistic benefits)
- Multilingualism leads to market competitiveness and can facilitate communication across cultures (economic and political benefits)

Figure 2.2   Summary of common arguments in support of multilingualism and diversity

to the integrity of families and ethnic communities and concerns about equal access to schools. Cognitive and politico-economic arguments address the benefits of multilingualism for both majority and minority language speakers (Figure 2.2).

IDENTITY, CULTURE, AND LANGUAGE

Language plays an important role in socializing children into the linguistic and cultural norms of a community. This holds true for the immediate environment (home, family, school) as well as the broader sociopolitical context. Parents, family members, and community members explicitly and implicitly teach about the world, impart cultural beliefs and value systems, reward acceptable, and reject unacceptable behavior. Through their daily interactions with adults and peers, children develop an **identity,** a sense of who they are. Language plays an important in this process of identity construction because it is an important medium to socialize children into the linguistic and cultural behaviors of their home and community (Berry, Phinney, Sam, & Vedder, 2006; Jones & McEwen, 2000; Phinney & Ong, 2007). Identities reflect "how people understand their relationship to the world, how that relationship is constructed across time and space, and how people understand their possibilities for the future" (Norton, 1997, p. 410). More broadly, the media (TV, newspapers, the Internet) also rely on linguistic means to send strong messages about what is valued and who we are. The official language is a powerful symbol of a national identity and of who can claim membership in that national community.

Although identities can also be expressed through music, clothing, and other symbols, language is an integral and noticible part of a person's and a nation's identity that expresses who they are, where they belong, and their ways in and views of the world. The following description by Sophie, a deaf girl in the United Kingdom, illustrates the impact that the school environment can have on a student's sense of self.

It was absolutely brilliant, suddenly I was just with everyone signing, people signing, telling stories, lots of jokes, making good friends really quickly and it was really good. The teachers, they could sign so that was really excellent and I just fitted in I just felt really happy about it. (Skelton & Valentine, 2003, pp. 456–457)

Sophie's affirmation of her identity as a Deaf girl[1] once she enrolled in a secondary school for the deaf made a significant difference to her and her relationships with others. In her oral-based elementary school, her deafness was an exception, a handicap, and always questioned. At the school for the deaf, however, deafness and signing was the norm; she did not have to prove that despite her deafness she was equal to others. Her identity as a Deaf girl was given a very different space in her new school.

Identities can be communicated through the choice of language code (e.g., speaking English or Russian or speaking standard or nonstandard varieties) but also through how people use language to express their values, world views, and so forth. The Polish American author Eva Hoffman (1989) reveals how closely language and identity can be linked as she decides which language to use in a diary she has received from a friend.

If I am indeed to write something entirely for myself, in what language do I write? I open the diary and close it again. I can't decide. Writing in Polish at this point would be a little like resorting to Latin or ancient Greek—an eccentric thing to do in a diary, in which you're supposed to set down your most immediate experiences and unpremeditated thought in the most unmediated language. Polish is becoming a dead language, the language of the untranslatable past. But writing for nobody's eyes in English? That's like doing a school exercise, or performing in front of yourself, a slightly perverse act of self-voyeurism. . . . Because I have to choose something, I finally choose English. If I'm to write about the present, I have to write in the language of the present, even if it's not the language of the self. As a result, the diary becomes surely one of the more impersonal exercises of that sort produced by an adolescent girl. (E. Hoffman, 1989, pp. 120–121)

The link between language and identity is currently conceptualized as dynamic and complex. Earlier work considered language and ethnic identity in a one-to-one relationship, that is, individuals were expected to identify with either one group or another and language choice was considered an important indicator of this group affiliation. Early acculturation models described the immigrant adaptation process (at the group level) as a development from identification primarily with the minority culture (cultural maintenance) to (the desired) identification with the majority culture (assimilation). In these models, the frequent use of the native language implied a lower level

---

[1]It is common in the literature to capitalize the *D* in the cultural definition of Deafness. In this view, being Deaf is seen as belonging to a unique cultural group and not as a handicap. Interpretations of deafness as a physical condition are typically referred to with a lowercase *d*. Following Skelton and Valentine, both forms are used here.

of acculturation. The notion of biculturalism, as a way of simultaneously belonging to two groups, was initially excluded from these theories. Later, the bimodal model was replaced with a more complex matrix of possible outcomes of group contact: segregation (the minority group elects to remain separate), marginalization (the minority group is forced by the majority group to remain separate), assimilation (the minority group is oriented toward the majority culture), and integration (the minority group aims to integrate the native and the host culture) (Berry, 2005).

In today's holistic framework, identities are seen not as singular and separate but as multiple and hybrid. These identities are shaped along multiple axes, including age, race, gender, sexuality, social status, institutional affiliation, as well as language and ethnicity (B. Bailey, 2007; Garret, 2007; Pavlenko & Blackledge, 2004; Rampton, 2005). Research has demonstrated that identities are not fixed. Two studies based on interviews with Asian college-age students (Hinton, 2000; Tse, 2001), for example, describe a pattern that begins with the subjects' rejection of their home language and culture during their elementary school years, and then changes to their accepting and seeking out connections with their heritage language and culture during their high school and college years through comic books and other forms of popular culture. Moreover, the link between language and identity can exist regardless of the level of proficiency in the language. Limited proficiency in the home or heritage language does not necessarily diminish its importance for young children's identification with their culture. In one study (Bearse & de Jong, 2008), U.S.-born, English-dominant Hispanic adolescents still identified with their parents' ethnicity (Guatemalan, Salvadoran) and language (Spanish) rather than only American or English. Many Native American youngsters may not speak their parents' language well but have close links with their Native American culture (Deyhle, 1995).

Since identity is not fixed or one-dimensional, scholars prefer to talk about identities, recognizing that individuals construct multiple identities and that these identities shift and change according to the context (Pavlenko & Blackledge, 2004). The identities of children who grow up in diverse language contexts become more complex as they develop membership in communities with different languages and cultural norms. A boy growing up in the United States in a Mexican family, for example, may speak an indigenous Mexican language at home, Mexican Spanish in the community, and English at school. His identity will be connected to the experiences in each of these environments. It is important for their well-being that children like him have opportunities to explore and develop these multiple and at times conflicting identities (Berry, 2005; LaFromboise, Coleman, & Gerton, 1993; Padilla, 2006). In a study among elementary school students, Commins (1989) noted that a strong desire to assimilate (rejection of native culture) that is met with rejection by members of the majority culture can lead to the social and academic marginalization of minority students.

Multilingualism, defined as the ability to engage in multiple languages and cultural norms, is tied first and foremost to acknowledging and respecting the multilingual realities of a child's life. Much of one's identity is rooted in language and constructed through language use across different contexts. Children who encounter different languages and cultural norms in their everyday lives need to be able to communicate in these various contexts. They need opportunities to appropriate or change cultural and linguistic practices to meet their own (identity) needs (Leung, Harris, & Rampton, 1997). When the link between languages and identities is severed, it becomes more difficult for children to participate fully and meaningfully in their home, community, school, and other domains. Multilingualism allows children (and adults) to negotiate their different life worlds more effectively and affirms who they are. The denial of the use of the language or languages that children are socialized in can be seen as a denial of their humanity (Skutnabb-Kangas, 2001). Crawford (2000) argues that it is a matter of social justice to allow the development and use of native language, because its demise is linked with "identity loss, loss of self-worth, and limiting the human potential" (p. 63).

EDUCATIONAL BENEFITS

The schooling of linguistically and culturally diverse learners should build on their strengths (what they know and are able to do). This is a basic pedagogical principle. Effective learning involves engaging prior understandings and background knowledge and integrating factual knowledge with conceptual frameworks by encouraging deep understanding. Applying this learning principle to multilingual learners implies that they should be able to use their entire linguistic and cultural repertoire for learning. This means building on the knowledge (including language and literacy skills) that has been acquired in languages other than the school language. As student views and research confirm, doing so facilitates learning.

Case studies of successful bilinguals mention caring bilingual teachers and bilingual instruction as important factors for school success. Chinese high school students in Canada found that being able to negotiate academic content through the native language facilitated their academic achievement (Goldstein, 2003). Native language instruction has been shown to prevent early drop-out for girls in Africa (Benson, 2005b). In one study (Whitemore & Crowell, 2005), a former bilingual program student, Marisela, comments:

> Since it was a bilingual class, and the students helped me . . . it was much easier for me. I think it was because I could speak Spanish to some people and then they would teach me, for example, a word and how to say it English. . . .

So it wasn't that hard like it would have been if I had been in an English-only classroom. (Whitemore & Crowell, 2005, p. 278)

As early as 1953, UNICEF declared, "We take it as axiomatic . . . that the best medium for teaching is the mother tongue of the child" (UNESCO, 1953, p. 1). Chapter 7 discusses program effectiveness in detail and outlines some of the challenges of that research. It is sufficient here to note that the pluralist discourse references a consistent pattern across studies that have identified significant and positive relationships among bilingual proficiency, valuing the native language at home and at school, biliteracy development, and academic achievement. These patterns have been observed in the United States (Krashen & McField, 2005; Thomas & Collier, 1997; Thomas & Collier, 2002) and other countries around the world (Benson, 2005a; Cummins, 2001; Dutcher, 2003; Golash-Boza, 2005).

The use of the students' languages in school also influences the relationship between parents and the school. Immigrant parents feel more at home and are more likely to come to school when bilingual personnel are accessible, and when homework is in the native language, parents can better assist with homework (Ramirez, Yuen, Ramey, & Pasta, 1990). Thus, bilingual services can provide an important bridge for parents as well as children. Parents often ask teachers whether they should speak their native language at home since they are concerned that their children learn English. Dolson (1985) found that children in bilingual home environments (where Spanish was used) performed better in school on measures of Spanish and English achievement and were better adjusted socially and psychologically than children growing up in homes where English was replacing Spanish.

To engage multilingual students in "deep" learning (like what we do with monolingual students), we must not limit their instruction to drawing on just a small portion of what they know and are able to do. If students are expected to process new conceptual knowledge solely through a language they are not yet proficient in and if this conceptual knowledge is not taught elsewhere through their native language (e.g., with the help of tutors or parents), they may not fully grasp the content of what is being taught. This practice can result in wider and wider knowledge and skill gaps and lack of access to the curriculum. A careful negotiation of linguistic and cognitive development is therefore important for educational success. For many bilingual learners, using more than one language for learning becomes essential to their ability to access equitable and challenging learning environments.

COGNITIVE AND LINGUISTIC BENEFITS

Since the introduction of intelligence testing in the early 1900s, researchers have tried to uncover the relation between cognitive and language development in bilingual children and the interaction of this relation with educational programs (Bialystok, 2001, 2009; Diaz & Klingler, 2001; Hakuta, 1996; Lee, 1996). Early studies found a negative relation between cognitive and language development and set the stage for the argument that bilingualism causes developmental delays. More recent (and more sophisticated) studies have documented a wide range of cognitive advantages to bilingualism.

The IQ test, a standardized test to measure general intelligence, was originally intended to provide students with extra support in school. Its inventor, Alfred Binet, did not believe that one's IQ is an innate and fixed trait (Hakuta, 1996). Binet's intent rapidly changed under the influence of American researchers who adapted and used IQ tests to screen and sort individuals according to a fixed scale. Intelligence became innate ability that could be accurately and scientifically measured through tests. IQ tests were subsequently used to justify preventing individuals from certain countries to immigrate to the United States and to screen and sort students in order to place them into separate tracks with separate curricula.

When intelligence tests were used to compare bilingual and monolingual children, bilinguals scored lower than monolinguals. This finding fueled the belief that bilingualism can cause retardation and mental confusion. Bilingualism was framed as an abnormality, a deviation. According to what was referred to as the "balance effect," the development of one language occurred at the expense of cognitive space necessary for learning another language. By having another language, bilingual children had less cognitive capacity. Developing that language further would be even more detrimental to their ability to become fully proficient in the societal language. The implication of this container view of language was to avoid bilingualism and emphasize learning the societal language in schools.

The early studies were criticized in the 1960s because they did not control for important variables that could also influence the results on the tests, such as context (rural/urban areas), second language proficiency level, and socioeconomic background. In a now famous study published in 1962, Peal and Lambert (cited in Hakuta, 1996, pp. 33–34) set out to address these concerns. Controlling for proficiency level in both languages and for social class, their study found that bilinguals outperformed matched monolinguals on measures of verbal intelligence and nonverbal measures, cognitive flexibility, concept formation, picture completion, and figure manipulation.

Since this landmark study, researchers have found positive effects of bilingual proficiency for young children as well as school-age children on a number of different measures, including cognitive functioning, learning styles, cognitive flexibility, and abstract reasoning. Much of this research uses different measures of bilingual proficiency and a range of cognitive tasks, which makes it challenging to generalize the results. In an effort to sort through these findings, Bialystok (2009) concludes that bilingualism can shape cognitive functioning but "not in a way that can simply be defined as better, worse or indifferent" (p. 8).

Besides general cognitive measures, research has also shown that multilingual children become much earlier aware of how languages work than do monolingual children. This so-called **metalinguistic awareness** includes sensitivity to the details and structure of language, early word-referent distinction, recognition of ambiguities, control of language processing, and correction of ungrammatical sentences (Bialystok, 2001). The most common explanation of these various cognitive benefits is that bilinguals have access to and must negotiate multiple systems and meanings as they switch between languages (Bialystok, 2009). Finally, studies that take a long-term perspective have also found that early childhood bilingualism slowed down a decline among elderly people in the ability to focus attention on a particular task by almost 4 years as well as the onset of symptoms of dementia (Bialystok, Craik, & Freedman, 2007; Bialystok, Craik, Klein, & Viswanathan, 2004).

One important characteristic of these studies is that they focus on bilinguals who have achieved high levels of proficiency in both languages. Scholars became interested in comparing "high" and "low" bilinguals to see whether there were differences in levels of achievement. Lindholm-Leary (2001), for example, found that students who scored higher on language tests in both languages also scored higher on an academic achievement test. Moreover, knowing two languages makes learning a third language easier (Cenoz & Hoffman, 2003; Cenoz & Valencia, 1994; Clyne, 1997; Dijkstra & van Hell, 2004; C. Hoffman, 2001; Sanz, 2000). Though these findings involve only correlations and therefore not causal relations, they have been interpreted to mean that individuals should reach a certain proficiency threshold in both languages in order to realize the cognitive benefits associated with bilingualism. The **threshold hypothesis** (Cummins, 1979) has led to an emphasis on bilingual learning environments that promote high levels of competence in both languages and where the introduction of the second language does not mean the loss of the first language.

Even though comments about the potential of "language confusion" in bilinguals continue to be heard today, the notion that bilingualism is harmful is outdated and inconsistent with the current research that has clearly demonstrated cognitive advantages for bilingual children and adults. The brain is not wired for monolingualism, as suggested by the early research on bilingualism, but has capacity for learning multiple languages. Current research findings also point to the need to ask different questions about the relation between bilingualism and cognitive functioning. The field has moved beyond the question whether bilingualism is "good" or "bad". Rather, research is needed that considers which conditions lead to what kind of cognitive and linguistic benefits. Further, there is a need for theories of multi-lingualism that clarify what we know about the relation between language and cognition.

ECONOMIC AND POLITICAL BENEFITS

Linguistic instrumentalism stresses the utilitarian purposes of language use, such as economic development, access to social goods, and improved inter-ethnic communication. Multilingualism is promoted on the grounds that it will increase economic competitiveness, and it can support military defense goals and contribute to peace efforts.

Recent trends toward globalization and modernization have stressed the need for a multilingual work force. Businesses call for bilingual qualifications and cross-cultural competence to access or maintain their position on the international marketplace. Market research has shown that consumers prefer on-line shopping in their native language and will buy more when products are presented in their native language. Building multilingual computer inter-faces for global marketing through the Internet will demand multilingual skills (see International World Stats, 2009).

With increased demand come economic incentives to learn other lan-guages. There is some evidence that bilinguals' earnings are higher than those of monolinguals, although the differential appears to depend on gender, region, and segment of the labor market (Christofides & Swidinsky, 1994; Cortino, de la Garza, & Pinto, 2007). In Miami, Hispanic bilinguals earned as much as an average $7,000 more than monolinguals (Fradd & Boswell, 1996). Knowing that proficiency in a particular language or languages can result in better jobs is a powerful incentive to learn that language or lan-guages or to maintain competence in one or more languages.

The political argument connects the development of multilingual competence with national defense and peace efforts (Spolsky, 2004). The advantages of multilingual skills for military purposes (e.g., intelligence gath-ering) have long been recognized. After World War II, American soldiers returning from Europe complained about their inability to communicate with people in different countries. The National Defense Act of 1954 played a major role in reviving foreign language teaching in the United States, includ-ing experimentation with intensive foreign language teaching in elementary schools. In 2006, President George W. Bush announced the National Secu-rity Language Initiative, which allocates $12.9 million to the development of languages deemed most important for national security and commerce, such as Arabic, Farsi, Korean, and Chinese. A recent report by the U.S. Gen-eral Accountability Office (2009) notes that 31% of foreign service workers in language-designated positions do not meet proficiency requirements for their positions. The report points out that this sad state of affairs can "have adverse impacts on security, public diplomacy, consular operations, economic and political affairs, and other aspects of U.S. diplomacy" (p. 8).

A different political angle is taken by those emphasizing the importance of linguistic equality for peace. This argument considers the principle that systematically excluding certain groups from access to certain political and economic sectors of society by insisting on monolingual practices may lead to social conflict. Thus, the Organization for Security and Cooperation in Europe supports granting linguistic rights to national minorities, and the authors of the Universal Declaration of Linguistic Rights state the need for "a just and equitable linguistic peace throughout the world as a key factor in the maintenance of harmonious social relations" (UNESCO, 1996, p. 12). In this case, the promotion of multilingualism acts as an affirmation of a group's autonomy and identity as well as a communicative bridge between groups. Immigrant children often take on this bridging role for their parents to facilitate the interaction with dominant-language institutions, such as schools, hospitals, and the courts. Thus, rather than fragmenting societies, multilingualism can facilitate interethnic communication.

Politico-economic arguments, which are often formulated and supported by government agencies, tend to carry a lot of weight in public debates. Proficiency in certain languages is presented as a condition for access to school and top-level jobs. Critics of an approach to linguistic diversity that relies exclusively on instrumental rationales point out that these arguments are applied only to languages that are needed at the time (e.g., Russian during the cold war; Chinese and Arabic today) and to those with consistent widespread use and international status (Arabic, English, French, Spanish). Ricento (2003), for example, points out that languages that have national economic and political benefits (instrumental value) receive more attention and funding than those that support the integrity of ethnic communities (symbolic value). The National Security Language Initiative combined with the Foreign Language Assistance Program allocated $22 million into improving the language skills of native English speakers. In contrast, funding for bilingual education has been limited to indigenous languages, and is no longer allocated for native speakers of immigrant languages, under the 2001 Title VII of the Elementary and Secondary Education Act (No Child Left Behind).

Instrumental and symbolic values of language learning, however, are important. Students in South Africa indicated that they valued English for its access to economic means and for international communication but that they also valued Xhosa as a link to their ethnic culture and history. They saw Xhosa and not English as the marker of what they considered their authentic identity (Barkhuizen, 2002). The same language can be valued differently. Anglo students in a bilingual program emphasized the advantage of knowing Spanish for future employment and college entrance. Latino students in the same bilingual program stressed the importance of identity and the ability to communicate with parents and families (Bearse & de Jong, 2008).

Are There Advantages to Monolingualism?

Not everyone views multilingualism as a positive force in society. Concerns about (too much) linguistic and cultural diversity are grounded especially in the importance of having one (official) language to maintain political unity and prosperity and the danger that linguistic and cultural fragmentation pose to these processes. An additional argument is the cost and lack of efficiency of translation and multilingualism (Figure 2.3).

LINGUISTIC DIVERSITY AND SOCIOPOLITICAL FACTORS

The development of European nation-states required significant efforts by newly established governments to help what were relatively disparate groups see themselves as one community. In his book *Imagined Communities*, Benedict Anderson (1991) argues that, unlike family or village ties, the ties among people in nation-states are necessarily imaginary (i.e., in the mind), "because the members of even the smallest nations will never know most of their fellow-members, meet them, or even hear of them; yet in the minds of each lives the image of their communion" (p. 6). To become a national community, a group of individuals must therefore imagine what they have in common. The process of defining the **imagined community** requires setting boundaries to determine who is considered part of the community and who is not (who belongs) and is constructed in contrast to the images of other nations (Wodak, de Cillia, Reisigl, & Liebhart, 1999; S. Wright, 2004). The choice of the (official) language of the nation has traditionally played a central role in helping to establish this imagined community separate from other communities. Theodore Roosevelt exclaimed in 1914, "We must have but one flag. We must also have but one language. . . . The greatness of this country depends on the swift assimilation of the aliens she welcomes to her shores" (cited in Crawford, 1992, p. 85). The assumed direct link between a unified nation and language is still an integral part of debates in societies around the world today.

- Multiple languages and the absence of one common language will undermine political unity and cohesiveness
- Linguistically heterogeneous systems costs too much to maintain and lead to a breakdown of communication among people from different language groups (cost and efficiency)

Figure 2.3   Summary of common arguments in support of streamlining diversity

Applying the principle of "one language, one nation," many people argue that the more languages exist in a nation, the higher the likelihood of social unrest or poverty. The question for political separation of French-dominant Quebec in Canada or the conflicts between French and Flemish (Dutch) speakers in Belgium are often given as evidence for the divisive power of language. The assertion that English is "the glue that holds us together" reflects this concern and can be frequently heard in policy debates in the United States today.

Linguists and economists have examined the possible links between language, economic prosperity, and political systems. Early studies appeared to confirm a correlation between linguistic heterogeneity and prosperity as measured through gross domestic product (GDP) and other social variables (Easterly & Ross, 1997; Fishman, 1966; Pool, 1991). More recent work, however, finds no significant correlation between linguistic or ethnic diversity and economic development and denies a causal link between language and economy (Lian & Oneal, 1997; Nettle, 2000). As for diversity and political regime, Fish and Brooks (2004) note the significant role of economic development but failed to find linguistic, ethnic, or religious diversity to correlate with democracy. Even when only countries that have a low GDP are considered, a common denominator is difficult to find. One study Collier, Honohan, & Moene (2001) argues that countries with ethnic dominance (i.e., 45–90% of the population is of one ethnic group) may be more prone to major civil conflict than either more heterogeneous countries (less than 45% of one ethnic group) or more homogeneous countries (more than 90% of one ethnic group) because of higher levels of fractionalization. Other studies also find no relation between diversity and violence or civic strife (Fearon & Laitin, 1996, 2003).

To return to the two earlier examples, the real cause of the conflicts in Canada and Belgium is more economic than linguistic and the result of historical marginalization. In Quebec, a long history of the repression of French speakers by English speakers in the economic sector and the political domain preceded the language question. In Belgium, the linguistic division parallels a longstanding religious division (Protestant versus Roman Catholic) and access to economic resources. While language is certainly a hotly contested issue in both countries, it is a symptom rather than the cause of conflict. When groups are economically or politically marginalized, they are more likely to seek ways to improve their conditions. When these groupings line up with ethnic, racial, or linguistic differences, language easily becomes a rallying point.

COST, EFFICIENCY, AND EFFECTIVE COMMUNICATION

Another argument in favor of limiting the number of languages is one of cost and efficiency: it is simply too costly and cumbersome to duplicate everything in multiple languages. If everyone spoke the same language, communication would be more efficient and cheaper for the country. Grin and Vaillancourt (1997) argue that an economic cost and benefit analysis should be included in policies that mandate translations or interpretations in certain languages or access to native language instruction that takes into account the number of speakers of the languages. The European Union (EU) is often cited in discussions of such analyses because it provides translations in all its 20 official languages for major EU documents and interpretation services for its meetings. For 2007, the cost of translation and interpretation is expected to reach 800 million Euros. This is about 6% of the EU's total 126.5 billion Euro budget.

Other concerns relate to the effectiveness of communication: if people living in a nation cannot communicate with each other in the same language, conflict and fragmentation will inevitably result. The need for a shared communication system is rarely contested and many languages function as a **lingua franca**, the language used by native speakers of different languages in a particular area to communicate with each other, such as Arabic in the Middle East and Hausa in West Africa. Monolingualism, however, is not the only option for community building across groups; bilingualism could be equally effective, as illustrated under the political arguments for multilingualism. Moreover, monolingualism does not guarantee successful and conflict-free communication. Bilingual competence was a highly valued skill in colonial America, where traders, Native Americans, and colonists from various language backgrounds had to find ways to communicate with each other. By the mid 19th century, the shared English skills of the North and South certainly did not prevent the Civil War. If mandated monolingualism results in oppression, it may also result in more conflict. Similarly, examples of past and present strife among speakers of the same language are sufficient to show that a shared language does not lead to effective communication or to the absence of conflict.

These three arguments (political unity, economy, effectiveness) are made at the level of the nation. The most direct benefits of monolingualism at the individual or group level are limited to one specific group, that is, those who already possess the type of linguistic and cultural capital associated with the dominant language. For a white person growing up in a upper or middle class English-speaking household, a monolingual policy that favors English only (implying standard English) is unproblematic and will be considered beneficial. In fact, this person may feel threatened by the increased need for bilingual skills in the job market because he or she may not have access to a good foreign language class. A similar phenomenon occurred in many postcolonial nations. As Africans learned French or English and became part of the political and economic elite in power, it was to their benefit to advocate the European language as the official language and to sustain the idea that only competence in the European language could make one literate, well-educated, and successful.

It seems, then, that there are few documented advantages to promoting linguistic homogeneity, although this does not necessarily mean that those benefits occur with linguistic heterogeneity. Monolingualism may be beneficial to a particular group in a nation (i.e., those already speaking that language), but clearly an explicit policy of monolingualism must be tempered with other, more equity-oriented, policies. To avoid political and social fragmentation, nations must try to avoid practices that are perceived to be discriminatory and lead to unequal access to economic resources.

A Special Case: Arguments for Saving Endangered Languages

While the large number of languages in the world suggests an impressive linguistic diversity, scholars have cautioned that many languages are in danger of dying out (Krauss, 1992; Nettle & Romaine, 2000). Languages can be classified from "extinct" to "not endangered" or "safe" according to their size (number of speakers) and potential of being transmitted to the next generation (see Table 2.1 for definitions). It is estimated that only 600 languages (less than 10% of the total number of languages) can be considered "safe," that is, each has more than 100,000 speakers. Regional minority and indigenous languages are particularly at risk of dying out because they are used in fewer and fewer language domains and their speakers are shifting to using only the dominant language.

The decline in the number of languages and the number of speakers of individual languages has become a major global concern (Skutnabb-Kangas, Maffi, & Harman, 2003). Currently, it is estimated more than three-quarters of the world's languages are spoken by fewer than 1,000 people (Lewis, 2009). It is expected that within the next decade as many as half of the world's 6,000 languages will become **moribund languages** (no longer used by children) and another 40% **threatened languages** (i.e., decreasing number of children learning the language) (Krauss, 1992; Nettle & Romaine, 2000). In the United States, some 300 to 500 Native American languages were spoken by the peoples indigenous to what is now the United States and Canada prior to European contact; an estimated 34 (14%) are still being naturally acquired as a first language by children (McCarty, Romero, & Zepeda, 2006). Five of the native Indian languages in the United States have more than 20,000 speakers. Navajo is the only native language with more than 100,000 speakers. Of the 20 Alaskan languages, only two are transmitted directly through children.

TABLE 2.1	
UNESCO's Descriptors for Endangered Languages	
Status of Languages	**Description**
Extinct	No speakers
Critically endangered	No intergenerational transmission; language is spoken infrequently by grandparents and older
Severely endangered	No intergenerational transmission; language is spoken regularly by grandparents and may be understood by parent generation
Definitely endangered	No intergenerational transmission; children no longer learn the languages as mother tongue in the home
Vulnerable	Intergenerational transmission; most children learn the language but may be restricted to certain domains (e.g., home)

Scholars have argued for and against protecting these endangered languages, they have also argued for and against **language revitalization**, which are efforts to revive languages by increasing the number of speakers of a threatened language or, at minimum, to maintain the linguistic diversity that exists in the world (for extended overviews, see Baker, 2006; Crawford, 2000; Lo Bianco, 2005; Nettle & Romaine, 2000). Besides the arguments in favor of multilingualism already mentioned, supporters for the protection of endangered languages offer additional linguistic and cultural rationales and make an appeal to human rights.

Supporters warn that losing languages means losing a source for cross-linguistic analysis and thus the potential for understanding language universals and patterns of language acquisition. Others argue for the importance of intellectual diversity that is maintained through language. In this view, losing a language also means losing the knowledge encoded in that language. An example is knowledge about the medicinal use of certain plants that may be encoded only in one endangered language. A related argument focuses on a general loss of diversity when another way of viewing the world is lost. In both cases, linguistic homogenization implies cultural uniformity of viewpoint. The field of **linguistic ecology** considers language in relationship to other systems, including economic and sociocultural systems. It has extended these arguments for maintaining linguistic diversity into a framework that considers languages and cultures as ecologies that, like endangered species, have been upset, directly and indirectly, by the impact of globalization (Maffi, 2001; Muhlhausler, 2000; Pennycook, 2004; Skutnabb-Kangas, et al., 2003). Ecolinguistic arguments stress the loss of knowledge as a result of language loss. Singh and Scanlon (2003, in Lo Bianco, 2005) argue that sustainable management of unique bio-ecological systems is more feasible with intact traditional social systems.

Those who cite human rights as a reason to protect languages appeal to the dignity of humans and the importance of treating language with respect, arguing that nobody has the right to force individuals to give up their native languages because these languages are integral to their identities and to who they are as human beings. The **linguistic human rights movement** takes the argument one step further to also include governmental actions to support different languages. It presents a legal framework of the right to use and maintain the native language, the right to develop the native language through formal schooling, and the right not to be discriminated against for speaking a particular language (Phillipson, 1998; Skutnabb-Kangas, 2000, 2001, 2002; UNESCO, 2003). For indigenous peoples, the linguistic human rights movement has been closely linked to a process of self-determination and autonomy and the right to make their own decisions about their languages and cultures (Hinton & Hale, 2001).

Arguments against efforts to protect endangered languages from extinction range from a laissez-faire attitude to a sense of futility and suggestions that efforts to maintain threatened languages are a waste of resources. Many view the decrease in the number of speakers of a language as a natural outcome of a competitive process through which the language of the fittest will survive. Minority languages with less value will logically give way to dominant languages that have more value. Governments should let this process take its course and not interfere with individual linguistic choices. In this framework, language choices are perceived as motivated primarily by economic self-interest: individuals will choose the language that will bring them economic prosperity or gain (Edwards, 1994, 2001). As people choose to use one language over another, certain languages will naturally gain ground and other languages will lose ground, and thus, it is less a matter of formal policy than rational choice. Critics of the ecological approach to linguistic diversity argue that the biological analogy between species and languages does not hold: languages exist through their speakers; they are not independent species like plants or animals. Their continued existence therefore depends on speaker choices and these choices are influenced by issues of access to power and status (Mufwene, 2002; Pennycook, 2004). A final argument is that countering language shift and its ultimate outcome, language death, is a futile exercise. While language maintenance is perhaps worthwhile, these critics argue, such efforts will not succeed in stemming the tide and therefore vital economic and human resources should not be used to this end (for further discussion of these arguments, see Baker, 2006).

Multilingualism for All

The arguments presented in this chapter reflect pluralist and assimilationist discourses about linguistic diversity and the role of language for the individual and the group. Pluralist discourses ask what the short-term and long-term costs will be for the individual, for the group, and for society when different ways of communicating and meaning making are systematically excluded, and what benefits may be incurred when these skills are expanded on. Assimilationist discourses emphasize the "economy of language choice" when resources are perceived to be limited, and push us to consider whether there are perhaps limits to diversity under certain conditions.

The sociocultural, educational, cognitive, economic, and political benefits of multilingualism would argue for an asset approach: multilingualism as the norm, an enrichment, and not an abnormality. Thus, streamlining linguistic and cultural diversity into a monolingual, standardized form would limit the human potential for multiplicity and multilingualism. There is no reason to abandon children's languages and cultural experiences when they start school. Rather, the optimal choice would be to capitalize on the language and cultural resources they already possess.

These potential benefits of multilingualism are not extended equally to all individuals. Whereas majority or societal language speakers are encouraged to learn one or more foreign languages (elite bilingualism), folk bilingualism is controversial for children who come from homes where a minority language is spoken. For majority language speakers, multilingualism is an educational issue; for minority language speakers it is a political issue. This double standard prevails ("bilingual handicap" for some; enrichment for others) but is rarely acknowledged. In fact, fierce opponents of bilingual instruction for immigrant children have been known to openly support programs that provide extensive foreign language instruction to native English speakers without seeing the contradiction in their positions. These actions illustrate that more than language issues are at stake in discourses about linguistic diversity. The status of speakers and hence the status of the language they use play a central role in decisions we make about languages and language use in schools.

CHAPTER 2
Discussion & Activities

Critical Issues

1. Do you see evidence in your state or district of a double standard regarding the value of multilingualism? Give examples.
2. Consider the origins of language contact and language diversity discussed in this and the previous chapter. What factors can help explain the patterns that you observe?
3. Which of the arguments for or against supporting multilingualism presented in this chapter is the most convincing to you? Which one do you think would be most convincing to policy makers? To parents? To students?

Application and Reflection

4. Reflect on the linguistic diversity in your own setting (school, city, region, country). What language groups and languages are part of the immediate and extended linguistic environment (remember to include nonstandard varieties of language)? What are the origins of this linguistic and cultural diversity? What status does each language have in your setting?
5. For those growing up in monolingual settings, the powerful link between language and identity is often incomprehensible. How might you illustrate for colleagues and others why, for many, language and identity are so closely intertwined?

Recommended Readings

Baker, C. (2006). *Foundations of bilingual education and bilingualism* (4th ed.). Clevedon: Multilingual Matters.
> *This book is a comprehensive treatment of the issues surrounding language maintenance, bilingualism, and educational approaches that support bilingual development. It provides a wealth of information, including good examples of research and resources.*

King, K., Schilling-Estes, N., Fogle, L., Lou, J. J., & Soukup, B. (Eds.). (2008). *Sustaining linguistic diversity: Endangered and minority languages and language varieties*. Washington, DC: Georgetown University Press.
> *This collection of essays provides a good overview of the issues involving indigenous and regional minority language revitalization efforts with case*

studies from around the world, including Ireland, Eritrea, and South America.

Nettle, D., & Romaine, S. (2000). *Vanishing voices: The extinction of the world's languages.* New York: Oxford University Press.

This book documents the loss of linguistic and cultural diversity in the world and the cost for individuals and communities.

Valdés, G., Fishman, J. A., Chavez, R., & William, P. (2006). *Developing minority language resources: The case of Spanish in California.* Clevedon: Multilingual Matters.

This book discusses rationales for Spanish language maintenance and describes a wide range of initiatives to support Spanish language development and maintenance for the diverse Spanish-speaking population in the United States.

Multilingualism and Multilingual Development

GUIDING QUESTIONS

- *What is bilingual proficiency?*
- *How do multilingual children develop competence in more than one language?*
- *What is the relationship between the two languages involved in bilingual and biliteracy development?*

KEY TERMS

holistic view of bilingualism
communicative competence
continua of biliteracy model
fractional view of bilingualism
balanced bilingual
semilingualism
language dominance
simultaneous language acquisition
successive language acquisition
language attrition
code-switching
translanguaging
language brokering
additive bilingualism

subtractive bilingualism
ethnolinguistic vitality
social networks
simultaneous biliteracy development
language transfer
cognates
interdependence hypothesis
time-on-task argument
common underlying proficiency
  (CUP)
separate underlying proficiency
  (SUP)
social language proficiency
academic language proficiency

Pluralist and assimilationist discourses reflect different ideas about language and how we conceptualize language proficiency in more than one language. These notions, in turn, shape how educators think about and approach language development. This chapter presents some of the foundational understandings about bilingualism and biliteracy development at home and at school.

Multilingual Repertoires

What does it mean to be bilingual or multilingual? This section examines more closely how bilingualism and multilingualism have been conceptualized within pluralist and assimilationist discourses, in particular, how these discourses align with holistic (pluralist) and fractional (assimilationist) views of language and language proficiency.

HOLISTIC VIEW OF BILINGUALISM

"Bilinguals are not two monolinguals in one person." This statement by François Grosjean (1989) captures a key principle of the pluralist discourses about bilingual proficiency. Grosjean uses the analogy of a hurdler to explain his statement. Neither a high jumper nor a sprinter, a hurdler combines skills from both sports in a unique way. Comparing a hurdler to the other two specialists does not make sense; each athlete has a unique set of skills. Similarly, a bilingual person has a unique combination of skills. This **holistic view of bilingualism** encourages educators and researchers to consider an individual's linguistic repertoire as an integrated, interconnected whole. Delineating each language system separately and comparing them to those of native speakers of either language ignores the integration that is inherent in bilingualism (Grosjean, 1989) and multilingualism (Herdina & Jessner, 2002).

The second key principle of pluralistic discourses about bilingual proficiency is that people in multilingual settings will "develop their languages according to the differential needs for the two languages and/or the different social functions of these languages" (Grosjean, 1989, p. 4). From a holistic perspective proficiency is understood first and foremost as a matter of language use in context. Knowing a language is more than knowing the pronunciation of individual words or how words are put together in grammatically correct sentences. This grammatical knowledge is important because linguistic choices reflect ways that language is considered appropriate for a particular social context. When making a formal presentation, speakers will use complete sentences and specific vocabulary and may use more complex sentence structures than they would in an informal setting. Using the same linguistic features in a conversation with friends about the weekend would be considered inappropriate. This knowledge about language use and how it changes according to context is also referred to as **communicative competence** (Cazden, John, & Hymes, 1972). Multilinguals develop this competence within languages (e.g., style and register) and across languages through continuous interactions with members of particular communities. Speakers receive feedback from their listeners (explicitly and implicitly) on their ways of speaking and using language. Multilinguals will always have partial knowledge of language as a function of these social interactions—by definition not everybody participates in all existing social practices (Romaine, 2001; Wee, 2007).

Within a holistic view of bilingualism, conversations about proficiency or competence therefore must take into consideration the contexts in which languages are learned and used. If Spanish is used only at home and English is used in all other domains (such as school and work), proficiency in Spanish will reflect the communicative skills necessary to maintain intimate family relations. The children from such a household may not yet have developed English vocabulary for common household items when they go to school. This situation exemplifies the distributive nature of bilingualism, that is, language knowledge depends on the contexts in which each language has been learned (Oller & Eilers, 2002; Oller, Pearson, & Cobo-Lewis, 2007).

To capture this complexity, Hall, Cheng, and Carlson (2006) propose the term *communicative repertoires*. They take this term to refer to the range of language skills individuals develop in the course of their lifetime. These repertoires include appropriate use of nonstandard and standard varieties of the same language, as well as the ability to adopt different registers as the situation requires. Multilinguals develop these communicative repertoires within languages (e.g., varieties of Spanish, different styles or registers appropriate for the situation) as well as across languages (e.g., English and Spanish).

The idea that a bilingual's proficiency is a function of how he or she uses their languages extends to reading and writing skills (de las Luz Reyes, 2001). An influential approach to conceptualize biliteracy is the **continua of biliteracy model** developed by Hornberger (1989) and extended in Hornberger and Skilton-Sylvester (2000). In this model, Hornberger aims to capture the complexity of bilingual proficiency by describing it along various intersecting continua, from oral to written skills and from receptive to productive skills in either or both languages. The development of these skills is influenced by the languages themselves or by the medium (i.e., structural similarities and differences between languages), the context (the macro and micro contexts in which languages are used), and the content (the topics and perspectives represented in oral and written text). The more recent version of the model (Hornberger & Skilton-Sylvester, 2000) emphasizes the importance of including a power/status dimension to illustrate that the different ends of the continua are valued and distributed unequally in school settings. For example, schools in the United States value written literacy over oral literacy traditions (e.g., oral storytelling), and dominant culture perspectives over minority perspectives.

The holistic view considers the whole of an individual's linguistic repertoire within and across languages. For bilinguals, their languages do not operate as separate, isolated entities. Rather, their languages are cognitively and linguistically interconnected. Moreover, this view encourages us to think of bilingualism and biliteracy as a continuum of different configurations of competence as it relates to actual use (Valdés, 2005). Multilingual repertoires reflect multilingual abilities according to different skills (listening, speaking, reading, and writing), communicative functions, and domains where the languages are used (home, school, community).

FRACTIONAL VIEW OF BILINGUALISM

Grosjean considers his approach holistic because it takes the whole of the bilingual person's language proficiency and use into consideration. A contrasting view, which he labels a **fractional view of bilingualism**, treats each language as a separate system. In this view, put forth by Bloomfield (1933, p. 56), a bilingual is an individual with "native-like control of two or more languages." Bloomfield's definition sees bilingual competence as the sum of the proficiency of each of the two languages (Romaine, 1995). According to this perspective, the "real" bilingual person is referred to as a **balanced bilingual**, someone undistinguishable from a monolingual native speaker in either language.

This view of language proficiency uses linguistic criteria of what are considered clearly identifiable and fully developed language systems, generally assumed to be those of educated native speakers. In particular, the focus is on complete mastery of the language (its sounds, word formation, and grammar) across different skill areas (listening, speaking, reading, and writing). This monolingual model and its expectations of what it means to function like an (ideal) native speaker are applied to bilinguals.

The fractional view attaches significant importance to bilinguals' ability to keep their languages separate. Cognitive separation is considered an indicator of native-like proficiency, since it emulates monolingual speaker behavior. Maintaining distinct boundaries between languages in actual language use is a mark of native speaker behavior. Mixing languages or language varieties reflects a less competent speaker (or writer).

Another implication of the fractional view is that bilingual proficiency is measured according to the specific skills in each language. Rating scales, fluency tests, and other formal measures have been developed to try to describe proficiency levels in each language. From the comparison of performance in each language, an indication emerges of how bilingual a person is (i.e., to what degree he or she compares to an (ideal) native speaker). A multitude of terms has developed to describe bilingual individuals with different skills in each language. *Balanced, ambilingual, equilingual, maximal bilingual,* and *symmetrical bilingual* are used to describe the desired outcome: bilingual individuals who have equal and native-like proficiency in both languages. *Dominant bilingual, receptive* or *productive bilingual,* and *semibilingual* indicate uneven skill levels between the first and second language (Wei,

2000, pp. 6–7). One term in particular, **semilingualism,** continues to inform a fractional view of bilingual children. The term has been used to describe language behaviors considered deviant when compared to the native-speaker norm (Edelsky, et al., 1982). Originally used by a Swedish linguist, Nils Erik Hansegård, semilingualism is used particularly to denote the imperfect learning of two languages according to criteria such as vocabulary size, degree of automatism, ability to make new words, and mastery of the cognitive, emotive, and volitional functions of the language (Paulston, 1994; Romaine, 1995). When used to describe a less than complete mastery of both languages systems, semilingualism and similar labels have negative connotations, especially when applied to minority language speakers. Despite the negative connotations of the term, the idea behind semilingualism persists in common usage, in expressions such as, "He doesn't know either language well" or "She is limited in both languages."

Views of Bilingualism and Assessment Practices

Our perspective on bilingualism affects how we view bilingual children, including how we assess what they know. This section looks at the implications of the holistic and fractional views on how teachers and researchers approach bilingual learners, ways of assessing vocabulary, proficiency testing as part of identification and placement, and ways of evaluating school outcomes.

BILINGUAL LEARNERS AS BILINGUALS

The holistic view of bilingualism stresses the importance for teachers of getting to know bilingual children as bilinguals and for researchers to understand the conditions under which bilinguals acquire their languages. Educators and researchers need to ask questions about bilingual students' language histories and the roles and functions their languages play in their lives. After all, bilinguals' performance on tests may vary according to when and where their languages are learned, whether the person administering the tests shares their language background, and whether assessments are conducted in a monolingual or bilingual mode (Grosjean, 1998).

Brisk and Harrington (2000, pp. 130–140) list over 30 questions teachers can ask to get to know their multilingual learners. They include questions about students' immigration history as well as about parents' languages and education, home language and literacy practices, and students' reading and writing experiences in schools in the native language and the second language. These linguistic histories, as a reflection of what a child does with language in daily life, provide the basis for instruction. They emphasize the importance of assessing the child's entire communicative repertoire, not only what the child knows about a standardized second language (e.g., standard English as measured on a formal language test).

LOOKING AT VOCABULARY

Vocabulary development is probably the most visible area where monolingual and bilingual students vary. A range of studies have found lower standard scores for bilinguals when compared with monolinguals (Bialystok, 2009; Oller, et al., 2007). From a bilingual perspective, presenting the data in one language tells only half the story for bilinguals because it may not show what the child knows when combining the two languages. Because vocabulary is learned experientially and experiences in both languages can differ greatly, patterns of exposure to vocabulary will also vary. The distributive nature of bilingual proficiency makes it imperative that a bilingual child's vocabulary be considered across the two languages, not just one. Young bilingual children will know some words in one language or the other (singlets) and some words in both languages (doublets). As children continue to interact and learn both languages, the number of doublets increases, from around 30% for 2-year-olds, 60% for elementary school children, and 80% for college-age students (Pearson, Umbel, Andrews de Flores, & Cobo-Lewis, 1999). Another consideration is the measurement of conceptual knowledge (what words refer to) against that of lexical knowledge (the actual words) (Oller & Eilers, 2002; Pearson, Fernandez, & Oller, 1995). Bilinguals may have smaller vocabularies in each language (lexical items) but across language may have a comparable conceptual framework to draw from.

Since the monolingual perspective looks at each language separately, it assumes and expects the existence of doublets (the balanced bilingual) and may ignore the possibility of singlets in either language. When a bilingual student scores low on an English vocabulary test, the conclusion may be that the child is cognitively less developed or is a poor vocabulary learner because of his or her bilingualism. But that conclusion does not take into consideration that for bilingual children concepts can be encoded in either or both languages. Because of the emphasis given to vocabulary tests in assessing young children's readiness for school and their cognitive and linguistic development, it is important to critically examine these tests and how they are used for bilingual learners.

SCHOOL PRACTICES: IDENTIFICATION AND LANGUAGE DOMINANCE

Perhaps one of the most challenging implications of our understanding of multilingual repertoires is in the area of program development and evaluation. The notion of **language dominance**, for example, plays a key role in determining a student's placement in such areas as bilingual education and special education services. In this context, language dominance refers to the language that the child is most proficient in.

Identification of students for special language services is typically based on the results of a language test. When a bilingual student scores low on such tests in both languages, the assumption often is that the child is at risk and that a bilingual education placement will be "confusing," inappropriate, or too much for him or her. These assumptions are not well founded. In a study by MacSwan, Rolstad, and Glass (2002), kindergarten students who obtained a low score for both languages on a language assessment test were identified as "semilingual" and "at-risk." Upon closer examination, however, the label "semilingual" was found to be more a function of the use of the language test (how items and sections of the test were scored) rather than a valid indicator of actual language behavior (Valadez, MacSwan, & Martinez, 2003). Classroom observations showed that the students who had been considered at risk based on the test were in fact capable of using the same range of grammatical features as those who had been identified by the same test as fluent speakers.

For the purpose of special education testing, a child who is considered to be dominant in Spanish is generally tested in Spanish rather than English, the "weaker" language. The idea behind this practice is that making determinations based on the results of tests given in the stronger language is fairer than making them based on scores obtained through the weaker language. The challenge is not in the principle but in how language dominance is determined. Assessing language dominance requires a comparison of skills in two languages and forces a judgment about which of the two languages is "stronger" or "better." Typically, dominance tests will use similar items that assess the same kinds of (discrete) skills in both languages. A higher score in one language would indicate dominance in that language. Language tests that are often used to measure the degree of bilingualism of individuals are rating scales, fluency tests, or flexibility tests.

From a holistic bilingual perspective, it is easy to see why these kinds of tests are problematic. It is unlikely that children acquire their languages under exactly the same conditions or that they are exposed to the same language patterns in both languages. In the United States, children may hear English on television, speak Spanish with their parents and relatives, read Spanish and English books, and speak English and Spanish with siblings and friends. They may use particular languages for specific topics, such as English for school work or computer-related activities, Spanish for discussing religion or emotions. It is likely, then, that Spanish may be developed more to talk about certain topics and English may be the language of choice for other topics or in different domains. If a language test measures only one particular domain (e.g., school-related vocabulary), it easily overlooks important language skills that are demonstrated in other domains and underestimates what multilingual children are actually able to do with language.

SCHOOL PRACTICES: CURRICULUM AND PROGRAM OUTCOMES

If a school chooses to have bilingual or multilingual competence as a goal for students in a particular program or for all students in the school, they must consider how they will identify and assess the bilingual skills they want to develop as part of their program. A holistic view of bilingualism would call for a curriculum that focuses on the development of communicative competence across two languages. Through their curriculum and instructional approaches schools would identify the purposes for which they want students to be able to use their languages and then provide meaningful opportunities to develop these skills.

Assessment would reflect these linguistic repertoires. Assessment activities would be contextualized and functional, that is, they would involve communicative tasks that are representative of a particular domain or community. In schools, such authentic assessment tasks could range from making requests for information to explaining while conducting an experiment. Assessing this kind of language is rarely accomplished with a test of discrete language skills. Rather than asking students to pronounce individual words, repeat sentences, match vocabulary, holistic assessments require students to perform an authentic task with a real purpose, such as conducting an experiment, writing a lab report, or presenting the experiment to the class.

A study by Escamilla, Chavez, & Vigil (2005) offers an example of a holistic, bilingual approach to accountability. The researchers found that bilingual education was blamed for low state test scores in the Denver Public Schools. The researchers purposefully shifted the analysis from English-only to a bilingualism-as-resource perspective by including Spanish and English test scores. Using this analysis, they showed that students enrolled in bilingual education in fact scored at or above grade level on the Spanish version of the state test. The underachieving group in the school consisted of students enrolled in the mainstream classrooms, not those in the bilingual program. This bilingually oriented analysis turned the spotlight on why mainstream classrooms were not effective rather than automatically placing the blame on the bilingual program.

A holistic view also recognizes the need to provide opportunities for students to demonstrate what they know through their entire bilingual linguistic repertoire, by assessing in both languages. Escamilla (2000) gives the example of Leticia, a 3rd grader, who scored at the 40th percentile in Spanish on La Prueba, a Spanish-language achievement test, and a 25th percentile in English on the Illinois Test of Basic Skills. The teacher's conclusion was that Leticia read poorly in both languages and that biliteracy perhaps caused her confusion. Alfredo, a monolingual-English student in the same class, also scored at the 40th percentile in English. This time the teacher's interpretation was that he was doing fine and that he was one of her better readers. The absence of a bilingual perspective devalued Leticia's native language reading skills and her label as a "poor reader" may lead to low expectations and inappropriate instruction. As part of the Literacy Squared Project at the University of Colorado, researchers have developed a writing rubric that simultaneously displays native language, second language, and bilingual language knowledge and strategies that students demonstrate in their writing, such as phonetic spelling, using the sound structure from the native language, or the semantic transfer of vocabulary meaning (Escamilla, 2006; Escamilla, Hopewell, Geisler, & Ruiz, 2007). Moreover, Escamilla and Coady (2001) note differences in rhetorical conventions (e.g., text organization) as well as punctuation norms (e.g., expectations for when to be able to use accents accurately in Spanish). Their findings make the imposition of English writing norms on Spanish writing highly problematic.

An integrated functional view is not always reflected in documents that outline the nature of proficiency in the dominant language to be developed by minority language speakers. Language proficiency standards typically list separate listening, speaking, reading, and writing skills organized by grade and proficiency levels. They rarely make explicit reference to (the use of) native language and literacy skills as a way of demonstrating knowledge of language or literacy. In addition, the extent to which proficiency expectations have been tied to how children are expected to be able to use the language skills to communicate a range of language functions common to other content areas (e.g., math, science, social studies) varies. In the United States, the most recent standards for bilingual learners' proficiency in English (developed by the professional organization Teachers of English to Speakers of Other Languages [TESOL] and drawing from the standards previously adopted by a consortium of states, the World Class Instructional Design and Assessment [WIDA] consortium) do acknowledge that students must use language for social and academic purposes, specific to the content areas. The standards are organized by proficiency level and skill area as well as by subject area (e.g., tasks students must be able to complete in math or science in English).

Multilingual Acquisition

The process of mastering multiple language repertoires is often divided into **simultaneous language acquisition** and **successive language acquisition**. In the case of simultaneous or bilingual acquisition, children grow up speaking two or more languages early on (generally, before the age of 3 is used as a cut-off point). Successive acquisition or second language learning involves learning another language after one language has already been more or less established. For many, this involves going to school where a language other than the home language is used. These distinctions blur, however, when considering multilingual acquisition contexts, for example, bilingualism at home, learning a third language in school, monolingualism at home, or learning two languages in school.

GROWING UP MULTILINGUALLY

Multilingual scenarios are immensely diverse and depend on language practices in the home, the family, the community, and other specific domains (e.g., church, school, work). Romaine (1995) distinguishes six different home language scenarios based on the language or languages spoken by the parents, the relationship to the societal language, and the distribution of the languages at home and the community (Table 3.1).

A distinction is often made between the simultaneous acquisition of two languages from birth and the sequential acquisition of two languages in childhood, (typically after the age of three; McLaughlin, 1984). Most researchers have been interested in early multilingual acquisition. This research consists of case studies of individual children who acquire two languages simultaneously. Only a handful of studies have considered the simultaneous acquisition

---

TABLE 3.1

Bilingual Language Learning Configurations

Type 1. One parent–one language
One of the languages is the dominant language of the community; both parents are native speakers of different languages.

Type 2. Nondominant home language/one language, one environment
Both parents are native speakers of different languages; minority language at home, dominant language outside the home.

Type 3. Nondominant home language without community support
Parents speak the same native language, which is not the dominant language of the community.

Type 4. Double nondominant home language without community support
Parents are native speakers of different languages.

Type 5. Non-native parents
Parents are native speakers of the dominant language; one parent addresses the children in a language that is not the parent's native language.

Type 6. Mixed languages
Parents and community are bilingual.

Source: Romaine, 1995, pp. 183–185.

of three languages at home (De Houwer, 2004; Hoffman, 2001; Maneva, 2004; Quay, 2001). These bilingual and multilingual acquisition studies typically involve middle class, well-educated parents, often linguists studying the language development of their own children. These parents tend to maintain a one parent–one language policy in the home with the idea that this practice would provide their children with sufficient input and opportunities to support their complete development of two languages.

One of the earliest bilingual studies was conducted by Jules Ronjat (1913), who studied the development of French and German in his son, Louis. Leopold (1939) followed with three volumes documenting the vocabulary, phonology, and syntax/morphology development of his daughter, Hildegard (both studies are described in McLaughlin, 1984). The findings of these and more recent case studies (De Houwer, 1990; Deuchar & Quay, 2000; Saunders, 1988) have been fairly consistent in showing that there is no evidence to suggest that there is a limit to how many languages children can learn or that multilingual children are cognitively behind or language delayed (Genesee, Paradis, & Crago, 2003).

Bilingual children and monolingual children have similar developmental milestones. Speech perception research shows that bilingual infants can distinguish between different languages by 2 months of age. Babbling is distinct for both languages and emerges around the same time as it does in monolingual children. Bilingual children show similar rates of development in their mean length of utterance. Though much of this research has taken place under different conditions and with a small number of children, the research suggests that growing up bilingually parallels monolingual development without delays.

Although universal principles of acquisition appear to apply, bilinguals also show unique language behaviors because they are sorting out two language systems (McLaughlin, 1984; Menyuk & Brisk, 2005). It is now generally agreed that bilingual children separate their language systems early on and apply rules within and across languages as they master the structure and use of each language (Genesee et al., 2003). Studies have found that as early as almost 2 years of age, bilingual children know which language to use with whom and in what context. Fantini (1985) reports that his son would switch between the two languages at home (bilingual environment) but never in preschool (monolingual environment).

Some cross-linguistic differences are quantitative. For example, bilingual children make the same kinds of errors as monolingual children but more frequently and sometimes for a longer period because of influences from the other language. Döpke (cited in Genesee et al., 2003) found that German-English bilinguals went through the same developmental stages for word order in acquiring German as monolingual German-speaking children. The

TABLE 3.2

Some Unique Linguistic Developmental Patterns among Multilingual Children

Phonology
- When phonemes are differentially difficult, the easier phoneme will be applied in both languages.
- Words that are difficult to pronounce may be avoided completely.
- Blends may occur that take elements from both languages.

Semantics
- Synonyms seem at first to compete. Example: the child uses *please* (English) for formal situations, *bitte* (German) for informal situations.
- The meanings of words are extended to the other language.

Syntax
- Perceptual salience appears to play a role in the order of acquisition of certain structures in both languages. Example: the use of noun inflection for locative (Hungarian) appears earlier than the use of prepositions (Serbo-Croatian).
- Most of the differential acquisition patterns parallel those found in L1 acquisition (i.e., more complex patterns are acquired later). It also appears that rules found in both languages are applied before language-specific rules.

Sources: McLaughlin, 1984; Menyuk & Brisk, 2005.

bilingual children used the same kind of word order structures but made more errors that corresponded to the word rules of English than did monolinguals.

Other cross-linguistic differences are qualitative, that is, they reflect strategies for language learning that monolingual children do not use. For example, bilingual children may extend the meaning of a word in one language to the other language. Imedadze (described in Menyuk & Brisk, 2005) found that the Georgian word for ball to denote a toy, a radish, and stone spheres at a park entrance was transferred to Russian. Table 3.2 summarizes more uniquely bilingual acquisition patterns.

Early bilingual acquisition studies affirm that bilingualism does not confuse or delay development for multilingual children. Bilingual children understand early on which language to use according to the speaker or topic and under normal conditions do not demonstrate developmental delays. More important, multilingual children will learn their languages because there is an authentic communicative need to do so. A child's rate of development in two or more languages will therefore depend on in what contexts and how frequently each language is heard and used in his or her environment. Family-based studies have found that the one parent–one language strategy does not always result in children's speaking both languages. It is argued that frequency of parent language input, level of engagement with the language through interaction, and the use of bilingual discourse strategies may play a role in strengthening or undermining the use of the native language (De Houwer, 2007). Initial delays in one language usually disappear with sufficient input in that language alongside the other language (Menyuk & Brisk, 2005). Once the need to use the language is removed from the context, it will be more difficult to maintain competence in the language or develop competence without a real purpose. Some studies suggest, however, that receptive bilingualism may be sufficient to be later activated into productive bilingualism (Hurtado & Vega, 2004; Jisa, 2000; Meisel, 2007), so that bilingual exposure is not necessarily a futile exercise. If schools aim to develop multilingual competence, they must therefore consider what opportunities students have to engage with the language at school and at home.

Since acquisition contexts can change within a lifetime, multilingual development is rarely stable. New languages are added and skills can be lost when a language is no longer used (**language attrition**). Noam is a good example (Faingold, 2004a). Noam was born in Israel, where his parents spoke with him in Brazilian Portuguese and Spanish and a caretaker spoke with him in Hebrew. During this time, Noam used all three languages to express his communicative needs. When he went to preschool, the dominant language became Hebrew both at home and outside the home. A move to the United States introduced English when he was 6 years old and language use shifted accordingly. During this period Noam did not want his parents to speak any language other than English in public with him and he used only English. It was not until he was an adolescent that both Hebrew and Spanish re-emerged in Noam's life, one as a return to his Jewish roots (stimulated by his parents) and the other as a foreign language in school. His knack for word play and his ability to joke in three languages (Hebrew, Spanish, English) at that time illustrate his changed attitude toward his multilingualism.

CODE-SWITCHING OR TRANSLANGUAGING

One of the most common bilingual phenomena is the use of both languages within a conversation or text. When a bilingual person begins a conversation in one language and then switches to the other language is referred to as **code-switching.** Linguistically, a distinction is often made between switches within phrases or sentences, or intrasentential code-switching (e.g., "I want *una flor*"), and between phrases or sentences, or intersentential code-switching (e.g., "I want to have coffee, *pero mi taza está rota*"; "I went to school. *Después fui a mi casa.*"). While most research has focused on the use of both languages in oral communication, code-switching also occurs in writing (Escamilla & Hopewell, 2007).

A holistic view of bilingualism approaches code-switching as normal bilingual behavior and explores its diverse linguistic and functional characteristics. This research stresses that, first, code-switching is systematic and not random: it follows certain linguistic rules that govern which switches are allowed and which are not acceptable (Herdina & Jessner, 2002; Myers-Scotton, 2006b; Romaine, 1995). Second, code-switching is purposeful, that is, it fulfills specific communicative functions. There is now a large body of research on the different functions that code-switching has in natural conversation as well as in the classroom (Ferguson, 2006; Myers-Scotton, 2006a). In the classroom, for example, teachers use code-switching for pedagogical reasons (access to the curriculum, classroom management), for establishing relations, and for affirming students' identities (Gajo, 2007; Lin, 2006; Serra, 2007). Bilingual negotiations occur quite naturally among students and switching to the native language aids problem solving or task completion in cooperative learning groups (Anton & DiCamilla, 1999; Garcia, 2009; Reyes, 2004). García (2009, p. 155) presents the following example of how bilingualism functions as a way of meaning construction among three Spanish-speaking children with different bilingual ranges who are writing and drawing in English journals.

ADOLFO: [Looking out the window and talking to himself]
Está lloviendo mucho. "It is raining a lot."
Look [telling the others] It's washing there. There's washing *afuera* "outside."

GABRIELA: ¿*Está lloviendo?* [She asks him].
[Turning to me] He says raining. He speaks Spanish, only Spanish.
[Turning to boy] Adolfo, *raining.*

ADOLFO: Raining.

To capture the dynamic nature of this kind of language use across languages and its meaning-making dimension, García and others prefer the term **translanguaging**.

Language brokering is an area that deserves special mention for bilinguals. Many bilingual children translate for their parents or other family members in a wide range of contexts, such as immediate translation when someone comes to the door of the home and translation of notes or letters from school, businesses, and medical offices (Orellana, Dorner, & Pulido, 2003; Weisskirch, 2005). Language brokering plays an important role in the acculturation process for immigrant children (Tse, 1995) and in their second language acquisition (McQuillan & Tse, 1995), and it may contribute to their academic success (Buriel, Perez, De Ment, Chavez, & Moran, 1998). Overall, bilingual learners experience language brokering, or para-phrasing (Orellana, Dorner, & Polido, 2003) as an important and enjoyable part of their lives, even though at times they may be put in difficult or embarrassing situations with their elders.

Because translanguaging breaks monolingual rules, it is not surprising that the fractional perspective on code-switching has been one of interference. According to this perspective, code-switching is seen as confusion, an inability to keep the two languages separate, and an indicator of lack of competence in the language. Mostly, code-switching is seen as filling a lexical gap: the speaker does not know the word and inserts a word from their other language to communicate. Bilingual children's code-switching is subsequently interpreted as a sign of developmental delay or a crutch for learning that should have occurred in one language only.

While filling lexical gaps is one function of code-switching, several studies have found that code-switching is not primarily a strategy for those with limited proficiency. In fact, Zentella (1997) and Martínez-Roldán & Sayers (2006) found that the most fluent bilinguals engaged in more frequent code-switching. Zentella also notes that code-switching for lexical gaps may simply be a strategy in the moment rather than a reflection of not knowing the word in the other language. Rather than a handicap, code-switching is an important communicative strategy, and therefore it is important to create bilingual spaces where students can use these strategies as a resource for learning (García, 2009; Gumperz & Cook-Gumperz, 2005; Reyes, 2004).

Access to the Minority Language: Maintenance, Shift, and Loss

Most research into language development has focused on how children and adults can maintain and develop competence in the minority language, assuming that skills in the dominant language will be developed through media, schools, and other domains. This section highlights some of the contextual (societal, community, and home) variables that affect whether opportunities for the use of minority languages will expand, remain the same, or be restricted. These contextual variables will subsequently affect what schools can do and need to consider when their goal is to develop and expand multilingual repertoires for their students. (Chapter 5 discusses school-based approaches to support multilingualism.)

ADDITIVE AND SUBTRACTIVE ENVIRONMENTS

A common distinction used to explain differences in multilingual competence attainment is whether languages are learned in additive or subtractive bilingual contexts. The distinction was introduced by Wallace Lambert (1977) to explain the positive attainment of French-English bilingual competence in the

Canada context and the struggle of minority-language speakers in other settings to achieve the same outcome. As the two official languages of Canada, French and English have high prestige. They both have significant literary traditions and are used in the wider society. Lambert refers to the attainment of language proficiency in this acquisition context as **additive bilingualism** because it involves languages of social value and respect and "the learning of the second language does not portend the slow replacement of it for the home or the other language" (p. 18). As their languages are accepted and valued, students' sense of self and views of their own language are positive and supported.

In contrast, for speakers whose native languages are not valued there is differential prestige: one language is the high-status language (the societal language), the other language (the minority language) is assigned a low status. Consequently, proficiency in the high-status language is valued over proficiency in the minority language. For these speakers, learning the second language requires them to "put aside their ethnic language for a national language" and their degree of bilingualism will "reflect some stage in the subtraction of the ethnic language and associated culture, and their replacement with another" (p. 19). **Subtractive bilingualism** is also associated with a loss of identity or the development of a sense of self that is ambivalent when parents and students begin to perceive their own language and culture as inferior (Cummins, 1979). Recall Datta's (2000) shock at the level of shame and embarrassment among multilingual children in England who were able to speak or read and write languages other than English. They had come to accept the negative attitudes toward their native languages from school personnel and the society at large.

Multilingual competence develops more easily (though not necessarily automatically) in additive contexts, because both languages receive attention in schools and in society. In subtractive contexts, special attention must be given to the overlooked language, the minority language, if multilingual competence is to develop. Such attention may involve the enactment of specific school policies to counter the status differences between the two languages, such as an equal distribution of the two languages across the curriculum and the use of both languages for literacy development. The sociopolitical context is therefore an important variable that affects the maintenance of the proficiency in the minority language when it is surrounded by or interacts with other languages.

It is important to remember that the subtractive/additive distinction is not a mere matter of one language plus or minus another. As stated earlier, multilingual learners' multiple languages stand in a complex and dynamic relationship to one another (García, 2009). We will continue to use the term additive in this book with this dynamic nature in mind, as a principle of building on and extending multiple linguistic repertoires.

CONTEXTUAL VARIABLES AND LANGUAGE USE

Some scholars have used the concept of **ethnolinguistic vitality** to describe the potential of language communities to maintain their identities and languages when they come into contact with other communities. Bourhis (2000), identifies three sets of factors: status factors (economic, social, and symbolic), demographic factors (geographical distribution, interlanguage intermarriage, and urbanization), and institutional support factors (mass media, religion, administrative services, schooling in the minority language).

Others researchers have emphasized that language behavior changes in accordance with the **social networks** that surround individuals. Social networks are described in terms of size (how many people you know), frequency of contact, the amount of time spent with members in the network, the interconnectedness of different networks, and how important people within the network are to the individual (Marshall, 2004; Wierzbicki, 2004). The argument is that the more a language is used with people who are most significant in one's life, the more likely that that language will be used and maintained. Social networks include local networks but also those networks in the country of origin (Milroy, 2001). Weak networks in a particular language may, in contrast, threaten the continued use of a particular language and support a shift to dominant languages in the network.

A shift in social networks may also initiate a shift in language use. Baker (2006, pp. 79–80) discusses two landmark studies that nicely illustrate this process. Dorian (1981) explored the demise of Gaelic in a fishing community in East Sutherland, Scotland that was relatively socially and geographically isolated. As a result of the decline in the fishing industries, young people were forced to move out of the communities into the cities where English was the dominant language spoken. Intermarriage and increased contact with English speakers gradually eroded the use of Gaelic in daily lives.

Gal (1979) documented a similar pattern with German and Hungarian in Oberwart, a border area between Hungary and Austria. After World War II, speaking German was linked to modernization and "urbanness," whereas Hungarian was associated with farmers and "peasantness." Gal notes that in particular the women chose non-Hungarian-speaking husbands and through intermarriage and their partners' monolingualism in German, a language shift from Hungarian to German occurred. These two studies illustrate the influence of urbanization and industrialization on language shift, the link between language choice and (perceived) social and economic mobility, and how contact between two languages of unequal status can negatively affect the low-status language.

Other variables include the response of the host society to a particular group, the social distance between groups, access to the home country, the number of speakers, geographical distance, attitudes toward the language, and economic incentives, as well as issues of race, class, and gender. Individual variables also affect native language maintenance and second language acquisition, such as individual motivation to maintain the native language and learn a second language, literacy skills, cultural identity, and schooling experiences (Baker, 2006; Brisk, 2006; see Table 3.3). Studies based on census data show that immigrant language maintenance depends on the use of the native language at home (by both parents) and its use in the surrounding community. Spanish language use and maintenance can be more easily supported in the home in a geographical area like Miami in South Florida but will be more challenging in a rural area with few Spanish speakers (Alba, Logan, Lutz, & Stults, 2002)

These factors can both positively and negatively affect language use and hence encourage or discourage language maintenance or shift (within a group) or bilingual competence development (for the individual). For example, the number of speakers of Catalán in Spain is relatively small, as is the region where the language is used. Moreover, under the Franco regime (1936–1975), it was illegal to use the language. However, even under these conditions, Catalán is used in schools throughout the state and continues to be a key identifier of Catalonia's cultural and political identity. Group size (number of speakers) can be a hindering factor for minority language maintenance but may not play as dominant a role when combined other factors, such as strong historical, political, or territorial claims and autonomy (Paulston, 1994).

IMMIGRANT LANGUAGES AND LANGUAGE SHIFT

Of particular interest to policy makers and researchers has been the extent to which immigrant groups maintain their home languages. Whether such language maintenance is seen as desirable or problematic depends on one's view of linguistic diversity. Within the assimilationist, monolingual discourse, there is a deep concern for whether immigrants are learning the dominant language as an important indicator of their level of assimilation into mainstream society; native language maintenance is interpreted as a hindrance to this process. Pluralist, multilingual discourses see a shift to the dominant language as the potential breakdown of the integrity of ethnic communities and families; maintaining the native language does not imply not speaking English and supports the development of valuable bilingual skills. To ascertain societal or group patterns of language maintenance or shift toward the societal language, researchers rely mostly on census data. Before presenting the general trends of these studies, it is important to point out the limitations of these data.

TABLE 3.3

Language Maintenance Factors

Language Retention	Language Loss
Political, Social, and Demographic Factors:	
Large number of speakers living in concentration (ghettos, reservations, ethnic neighborhoods, rural speech islands)	Small number of speakers, dispersed among speakers of other languages
Recent arrival and/or continuing Immigration	Long, stable residence in the United States
Geographical proximity to the homeland; ease of travel to the homeland	Homeland remote and inaccessible
High rate of return to the homeland; intention to return to the homeland; homeland language community still intact	Low rate or impossibility of return to homeland (refugees, Indians displaced from their tribal territories)
Occupational continuity	Occupational shift, especially from rural to urban
Vocational concentration, i.e. employment where coworkers share language background; employment within the language community (stores serving the community, traditional crafts, homemaking, etc.)	Vocations in which some interaction with English or other languages is required; speakers dispersed by employers (e.g. African slaves)
Low social and economic mobility in mainstream occupations	High social and economic mobility in mainstream occupations.
Low level of education, leading to low social and economic mobility; but educated and articulate community leaders, familiar with the English-speaking society and loyal to their own language community.	Advanced level of education, leading to social and economic mobility; education that alienates and Anglifies potential community leaders
Nativism, racism, and ethnic discrimination as they serve to isolate a community and encourage identity only with the ethnic group rather than the nation at large	Nativism racism, and ethnic discrimination as they force individuals to deny their ethnic identity in order to make their way in society

Cultural Factors:

Mother-tongue institutions, including schools, churches, clubs, theatres, presses, broadcasts	Lack of mother-tongue institutions, from lack of interest or lack of resources
Religious and/or cultural ceremonies requiring command of the mother tongue	Ceremonial life institutionalized in another tongue or not requiring active use of mother tongue
Ethnic identity strongly tied to language; nationalistic aspirations as a language group; mother tongue the homeland national language	Ethnic identity defined by factors other than language, as for those from multilingual countries or language groups spanning several nations; low level of nationalism
Emotional attachment to mother tongue as a defining characteristic of ethnicity, of self	Ethnic identity, sense of self derived from factors such as religion, custom, race rather than shared speech
Emphasis on family ties and position in kinship or community network	Low emphasis on family or community ties, high emphasis on individual achievement
Emphasis on education, if in mother-tongue or community-controlled schools, or used to enhance awareness of ethnic heritage; low emphasis on education otherwise	Emphasis on education and acceptance of public education in English
Culture unlike Anglo society	Culture and religion congruent with Anglo society

Linguistic Factors:

Standard, written variety as mother tongue	Minor, nonstandard, and/or unwritten variety as mother tongue
Use of Latin alphabet in mother tongue, making reproduction inexpensive and second language literacy relatively easy	Use of non-Latin writing system in mother tongue, especially if it is unusual, expensive to reproduce, or difficult for bilinguals to learn
Mother tongue with international status	Mother tongue of little international importance
Literacy in mother tongue, used for exchange within the community and with homeland	No literacy in mother tongue; illiteracy
Some tolerance for loan words, if they lead to flexibility of the language in its new setting	No tolerance for loan words, if no alternate ways of capturing new experience evolve; too much tolerance of loans, leading to mixing and eventual language loss

The Use of Census Data

Census data are in general problematic for several reasons. First, questions about language and languages are often changed significantly from one census to the next, making it difficult to compare data. For example, the 2001 Canadian Census framed its language ability question for its two official languages, French and English, as "being able to hold a conversation." In the earlier 1986 census, the interpretation was more stringent: being able to hold a "lengthy conversation on a variety of topics."

Another factor is the validity of the answer itself, which is embedded in the sociopolitical context at the time the census is taken. Often individuals respond to societal attitudes about the language, downplaying their competence in a language if it is perceived negatively or overestimating their competence if it is seen as a desired behavior. Significantly more individuals indicated they spoke Irish in 2001 than in 1991. While it is possible that there were indeed more speakers of Irish, another factor that may have influence the responses was the declaration of Irish as the official language of Ireland. From being a stigmatized language, speaking Irish had become a positive marker of Irish cultural identity. Unlike 10 years before, claiming Irish proficiency was now desirable.

Finally, it is important to remember that the way census data are collected is not neutral. The U.S. Census is an interesting barometer of the role that language (and race) has played in defining the national identity. The original purpose of the census was to determine who could be taxed and where voters lived. Since then, its use has been expanded and it is now used to determine, for example, health service provisions (e.g., to identify appropriate emergency provisions in areas with many elderly people) and to identify voting, economic, and employment discrimination. While to most of us the census seems to be an objective tool because of its focus on numbers and statistical analyses, it is in fact a product of how diversity is constructed by the national government. What gets reported, how data are presented, and how data are interpreted reflect particular ways of thinking about a population and who is counted in the national community (Leeman, 2004; Stevens, 1999).

The first U.S. Census in 1790 defined the population in terms of race (white and other), sex (male and female), age (under and over 16 years), and position in society (free and slave). Native Americans were not counted and language issues were excluded as well, an indication of the importance of race, rather than language, in defining the nation, even though many languages were spoken at the time. It was not until 1890, in the heyday of immigration from non-English-speaking countries, such as Poland and Italy, that language was included as a question. The "old" immigrants were very concerned about being able to assimilate these new immigrant groups into

Since 1990, the Census asks a three-part series of questions:

A. Does this person speak a language other than English at home?

(For those who speak another language)

B. What is this language? _____

C. How well does this person speak English? — very well, well, not well, not at all

Figure 3.1   The 2010 Census language questions. Source: http://www.census.gov/population/www/socdemo/lang_use.html

their existing society in an era of rapid economic change. Measuring who spoke English and who did not became more important during this period. The clear relationship between the census and immigration re-emerges in the 1940s and 1950s (both periods of low immigration) when the language question was dropped. Concerns about how well a person could speak English began in another era with growing immigration, the 1980s.

The census questions about language changed several times before the government settled on the current set of three questions (Figure 3.1). In the past, the questions have asked about a person's ability to speak English (yes, no) and what language was spoken in the person's home. The question about how well the person speaks English was introduced in the 1980 census and has been asked, along with the other two that appear in Figure 3.1, in each succeeding census, including in the most recent 2010 American Community Survey. These three language questions reveal how the census represents linguistic diversity and multilingualism today.

The first question presents linguistic diversity as anything other than English. It takes English as the norm and knowing a language other than English as varying from that norm. The census could as easily have asked, "What language(s) does this person speak at home?" recognizing bilingual and multilingual families. Linguistic diversity is also restricted to speaking a language other than English at home. This restriction may lead to an underestimation of the diverse language resources in this country, because, for example, it leaves out individuals who may speak English at home but other languages in other domains, such as work or school. It also excludes those who may have literacy skills in a language other than English but may not use a language other than English orally at home.[1] To date, the census has reflected no interest in documenting multilingual competence. A yes answer to Question 11a leads to further questions about the person's English-speaking ability but not to questions about oral or literacy abilities in his or her other language or languages.

---

[1]The use of an indicator such as "speaking well" is also problematic because it is subject to different interpretations of what it means.

In reporting the census data, researchers have to select how to present their findings. Interestingly, even though there are four categories for Question 11c, census tables typically cluster the last three English ability ratings (well, not well, not at all) as one rating and report them under the heading "Speaks English not very well." The rating "Speaks English very well" is presented as a separate category. Why the category "Speaks English well" is included in the "Speaks English not very well" is unclear. Notice how this can skew the data to create an image of less English ability.

The U.S. Census contributes to the definition of the imagined community of the United States by determining who gets counted and who remains invisible. It has also been sensitive to political and social events in a given period, initially stressing the importance of race and property (excluding African Americans and Native Americans), and later, in response to immigration trends, including questions about language. In matters of language, the census has been guided more by an assimilationist than a pluralist discourse, revealing that it is concerned with English and ability in English. The fact that the census does not include questions about proficiency in languages other than English shows its preoccupation with English as the dominant language, whereas the (potential of) multilingualism remains invisible. What questions are asked (and what questions are not asked) and how they are asked are therefore important to keep in mind when analyzing census data.

Losing Bilingual Skills

Excluding Native American languages, the 1790 U.S. Census estimated that about 49% of the national population was of English origin, while nearly 19% was of African origin, 14% of Spanish origin, and 15% of Scotch, Scotch Irish, or Irish origin (Ricento, 2005, p. 350). By 2000, 82% of those surveyed stated that they spoke only English at home. One indicator of the move toward monolingualism in the United States has been the intergenerational shift among immigrant groups and indigenous language speakers from the use of the native language to the use of English (i.e., language shift). By the third generation, language and cultural maintenance has become very difficult because of the shift of the language at home to English (Padilla, 2006).

The three-generation language shift pattern appears to be fairly consistent for many immigrant groups in the United States, though with exceptions, such as the Greeks and Italians, who have maintained their languages across four generations. Even the continued influx of new immigrants has not reduced the shift to English. Study after study on Hispanics (Alba, 2005; Alba, et al., 2002; Portes & Rumbaut, 2001; Portes & Schauffler, 1994; Rumbaut, Massey, & Bean, 2006; Veltman, 1983) has documented a preference for the use of English among the most recent groups of Spanish-speaking immigrants. Some argue that the shift occurs even faster today: young and adolescent immigrant children prefer English within a few years of their arrival in the United States (Hakuta & D'Andrea, 1991). This is true for adults as well. The number of immigrants wanting to enroll in adult English as a second language classes greatly outnumber the number of classes being offered, resulting in long waiting lines (Tucker, 2006). Alba et al. (2002) conclude that, despite claims of some to the contrary, there is absolutely no threat to English in the United States. For current immigrant groups the issue is not whether they learn English—they do and want to—but what is the viability of their bilingualism.

The rapid shift to English, however, has significant consequences. Children's shift to speaking only the dominant language can lead to the deterioration of family ties and intergenerational communication (Fillmore, 1991; Portes & Hao, 1998; Tseng & Fuligni, 2000). When children experience language attrition and eventually no longer share their language with their parents, the change can limit the kind of parent-child interactions that take place. While parents may still be able to discuss everyday matters, they may be less able to address deeper and more complex topics with their children, including cultural beliefs and values. Fillmore (1991b), who examined language loss in young children, explains the significance of this phenomenon well:

> What is lost is no less than the means by which parents socialize their children: When parents are unable to talk to their children, they cannot easily convey to them their values, beliefs, understandings, or wisdom about how to cope with their experiences. . . . Talk is a crucial link between parents and children: it is how parents impart their culture to their children and enable them to become the kind of men and women they want them to be. When parents lose the means for socializing and influencing their children, rifts develop and families lose the intimacy that comes from shared beliefs and understanding. (Fillmore, 1991).

In his autobiography about growing up as a Mexican American boy in California, Richard Rodriguez (1982) describes how his relationship with his parents changed as he spoke more English and lost his command of Spanish.

> Matching the silence I started hearing in public was a new quiet at home. The family's quiet was partly due to the fact that, as we children learned more and more English, we shared fewer and fewer words with our parents. Sentences needed to be spoken slowly when a child addressed his mother or father. (Often the parents wouldn't understand.) The child would need to repeat himself. (Still the parent misunderstood.) The young voice, frustrated, would end up saying, "Never mind"—the subject was closed. (Rodriguez, 1982, p. 23)

Shin (2005) found a reaction similar to Rodriguez's in her study with Korean parents. Fifteen percent of the parents indicated that miscommunications with their children (in English) were resolved with the child's giving up or saying, "Never mind." Moreover, in over 30% of the cases, parents would ask the child to explain it again in Korean, illustrating the importance of the children's bilingual skills.

Minority families have the challenge of negotiating child rearing within the cultural and linguistic practices that are familiar to them but in a context that expects socialization in another language or other languages and cultures as well. In this process, real tensions may emerge out of conflicting expectations at home, among peers, and in the community, the school, and the larger society (Phelan, Davidson, & Cao, 1991). Patanaray-Ching, Kitt-Hinrichs, & Nguyen (2006) describe how Vietnamese parents were very supportive of school for their daughter, Han. They gave native language support, practiced with homework, valued education, and stressed school achievement. Yet, consistent with the Vietnamese culture, the father believed that, while his daughter should learn English, he did not want her to become too educated to find a husband. A complex set of factors thus mediates parents' attitudes toward bilingualism, their actual language use in the home and with their children, and the extent to which children will subsequently develop and use their minority language (Pawels, 2005).

The research on language maintenance and shift in the United States is often a direct response to fears that the "new" immigrants will not assimilate in the same way previous immigrant groups did before them. Many studies try to alleviate this fear and negate the image of the new immigrants' not learning English. Using census data, they can demonstrate that immigrants are indeed learning English and that immigrant groups are experiencing drastic language shifts. The linear trend toward linguistic assimilation (from monolingualism in the native language through bilingualism to monolingualism in English) is not questioned. This assimilationist paradigm assumes that a shift to English is both necessary and desirable and that bilingualism is a transitional phase between the two monolingual ends of the continuum. Linton (2004) argues, however, for a more additive approach. Citing the benefits of bilingualism for the individual and the group (see Chapter 2), she proposes that bilingualism could be considered a desirable endpoint and indicator of immigrant integration. From this perspective language maintenance along with English proficiency becomes the desired pattern. Taking up the latter paradigm would change how languages are supported and used in various domains, including schools.

Bilingualism and Biliteracy in School

While many studies have documented simultaneous bilingual acquisition, fewer studies exist that have considered **simultaneous biliteracy development**.

Literacy is often not introduced formally until children go to school and hence the focus has been more on second language literacy development without much attention to literacy skills in other languages. For some, the language of school may in fact be their third language or the school may introduce two more languages in a trilingual education model (e.g., Aronin, 2005; Cenoz, 2003, 2005; Cenoz & Valencia, 1994). While developing literacy skills in more than one language is an option for some students, for many children going to school means exclusive exposure to the dominant language.

BILITERACY DEVELOPMENT

For many bilingual children, biliteracy development begins when they are exposed to literacies in different languages as part of their home and community and in school, including preschool. Children observe their parents reading or writing in different languages, such as writing letters to family members (Schwarzer, 2001). Older children may engage their younger siblings in literacy activities at home that they have learned in school (Gregory, 1998). Volk and De Acosta (2001) noted Puerto Rican children's participation in church-based literacy activities, such as reading the Bible aloud in Spanish and incorporating their own versions of prayer in their play. Before going to school, multilingual children have therefore already built up expectations and ideas about what literacy is in the languages of their home and community.

Because there are so few bilingual programs, our understanding of formal simultaneous biliteracy development is still relatively limited. Research has mostly focused on second language reading or writing (at a later age) and not on the simultaneous development of literacy in both languages. While the second language acquisition research includes research on the influence of the native language on learning another language (Odlin, 1989), it tends to be more interested in how children and adults master various aspects of reading and writing of their second language than how they negotiate literacy in and through two or more languages. Other studies have taken a more holistic, pluralist approach, trying to describe the processes of biliteracy and the conditions that promote biliteracy development (Moll & Dworin, 1996; Reyes & Azuara, 2008; Walters, 2005). From this latter research, three important understandings have emerged.

First, research has stressed the importance of an integrated approach to the development of literacy in a second language, allowing students who are learning a second language to use all their linguistic and cultural resources, including knowledge and skills in their first or native language, rather than limiting them to what they know in their second language (Edelsky, 1986; Hudelson, 1984). As early as the 1980s, Hudelson (1987) demonstrated the importance of approaching biliteracy from this perspective. Her study took place during a time when it was believed that oral language development had to precede literacy development, an assumption based on experiences with monolinguals. She argued that this assumption did not hold for bilingual writers. In her study, bilingual writers used their knowledge from their first language and applied it to what they were learning their second language, even without a sophisticated oral language base in the second language. Rather than postponing writing until bilingual children have developed high levels of oral proficiency in their second language, she therefore advocated the integration of reading, writing, listening, and speaking.

Second, studies have documented the interconnectedness of the two languages for bilingual learners, or **language transfer**. These studies have found that literacy skills in the first language are strongly correlated to literacy levels developed in the second language for languages that have the same alphabet as well as between languages with different orthographies (Cummins, 2000; Oller & Eilers, 2002). Jiménez, García, and Pearson (1995) documented reading strategies of a fluent bilingual reader, including the use of **cognates** between English and Spanish, that is words from both languages that have similar sounds and meanings, such as famous/famoso. They also found that students monitored their comprehension in both languages. Others have shown how children compare and contrast the writing systems of their language, apply writing behaviors in their first language to their writing in the second language, and use rules of one language when writing the other (Escamilla & Hopewell, 2007; Gort, 2006; Kenner, 2004; Reyes & Azuara, 2008). Even when they have not yet received formal instruction in the second language, children will transfer their understandings of their first language literacy to literacy activities in their second language (de las Luz Reyes, 2001; Peréz, 2004).

Language transfer is bi-directional, that is, from the first to the second language and from the second to the first language (Cook, 2003; Gort, 2008). As some have pointed out, this phenomenon makes it difficult to use labels such as "native," "first," and "second" language. Students can be more proficient speakers in Spanish than in English but better readers in English. With some assistance, many of these children can use their English reading proficiency (their knowledge of reading strategies) to develop their "first language" reading in Spanish (Dworin, 2003).

A third finding from biliteracy studies is that there are many pathways to biliteracy (de las Luz Reyes, 2001; Gort, 2006; Peréz, 2004). Some bilingual children choose to write in one language before beginning to read in that language. Others prefer to write in one language when given the opportunity, even if they are fluent writers in two languages. For example, in a study by Dworin (2003), Kathleen was an African American student whose Spanish receptive skills were higher than her productive skills. She began to write in Spanish before reading in Spanish. These pathways to biliteracy are shaped by the history of the student, the social contexts available for learning, and the support the children receive to engage with topics and texts in both languages (Moll & Dworin, 1996). Gort (2006) suggests that transfer of literacy processes and skills may be contingent on the relative strength in the bilingual's first and second language literacy. Looking at four case study children, de la Luz Reyes (2001) identified two key factors that supported the children's biliteracy development: learning environments that build on children's linguistic and cultural resources, and social play. Working in and across languages allows students to use their cultural experiences and linguistic knowledge for personal, social, and academic purposes. Using school routines around literacy helps students interpret literacy in the second language. Literacy for bilingual children is not associated with one language; they use what they know about literacy across languages.

CUMMINS'S INTERDEPENDENCE HYPOTHESIS

Transfer phenomena and recent biliteracy research confirm as well as extend an important principle of bilingual education, the **interdependence hypothesis**, developed by Jim Cummins (Cummins, 1979, 1981, 2000) to explain the seemingly contradictory outcome that students instructed through two languages perform better or similarly in the societal language when compared with students instructed in only the societal language. In other words, students who spend less time in the second language and receive instruction through their first language can do as well as students who spend all their time in the second language. This finding contradicts the **time-on-task argument**, according to which the amount of time spent in a language is the most important variable in second language learning.

Cummins argues that this outcome can be explained by thinking of the two languages as a think tank reinforcing each other through interdependence and transfer, and not as two separate, isolated containers with limited capacity. He juxtaposes the think tank model, which is also referred to as **common underlying proficiency (CUP)**, and the balance metaphor or the container view that dominated early work on cognition and bilingualism and was referred to as the **separate underlying proficiency (SUP)** model. This distinction follows the distinction between the holistic and the fractional view of bilingualism described earlier.

The interdependence hypothesis focuses on the relationship between the native or first language, L1, and the second language, L2. Cummins (1979) argues that "the level of L2 competence which a bilingual child attains is partially a function of the type of competence the child has developed in L1 at the time when intensive exposure to L2 begins" (p. 75). Transfer involves applying cognitive and linguistic abilities from their first to their second language and using general concepts and knowledge developed in their native language to learn content in the second language. Understanding certain mathematical concepts in Korean, for example, will greatly help learning the same math concepts in English. Finally, if languages are related, transfer also involves the use of language-specific strategies, such as cognates (Cummins, 2000).

Cummins's framework and assumptions are supported by the findings of early biliteracy development described above. Bilingual children use what they learn in one language as a resource for learning in the other language. At the same time, the notion of bidirectionality stresses that Cummins's framework should not be limited to an interpretation of unidirectional transfer from first to second language but should be expanded to include second to first language and literacy influences. While language transfer occurs, research also suggests that is not always automatic and it does not occur across all language features. Explicit cognate instruction was necessary for many students to make links between Spanish and English when reading text. When applied, the use of cognates can positively affect literacy development (August, Carlo, Dressler, & Snow, 2005; Carlo, et al., 2004).

The interdependence hypothesis also stresses that, as a function of language use, multilingual competence is sensitive to the extent to which there are opportunities for communication in a particular language. Especially in communities and societies where one language dominates (e.g., English in the United States), it may be challenging for individuals and communities to maintain and develop bilingual or multilingual competence across multiple domains and across skills (i.e., oracy and literacy). Effective second language teaching is therefore as important as ensuring access to instruction in the students' first language. Because of the way language knowledge and skills are integrated in literacy development, students must have high-quality instruction in first as well as second (and third and fourth) languages and multiple opportunities for using the languages for a range of social and academic purposes. Effective biliteracy development requires students to "read and write in both languages for academic purposes, where biliteracy is an integral and legitimate part of the intellectual culture of the classrooms and where both languages are involved *substantively* in academic tasks" (Moll & Dworin, 1996, p. 240).

SECOND LANGUAGE AND LITERACY LEARNING IN SCHOOL

Learning the dominant language as a second language is more common in school settings than the experience of simultaneous bilingualism and biliteracy development described earlier. For most multilingual children, going to school means switching to a language other than the language or languages used at home with limited access to those languages. While some second language acquisition research considers the role of the first language, most studies focus on how learners develop communicative competence in the second language, with the implicit assumption that the first language system is relatively stable and well-developed.

Extensive studies in the field of second language acquisition offer insights about second language acquisition that are relevant for educators of bilingual learners (for overviews, see Brown, 2006; Lightbown & Spada, 2009; Mitchell & Miles, 2004; VanPatten, 2003). The driving force behind learning a second language, these studies agree, is meaningful communication. Children will learn and practice the language if they have authentic reasons to do so for different communicative purposes and see the value of the language and the purpose of reading and writing. Providing opportunities for meaningful interaction with native or more fluent language speakers can enhance this process (Fillmore, 1991a; Mackey, 2007).

The studies also agree that becoming proficient in a second language takes time, particularly if the goal is for the learner to acquire content in and through that language, as it is in schools. In this regard, a distinction is often introduced between language that is used for social, interactional purposes (**social language proficiency**) and language that is necessary for academic learning and representation in school (**academic language proficiency**) (Cummins, 1981, 2000). Cuevas (2005), for example, describes the complexities of the language of mathematics, which includes words that have other meanings outside of mathematics (e.g., *table*, *square*) and unique syntactical structures ("if . . . then," "larger than," "in all"). Word problems are often linguistically complex and may contain cultural bias, that is, they require cultural background knowledge to make sense of the problem.

Mastering the discourse of each of the content areas (science, social studies, math), as well as the language and literacy demands of language arts, is a lengthy and challenging process. When proficiency is defined as being able to score at the same level as an average native English speaker on a standardized reading test, research suggests that it may take 7 to 9 years for English language learners catch up with native English speakers (Collier, 1989; Hakuta, Butler, & Witt, 2000). The demands on English language learners in school are thus significant: not only must they learn the language, they also must learn grade-level content through that language, orally and in writing (Gibbons, 2002). Whitin and Whitin (2006) describe Mirella Rizzo, a 2nd grade teacher in an urban school setting with several English language learners. She used the book *How Many Snails?* to teach comparison and sets but was disappointed by the response of her bilingual learners. She soon realized that they were misunderstanding the book's comparative terms. When she used the wordless book *More, Fewer, Less* to help her class understand the relationship between details and sets and verbalize these for themselves, her second language learners were able to apply their mathematical understandings.

Learning a second (or third) language is a developmental process. Students move through stages where they can use the language in more complex ways for a wider range of purposes. Initially, students may go through a silent stage, where they are actively engaged in processing the language and figuring out how it works but they do not say anything yet. Next, they may begin to use single words or two-word phrases and then move to short phrases and simple sentences. Gradually, their sentences become longer and more complex and they learn to use the language in ways consistent with their new language community (Krashen & Terrell, 1983). Similar stages from simple to more and more complex language use have been identified in writing (e.g., Peregoy & Boyle, 2008). Research that has focused on the linguistic aspects of this process has found that learners go through certain predictable stages to master specific aspects of a language. Negation in English, for example, often begins with placing *no* or *not* before the verb or at the beginning of a sentence ("No food"; "I not like it"). In later stages, the learner begins to figure out that negation requires the insertion of the appropriate form of *to do* (*does*, *do*) and *not* and is able to matching person, time, and tense (Lightbown & Spada, 2009).

Finally, it is important to keep in mind that second language acquisition shows much variability and is influenced by a range of factors. Whereas all children typically learn to speak their first language, oral language production in a second language shows significant differences for individuals at the sound (phonology), word (morphology), sentence (syntax), and interactional (pragmatics) level. Research has identified cognitive, linguistic, psychological, social, and cultural factors that affect rate of and attainment in second language acquisition, including first language features, age, learning style, attitudes and motivation, aptitude, anxiety, and personality (Brown, 2006; Gass & Selinker, 2008). It is therefore also important to consider each child's second language process individually.

These insights are also important for second language literacy development. Successful literacy development is tied to meaningful and authentic communication. Students go through stages of reading and writing development, which is influenced by what they know about literacy and features of their native languages as well as their emerging understandings of how the second language works. While the debate about what makes for good reading instruction continues (Allington, 2002; National Reading Panel, 2000), a balance between top-down (using background knowledge, applying understandings about text structures and genre, beginning with the whole of the language and then breaking it down) and bottom-up approaches (beginning with the sounds, then words, then sentences, then paragraphs, then larger texts) is important (Birch, 2007; Grabe & Stoller, 2002). It is also evident that without access to meaning, it is more difficult for second language learners to make connections between oral and written language and to understand written text. Building prior knowledge, building on what students already know in the second language, and developing vocabulary make important contributions to literacy development for second language learners, in addition to providing specific opportunities for developing understandings about sound-letter correspondences (phonics), word formation, and sentence structures (August & Shanahan, 2006; Freeman & Freeman, 2001; Genesee, Lindholm-Leary, Saunders, & Christian, 2006).

Dynamic Approaches to Multilingualism

Schools operate in the wider context of home and community patterns and pressures in support of language maintenance and shift. Educators' understandings about and attitudes toward bilingualism and bilingual competence development will shape their communication with students and parents. If they intend to organize their school on the idea of additive rather than subtractive learning environments, educators need to design their programs in response to existing and desired multilingual repertoires of their students. These programs will depend, in part, on opportunities available at home and in the community to use the minority or the majority language and student and parent attitudes toward bilingualism, the minority language, and the dominant language.

To effectively support multilingualism, educators need to understand how multilingual development occurs in the home and in school. The difference between a holistic, bilingual view of bilinguals and a fractional, two-monolinguals-in-one view, is fundamental to understanding how policy makers and educators have responded to linguistic diversity in schools. Both views make different assumptions about the value of bilingualism and biliteracy, how the two languages are related to each other, and multilingual competence development. These assumptions, in turn, affect educators' understanding and response to bilingual language behaviors (including code-switching and expectations about bilingual vocabulary development), their support for scaffolding for multilingual competence, and assessment practices.

CHAPTER 3
Discussion & Activities

Critical Issues

1. One argument against bilingual approaches in education is that using more than two languages for instruction will result in students' not knowing either language well. Therefore, the argument goes, it is better to teach in only one language. Drawing on the information in this chapter (and Chapter 2 as well), how might you respond to this statement?

2. Consider the following questions to help establish the definition of who is bilingual (adapted from Wei, 2000, pp. 5–6, citing Baker & Prys-Jones).
   - Should the definition be based on (oral) fluency?
   - Should it include only individuals with equal competence in both languages?
   - Is proficiency the only criterion for assessing bilingualism or should we also include the use of two languages?
   - Does bilingualism include all four skills (listening, speaking, reading, writing) receptively and productively?
   - Should self-perception and self-categorization be considered part of the definition?
   - Is bilingualism stable or may there be degrees of bilingualism?
   In what ways does each of these questions present a holistic or a fragmented view of bilingualism? Which questions will matter most to you as a teacher?

3. Interview bilingual individuals about their definition of *bilingualism*. In what ways do they consider themselves bilingual and in what ways do they think they are not? How do their definitions differ from or equate with those presented in the chapter? What is your definition?

Application and Reflection

4. Write your own linguistic autobiography, answering the following questions. What languages (and language varieties) did you learn, when, and with whom? What skills did you develop, and for what purposes did you use each language? How have these experiences shaped your view of bilingualism and learning another language?

5. Consider the contexts of literacy development at home and in school for your students who are bilingual learners. Look around to see what

representations are visible in languages other than the dominant language in your school and your students' community. Ask your students about literacy practices in their homes. (Remember that *literacy* is a broad term that includes a wide range of interactions with written text and includes language on posters, labels on products, newspapers, religious pamphlets, language in computer games, and so forth.)

6. Grosjean argues that a bilingual view of bilinguals has significant implications for doing research in the field of bilingualism. What are some of these implications, for example, for determining how to assess proficiency and what background variables to take into consideration, and for identifying valid comparison groups?

Recommended Readings

THE SOCIOLOGY OF LANGUAGE

Fishman, J. A. (1972). *The sociology of language: An interdisciplinary social science approach to language in society.* Rowley, MA: Newbury House.

> *Fishman is one of the leading scholars in the area of language maintenance, shift, and revitalization. His work spans four decades. In this classic foundational book, he looks at language use in its societal contexts.*

García, O., Peltz, R., Schiffman, H. F., & Fishman, G. S. (Eds.). (2006). *Language loyalty, continuity, and change: Joshua A. Fishman's contributions to international sociolinguistics.* Clevedon, UK: Multilingual Matters.

> *This book provides an excellent overview of Fishman's work.*

BILINGUALISM AND MULTILINGUALISM

Auer, P., & Wei, L. (Eds.). (2009). *Handbook of multilingualism and multilingual communication.* Berlin: Mouton de Gruyter.

> *This book explores the processes of developing and maintaining bilingualism and addresses multilingual language behavior and the societal issues that arise in multilingual contexts.*

Bhatia, T. K., & Ritchie, W. C. (2006). *The handbook of bilingualism.* Malden: Blackwell.

> *This book provides an overview of key linguistic and psycholinguistic perspectives on bilingualism. The final section presents examples of bilingual practices from around the world.*

Grosjean, F. (1982). *Life with two languages: An introduction to bilingualism.* Cambridge: Harvard University Press.

> *Grosjean explores what it means to be bilingual, the advantages of bilingualism, and patterns of bilingualism in society and the individual. This book is a classic in the field.*

Romaine, S. (1995). *Bilingualism* (2nd ed.). Malden: Blackwell.

   Romaine's sociolinguistic approach to bilingualism illustrates the complexity and variation of bilingual individuals, communities, and societies. This book is an excellent introduction to the issues.

Linguistic Diversity and Globalization

4

GUIDING QUESTIONS

- *In what ways is globalization both homogenizing and diversifying?*
- *What conditions make it difficult for language revitalization efforts to succeed?*
- *Does the spread of English threaten linguistic diversity?*

KEY TERMS

globalization	outer circle
glocalization	expanded circle
transnationalism	linguistic imperialism
intergenerational language transmission	anglocentricity
	orientalism
hegemony	appropriation
inner circle	world Englishes

Pluralist and assimilationist discourses can also be found at the global level. The current interconnectedness of the world resulting from advances in technology and continued migration has seen the emergence of global trends toward linguistic and cultural homogenization as well as diversification. This chapter explores these trends as they affect discourses about endangered languages and the spread of English as a lingua franca across the globe.

Globalization and Language Issues

Globalization is a process that involves "the widening, deepening and speeding up of worldwide interconnections in all aspects of contemporary social life" (Dewey, 2007, pp. 323–333). It has been simultaneously identified as encouraging innovative forms of interaction and language use (diversification) and contributing significantly to the world's declining linguistic and cultural diversity (homogenizing impact).

Pluralist trends can be seen in the increased linguistic and cultural contact around the world that breaks down traditional boundaries between language, identity, and culture and allows for new exchanges of knowledge and skills. As an outgrowth of globalization, multinational companies that have a global reach have adapted their practices to specific localities. For example, McDonald's menu accommodates the dietary customs and restrictions of the country in which each restaurant is located. This phenomenon is referred to as **glocalization**. Diversity has become a positively valued commodity, at least for some languages. Businesses and some governments are promoting multilingualism and businesses are using consumers' native languages to encourage online shopping. Europe's Framework Strategy for Multilingualism stresses the importance of multilingualism for economic competitiveness as well as international collaboration. The emphasis is on English, the national language, and a third, international language (Commission of the European Communities, 2005).

Technology in particular has become a resource to support smaller languages and different cultural expressions. Technology has supported new ways for migrants to remain connected with social networks and developments in their home countries; this phenomenon of moving back and forth between countries is referred to as **transnationalism**. Moreover, English is not the only language on the Internet; the representation of other languages than English is increasing and more and more speakers of languages other than English make use of the Internet. Indigenous social movements have been able, as never before, to gain international attention for their plight and connect with and obtain support from other indigenous groups (Dewey, 2007). These examples suggest that increased interconnectedness has supported pluralism and diversity.

Globalization, however, has also been equated with a cultural and linguistic homogenization and westernization that is crowding out other languages and ways of being. Recent worldwide economic and political agreements are seen as contributing to this effect. Since 1995, international trade agreements, such as those negotiated by the World Trade Organization (WTO) and the General Agreement on Trade in Services (GATS), have regulated the spread of cultural goods. Mega mergers, the corporatization and concentration of ownership, and centralized control over production have resulted in a creative industry that is less diverse, less local, and all about economic benefits (Chan-Tibergien, 2006). Publishing in the native language (and tapping into local knowledge) in African countries has been greatly undermined as a result of continued (forced) reliance on foreign publishing houses.

A World Bank loan to the Central African Republic, for example, was contingent on the country's importing French-language textbooks from France and Canada. Since textbooks represented 90% of the book market in Africa, the lack of access to the local market greatly disadvantaged the local publishing and printing industry. It also undermined efforts to use native languages in schools (Brock-Utne, 2001a; Hunt, 2007).

Globalization also contributes to the homogenization of language and culture by intensifying unequal economic conditions and power relationships between countries, causing a typically one-sided flow of information and expertise. Research on the SOCRATES exchange program, a university faculty and student exchange program in the European Union, for example, shows an unequal flow from western to eastern Europe (Slowinski, 1998). Furthermore, westernized bases of knowledge and western worldviews dominate in knowledge-generating industries (including universities) and they are assumed to be appropriate across contexts. As a result, indigenous knowledge and views of the world are rarely reflected in mainstream school curricula and textbooks. Insights from research in industrialized countries are applied uncritically to other contexts, reinforcing the idea that this knowledge base is universal rather than particular to its western context. The implied message is that other ways of knowing are less valid, less important, and less relevant.

PROTECTING DIVERSITY: LANGUAGE RIGHTS

Calls for protective and direct action from governments and other organizations have resulted in a proliferation of laws, treaties, and agreements, as well as agencies and organizations, to protect minority languages (Skutnabb-Kangas, 2000). Among the organizations established in Europe to support linguistic diversity and help protect minority languages are the Mercator Network and the European Bureau of Lesser Used Languages (EBLUL). Organizations such as Terralingua and the Foundation for Endangered Languages advocate for and document linguistic diversity around the world.

The recognition of increased language endangerment has led to legal protection of minority languages internationally. Besides an active agenda to support multilingualism through expanded foreign language education opportunities (Framework Strategy for Multilingualism, 2006), the European Union has regulations to protect the use of regional minority languages within its member countries through its European Charter for Minority Languages (1992) and, more recently, the Lisbon Treaty, which was signed in 2007.

In response to the Declaration of Human Rights, most countries now recognize an individual's right to be protected against discrimination based on language (de Varennes, 1996, 2004; Kymlicka & Patten, 2003; Skutnabb-Kangas, 2002). Several treaties and agreements also acknowledge the right to use and develop the native language in and through private institutions, including businesses and the arts. In contrast, the obligations of government (public) institutions to provide services (including education) in different languages are less clear and are framed primarily in terms of reasonableness of required accommodations. Moreover, a "sliding scale" of numerical strength is often in effect: the greater the number of speakers of languages other than the official government language, the greater the obligation to provide multilingual services (de Varennes, 1996). In September 2007, after 22 years of negotiation, the UN General Assembly approved the *Universal Declaration on the Rights of Indigenous Peoples*, which protects the right to self-determination, including language and culture (Rizvi, 2007). Other international charters and agreements also provide legal interpretative frameworks for indigenous and regional minority language rights and cultural maintenance. While such policies may not necessarily change language use patterns, they do legitimize minority language groups' claims for self-determination and create possibilities for the allocation of national and international resources to support language revitalization, maintenance, and development.

LANGUAGE MAINTENANCE AND REVITALIZATION EFFORTS

For both immigrant and indigenous language speakers, language maintenance is a complex and difficult process (see Chapter 3). Language revitalization efforts focus on improving the language skills of the future generation in the hope of rekindling or ensuring **intergenerational language transmission** from parents to children. This process of children acquiring the minority language as their home language from their parents is considered a precondition for maintaining (the use of) minority languages (Fishman, 2001). Language maintenance and revitalization efforts include the alphabetization of nonliterary languages, the development of textbooks and other texts, community-based celebrations of art, music, and other cultural expressions, and the development and implementation of immersion or bilingual programs (Fishman, 2001; Hale, 1992; Hinton, 2003; Hinton & Hale, 2001; Hornberger, 1998; Hornberger & Lopez, 1998; Huss, Grima Camilleri, & King, 2003; King, 2004; King & Benson, 2004; May, 2000; May & Aikman, 2003; Spolsky, 2003). Increasing minority language use and competence in the next generation has been particularly important because indigenous languages must rely solely on existing speakers. Unlike immigrant languages, indigenous languages have no continued influx of new speakers from other countries.

Most minority language parents have a pluralistic perspective on bilingualism: they want their children to belong in their new culture and at the same time become bilingual and maintain their ethnic identity, and they generally feel positive about bilingual education programs to support this goal

(Amaral, 2001; Craig, 1996; Giacchino-Baker & Piller, 2006; Lao, 2004; Ramos, 2007). However, daily decisions about whether, when, and how to use the minority language and dominant language at home are highly contextualized (Bayley & Schecter, 2003; Bayley, Schecter, & Torres-Ayala, 1996; G. Li, 2006; Pease-Alvarez, 2002; Schecter & Bayley, 1997, 1998; Shin, 2005). Looking at this individual level, it becomes clear how diverse language choice can be. No family follows the same path, even within the same community. And within families, children will vary in their proficiency in the minority language. It is quite common for the oldest child to be fluent and comfortable in the minority language and for younger siblings to prefer the dominant language. In an ethnographic study of three immigrant families, Pease-Alvarez (2002) found that the parents' perceptions of their language and literacy skills in the minority language affected their confidence in using the language at home and teaching it to their children. One family in her study who wanted their children to become bilingual nonetheless decided not to place their children in the bilingual program offered by the school because they had serious concerns about the quality of instruction. She also found that language choices were influenced by the pressure to assimilate, the availability and quality of school programs, and the attitudes in the community.

Maintaining a strong native language presence and sustaining opportunities for using the language can be difficult because of the dominance and power of the societal language in school, the media, and the public domain. Lao (2004) found that even though Chinese parents wanted their children to become bilingual, they used a significant amount of English at home in response to the fact that their children brought the dominant language home from school and used it with their siblings. A similar shift in favor of the dominant language has been observed when children begin to attend a preschool that does not offer instruction in the minority language (Fillmore, 1991, 2000).

Societal discourses about linguistic diversity in general and minority language in particular thus play an important role in the linguistic choices children and parents may (feel they have to) make. In most countries, indigenous languages were violently repressed for many years. Language policies excluded indigenous languages from public life and dismissed these languages and language varieties as useless, worthless, irrelevant, and backward. These negative perceptions and attitudes have become so ingrained in society that both majority and minority language speakers have accepted and "bought into" the idea of the superiority of the dominant language. This acceptance of the normalcy of these language hierarchies is also referred to as **hegemony**.

Today, this discourse of marginalization is often reinforced in the context of globalization. Globalization discourses emphasizes access to the international market and political arena. While efforts to recognize indigenous languages and cultures in school curricula are becoming more common, the relevance of indigenous knowledge for a nation's development continues to be minimized. Indigenous knowledge is often positioned as something that is tied to a far and distant history or origin of the ethnic group, and as such, is seen as static, historical knowledge that may once have been important but is largely irrelevant for the present. When indigenous ways of knowing and doing are contrasted to modern life, they are often viewed as a reactive and traditional, with no potential link to the future and progress (Stroud, 2001, 2003). In this discourse, indigenous languages are often positioned as oriented to the past, whereas the national language and other European languages (and particularly English) are linked with progress and modernity and thus oriented to the future.

These discourses about regional minority, indigenous, and immigrant languages in relation to colonial, national, and official languages are subsequently reflected in institutional practices that reinforce monolingualism in the standard variety of the national language as a condition for advanced schooling or economic success. The use of the European or standard language in the social, economic, and political post-colonial system values and rewards competence in and knowledge that is presented in the European language in almost all of the nation's institutions, including its schools and work places (Milroy & Milroy, 1999).

Convincing minority language speakers (as well as majority language speakers) to invest in indigenous language development therefore requires overcoming a long history of stigmatization and devaluation. Even though parents may value bilingualism, if they perceive that instruction in the native language will prevent their children from access to the societal language, they may not support native language maintenance (Bamgbose, 2003). In a 1996 study by Lambert and Taylor, socioeconomically middle and lower class Cuban parents in Miami valued Spanish and bilingualism. However, the lower-class parents insisted on English-only instruction and more English at home because they wanted to ensure access to mainstream institutions. Already more secure in that access, middle class Cuban parents supported Spanish and bilingual practices at home. Mufwene (2002, 2006a) argues that parents and children will ultimately select the language they see as linked to future socioeconomic benefits. If that language happens to be the dominant language, the argument goes, then choosing to use that language is a useful adaptive strategy. When competence in the societal language continues to be the only or primary vehicle for social mobility, the cost of maintaining the native language may be perceived by parents and children as too high. Mufwene's argument reminds us that language choices are embedded in the wider historical and sociopolitical contexts. Unless the socioeconomic context also changes, it may be more difficult for language revitalization efforts to succeed, especially if the rationale for such revitalization stresses instrumental reasons (Edwards, 2001; Rappa & Wee, 2006). However, minority languages continue to be actively used despite their marginal status, and speakers of these languages continue to resist the hegemony of the dominant language, also suggesting that more than just socioeconomic factors play a role in decisions about language maintenance and use.

Those involved in revitalization efforts need to negotiate these discourses. A national government statement declaring the indigenous language a legitimate medium of instruction will not be sufficient to counter this hegemonic discourse. Especially in contexts where access to the minority language may be restricted at home (because of a limited family network or the lack of connection to the home country through travel back and forth), parents and communities have to engage in activities designed to maintain proficiency and use in the minority language. Conversations with parents as well as teachers and students about the value of the indigenous language for social identity, literacy, and learning are crucial to counter negative language attitudes (Hornberger & Skilton-Sylvester, 2000). Moreover, most language policies and programs target only minority language speakers, leaving majority language speakers and mainstream education largely untouched. Without a broader policy that addresses the role of multilingualism and intercultural education for all learners in a particular country, it is unlikely that the unequal power relationships and attitudes will change.

The Spread of English: Threat or Benefit?

Kachru (1985) uses three concentric circles to represent the spread of English: inner, outer, and expanded. Although the boundaries between the circles Kachru describes are rapidly changing, his model helps illustrate how diverse the use of English has become. Initially, English spread through speaker migration, that is, English speakers settled in new areas, and their language became the language for that particular region. This spread happened first in the British Isles (Scotland, Ireland, Wales), then in early colonies in America, Australia, and New Zealand. These native speaker countries make up the **inner circle**. In these settings, English typically replaced and displaced languages in existence prior to contact. Next, English spread through the British Empire as Britain colonized Africa and Asia. As the British established English as the official language of government, economics, and schooling, English become a major public language. Most postcolonial nations in this **outer circle** maintained the high-status position of English, even though it was not the native language of the great majority of people. Finally, English is used in the **expanded circle** of countries, where it is contained to specific domains (e.g., academic study, business transactions) but does not constitute the main means of communication in daily life. The expanded circle includes most European nations, and countries such as China, Korea, and Japan, where English is taught in school. In these countries, English is the language associated with modernization, globalization, and access to the international economic market.

The dominant status of English has also been identified as a threat to linguistic diversity and its spread has raised many concerns about the position and survival of other languages. At the same time, the role of English is not the same in every context and, accordingly, its impact on the (continued) use of official, national, and local languages is complex and varied (Bamgbose, 2003). Moreover, as English has become appropriated as an international language by non-native speakers, new forms of and functions for the language have emerged.

THE DOMINANCE OF ENGLISH

There is little doubt that English is a dominant language in the world. Today there are about 350 million native speakers of English and between 400 million and 1 billion second or foreign language speakers (Graddol, 2006). In 1995, the British Council administered a survey to almost 1,400 individuals worldwide and found that 78% believed that no other language would challenge English in the next decades and 95% agreed with the statement that English would be the world language for the next 25 years and continue its central role in world media and communication (Bamgbose, 2001). The more people are able to speak English, the more English will become the default option for communication, and the less likely it is that the spread of English will come to a halt (Van Parijs, 2000). In today's world, English therefore has a unique position as a lingua franca: it has a wider geographical use area than any other international language (e.g., Latin) ever before.

The inner circle often has English-only policies to further reinforce the position of the national language. In the expanded circles, English, as a former colonial language, dominates secondary and higher education, government, and business. Although in many African and Asian countries languages other than English are used at the elementary level, subjects are often taught through English when students enter secondary school. As the language of international communication in the outer circles, the position of English is virtually uncontested (Phillipson, 2003). A Eurobarometer (2005) survey of 30,000 individuals 15 years old and older shows English the first foreign language listed in all but eight of the European Union nations; all but one lists English as one of the top three foreign languages known. English is increasingly introduced in the early elementary grades in the outer and expanded circles as well. Korea and Japan begin teaching English by 3rd grade; other countries are experimenting with early partial immersion programs. In Finland, for example, bilingual programs introduce 20% of English instruction in kindergarten (Bjorklund, 2005). Another trend is that the policy of using content as a language teaching technique to promote second language learning is increasingly shifting to one of teaching specific content areas through English (Wannagat, 2007).

English has also encroached on domains traditionally reserved for the preparation of individuals for the highest paying jobs (Berg, Hult, & King, 2001; Boyd & Huss, 2001; Brock-Utne, 2001b; Dronkers, 1993; Ljosland, 2007). While both the national language and English are used in these domains, an increasing number of courses are offered in English at competitive universities, partially in response to increased internationalization through student exchange programs. English has been noted as the socially more accepted language of dissertations in the sciences. Further, there is clear pressure for international scientific publications (mostly in English) and, increasingly, proficiency in English as a prerequisite for higher-level positions in businesses. In the European Union, despite efforts to ensure multilingualism in its official communications, English has become the unofficial working language among many European officials. Rather than waiting for translation, many European employees rely on English for expediency of communication (Phillipson, 2003).

Though the dominant position of English is visible in each of the circles, it must be remembered that other important lingua francas exist, including Spanish, French, and Arabic. At a 2009 symposium, the Google CEO Eric Schmidt predicted that Chinese-language content will be dominating the Internet 5 years from now. Some have argued that once English proficiency becomes more universal, multilingualism will become the competitive edge of the future (Graddol, 2006). In other words, the story of English and its relationship to other languages continues to change.

LINGUISTIC IMPERIALISM

Phillipson (1992) considers the spread of English a relatively deliberate process of **linguistic imperialism**, a process whereby "the dominance of English is asserted and maintained by the establishment and continuous reconstitution of structural and cultural inequities between English and other languages" (Phillipson, 1992). Linguistic imperialism occurs through specific policies as well as discursive practices.

The British Council and British colonial policies introduced and promoted British English as the norm (also referred to as **anglocentricity**). English was the sole medium of instruction in school in British colonies and the curriculum represented the British culture and value system (including the British literacy canon as required reading) as superior to the indigenous cultures and languages. British-English linguistic and cultural norms guide testing practices and textbook choices, and other material development (Phillipson, 1992, 1998, 2001). Applicants' scores on the Test of English as a Foreign Language (TOEFL) play an increasingly important role in university admissions. Teaching (British) English as a foreign language has become a lucrative business: it brought over 570 million pounds into the country, about 1% of its gross domestic product.

Phillipson's theory of the spread of English also references the powerful discourse that appears to make the choice for English as the language of communication natural and inevitable. According to Pennycook (1994), this argument goes as follows: English is the logical result of global forces (claim to naturalness), non-native speakers prefer the language because it is not hindered by nationalistic attachments (claim to neutrality), and it is an efficient tool for international communication (claim to relevancy). English is seen as the language of progress or modernity and the language of access to knowledge and the world. Because of available resources and training opportunities, English becomes a logical and natural choice.

Implied in this discourse is that other languages are not suitable for these functions for intrinsic reasons (e.g., the language is not "developed" enough) or extrinsic reasons (e.g., available resources are lacking). In analyzing this discourse of English as an international language, Pennycook (1994, p. 12) sees the need to "problematize the notion of choice." The choice to use English is not always by free will exercised among equals. Rather, it is the result of historical, political, social, and economic development conditions that constrain individuals' language choices.

A CRITIQUE AND ALTERNATIVE THEORY

Phillipson's explanation has been criticized for assuming too much in identifying a deliberate, consistent, and top-down language policy as part of British foreign policy. Other scholars have argued that British colonial language policy was often determined by individuals and the local context and was ambivalent in its attitude toward English and the use of native languages in school (Brutt-Griffler, 2002). It seems to have been simultaneously shaped by often contradictory forces: anglicism and orientalism, in addition to colonial imperialism and local governance (Pennycook, 1994, 1998, 2001).

Anglicists promoted the teaching of English to provide educational, cultural, and moral benefits to the colonies. Their "civilizing mission" was an important force driving the use of English as medium of instruction. Others argued in favor of using the local languages in school and not uprooting the colonized but often insisted on teaching western knowledge and institutions. This discourse is referred to as **orientalism.** Ambiguity existed about who should be taught English and how much education (in English) children should receive. The use of the local languages was often rationalized by perceived intellectual limitations on one hand and a fear of unrest or revolt if people became too educated (in English) on the other hand. In response to the latter, the British actually engaged in a "policy of containment" which limited (English) education to local elites rather than promoting English for all (Brutt-Griffler, 2002).

Phillipson's linguistic imperialism model also leaves little room for agency by speakers of indigenous languages in appropriating English for their own uses. Canagarajah (2000) describes various strategies of **appropriation** to illustrate how English has been used creatively by non-native speakers in previously colonized countries without blindly accepting anglocentricity. For example, Saivite schools taught English using Hindi-informed ways of acting and believing, rather than a western discourse (referred to as a "strategy of discursive appropriation"). He also points out that without the use of English and its global place it would have been difficult to gain access to revolutionary thinkers and use the discourse of independency and self-determination against the colonizers (which he refers to as a "strategy of reinterpretation").

In response to Phillipson's linguistic imperialism, Brutt-Griffler (2002) proposes an alternative framework to explain the spread of English. She argues that a world language is characterized by four features: its econocultural functions, its transcendence to the role of an elite lingua franca, its coexistence with other languages in bilingual and multilingual contexts, and language change through world language convergence and divergence (pp. 110–124). English has increasingly been characterized by all four features because of global economic development dominated by the English-speaking United States and political integration (e.g., the European Union) rather than deliberate British language policy. As the use of English increases, it has become a more logical linguistic option for more people, that is, if you are more likely to be able to communicate with people in English than in any other languages, you will first invest in English. As a result of the clear dominance of English around the world in so many different domains, the desire to learn English has moved beyond individuals who want to learn English. Instead, what has had a tremendous impact on the spread of English is the fact that entire communities elect to develop proficiency in English in order to gain access to knowledge, international trade opportunities, cultural events, and the like. Such adoption of a language by an entire group is referred to as macro acquisition (Brutt-Griffler, 2002).

ENGLISH DOMINATES BUT DOES IT REPLACE?

Summarizing the lessons of colonial language policy, Pennycook (2001) warns that any analysis must maintain the complexity and the historical and contextual location of language policies. Individuals' actions and choices must be seen in relation to sociohistorical and political processes. Moreover, we must "learn to step outside the English-versus-other-languages dichotomy" (p. 216) to allow English as well as local languages to be used for different ends. The notion that the spread of English implies displacement or replacement of other languages (the homogenization argument) needs modification and contextualization. English does not serve the same function in the different circles and hence its relationship with local, indigenous, regional, and national languages differs (Bamgbose, 2003).

In the inner circle, English is the language of national identity and standard English has been institutionalized as a condition for socioeconomic, educational, and political success. The effect, however, tends to be subtractive language learning: for many children and adults in these settings, learning English comes at the cost of giving up the native language. As discussed in Chapter 3, children of immigrants and immigrant children learn English more quickly and prefer English over their native language in most domains. Despite efforts at language maintenance or language shift reversal, English dominates and generational language shift occurs in the face of pressures to acquire the dominant societal language.

In other countries, English is the lingua franca rather than the language of daily communication, that is, it is the language used by those who do not speak the same native language. In this role, English is not necessarily equated with the national or group identity, and therefore, some have argued, English does not necessarily threaten to replace the daily use of national languages for communication (Hause, 2003; Mufwene, 2002, 2006b). For example, there is no current danger that English will become the language of daily communication in western and eastern Europe. More than 97% of the population of the European Union claim their country's official language as their mother tongue (Eurobarometer, 2005). For majority language speakers in these countries, learning English is an additive process with little threat to the position of the national language as it continues to be used as the language of communication in all domains. Similar observations can be made for Korea and Japan, where Korean and Japanese continue to be the main national languages.

The potential of English to threaten the use of local languages as the daily language of communication (and hence intergenerational transmission) has also been questioned with respect to Africa (Mufwene, 2005, 2006a, 2006b). While former European colonial languages are lingua francas and are used for higher education, most Africans living in former British, French, and Portuguese colonies continue to speak local languages. And though these languages are now at risk, according to Mufwene, the threat to their survival does not only come from English and the other European colonial languages but from other processes, such as urbanization. As local language speakers move from rural to urban areas to improve their socioeconomic conditions, they often leave their native languages behind and adopt the urbanized African national language rather than the European language for daily communication. In Senegal, Wolof has become the lingua franca and the language of urbanization, and it is perceived by smaller language speakers as a threat to their language and identity (McLaughlin, 1995). A similar "takeover" has been observed in Tanzania, where Kiswahili has replaced local language use, even in rural areas (Brock-Utne, 2007).

These developments illustrate that the spread of English or dominance of other European languages does not automatically lead to replacement and displacement. Other developments suggest that the impact of the high status of English may be indirect. One relatively unexamined area, for example, is how the trend toward internationalization through English may result in an ambiguous relationship with educational language policies directed at indigenous or regional minority language development. In Taiwan, for example, though policies have been implemented to support both English and indigenous language development, an analysis of curriculum and material development and teacher preparation reveals that English has been clearly favored at the cost of indigenous language development (Chen, 2006).

A second trend relates to the potential impact of the pressure to introduce (more) English earlier in the elementary curriculum. Under the assumption "the younger, the better," proposals have been put forward to lower the age of instruction to kindergarten or 1st grade and even to as early as preschool. These proposals have raised concerns about the impact of introducing English on the development of national language and culture (Knell, et al., 2007). The fact that Korean mothers are beginning to teach their children English at home to better prepare them out of concern that school will not be sufficient suggests that the pressure to learn English may have an impact beyond school into home literacy practices (Yoo & Lee, 2006).

Finally, although English as a lingua franca may not necessarily replace current indigenous languages, its role in the internal economy must be critically examined. While claiming no evidence that English replaces other languages, Brutt-Griffler (2002, p. 122) modifies this conclusion by noting that the claim may hold only "as long as the world language does not become the language of the internal (domestic) economy (market)." Hyltenstamm (1999, cited in Ljosland, 2007) warns of the emergence of a two-tiered society divided by English competency. The fact that in European, African, and Asian countries English proficiency is directly and consistently linked with access to (certain levels of) tertiary education leading to high-prestige and white-collar, managerial leadership positions has aligned social class with English competence (Walby, 2000). In many Asian countries, increased proficiency in English is obtained though private tutors, a resource available only to certain groups of parents. A different dimension of the two-tiered society is illustrated by Yang (2005), who argues that English teaching and learning is not distributed equally between urban and rural areas in China. Besides differences in resource allocation (textbooks, teacher quality), the position of English varies according to region. English is a valuable commodity in cities on the eastern coast where increasing numbers of international trade companies are located, and in these areas an investment in English learning (also referred to as the "craze" about English) is visible. The same cannot be said, however, for rural western China, where Mandarin Chinese, not English, provides access to higher education and better jobs locally.

In the expanded and outer circles, though English has spread, it is not necessarily replacing or displacing national languages from their daily communicative functions. Often, however, it has more market value than the national language or languages when it comes to accessing higher education, higher paying jobs, and other positions of leadership and power, raising concerns about new social and economic inequalities. Future research will have to tell whether pressures to increase English competence may ultimately affect home language use and the development of literacy skills in the native language or whether bilingualism or multilingualism that includes local home languages will be defined as the desired outcome.

English and Diversification

While the spread of English suggests linguistic and cultural homogenization, there is also evidence of diversification. Unlike other languages, English has fewer native speakers than non-native users of the language, and this imbalance has had an important impact on the language as well as on English language teaching.

WORLD ENGLISHES

The spread of English has been accompanied by structural changes. The use of English by non-native speakers to communicate with other non-native speakers has sparked debates about linguistic features of English as an international language (EIL) and issues of minimum intelligibility (Dewey, 2007; Seidlhofer, 2004). Moreover, as English is appropriated at the local level in postcolonial settings, it continues to change lexically and syntactically. Several indigenized, English varieties (also referred to as **world Englishes**) have emerged, such as Indian, Nigerian, and Singaporean English. The existence of the journal *World Englishes* and a new handbook devoted exclusively to this topic (Kachru, Kachru, & Nelson, 2006) illustrate the increased legitimacy of these English varieties as a field of research. Although these indigenized varieties occupy low-status with respect to standard English, they function as an important marker of linguistic and cultural identities for those using these varieties (Pennycook, 2003; Sakai & D'Angelo, 2005; Wee, 2005).

The recognition of English varieties has led to a re-examination of the native speaker paradigm (Brutt-Griffler & Samimy, 2001). The inappropriateness of using this paradigm to describe the competence of multilingual speakers is discussed in Chapter 2. In the context of world Englishes, an additional dimension is that few learners of EIL desire or need native speaker competence. For many learners of EIL, the need to use English for very specific purposes shapes their reasons for learning English. These goals may or may not require what traditionally has been considered "native speaker" competence. Together with the notion of world Englishes, EIL questions the usefulness and appropriateness of using the native speaker as norm to guide English language teaching (Afendras, et al., 1995; Bamgbose, 1998; Brutt-Griffler & Samimy, 2001; Cook, 1999; Davies, 1989; Paikeday, 1985).

TEACHING ENGLISH AS AN INTERNATIONAL LANGUAGE

Pointing out that the existence of multiple varieties and purposes affects the teaching of EIL, McKay (2003) re-examines the assumed superiority of communicative approaches to language teaching. Her argument is similar to that of Pennycook (1994), who criticizes the assumption that what works in adult English intensive courses for small groups of elite students will transfer to other contexts, (e.g., large groups of students from diverse backgrounds. Canagarajah (1999) questions the inherent assumption that process-oriented approaches are empowering. Citing Tuman, he illustrates that process approaches may give the illusion of equality and freedom while maintaining dominant cultural and linguistic assumptions. Similar concerns have been raised about speakers of non-standard English (Delpit, 1995) and linguistically and culturally diverse learners (De la Luz Reyes, 1992) by scholars who argue that process approaches may not adequately provide access to the "power code" for minority language speakers. Non-native teachers' responses to the use of communicative teaching in and elsewhere underscore the importance of understanding local conditions for teaching (Canagarajah, 1999; D. Li, 1998; Nunan, 2003).

McKay (2003) also highlights the changing role of culture in EIL. Whereas traditional English teaching comes out of a second language teaching tradition in which language and culture are intimately intertwined, the anticipated interactions with native speakers that drove this tradition are not relevant to EIL teaching. In many instances, English will be used by non-native speakers to interact with other non-native speakers. Dewey (2007) suggests that these "lingua franca interactions" have raised important issues around intelligibility and communicative strategies.

In short, the spread of English and its adoption by elites and non-elites in various countries has diversified the English language structurally, the purposes of English language teaching, the definition of English competence, and the approaches to teaching culture. While these notions have not necessarily entered the mainstream through teacher preparation or testing and assessment practices, they are pushing the static limits of an idealized English norm.

Moving beyond Dichotomies

Multilingualism has become a valuable commodity in the world today. Increasingly, information can be accessed in multiple languages and corporations fully exploit the advantages of native language advertisement through the Internet and traditional media. Indigenous groups have taken advantage of the Internet to gain the world's attention to their concerns about their economic, political, linguistic, and cultural survival. Clearly, EIL is a growing and booming business, increasing multilingual competence for individuals around the world. It has given rise to new varieties of English and different ways of thinking about language, identity, nativeness, and culture in language teaching.

At the same time, the consolidation of multilingualism to English plus the national language has led to concerns about the survival of indigenous and smaller regional languages. The extent to which English represents western ways of knowing, teaching, and learning to the exclusion of other world views raises questions about cultural homogenization. When English becomes a gatekeeper for social mobility, the notion of "choosing" to learn English is questionable. Under these conditions, people "choose" to learn English not because they want to but because they need to in order to survive or better their social conditions (Bamgbose, 2003). When this choice can occur only at the cost of the native language, issues of social justice emerge. If fairness demands "free" individual choice, a choice must be available. But unless learning the native language at home, in the community, and in the larger society is desirable and feasible, few minority language speakers will be able to make a choice. Rather, the choice will be made for them by the dominant society (Van Parijs, 2000).

The impact of globalization and the spread of English cannot be simplified as either positive or negative. Homogenizing and diversifying forces are simultaneously at work with direct and indirect effects. The future of linguistic and cultural diversity must be understood in the context of "glocalized" practices, where macro and micro developments come together.

CHAPTER 4
Discussion & Activities

Critical Issues

1. Robert Phillipson (2003) argues that "linguicism" is analogous to other "isms" that we often hear about, such as racism and sexism. Do you agree that discrimination based on language is or can be similar to discrimination based on race or gender? If you are a non-native speaker of the official language or a speaker of a non-standard variety of the standard language, have you encountered discrimination based on your language? Think of other examples where linguicism may occur, other than, for example, in the work place, in schools, in health care institutions.

2. Mufwene argues that economic considerations may overshadow children's and parents' decisions to give up their native language in favor of learning the societal language. Do you think this is always true? What other motivations may be important for parents? For adolescents? For young adults?

3. What role can schools play in mediating language loss or language revitalization? In what ways might they be limited in their impact on resisting language shift to a majority language (see also Chapter 3)? In what ways can they make a significant contribution to efforts at language revitalization?

Application and Reflection

4. The literature on world Englishes stresses the multiplicity of the English language across the world. How might you reflect this pluralist view in your curricular or pedagogical choices if you were teaching English to school-age children? Might your approach differ depending on whether you are teaching in an English-dominant context (e.g., the United States, Australia) or a less English-dominant context (such as Korea or China)?

5. In what way could one consider the spread of English as simultaneously aligning with and disagreeing with pluralist discourses? How would those within the monolingual discourse consider the phenomenon of language spread?

Recommended Readings

Brutt-Griffler, J. (2002). *World English: A study of its development.* Clevedon: Multilingual Matters.

> *This book explains how and why English has expanded its role and use around the world and considers the implications for the future role of English and other languages.*

Crystal, D. (2003). *English as a Global Language.* (2nd ed.). Cambridge: Cambridge University Press.

> *This book reviews the past and present status and role of English in the world and considers future trends and development of World Englishes.*

Phillipson, R. (1992). *Linguistic imperialism.* Oxford: Oxford University Press.

> *This book, like Brutt-Griffler's (2002), discusses the spread of English around the world. Phillipson, however, in contrast to Brutt-Griffler, takes a critical approach to the encroachment of English in Europe. Students might find it useful to read the two books together.*

Phillipson, R. (2003). *English-only Europe? Challenging language policy.* London: Routledge.

> *This book provides a good overview of language policies and language use patterns in the European Union, and their impact on minority languages.*

Language in Education

GUIDING QUESTIONS

- *What are some program models designed to develop bilingual or multilingual competence (additive bilingual models)?*

- *What are some program models designed to develop proficiency only in the societal dominant language (subtractive models)?*

- *In what ways are educators language planners?*

- *How are multilingual/pluralist and monolingual/assimilationist discourses reflected in issues related to language policy?*

KEY TERMS

language policy

Question 2

corpus planning

status planning

acquisition planning

language-as-problem orientation

language-as-right orientation

language-as-resource orientation

standard language ideology

heritage language classes

community-based language schools

mainstream multilingual and bilingual models

European school model

Canadian immersion programs

maintenance bilingual programs

integrated bilingual education

two-way immersion (TWI)

transitional bilingual education (TBE)

integrated transitional bilingual education

pull-out second language classes

push-in second language model

self-contained second language programs

structured English immersion (SEI)

sheltered English instruction

specially designed academic instruction in English (SDAIE)

newcomer program

In today's multilingual and multicultural societies, schools are key sites where some linguistic and cultural resources are reinforced and others devalued. A school's language policies and practices have a great impact on the schooling experiences of language minority students. Despite the central role of language (and literacy) in education, discussions about schooling for minority language speakers have tended to focus on a singular issue, whether a language other than the dominant language can and should be used as a medium of instruction. While the decision about how to resolve this issue is important, especially for minority language speakers, an exclusive focus on medium of instruction can hide the myriad of other language decisions made in schools that also shape the experiences of multilingual learners. These other decisions, together with a formal choice of medium of instruction, communicate the value of students' native languages and legitimize certain languages as tools for learning and meaning making. This chapter illustrates the pervasive role that language plays in schooling and the wide range of language decisions that shape schooling for bilingual learners.

Language Policy and Education: A General Framework

Decisions about how language is used in school can be overt and covert. The formal, explicit dimension of **language policy** involves "what the government says and does through its laws, legislative statutes, regulations, and bureaucratic practices that affect the use of one or more languages used by the people it represents" (Heath, 1983a, p. 56). Other, less visible, decisions about language are enacted through the ways that we use language on a daily basis. When a teacher indicates to her students that she does not tolerate the use of nonstandard forms of the English language, she is making a decision about which languages are permitted. A useful framework for analyzing the complex dimensions of language policies and their relationship to education is one proposed by Cooper (1989). Cooper suggests that language policy and planning involves the answer to the question, "Who plans what (language practices) for whom, how, under what conditions, and for what purpose?" This question helps illustrate some of the issues that emerge when thinking about language policy as it relates to primary and secondary education.

WHO DECIDES?

The "who" of language policy refers to levels of decision making. Laws and official language policy statements have long been the focus of language policy studies (Ricento, 2000). Examples of such top-down policies are official language declarations and federal and state laws regarding which language may or must be used as medium of instruction in school. Of the more than

6,500 languages in the world, only a few have been declared an official language, that is, the language officially recognized in the country's constitution as the language of government business, including schools. Faingold (2004b) analyzed 187 constitutions around the world and found that 110 had declared one or more official languages. The United States is one of the countries without an official national language, even though English is clearly recognized as the national language of communication and more than 20 states have declared English their official language (see Chapter 6).

Few countries have enacted constitutional language policies without simultaneously considering the position of minority languages. In Feingold's analysis, of the 110 countries with an official language, all but 14 also have provisions for the protection of national languages, minority languages, or the linguistic rights of all citizens. Depending on the strength of these protections, minority language speakers may be entitled to be taught through their own language, in addition to learning the majority language. In other contexts, policies and laws may permit but not require schools to implement programs that use the native language and the majority language. In the latter case, a school's choice to provide bilingual instruction depends on whether their educational outcomes include competence in more than one language.

Because language policies are developed at several levels, including the district, school, and classroom levels, decisions that individuals make at each level may not be in agreement with one another, and as a result, implementation may be inconsistent. For example, in 1971 Massachusetts was the first state in the United States to mandate bilingual education. Thirty years later, in 2002, the initial law was amended and replaced by a mandate to place English language learners in an all-English program unless parents (and the district) requested a waiver (**Question 2**). Districts and schools have responded to this mandate in different ways, ranging from placing students in a standard curriculum classroom to implementing a specialized English-only program or a bilingual program through the waiver process (de Jong, Gort, & Cobb, 2005; Gort, de Jong, & Cobb, 2008). At the classroom level, the law states that teachers can use "a minimal amount of the child's native language when necessary." The interpretation of this phrase has depended on individual teachers' view of the role of the native language for teaching ELLs and the value of bilingualism. A teacher who is supportive of the use of the native language and interprets the law broadly explains:

> I try to show them that it's so important to know both languages. If they explain or use Portuguese there's nothing wrong with that. Because they will get the English they need but in the meantime I always say if you want to take books home because they go to the library and you want to read in Portuguese fine with me. (de Jong, 2008, p. 359)

Decisions about languages in schools thus involve the interaction of multiple policy layers and ways that the meanings of a policy for practice are negotiated by individuals at each level. Policies are often so highly contested at each level that they result in contradictory practices from one context to another. It is therefore important to look beyond the formal language of a law or policy statement into the practices that are enacted at different policy levels.

WHAT IS THE (LANGUAGE) PROBLEM?

The "what" of language policy refers to the activities considered part of language planning and what issue the policy is trying to address, that is, how individuals define the language problem to be solved. Language planning has traditionally been divided into three types of planning activities. **Corpus planning** refers to the "creation of new forms, modification of old forms, [and] selection from alternative forms in spoken and written code" (Cooper, 1989, p. 31). Creating an alphabet or new vocabulary to use to talk about science or technology are examples of corpus planning. **Status planning** involves deliberate efforts to influence the status of a particular language by extending the domains where it is used, such as in the home or in church, school, government, and the courts. Language status can be increased by formally allocating time in the school curriculum. For example, before independence, no local languages were officially used in many colonized nations. After independence, several nations elevated the status of certain local languages to national (widely used) or official languages (used in governmental institutions, including the courts and schools). Finally, to increase the number of speakers of a particular language, language policy makers can engage in **acquisition planning**. Communities often turn to schools for this role by offering formal language programs (such as foreign language programs or bilingual programs), but private and voluntary organizations are also often actively involved by establishing after-school programs and Saturday schools, or by organizing cultural events. Governments can provide incentives to promote communicative competence by requiring bilingual proficiency for certain jobs.

Defining the problem is crucial because that definition will determine which solutions will be sought and what will be excluded from consideration (Bacchi, 2000). Whether low student achievement is attributed to lack of parental support or to an inappropriate curriculum will affect what type of solutions will be considered (e.g., offering parent workshops or teacher training or changing textbooks). Ruiz (1984) provides a useful framework for examining this second aspect of the "what" question. He identifies three orientations: language-as-problem, language-as-right, and language-as resource. In his framework, Ruiz is concerned with how minority languages as spoken by minority language community members are treated in public policy at the national level, with a focus on language-in-education policies, that is, policies that affect the use of minority languages for minority language speakers in formal schooling contexts.

The **language-as-problem orientation** treats linguistic diversity as a problem to be remedied. Lack of fluency in the standard societal language is seen as a major cause of social, economic, and political problems and educational underachievement by minority students. To ensure social and political cohesion within the nation-state, multilingualism must be streamlined into monolingual paths (Wiley & Lukes, 1996). The natural solution to the problem is to focus on teaching the standard variety of the societal language. The **language-as-right orientation** appeared in the United States in the 1960s and 1970s and has emerged internationally in the debate about linguistic human rights (Skutnabb-Kangas, 2000). In its weaker version, language planning conducted in this tradition emphasizes the right to not be discriminated against on the basis of language. A stronger version argues for linguistic rights as a human right (Chapter 4).

Ruiz criticizes the language-as-problem orientation for reinforcing deficit thinking for bilingual children. He is skeptical of the language-as-right orientation in the absence of legally recognized rights based on group status and warns that compliance-driven native language use may hinder the quality of implementation. He thus proposes the **language-as-resource orientation**, which aims to reframe subordinate languages from being perceived as deficits (or problems) to being viewed as assets. Within this orientation, educational language policies are grounded in the assumption that "language is a resource to be managed, developed and conserved" and it considers "language-minority communities as important sources of expertise" (Ruiz, 1984, p. 28). Multilingualism is seen as a positive force in a diverse society that can benefit homeland security, international diplomacy, the national economy, and the ethnic community.

HOW ARE POLICIES IMPLEMENTED?

Language policies aim at influencing people's linguistic behaviors, so persuasiveness becomes an important element of implementation. Sometimes, force is used to achieve this goal. Many indigenous language and immigrant language speakers recount stories of being physically punished for speaking their native language in school. Less overt are discursive strategies used to legitimize a particular language as the "proper" one to be used in high-status domains, such as the government or education. Other languages are positioned lower in the linguistic hierarchy and are assigned less value. In this scenario, a particular language group (typically the social or political elite) uses schools, the media, and other ways of communication to reinforce this hierarchy and to create a shared understanding about a language and what role it plays in society. Eventually, this language ideology becomes the norm and is no longer questioned, that is, it becomes a commonsense understanding (Woolard & Schieffelin, 1994). When the dominant group can convince others that their language is the only standard or norm, linguistic hegemony emerges. Such hegemony "is ensured when they can convince those who fail to meet those standards to view their failure as being the result of the inadequacy of their own language" (Wiley, 1996, p. 113).

The assumed superiority of a standardized language over nonstandard varieties (dialects) is an example of such a language ideology. What we now refer to as standard English has come to this high-status position historically through complex sociopolitical processes whereby those speaking the language could impose it as the more desirable norm and position it as the inherently more educated, sophisticated, and complex language. In contrast, other (nonstandard) varieties are viewed and described as barbaric, immature, incomplete, or with little use. The **standard language ideology** transfers the qualities assigned to the language to its speakers. Speaking the standard variety is associated with an individual's intelligence, sophistication, and creativity. This language ideology becomes engrained in institutional processes as the standard language becomes the variety required for participation in school, for getting a job, and for running for a political office (Lippi-Green, 1997; Silverstein, 1996; Woolard & Schieffelin, 1994). Those who speak a nonstandard variety of English, such as African American Vernacular English, and are told that their speaking that language is the cause of their school failure, often feel compelled to ignore or devalue their own language in favor of standard English (Delpit & Dowdy, 2002; Rickford, 1996).

POLICIES FOR WHOM AND UNDER WHAT CONDITIONS?

The "for whom" dimension considers the target group the policy is meant to affect, that is, whose language behavior or language competence is to be influenced. Multiple target audiences can be imagined for educational language policies, according to the answers to such questions as, Does it aim to affect the language behavior of children or adults? Does it include majority and minority language speakers? Is it intended only for older immigrant youth? Some policies are more exclusive, geared to only one group, while others are directed at a broad range of groups. Although the latter can seem to be more inclusive (e.g., all immigrant children in K–12 schools), a policy "for all" may overlook important differences, for example, elementary and secondary immigrant children have different needs and may need different approaches.

Particularly for minority language policies, there often is a mismatch between those who formulate the policy and those most affected. Majority language speakers frequently make decisions about minority language speakers and their languages. When Arizona, California, and Massachusetts passed ballot initiatives to abolish bilingual education, most voters were white, monolingual, majority language speakers. In each of these states, the group most affected by the ballot initiative, Hispanics, had overwhelmingly voted against the measure. Similarly, indigenous language groups have long been kept from deciding about when and how to use their own languages in their own communities by policies set in motion by their colonizers.

Without the necessary human and material resources it is difficult to effectively achieve policy goals. The "under what conditions" phrase considers the extent to which a formal policy has financial as well as ideological support at different policy levels. Often a gap emerges between policy and practice when policies are implemented. In Ireland, for example, policy makers sought to increase the status and use of the Irish language, which was in decline as a result of British control. Irish was declared an official language and the government initiated several Irish immersion programs. The government also created an incentive to become fluent in Irish by making it a requirement for government employment. At the national level, the policy framework was therefore quite strong in support of Irish language development. But when researchers documented actual language practices in the school, it became clear that English dominated teacher and student interactions inside and outside the classroom. When examining language policies and their impact, it is important to consider both the official, stated policy and also actual practices that emerge in response to the policy (Coady & O'Laoire, 2002).

THE SOCIAL NATURE OF POLICY PROCESSES

As the preceding discussion makes clear, language policy formulation and implementation are socially negotiated processes that take place in specific contexts as individuals interpret particular policies (Shohamy, 2006; Sutton & Levinson, 2000). Cooper's framework illustrates that different interpretations and views begin with how the nonstandard language or languages are viewed (as problem, right, or resource) and affect how solutions are sought (who decides, how resources are allocated), which solutions are selected and how they are presented (language ideologies), and ultimately how speakers (including educators) respond to the policies in their daily lives (meaning-making processes). Different views of what language and which language practices are valued compete for dominance and legitimacy in the high-status domains of school, government, and the work force.

The diversity in responses to "Who decides what for whom under what conditions?" reminds us, first, that the stated goals of a formal language policy and actual language practices that follow it do not always match. When considering language policy it is important to look at the policy-to-practice realities, in addition to analyzing the wording of the language law or language policy statement. Also, because policy processes are constructed as individuals talk about the policy and consider what the policy means for practice, language policy processes are not neutral. Cooper (1989) points out that language policies that seem on the surface to deal with language are in fact rarely about language. Rather, they reflect the power and status relations in a particular society.

Language Policy in Schools

Decisions that schools make about language and language use carry significant weight at local and societal levels. The sections that follow first explore the explicit and overt policies schools make about medium of instruction (program models). However, since language is one of the most important symbolic tools used to socialize students into certain ways of thinking, being, and doing, these sections then look at more implicit and covert language policies in the form of informal daily language and literacy practices.

MEDIUM OF INSTRUCTION: PROGRAM MODELS

Languages that are formally recognized (and supported by the government) as languages of instruction in schools typically have a higher status than those that do not. The choice of the medium of instruction is therefore an important symbolic gesture with significant impact on different speech communities in society. When a language is declared the official language of a nation, its status is elevated and it becomes the language of the government, the media, and schools. Those fluent in that language have a clear advantage over those who may speak another language.

Formal language-in-education policies often translate into different program models that are permitted or mandated to develop linguistic skills. The terminology that surrounds these various models, however, can be confusing, especially since not everybody uses the same label for the same practices. Moreover, the same label can reflect significant variation in implementation. Despite the numerous classifications and labels, there are three basic questions that can be used to distinguish various models.

1. What are the desired language outcomes of the program: multilingualism, bilingualism, or monolingualism in the societal language?

2. For whom is the program intended: majority language speakers, minority language speakers, or both groups?

3. What languages are used as medium of instruction: one, two, or multiple languages?

Using these questions as a guideline, the following sections discuss program models for developing multilingual competence (additive approaches[1]) and monolingualism in the societal language (subtractive approaches), respectively.

Additive Bilingual and Multilingual Program Models

Additive bilingual models build on and extend students' existing language competencies and aim to broaden students' multilingual linguistic repertoire.[2] Table 5.1 provides an overview of common program types that aim for bilingualism or multilingualism for majority and minority language speakers. Descriptions and examples of each model follow.

The focus here is not on the full range of possible language programs for any student but on bilingual education models that involve teaching more than one language and subject through those languages. Options for teaching a foreign language as a subject for majority language speakers are therefore not included (for an overview, see Genesee, 2004). The discussion here also does not include other important ways that minority language maintenance can occur through schooling, for example by offering **heritage language classes** designed specifically for minority language speakers with varying abilities in the language or through **community-based language schools** organized by the ethnic community, such as Saturday schools (see Valdés, Fishman, Chavez, & William, 2006; Conteh, Martin, & Robertson, 2007).

Bilingualism and Multilingualism for Societal Language Speakers

Programs for native speakers of the societal language (majority language speakers) are typically enrichment programs. These are optional programs for parents who want their children to develop high levels of bilingual or multilingual competence. This form of elite bilingualism is largely uncontroversial and supported as an enrichment possibility for majority language speakers for personal development and access to global economic opportunities.

Mainstream multilingual and bilingual models aim for multilingualism

---

[1]García (2009) rejects the term "additive" because she argues that this term suggests a simplistic notion of *one language + another language = two languages*, which reflects a relatively static, linear notion of bilingualism. García prefers the term "dynamic bilingualism", which she argues reflects the dynamic, interactive nature of the languages that make up a bilingual learners' linguistic repertoire. We retain the use of the term "additive" here because it is heuristically useful for educators and policy makers. However, like García, we emphasize a dynamic, recursive view of multilingualism.

[2]Some scholars refer to additive bilingual programs with the umbrella term *dual language* education, to set them apart from transitional bilingual programs that use two languages for instruction but do not aim for high levels of bilingualism and biliteracy and do not use both languages for literacy and content instruction for a sustained period (typically about 5 years) (Howard, Olague, & Rodgers, 2003).

TABLE 5.1				
Additive Bilingual and Multilingual Program Models				
Program label	**Language goals**	**Target population**	**Language use and distribution**	**Policy orientation**
Mainstream bilingual or multilingual education	Multilingualism	Majority, international	L1 and L2 (and then L3, L4)	Language-as-resource
Canadian immersion programs	Bilingualism	Majority	L2, then L1	Language-as-resource
Maintenance bilingual/heritage language education	Bilingualism	Minority	L1, L2 (sometimes L3)	Language-as-resource/ language-as-right
Bilingual education for the deaf	Bilingualism	Minority	L1 and L2	Language-as-resource/ language-as-right
Integrated bilingual education: two-way immersion (TWI)	Bilingualism	Minority and majority (integrated)	Long-term L1 and L2 use	Language-as-resource/ language-as-right

Sources: Baker, 2006; Brisk, 2006; de Jong, 2007.

for majority language speakers. One well-known example is the **European school model**. The European schools were originally designed for children of parents who worked for the European Coal and Steel Community and could be considered a multilingual variant of mainstream bilingual education. There are now 12 European schools in Luxembourg, Belgium, Germany, Italy, the Netherlands, and Great Britain enrolling primarily the children of civil servants working for the European Union. The schools follow a common model with the goal to maintain and develop the students' native language, to develop proficiency in multiple other languages, and to develop positive cultural identities including a strong European identity.

Luxembourg has trilingual education for all students enrolled in the school system. Mandatory preschool education begins in Luxembourgish and this language continues as a language of instruction and as a subject throughout elementary school. German is introduced as a subject the first year of primary school and then intensifies as a subject and medium of instruction until 6th grade. French is introduced as a subject in 2nd grade and then increases its role in the curriculum to be the exclusive language used in instruction by the age of 15. Foreign language education is introduced at the secondary level as well, including English, Latin, Spanish, Italian, or Greek (Baetens Beardsmore, 1995; Hoffman, 1998; Horner & Weber, 2008).

An example of mainstream bilingual education can be found in some of the International Schools, which are mostly private schools that offer a full curriculum through two languages. Typically, these schools cater to the children of business people, government officials, and other international sojourners (Baker, 2006; De Mejia, 2002), although local families increasingly enroll their children in these schools as well. The curriculum is often equally divided between the two languages and tends to follow the curriculum of the "home country," for example, French is taught using the national curriculum from France.

Probably the best-known bilingual enrichment programs for dominant language speakers are **Canadian[3] immersion programs**. French immersion programs were developed in the late 1960s in response to demands from middle class Anglophone parents living in predominantly French-speaking Montreal to help their children develop a functional level of bilingualism. Immersion models differ with regard to the timing of the introduction of the second language (early or late immersion) and the amount of time spent in the second language (full or partial immersion). In early, full immersion programs, the target (second) language, French, is introduced before the student's first language during the first 2 years of elementary school. By 3rd grade, the student's native language (English) is formally introduced in the curriculum and both languages are used for equal amounts of time for the rest of the program. In late immersion programs, the second language is introduced either at the upper elementary or at the secondary level (Genesee, 2004). Canadian-style immersion programs have expanded internationally as nations try to respond to increased demands for multilingual competence in order to compete in the global market (Christian & Genesee, 2001; Fortune & Tedick, 2008; Johnson & Swain, 1997).

Bi/multilingualism for Minority Language Speakers

Minority language speakers generally do not have a choice about becoming bilingual. For these groups, learning a second language is necessary for survival and access to the society in which they live as a result of conquest, forced migration, or voluntary immigration. Especially for immigrant children and children of immigrants, bilingual competence receives little support from majority language speakers because it is viewed as hindering their linguistic and cultural integration into the mainstream.

---

[3]Following Brisk (2006), the term *Canadian* is added to distinguish these bilingual programs from (monolingual) English immersion programs for minority students that aim for second language proficiency rather than bilingualism.

Maintenance bilingual programs aim to develop, maintain, and revitalize minority languages. In the United States, language revitalization efforts have focused on increasing the number of speakers of Native American, Alaskan, and Hawai'ian indigenous languages through language immersion programs, apprenticeships, and the use of technology (Burnaby & Reyner, 2002; Hinton & Hale, 2001; Reyhner, Cantoni, St. Clair, & Yazzie, 1999). Internationally, such language revitalization efforts can be noted in New Zealand, Hawai'i, and South America. The Māori in New Zealand provide full immersion in the minority language in preschool (through Te Kōhanga Reo programs or "language nests") and elementary schools (Kura Kaupapa Māori), before introducing English as a medium of instruction (Benton & Benton, 2001; May, 2002; Spolsky, 2003). With an emphasis on community involvement, indigenous languages and cultural practices are included in the curriculum in several South American countries, in addition to the official language, Spanish (Hornberger & Lopez, 1998; King, 2004). Maintenance or development programs for immigrant or heritage language speakers have been noted for French speakers in Vermont (Thomas & Collier, 2002) and for Hispanic students in Texas (Tong, Irby, Lara-Alecio, & Mathes, 2008).

Maintenance bilingual education efforts in non-English-speaking countries increasingly include a multilingual component through the addition of a third, high-prestige language such as English to the regional minority language and the societal language. Such trilingual experiments are more common today on the European continent in response to a multilingually defined European identity and the globalization of the world market (Ytsma, 2001). At the elementary level, trilingual programs initially use a regional minority language and the society language as instructional languages, and then add a foreign language, generally English. Trilingual programs in Spain (Catalan, Spanish, English and Euskera, Spanish, and English) have been documented extensively (Cenoz, 2005; Lasagabaster, 2001; Sanz, 2000). In Lauro Ikastola, a school in the Basque Autonomous Community in Spain, the Basque language is used as a medium of instruction from kindergarten through secondary school. Spanish and English are initially included as a subject at the elementary level; English is then also used as a medium of instruction at the secondary level. German and French are offered as optional foreign languages (Azurmendi, Bachoc, & Zabaleta, 2001). In the Netherlands, schools are experimenting with the equal distribution of Frisian and Dutch and the introduction of English as a medium of instruction in 5th and 6th grade (Gorter, 2005).

Bilingual programs for the deaf teach content through sign language and the written form of the societal language. Approaches to language (the use of different sign systems) and the curriculum vary greatly from program to program and are often constrained by teachers' lack of proficiency in sign language (LaSasso & Lollis, 2003; Strong, 1995). Deaf culture and identity is an important component of the bilingual program to counter deficit views of individuals who are deaf or hard of hearing (Allen, 2002; Lane, 2005; Reagan, 2002; Smiler & McKee, 2006).

Integrated Bilingual Education

Additive models of **integrated bilingual education** integrate majority and minority language speakers and aim for dual language proficiency. To some extent, the European school model is an example of an additive integrated bilingual model. To promote an integrated European identity for a multilingual and multinational student population, the European school model integrates its students in the "European hour," during which students from multilingual backgrounds engage in cooperative and hands-on learning and content is taught from a European perspective (Baetens Beardsmore, 1995; Muller & Baetens Beardsmore, 2004). The most developed integrated bilingual education model, however, is **two-way immersion (TWI)** education. In this integrated model, native English speakers and native speakers of a minority language are educated together for most or all of the day and receive content and literacy instruction through both English and the minority language. Its goals include academic achievement, bilingualism and biliteracy development, and cross-cultural competence for all students (Howard, Sugarman, & Christian, 2003; Howard, Sugarman, Christian, Lindholm-Leary, & Rogers, 2007).

TWI originated in Miami Dade County, Florida, in response to the rapid influx of Cubans fleeing Fidel Castro's regime in the early 1960s. While in the rest of the country negative attitudes toward bilingualism prevailed, here a different educational response was developed in recognition that, in addition to learning English, maintaining Spanish was desirable for Cuban political refugees and their children in preparation for their return to Cuba as soon as Castro was defeated. In 1963, the first, now well-known, TWI school was established at Coral Way Elementary School. Early research on TWI by leading experts in immersion and bilingual education through the federally funded Center for Language Education and Research (1985–1989) led to the establishment of a number of new programs and increased awareness and interest in the model. By the late 1980s, 30 programs were identified nationwide, spanning seven states and the District of Columbia (Lindholm, 1987). According to a national database maintained by the Center for Applied Linguistics, there are currently over 300 TWI programs in the United States (a directory is available at http://www.cal.org/twi/directory). Today, the great majority of TWI programs use Spanish and English as instructional languages (93%), although Arabic, French, Korean, Mandarin, Portuguese are also used in a few programs. Further, most TWI programs

(79%) are implemented at the elementary (kindergarten through grade 5) level; it has been difficult to continue or begin programs at the secondary level.

Although different models have been developed, all TWI programs have three essential features:

- TWI programs are considered enrichment programs that aim at three interrelated goals: high levels of bilingualism and biliteracy, grade-level academic achievement, and cross-cultural competence.

- TWI programs enroll approximately equal numbers of native speakers of English and native speakers of the minority language, and integrate these two groups of students for most or all of the day.

- All TWI students receive content area instruction and literacy instruction through both languages, with at least 50% of the instruction in the minority language.

Like other bilingual programs, TWI programs have many designs (Christian, Montone, Lindholm, & Carranza, 1997). TWI programs are often one strand within a school and can also be a whole-school approach where all students are enrolled in TWI. Two common models are the 90:10 and 50:50 model. In a 90:10 model, native English-speaking and native Spanish-speaking students are integrated for all subject areas. Spanish is the prevailing language in grades K–3 for all students with 10% of English instruction in K–1, 20% of English instruction in grades 2 and 3. Instruction is balanced between the two languages in grades 4 and above. The students develop their literacy skills in Spanish first and formal English reading is introduced in 3rd grade. The 90:10 model follows the Canadian immersion program design most closely and is implemented particularly in the Southwest (Lindholm-Leary, 2001). In a 50:50 model, native English speakers and native Spanish speakers are also integrated for all subject areas at all times. Beginning in kindergarten, they receive half of their instruction in English and half in Spanish, often alternating weeks (i.e., 1 week in Spanish, 1 week in English). Literacy development takes place in both languages simultaneously. One of the oldest TWI programs in the nation, Oyster Elementary in Washington, DC, implements a 50:50 model, often with two teachers working together in the same classroom (Freeman, 1998). The Amigos program in Cambridge, Massachusetts, also uses this model (Cazabon, Nicoladis, & Lambert, 1998; Lambert & Cazabon, 1994). The 90:10 and the 50:50 models both integrate students throughout the day. A third model has emerged, differentiated TWI, that integrates students extensively but also includes some instructional time where the two groups of students are grouped by native language (or second language proficiency), mostly for language arts. The amount of native language/second language grouping varies from program to program and generally decreases as students move up the grades (Christian et al., 1997; de Jong, 2002).

Subtractive Bilingual and Monolingual Programs

Not all programs for minority language speakers aim for multilingualism. Many nations have responded to multilingual realities with an assimilationist approach to reduce linguistic diversity and teach almost exclusively through the societal language (Table 5.2). Subtractive models focus on developing proficiency in the societal language with limited or no development of the students' native language or languages.

Some schools have developed specialized programs for minority language speakers that focus on societal language development for students who have been identified as not fluent in that language. The term *submersion* refers to the placement of these students in a standard curriculum classroom designed for native speakers of the societal language without any special accommodations. In the United States, submersion is in violation of federal

TABLE 5.2				
Subtractive Language Programs for Minority Language Speakers				
Program label	**Language goals**	**Target population**	**Language use and distribution**	**Policy orientation**
Standard curriculum (submersion for minority language speakers)	Monolingualism in societal language	Fluent English speakers (minority language speakers are invisible)	Societal language only	Language-as-problem
Transitional bilingual education (TBE)	Proficiency in L2	Minority	L1 for limited amount of time and L2	Language-as-problem
Integrated TBE	Proficiency in L2	Minority	L1 for limited amount of time and L2	Language-as-problem
Pull-out second language instruction	Monolingualism in societal language	Minority	L2 only	Language-as-problem
Self-contained second language program (structured L2 immersion)	Monolingualism in societal language	Minority	L2 only, sometimes with L1 access	Language-as-problem

law, which requires schools to take appropriate action to overcome language barriers (see Chapter 6). Taking no action (i.e., submersion) is insufficient, though districts can choose to implement subtractive models, including bilingual and monolingual models.

Subtractive Bilingual Programs

In most nations, including the United States, **transitional bilingual education (TBE)** is the most common bilingual approach to teaching the official language to minority language speakers. In TBE, the student's native language is used only for an initial period of literacy development and content learning to assist the transition to literacy and content learning in the societal language. Unlike the additive bilingual education models, the goal of TBE is not to maintain or develop the student's native language but to provide access to the language of school. Students are typically expected to enroll in the program for 2 to 3 years and then exit the program into a standard classroom or instruction in the societal language only (early-exit TBE).

In many African postcolonial nations, bilingual education that includes local languages other than the national language is often transitional and experimental. In Mozambique, ciNayanja or xiTsonga is used as the main medium of instruction at the lower elementary grades until Portuguese is introduced in 4th grade (Matsinhe, 2005). Students in these programs often experience a "hard" transition from instruction in their native language to the European language (Ferguson, 2006). Other TBE programs attempt to provide a more gradual transition (late-exit TBE). In Framingham, Massachusetts, students began literacy and content instruction in their native language, with English as a second language (ESL) instruction. In 2nd grade, students began formal literacy instruction in their second language. In 3rd grade, instruction was increasingly balanced between the two languages across subjects, often using an approach where the native language was used to preview major concepts and activities occurred in English. Academic English instruction continued to increase by the second half of 3rd grade and students were expected to exit the program at the end of 4th or 5th grade (de Jong, 2006).

A special case of TBE is the integrated model. The purpose of **integrated transitional bilingual education** is not to promote bilingualism but to counter the negative impact of segregating minority language students while they are becoming familiar with the new language and culture. In the Belgian Foyer model, Turkish-speaking students receive half of their instruction in preschool and kindergarten separately as an ethnic group and half of their instruction with majority language speakers. By 3rd grade, 90% of the instruction is integrated with majority language speakers with 10% native language and culture (Leman, 1990). "Coordinated" classes in Sweden and Denmark promote native language instruction through separation and provide for integration with majority language speakers through hands-on activities in the second language (Glenn, 1996).

In integrated TBE models in the United States, minority language students are separated for some specialized instruction in their native language and integrated with native English speakers for specific subject areas for varying amounts of time (Brisk, 1991, 2006; de Jong, 2006). Brisk (1991) describes a model that integrated two 5th grade classes, one transitional bilingual classroom and one monolingual classroom. Students were grouped by their own homeroom (the monolingual or the transitional bilingual classroom) for morning activities, social studies, and ESL but were integrated for reading and language arts, math, and science. Flexible grouping practices were important to the success of the program: students had access to Spanish-only, English-only, or bilingual instruction throughout the school day, according to their individual linguistic and academic needs.

Despite their use of bilingual instruction, TBE programs are, in intent and design, subtractive within the school context. Of course, students may continue using their native language at home and in the community and maintain bilingual competence without the support of a school-based program. Unlike additive bilingual programs, however, TBE programs do not intend to build on and expand students' native language repertoires in school.

Monolingual Programs

Nonbilingual approaches provide specialized support in second language development without native language development. These supports can be linked to a standard curriculum classroom or exist as separate services. **Pull-out second language classes** are in general use around the world to meet the needs of immigrant children. Specialist teachers take second language learners out of their standard curriculum classroom for a portion of the day to teach the societal language; the amount of time spent in these classes is determined by each student's proficiency level. Increasingly, these teachers are asked to go into the standard curriculum classroom to provide in-class support (**push-in second language model**). The latter model is often preferred because it avoids segregating students from their peers and ensures better access to grade level curriculum content.

Finally, there are **self-contained second language programs** in which students spend most of their school day. These programs teach the societal language itself as well as content matter through the societal language by using instructional strategies designed for language and literacy development and content teaching. Note the difference between this type of immersion and the Canadian immersion programs described earlier. In addition to the sociopolitical context (both French and English have official status in Canada) and target population status (majority language speakers in Canada; minority language speakers in the United States), the goals of the two programs are distinctly different. Whereas Canadian immersion is an additive bilingual program (the native language is an integral part of the program), majority language immersion programs lead to monolingualism in the societal language. In the United States, the terms *English immersion* or **structured English immersion (SEI)** are also sometimes used to describe these classes. Another term is **sheltered English instruction** or **specially designed academic instruction in English (SDAIE)**. The latter two terms refer to a set of instructional practices in content classes (like history, science) taught in the second language to "shelter" the language of the subject matter, such as visuals and simplified language structures (Genesee, 1999).

It is worth mentioning the **newcomer program** at the secondary level. In the United States, almost half of the newcomer schools provide instruction or tutoring or both in the students' native languages and thus could also be classified as an example under transitional bilingual programs (Boyson & Short, 2003; Short & Boyson, 2004). Newcomer programs emerged in the United States to meet the needs of newly arrived immigrant children with no or limited English proficiency and limited literacy skills in their native language, often due to interrupted schooling (Friedlander, 1991; Short, 2002b). Neither traditional ESL nor bilingual programs are typically designed to meet these students' needs because they assume grade-level knowledge and skills in the native language. According to a nationwide survey of newcomer programs, 77% of the newcomer programs are programs within schools, 17% are at a separate site, and 6% are whole school models. Effective newcomer schools are characterized by flexible scheduling, ungraded programs, and a range of supporting services for families (for case studies, see Constantino & Lavadenz, 1993; Short & Boyson, 2003, 2004).

BEYOND MEDIUM OF INSTRUCTION: CLASSROOM PRACTICES

When teachers teach within a certain program model their language choices will be influenced by this structure. In a TWI program, one teacher often teaches solely in English and another teacher solely in the partner language. In an English immersion program, English will tend to dominate. Choice of program model is a visible aspect of language policies in schools. Educators are involved in additional language practices, however, that may be less explicit but no less significant in their impact on shaping the linguistic and cultural experiences of their students. A few examples can illustrate how pervasive language is and how important a teacher's decisions about language are.

In a study by Escamilla (2006), teachers who were shown writing samples in English and Spanish labeled them as evidence of "semi-literate" behavior.

These teachers interpreted bilingual strategies (such as spelling English words using Spanish rules) as signs of confusion, and they interpreted writing that differed from that of a native speaker as deficient. The solution, they felt, was a renewed emphasis on monolingual instruction. In contrast, a teacher taking a holistic approach might label the same writing samples as those of emergent bilinguals who had found creative ways to use what they know, and would see these strategies as part of a normal developmental pattern for bilingual learners. This teacher's strategy might be to continue building on both languages. In one scenario, the bilingual learner is positioned as a deficient monolingual, in the other as a competent bilingual. Subsequent interactions with the students about their writing ability in the two scenarios will be quite different.

Literacy is another area where cultural differences emerge (Pérez, 1998). Literacy practices in school are culturally embedded and reflect specific notions about what literacy is (and what it is not). Take the commonly used activity "show and tell" where students bring an item to school and talk about it to their peers. Teachers hold expectations about the structure of a typical show and tell event, for example, students should stay on one topic (the item itself) and use specific words to describe the item. Even though everyone may be able to see what a child is showing or doing, the child is expected to label the object by using a noun rather than referring to it by a pronoun (*he*, *she*, or *it*). These expectations differentiate the school show and tell as a formal literacy event from an everyday social conversation about an object where using implicit referents would be accepted. Familiarity with these school expectations is not universal and is not always made explicit by the teacher. Studies have found that the way teachers interact with students depends on whether students adhere to expected conventions or not. When students match the expectations, teachers tend to provide positive feedback and scaffold students' use of rich language through follow-up questions. When students do not meet these expectations (e.g., they shift topics or use implicit references), teachers typically interrupt, fail to provide useful feedback, or engage less with the student (Schleppegrell, 2004).

When teachers' ways of responding to or interacting with students coincide with majority norms, minority students can be at a disadvantage and can be systematically excluded from literacy activities that would be as meaningful to them as mainstream literacy activities are to majority students. Without teacher mediation, this unequal access disadvantages minority students and privileges those students already familiar with the literacy events that have become the (only) accepted norm in school. However, when teachers do mediate language and culture in their classroom, positive academic outcomes emerge. In a well-known experiment in Honolulu, teachers in the Kamehameha Early Education Program (KEEP) learned to match their talk more closely to the ways children were used to interacting with adults at home (Jordan, 1995). Making the home and school cultural practices more congruent positively affected student achievement.

The KEEP program shows that incorporating bilingual learners' experiences into the curriculum makes it easier for these learners to connect to school and enables them build on what they already know. This basic principle of learning is in place for majority students for whom there is a match between curriculum and cultural and linguistic experiences but becomes easily denied to those who come from different language backgrounds and cultures. Students who may have grown up with different linguistic and cultural norms are easily marginalized in classrooms that view majority norms as superior and take them for granted. Meanwhile, majority students who are socialized in these norms at home and in their community are in a better position to take advantage of what school has to offer. When both groups of students come to school, their experiences as learners will be distinctly different. Often, teachers lower their expectations for students in the minority group because they interpret the students' incomprehensibility or nonparticipation as a lack of cognitive ability or an unwillingness to work (motivation).

We All "Do" Language Planning

If language policy is narrowly defined as the formal legislative process, teachers may not think that they are engaged in language policy. Language policy involves much more than the passage of a formal law or regulation, however. Daily practices in and about languages and language varieties are included in the broad definition of language policy that we have used in this chapter. Schools do not have to declare a formal "English-only" or "dominant culture only" policy and openly denounce the students' native languages and cultures to reinforce the dominance, higher status, and desirability of monolingualism or speaking standard English. Simply by only using English and dominant cultural practices, a school already sends a powerful message to speakers of languages other than English about the value of their language and cultural experiences. Such policy by omission (ignoring linguistic and cultural diversity) can be more powerful than a policy of open repression (e.g., openly banning the use of the native language) because they are invisible and taken for granted by all, that is, they are hegemonic.

Educators need to understand the formal government policy so they know what is and is not permissible under the law. They also need to reflect how their own interpretation of a law relates to those of administrators and peers and how they view the impact of the law on their practices. They partake in discussions at the school and with colleagues about what program model best fits their goals and the student population. In addition, they make many formal and informal decisions about language in school every day: which language they use and for what purposes, which languages their students can use (and where), and what language or languages and views are represented in the curriculum and texts they select.

Because of the crucial role teachers play in language policy at different policy levels as they interact with parents, students, colleagues, administrators, politicians, and so forth, Ricento and Hornberger (1996) refer to teachers as the core of policy implementation. Using the metaphor of an onion, they argue that, once the outer (nation, state policies) and intermediate (e.g., district policies, the media) layers are peeled away, the core reveals the teacher directly shaping the experiences of students and families with and in school. Policy implementation and practices are mediated by a complex web of interpretations and negotiations of what a particular law or policy means for a specific context. These policy orientations (ideologies), in turn, affect how language problems are defined, what solutions are sought, and how resources are allocated.

CHAPTER 5
Discussion & Activities

Critical Issues

1. The idea of language policy as social practice is a relatively recent development in the field of language policy and planning. Give an example from your own experiences working in schools that illustrates how individuals interpret and construct the meaning of a particular policy differently (e.g., math reform, introduction of a new literacy program, new guidelines for special education placement)?

2. Analyze the additive and subtractive program models through the language orientation lens offered by Richard Ruiz. Which models would you categorize under the language-as-problem, the language-as-right, and the language-as-resource orientation? Could some models warrant a dual classification, i.e., reflect two orientations? Can you think of examples where all three orientations may co-exist but be applied to different languages (e.g., at the district level, at the state or national level)?

Application & Reflection

3. Thinking about your own language learning experiences in classroom environments, what was the language policy? In what ways did that policy work for you and in what ways was it not helpful? Compare these classroom-based language policies with learning a second language in a natural environment. What "policies" seem to be in place in these settings? When you are interacting with a bilingual learner and you share their native language, do you use bilingual strategies?

4. One of the main themes in this and other chapters is that of teachers as language policy makers (see also Chapter 1, Question 4 where you generated some examples of teachers' language decisions). Select a math, science, or social studies activity (e.g., an experiment, a math game, a role play) that you have taught or observed. Make a list of the language decisions that you or the teacher made while teaching this activity. Here is a brief list to get you started:

   • In general, which language/language variety was used and by whom, who had opportunities to talk, and what kinds of questions were asked?
   • If there were second language learners in the classroom, how did you/ the teacher accommodate their language for them?

- If students were grouped, did language play a role in deciding who worked with whom?
- If a written text was used, how did the content reflect the students' backgrounds and experiences? Were there references to other cultures or perspectives? What vocabulary did the text use? What was the reading level of the text? Did everybody read the same text?

5. Consider the composition of your school, school district, or selected geographical area (state, province, or nation) and determine what additive bilingual models might be possible there. What factors might you need to take into consideration when trying to make such a decision? If your setting does not already implement an additive bilingual program, what are some barriers that prevent this from happening? If you are implementing such an approach, what factors have facilitated the process?

Recommended Readings

Cooper, R. L. (1989). *Language planning and social change*. Cambridge: Cambridge University Press.

> *Cooper describes his framework of language policy as "Who plans what [language practices] for whom, how, under what conditions, and for what purpose?" While there are many excellent introductory texts to language policy, Cooper's analysis and integration of language policy into theories of social change remains a useful framework for thinking about language policy.*

Shohamy, E. (2006). *Language policy: Hidden agendas and new approaches*. New York: Routledge.

> *This book extends the definition of language policy beyond government documents, describing how language ideologies shape how policies are formulated and the role that the media, language testing regimes, and medium of instruction policies play in influencing language practices.*

Tollefson, J. W., & Tsui, A. B. M. (Eds.). (2004). *Medium of instruction policies: Which agendas? Whose agenda?* Mahwah: Lawrence Erlbaum.

> *This book explores language-in-education policies around the world, including in English-dominant countries (New Zealand, Wales), postcolonial nations (Hong Kong, Singapore, Africa), and countries where linguistic diversity has been negotiated in innovative ways.*

Language Policy in the United States

GUIDING QUESTIONS

- *How have policies and schooling options for immigrants and Native Americans changed historically? How do these options reflect pluralist and assimilationist discourses?*

- *What federal and state policies have shaped the schooling of English language learners?*

- *What rights and responsibilities do schools have according to the courts?*

KEY TERMS

meta-narratives
Americanization movement
nativism
Meyer v. Nebraska (1923)
Brown v. Board of Education (1954)
reluctant bilingual discourse
Elementary and Secondary Education Act (ESEA)
Bilingual Education Act (BEA)
Native American Languages Act
Lau v. Nichols (1974)

Lau Remedies
Castañeda v. Pickard (1981)
Flores v. Arizona (ongoing)
Plyer v. Doe (1982)
English-plus resolutions
No Child Left Behind Act (NCLB)
adequate yearly progress (AYP)
annual measurable achievement objectives (AMAO)
Proposition 227
Proposition 203
Amendment 31

Except for a brief period of repressive assimilationist policies before and after World War I (1914–1918), federal and state language-in-education policies throughout American history have simultaneously reflected pluralist and assimilationist tendencies (Schmidt, 2000). These policies reveal beliefs about what it means to be a member of this particular (national) community at a particular time. This chapter traces these discourses through U.S. federal and state policies and various court decisions.

Imagined Communities and National Identities

The construction of the "imagined national community" (Chapter 2) involves recognizing and legitimizing certain ways of thinking, doing, and being and contrasting those with the ways of thinking, doing, and believing associated with other groups. An imagined national community draws an imaginary boundary that defines how individuals or groups are positioned and how identities are constructed in relationship to the community. Some individuals and groups are said to belong, and others are not because they do share the same beliefs and practices associated with the group. This process of national identity construction is reflected in all aspects of society, including government policy, schooling practices, and the media.

Voting rights are a good example of an area that reflects decisions about whose voices are included and whose are excluded. Asian Americans were excluded from citizenship and therefore from voting in 1882, the year the Chinese Exclusion Act was passed banning Chinese labor. Not until 1870 did states ratify the 15th Amendment, which allowed African American men to vote. Women were excluded from voting until 1920; many Native Americans were effectively barred from voting until 1948. These decisions reflect the dominant concerns and discourses of their times. The U.S. Census also reflects the dominant concerns and discourses of a particular time and will be discussed in more detail below.

Language has traditionally played an important role in constructing national identities: language is a powerful symbol of community membership, and language is used to frame ideological discourses about the nation itself. Wodak and her colleagues (1999) talk about **meta-narratives** that have been constructed to support a particular version of national identity. Notions about language and the role of the national language for national unity are part of this "meta" narrative. In the United States, assimilationist discourses forge a close link between English proficiency, being an American, and academic success. This link has become integral to the image of the United States as an immigrant nation and reinforces the importance of English as a unifying force (Sonntag & Pool, 1987). At the same time, pluralist discourses have stressed the multilingual roots of the country and the strength in respecting and building on the linguistic and cultural diversity that exists in this country. Not surprisingly, language policies lead to heated debates because they tap into different narratives and different imagined (national) communities.

The following sections illustrate how different policies have emphasized assimilationist and pluralist versions of the imagined national community. The discussion covers four broad periods: the years before and after independence, the Americanization movement of the 1900s, the return to bilingual education in the 1960s and 1970s, and today's English-only movement.

Early Years: Tolerance and Repression

The years between the late 18th and early 19th century are often overlooked in overviews of educational policy for language minority students in the United States, which typically start after World War II. But this period is important because it illustrates a mostly pluralist stance toward immigrant languages at the beginnings of nation building. At the same time an overt assimilationist approach to Native American language speakers and the native languages of slaves also existed. These early years reflect a multiplicity and synchronicity of discourses.

LINGUISTIC DIVERSITY BEFORE INDEPENDENCE

Multilingualism was long the norm on the North American continent, where for centuries Native Americans lived throughout the area of what is now the United States and spoke about 300 different languages (Brisk, 1981, 2006; Conklin & Lourie, 1983; Kloss, 1998). The European colonists who settled colonial America spoke Spanish, French, German, Dutch, and English, as well as several other northern European languages. The first European language to take hold was Spanish in the early 1500s as Puerto Rico, Florida, and then California, Arizona, New Mexico, and Texas were settled by Spanish-speaking missionaries and explorers. The German-speaking population was the second largest ethnic group to arrive. Germans fleeing religious repression and war went to Pennsylvania and were the dominant ethnic group in an area that included Maryland and Virginia's Shenandoah Valley. By the time of the Revolution, Germans constituted one-third of Pennsylvania's population.

American colonies "abounded with speakers of languages other than English" (Read, 1937, p. 99). By the time New Netherlands ceded to British in 1664, at least 18 languages were spoken on Manhattan Island, not counting Indian languages (Crawford, 1999). Even at this time the English spoken was not one variety and included East Anglican English (spoken by indentured servants) and an English variety spoken by Scotch-Irish Ulsterites. By 1800, three varieties of French were spoken in Louisiana: the standard French of the original French settlers, Arcadian French (also referred to as Cajun), spoken by those who had been expelled from Nova Scotia during the French and Indian War between 1755 and 1763, and the Louisiana French Creole of West African slaves (Conklin & Lourie, 1983; Earle, 1992).

Like the ruling bodies of many other nations before them, the Continental Congress took up the question of an official language at the time of independence. While the various proposals were considered, Congress ultimately decided against declaring an official language and chose "a policy not to have a policy" (Heath, 1977, p. 10). As Heath explains, this decision was informed by several rationales. The nation's founders realized, first, the divisive impact that such a monolingual policy could have. They recognized the critical roles that multiple languages were playing in political and social life at the time. By declaring English as the official language they could potentially alienate powerful ethnic groups that were needed to support, unify, and legitimize the new nation. Second, language use was considered a matter of individual choice and not to be regulated by the government. The idea of a supranational language was too closely associated with the monarchical systems (such as those in Spain and France) that many were trying to escape. Finally, the Founding Fathers were confident that assimilation into greatness of American culture would naturally occur and needed no coercion through social engineering. The majority of individuals living in the 13 colonies spoke some variety of English and it was taken for granted that English would become the natural choice of communication as the nation expanded. For pragmatic and political reasons, then, Congress decided not to have a formal and explicit language policy. The Founding Fathers were correct in predicting that English would become the language of public life. Today English is spoken by the great majority of the people. According to the 2007 American Community Survey, only 8% of the total U.S. population reports not speaking English at all.

SUPPORTING MULTILINGUALISM

In the early years of U.S. nation building, speaking English was not a precondition to being or becoming a citizen or for being considered American; rather, subscribing to the ideals and principles of the "New Nation" (liberty, equality, democracy) defined the American identity. Recall that the census did not include any questions about language during this period. The Founding Fathers and other leaders valued multilingualism for individuals and national service because it provided access to knowledge and learning and advocated for the recognition of local, regional, or special interests.

Federal and state declarations and laws were printed in German and French. Non-English languages were officially recognized along with English in state constitutions as new states joined the union, including Louisiana (French), California and New Mexico (Spanish), and Pennsylvania (German). The use of the ethnic language was an expected and natural part of the acculturation process of immigrants. The colonial and early immigrant languages were used regularly, along with English, to conduct government business. They were used in church services and local media, including books, pamphlets, and, in particular, newspapers. Cultural events (theater, choral concerts, celebrations) also continued to be conducted in non-English languages for many years (Kloss, 1998).

Public, private, and parochial schools were established that used the native language out of a desire to maintain the native language and culture as well as out of necessity in the absence of English-speaking teachers (Crawford, 1999, 2000). Andersson (1971) credits German-English bilingual schools in Cincinnati, Ohio with the origin of bilingual schooling in the United States in 1840. To strengthen public education and attract children from the German community, the State of Ohio passed a law that required the provision of German or German and English schools if parents requested it. By 1900, at least 600,000 children in the United States were receiving part or all of their instruction in German, about 4% of the elementary school population. Cincinnati public schools continued to enroll over 15,000 students annually in their bilingual schools until the end of World War I (Schlossman, 1983a).

During this same period, Swedish, Norwegian, and Danish were used in public schools in Wisconsin, Illinois, Minnesota, Iowa, North and South Dakota, and Washington. Dutch was used in Michigan, and Polish and Italian were used in Wisconsin. Spanish was used extensively in the Southwest, in particular in New Mexico (Ovando, Collier, & Combs, 2003). New Mexico had previously been Spanish, then Mexican territory and bilingual practices had been typical until the 1880s. Anglo merchants learned Spanish, and New Mexico was seen as a bilingual society. A shift in numbers and the power structure changed this favorable attitude toward bilingualism (and the use of Spanish). English became the mandated language, although bilingual practices (e.g., the use of bilingual textbooks) continued (Getz, 1997). Today, New Mexico is one of four states that have endorsed resolutions in favor of bilingualism. At the time of the outbreak of World War I, about a dozen states allowed bilingual schooling for their citizens.

REPRESSION FOR NATIVE AMERICANS

While a pluralistic discourse characterized the treatment of the colonial and the first immigrant languages during the early years of the republic, policies toward Native Americans and West African slaves were openly repressive and characterized by coercive assimilation during this same period (Wiley, 2000). West African slaves were taken from Senegambia, the Gold Coast, the Bight of Biafra, and Southeast Asia to work on the southern plantations (Fogleman, 1998), though some worked as slaves (servants) in the Northeast as well (Berlin, 1980). In the Chesapeake area (Virginia), slaves were grouped into multilingual units and separated from their families and other group members who could speak their language. Unable to use their native languages, slaves throughout the south developed a language to communicate among themselves that developed into what we now refer to as Black English or African American Vernacular English (AAVE), which still has traces of African languages.

U.S. policy on Native American languages is perhaps historically the most coercive of all language policies in the country. Initial contact with Christian missionaries led to the development of alphabets for several Native American languages. However, since cultural and linguistic assimilation was their goal, missionaries used the students' native languages to provide religious instruction and found the method to be highly effective. Mr. Janney, a Quaker, wrote in a report to the Board of Indian Commissioners in 1871, "Theirs is a phonetic language, and a smart boy will learn it in three or four weeks; and we have found it far better to instruct them in their own language, and also to teach them English as fast as we can" (Annual Report, 1971, p. 168; cited in Reyhner, 1993, p. 38).

The use of the native language for schooling also appeared in a congressional treaty with the Cherokee nation in 1828, which states, "It is further agreed by the U.S. to pay $1,000 . . . towards the purchase of a Printing Press and Types to aid the Cherokees in the progress of education, and to benefit and enlighten them as people, in their own language" (Castellanos, 1983, p. 17). The Cherokees would operate 21 schools and two academies in Cherokee and English. The existence of a written language (the Sequoya syllabary) played a crucial role in the development of bilingual newspapers, pamphlets, and the like. By 1852 the Cherokee had higher literacy levels in English than the white population in either Texas or Arkansas. Unfortunately, subsequent English-only policies had a devastating impact on literacy levels, and by 1967, the literacy rate had dropped to 40% (Dicker, 2003).

This assimilationist 'bilingual' approach was short-lived. Starting in the 1860s, the federal government began its systematic eradication of the languages and cultures of the Native Americans. The 1868 *Report of the Indian Peace Commissioners* identifies language and cultural differences as the problem for the Native American Indian: "In the difference of language to-day lies two-thirds of our trouble. . . . Schools should be established, which children should be required to attend; their barbarous dialect should be blotted out and the English language substituted" (quoted in Reyhner, 1993, p. 39). Based on a mission to "save the savage," this assimilationist discourse dominated schooling for Native Americans well into the 1930s and was combined with territorial policies that systematically diminished the land owned by Native American tribes (Adams, 1995).

Native Americans were forcefully moved onto reservations, and children were taken away to off-reservation boarding schools, often for several years, where English-only policies were strictly implemented. As the commissioner of Indian affairs, John Atkins, stated in 1887: "The instruction of the Indians in the vernacular is not only of no use to them, but is detrimental to the cause of their education and civilization, and no school will be permitted on the reservation in which the English language is not exclusively taught" (quoted in Reyhner, 1993, p. 40). Children were physically punished for speaking their native language and torn from their cultural roots, in terms of values and physical attributes such as clothing and hair style (Adams, 1995). The curriculum focused on religious instruction with limited opportunities for developing practical skills. There was no expectation that Native Americans would rise to positions of leadership in the new nation.

War, disease, coercive assimilation, and forced migration onto reservations reduced the number of Native Americans and marginalized them as a group in the United States. This marginalization has led to the disappearance of many indigenous languages and cultures to the extent that there are only about 150 Native American languages recognized today (Estes, 1999). In California alone, approximately 150 indigenous languages were spoken at the time the Europeans arrived. Only 50 are still spoken today, mostly only by elders; and virtually 100% of California's indigenous languages are no longer learned by children (Hinton, 1994).

Immigrant Era: Focus on Assimilation

In the late 19th and early 20th centuries, a time of industrialization, urbanization, and the advent of compulsory public education, the number of immigrants arriving in the United States grew exponentially. At 14.7%, the 1910 foreign-born population is still proportionally the largest in U.S. history (see Figure 6.1). These immigrants came from more diverse and different backgrounds than the early northern European immigrants, most of whom were Anglo-Saxon and Protestant. Although previous immigrant groups continued to arrive (e.g., Swedes, Norwegians, Germans), the majority of the new immigrants came from eastern Europe (Czechs, Poles, Russian Jews) and southern Europe (Greeks, Italians). Most were Roman Catholic or Jewish and upon arrival moved into urban rather than rural areas.

The majority of the new immigrants did not speak English when they arrived. In 1910, 23% or about 3 million out of the 13 million foreign-born individuals 10 years of age or older were unable to speak English (compare with 8% in 2007). Their religious backgrounds and cultural habits were perceived as being distinctly different from those of the existing native "stock." These demographic and economic developments were subsequently joined by the threat of and entry into World War I (1914–1918); together they raised new questions about American identity.

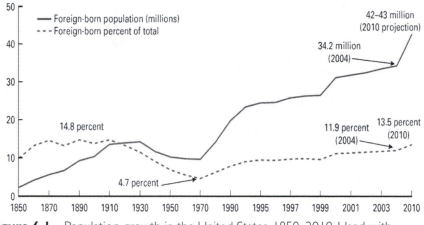

Figure 6.1   Population growth in the United States, 1850–2010. Used with permission of The Urban Institute.

THE AMERICANIZATION MOVEMENT

The dominant response to the new diversity was to try to streamline it to promote assimilation into a view that defined American identity as English-speaking, Protestant, and Anglo-Saxon. The **Americanization movement** that emerged during these years focused assimilating the new immigrants into American society (Handlin, 1982; Hartmann, 1967; Higham, 1998; Hill, 1919). Between 1917 and 1922, more than 30 states passed Americanization laws, requiring those unable to speak or read English to attend public evening schools (Pavlenko, 2005).

This movement included proponents of **nativism** (opposition to any foreign influences) and reformers genuinely concerned with improving the impoverished health and working conditions of the new urban immigrants (Olneck, 1989). Americanization efforts focused on providing classes in English civics primarily to adult, male immigrants. In addition, groups pushed for legislation to limit immigration in general or exclude certain groups from entering the country. These included anti-Catholic laws that had been passed in the early 1880s in response to the increased presence of Irish, and the Chinese Exclusion Act of 1882. Laws restricting Japanese, passed between 1905 and 1924, were followed in the 1920s and 1930s by laws retracting Filipinos (Daniels, 1990). Legislative anti-immigrant efforts cumulated in the Immigration Act of 1924, which put quotas on the number of immigrants allowed to enter from certain (nonwestern European) countries. By basing the quotas on the 1890 census, law makers privileged immigrants from northern European countries.

Language became a central issue in the immigration debate, especially as World War I approached. The 1906 Nationality Act made the ability to speak English a requirement for naturalization, and the 1917 Immigration

Act excluded aliens who were illiterate (in any language) from entering. In this climate, the use of languages other than English in school was un-American and undesirable. Speaking English became a condition for being a good (real) American. Several states passed legislation that prohibited the teaching of foreign languages to young children and 37 states passed laws making English the official language of the state during this period.

SCHOOLING FOR IMMIGRANTS

Educational policies directed at immigrant children during the early 1900s were primarily ones of neglect: students were submersed in English-only classrooms without any accommodations. Newcomers were often placed in 1st grade classrooms regardless of their age, causing many early dropouts. Intelligence testing in English led to the disproportionate placement of immigrant children in special education classes. In some instances, minimal accommodations were made through separate classes. Educators in New York and other major cities began to recognize that special classes were needed to help students who did not speak English. William Maxwell from the New York Board of Education argued in 1912, "It is absurd to place the boy or girl, 10 or 12 years of age, just landed from Italy, who cannot read a word in his own language or speak a word of English, in the same classroom with American boys and girls five or six years old" (quoted in Berrol, 1995, p. 49). New York established "C" or steamer classes for students older than 8 years who had recently arrived. Also referred to as "vestibule" classes, steamer classes, which lasted for 6 months to 1 year, segregated students from native peers and focused solely on teaching oral English skills (Berrol, 1995; Brumberg, 1986). Students were punished for using their native language. Similar classes were implemented for immigrant children in Boston and Chicago.

Segregated schools were also the solution for the "Mexican problem" in the Southwest beginning in the early 1900s, in particular California and Texas (Gonzalez, 2001). The establishment of these Mexican schools for Spanish-speaking students had been based on the rationale that the students did not have the level of command of English needed and would hold Anglo students back, and that segregation would permit more individualized instruction. Furthermore, it was believed, "Hispanic students attended school less regularly and so disrupted classroom continuity" (Schlossman, 1983b, p. 893). Like segregated schools for African American students (and boarding schools for Native Americans), Mexican schools had fewer resources and less qualified teachers (Donato & Garcia, 1992; Donato, Mechaca, & Valencia, 1991). The schools focused on teaching English, often punished students for using any Spanish, and portrayed Mexico and the Mexican people as inferior and backward.

Many immigrant children did not finish school during this period or were allowed to graduate with only minimal skills due to a greatly reduced curriculum. While achievement patterns varied from immigrant group to immigrant group and across different cities, the typical pattern was minimal school attendance and low high school and college attendance by the majority of immigrant children. Perlmann (1990) found that 13% of 12-year-old students whose parents were foreign-born went on to high school (compared with 32% of white children of native parentage). Native-born students with English skills did much better than immigrant children in school attendance and high school graduation rates. Poverty played a significant role in these patterns. According to Berrol (1982), "Most immigrant families, for at least two generations, needed whatever money their children could earn" (p. 38). A rapidly expanding economy that could absorb many low-skilled laborers, followed by a sharp reduction in immigration, explains the economic and social mobility that has been observed for the early 1900s rather than school success. The myth that submersion in English and giving up cultural ties has continued, however, as part of the meta-narrative of the country's national identity. As Berrol notes, by the 1950s when black and Hispanic migrants came to New York City, "most people had forgotten . . . that the public schools had not been successful with most of the poor and foreign children who had come earlier" (pp. 40–41).

PROTECTING LANGUAGES OTHER THAN ENGLISH

Pluralist views were pushed far into the background during this same period. Two trends, however, that opposed the insistence on assimilationism are worth mentioning. First, the federal government changed its policy toward Native Americans, at least for a while. Ironically, whereas during the early colonial years immigrant languages were tolerated and indigenous languages rejected, this period witnessed the reverse pattern of treatment. During the 1920s and 1930s, John Collier, director of the Bureau of Indian Affairs, was initiated a return to on-reservation day schools and the development of native language textbooks, promoting a greater emphasis on native cultures and languages. Funding for his efforts unfortunately ended with World War II and did not return until the 1970s.

Second, some court decisions maintained a more nuanced perspective (O'Brien, 1961). In **Meyer v. Nebraska (1923)** the Supreme Court constrained the scope of the English-only laws to those areas where the state could demonstrate a compelling interest in not allowing languages other than English to be taught. The case involved a teacher in a parochial school who was accused of teaching the Bible in German to an 8-year-old. At the time, Nebraska's English-only law forbade the use of languages other than English for children younger than 10 years of age. The Court sided with the plaintiffs because, in their judgment, the ends (teaching English) did not justify the means (restricting the parents' right to choose instruction for their children and a teacher's right to teach).

Return to Bilingual Education

Pluralist discourses slowly found their way back into educational policy after World War II. The shift from assimilationist policies to recognition of different languages and cultures in school was due in part to a steady decline in immigration that had begun with the implementation of legal restrictions and continued during World War II. By 1950, only 8% of the total population was foreign-born, down from 15% in the early 1900s dropping even further to 4.7% in the 1970 census. This trend greatly lessened the pre–World War I anxieties about immigrants and their ability to assimilate. Later, the civil rights movement set the stage for the recognition of minority group rights and antidiscrimination legislation. The landmark Supreme Court case ***Brown v. Board of Education* (1954)** that declared separate educational facilities inherently unequal began an era of integration and desegregation. The case played a major role in making equal educational opportunity a central focus of educational policies. Further, World War II had increased awareness of the need for knowing foreign languages and, under the influence of the cold war and competition with Russia, major initiatives were undertaken by the federal government to ensure a competitive act. One of these was the National Defense Education Act of 1958, which promoted extensive foreign language programs for language majority speakers.

In the 1960s, a pluralistic experiment in bilingual education was initiated in Miami, Florida. In a unique move, Coral Way Elementary School made the bilingual option available to native English speakers as well as Cuban refugees (Chapter 5). For both groups, bilingualism was considered an asset and enrichment. The school's demonstrated success with both groups in both languages encouraged several other schools in Miami and other states (Arizona, California, Illinois, Texas, Washington, DC) to take a similar approach (Andersson, 1971; Mackey & Beebe, 1977). However, this pluralist educational approach was the exception. Most language policies initiated during this period were based on an assimilationist approach, though these policies promoted assimilation in a more gentle way than those advocated during the Americanization movement in the 1920s. Bilingual approaches were endorsed and implemented but mostly with an assimilationist intent (Spener, 1988). The assimilationist bilingual discourse, or **reluctant bilingual discourse** (Zhou, 1997), sees the student's native language as a temporary bridge to learning the societal language, English. Though room for more pluralist interpretation existed (at the local implementation level), this "reluctant bilingual discourse" dominated federal legislation as well as court decisions and their enforcement.

BILINGUAL EDUCATION ACT (1968–2000)

The **Elementary and Secondary Education Act (ESEA)** of 1965 was a major effort by the Johnson administration to address the effects of poverty on educational and economic achievement. Programs such as Headstart (preschool) and Title I (supplemental support services for at-risk students) were initiated under this law. Combined with the Equal Educational Opportunity Act of 1974, Title VII of the ESEA, the **Bilingual Education Act (BEA)** of 1968, was to shape much of the schooling of minority students, in particular ELLs (Figure 6.2 and 6.3).

The BEA was the first comprehensive federal intervention in the schooling of language minority students. Its uncontroversial passage in 1968 reflected agreement over the underachievement of a steadily increasing number of language minority students in schools. The BEA was introduced by Senator Ralph Yarborough of Texas, who noted that Spanish-speaking students in his state completed, on average, 4 years of schooling less than their Anglo peers. The lack of resources and trained personnel and the absence of special programs to meet the needs of these students contributed to this educational failure. Yarborough proposed bilingual education as a solution to what he perceived was a problem of English proficiency.

> The problem is that many of our school-age children come from homes where the *mother tongue is not English*. As a result, these children enter school *not speaking English* and not able to understand the instructions that is [sic] all conducted in English. [There is] an urgent need for this legislation to provide equal educational opportunity for those *children who do not come to school with English-speaking ability*. We received almost unanimous enthusiasm and support for this legislation as being an effective *remedial* program. (US Congress 1967:37037; cited in Bangura & Muo, 2001, p. 58; italics added)

Note that Yarborough presents bilingual education as a remedial program, not an enrichment program like the bilingual education program at Coral Way. Only with the 1974 re-authorization of the BEA was bilingual education formally defined as a program where "there is instruction given in, and the study of English, and, to the extent necessary to allow a child to progress effectively through the educational system, the native language of the children of limited English-speaking ability" (Lyons, 1990, p. 68).

The BEA was not a mandate for bilingual education. Since education is the responsibility of the states, the federal government can only create financial incentives through grant programs. The federal government's influence is in setting the criteria for the allocation of funds: if states or districts want

1968   First Bilingual Education Act. Targets low-income nonspeaking and limited-English-speaking students; no definition of bilingual education.

1974   Mandates equal educational opportunity through bilingual education, defined as "There is instruction given in, and study of, English and, to the extent necessary to allow a child progress effectively through the educational system, the native language of the children of limited English-speaking ability." Low-income criterion is dropped and the eligibility criteria changes to limited English proficient (LEP). Native Americans are included as a target group, as are native English speakers. Funds are made available for professional development and dissemination of instructional materials.

1978   Declares that instruction in English should "allow a child to achieve competence in the English language" and that increased parental involvement in planning programs and school districts must have a plan for institutionalization of the program after the grant has ended.

1984   Declares that transitional bilingual education programs are to provide "structured English-language instruction, and, to the extent necessary to allow a child to achieve competence in the English language, instruction in the child's native language." Three-quarters of the funding allocated to transitional bilingual education (TBE) programs. An unspecified amount is allocated for developmental[1] bilingual education. Funding is also provided for special alternative instructional programs (SAIPs), which do not use the native language (4%).

1988   Defines grant categories similar to those provided in 1984. SAIPs now receive 25% of the funds. Participation in TBE or SAIPs may be up to 3 years.

1994   Goals: "to ensure that limited English proficiency students master English as they develop high levels of academic attainment in content areas." Further, "the use of a "child's native language and culture in classroom instruction can (A) promote self-esteem and contribute to academic achievement and learning English [and] . . . (C) develop our nation's national language resources thus promoting our nation's competitiveness in the global economy." Preference is given to programs that develop bilingual proficiency in both English and another language for all participating students. Target group specified: LEP, indigenous language populations, recent immigrants. 25% cap on SAIP can be lifted if applicant has demonstrated that bilingual education is not feasible.

2001   BEA is discontinued. No Child Left Behind provides for indigenous language maintenance only through Title VII. For ELLs, Title III specifies that the goal is to "attain English proficiency, develop high levels of academic attainment in English, and meet the same challenging . . . achievement standards as all children are expected to meet." Further, districts should "develop high-quality language instruction educational programs . . . to prepare limited English proficiency students . . . to enter all-English instruction settings."

[1]The BEA's use of the term "developmental" here parallels the use of "dual language" (Chapter 5), including maintenance bilingual education and two-way immersion.

Figure 6.2   Key changes in the Bilingual Education Act (BEA), 1968–2000

> **Title VI of the Civil Rights Act (1964).** "No person in the United States shall, on the ground of race, color, or national origin, be excluded from participation in, be denied the benefits of, or be subjected to discrimination under any program or activity receiving Federal financial assistance." In general, programs should not be discriminatory in intent or effect.
>
> **Elementary and Secondary Education Act (1968–2000): Title VII Bilingual Education Act.** Federal law that provides funds to states that decide to implement bilingual education programs, provide bilingual teacher preparation, and engage in bilingual program development. The provision ended with the 2000 reauthorization of the ESEA.
>
> **Equal Educational Opportunity Act, section 1703 (f) (1974).** No educational agency "shall deny equal educational opportunity to an individual on account of his or her . . . national origin" by failing to "take appropriate action to overcome language barriers." This law extended the *Lau v. Nichols* decision to all districts, not only those receiving federal funding.
>
> **Elementary and Secondary Education Act (2001–present): No Child Left Behind.** Latest reauthorization of the ESEA; stresses accountability for all learners by setting annual targets for the percentage of students achieving proficiency on state achievement test.

Figure 6.3   Federal law and ELLs

the money, they have to meet the federal requirements. Under the BEA, districts had to implement bilingual education programs for the specified target groups in order to receive federal funding. It thus provided an incentive for districts to consider bilingual instruction options.

The history of the re-authorizations of the BEA (1974, 1978, 1984, 1988, 1994) reveals changes in the political climate and changing views about the place of linguistic diversity in American society (Gándara, Moran, & García, 2004; Wiese & Garcia, 1998). The early re-authorizations (1974, 1978) restricted the BEA on students with limited English proficiency and maintained a transitional focus, ambiguous enough for both reluctant bilingual and additive bilingual interpretations (see Figure 6.2). More assimilationist provisions (focus on English language acquisition, quick mainstreaming into all-English education, and funding for nonbilingual programs, such as Special Alternative Instructional Programs) were added to the BEA in 1984 and 1988 under the Reagan administration. Reagan's secretary of education, William Bennett, declared bilingual education a failure and proposed English as a second language as a better alternative. Bennett decried the loss of focus on the goal of the BEA, which he saw as "fluency in English" (Crawford, 1992, pp. 359–362). Only the 1994 reauthorization of the BEA by the Clinton administration was pluralist in scope because it funded bilingual programs aimed at language maintenance and development and focused on content as well as language and literacy development.

Legislation for Native Americans has taken a slightly different route.

After the brief renaissance of instruction in Native American languages in the 1930s, the period immediately after World War II saw a return to assimilationist practices. The federal government dismantled reservations and prompted a major migration of Native Americans to urban areas. Though the government's actions were intended to fragment the indigenous population, the shared experience of loneliness and stress often ensured closer connections. Native American education was not put on the agenda until the 1960s, first under the 1966 ESEA and then as part of the 1968 BEA. The 1970s saw a renewed interest in Native American bilingual education, increased control over educational programming by the Native American community with passage of the Indian Education Act of 1972 and the 1975 Indian Self-determination and Educational Assistance Act, and a growing network of Native American educators through the establishment of organizations such as the American Indian Language Development Institute. An important piece of legislation was the **Native American Languages Act (1990),** which granted the right of indigenous language groups to maintain their language and culture (Glass, 1988; Havighurst, 1978; McCarty, 1993, 1994, 1998; Reyhner, 1993; Russell, 2002; Szasz, 1983).

KEY COURT DECISIONS

The courts also have played an important role in shaping the education of ELLs (Figure 6.4). The landmark Supreme Court case *Lau v. Nichols* (1974) and the Office of Civil Rights' Lau Remedies that followed were turning points for bilingual education. No longer relying on voluntary measures like those of the BEA, the courts and the Office of Civil Rights began putting stronger demands on school districts to take affirmative steps to aid language minority students. Subsequent court decisions initially supported the guidelines proposed by the Lau Remedies but by the 1980s districts were given more flexibility.

In **Lau v. Nichols (1974),** Chinese parents in San Francisco argued that their children did not have equal access to the educational system if the language of instruction was in a language their children did not understand. The Supreme Court agreed, stating that "under these state-imposed standards there is no equality of treatment merely by providing students with the same facilities, textbooks, teachers, and curriculum; for students who do not understand English are effectively foreclosed from any meaningful education" (cited in Teitelbaum & Hiller, 1977, p. 7). In *Lau,* the Court made the important observation that same does not imply equal. For ELLs, equity is not served by providing them with the same instruction while making specific accommodations for their needs. *Lau* was not a guarantee of bilingual education, however, nor did it assert any language rights. The Court was quite specific on this point.

> *Meyer v. Nebraska* (1954). Supreme Court case that struck down a prohibition against teaching in languages other than English. There was no compelling state interest to interfere with parents' rights to determine the education of their children.
>
> *Lau v. Nichols* (1974). Supreme Court case that involved about 1,800 Chinese students in San Francisco. The court argued that when English is the sole medium of instruction without any additional steps taken, "[i]t seems obvious that the Chinese-speaking minority receives fewer benefits that the English-speaking majority from respondents' school system which denies them a meaningful opportunity to participate in the educational program—all earmarks of discrimination banned by the regulations." The *Lau* decision requires districts to take steps to remedy the situation but does not specify how.
>
> *Plyer v. Doe* (1982). Supreme Court case that struck down a Texas state law denying public school funds for children who had not been legally admitted to the United States. The Texas law, the Court determined, "imposes a lifetime hardship on a discrete class of children not accountable for their disabling status." The decision further states: "The stigma of illiteracy will mark them for the rest of their lives. By denying these children a basic education, we deny them the ability to live within the structure of our civic institutions, and foreclose any realistic possibility that they will contribute in even the smallest way to the progress of our Nation." The Court concluded that the state had no compelling right to deny undocumented children access to education.
>
> *Castañeda v. Pickard* (1981). Defined for the first time what criteria the courts would apply to determine that districts had taken affirmative actions to meet the needs of limited English proficient students. The three prongs focus on (1) theoretical justification; (2) sufficient resources to implement remedy; and (3) program effectiveness.

Figure 6.4   Key court cases and ELLs

> No specific remedy is urged upon us. Teaching English to the students of Chinese ancestry is one choice. Giving instructions to this group in Chinese is another. There may be others. Petitioners ask only that the Board of Education be directed to apply its expertise to the problem and rectify the situation. (Teitelbaum & Hiller, 1977, p. 144)

The *Lau* decision ensured that schools could no longer simply submerse students in English-only classrooms with no adequate linguistic support. They were under an obligation to provide special language services for language minority students with limited English abilities but it was up to the school to decide whether those were to be bilingual services or English-only services.

Besides the BEA, the real push for bilingual education came from the Office of Civil Rights, which was charged with implementing the *Lau* decision and developed the **Lau Remedies** to guide compliance. The Lau Remedies required school districts to show how they intended to identify each student's primary or home language, to assess their language proficiency and educational needs, to provide adequate notification in the parents' home language, and to evaluate the effectiveness of the program. They also required districts that were out of compliance to implement bilingual programs at the elementary and intermediary levels but allowed for English as a second language (ESL) programs for high school students. Their reasoning for this distinction was that "because an ESL program does not consider the affective nor cognitive development of students in this category and time and maturation variables are different here than for students at the secondary level, an ESL program is *not* appropriate" (Baker & De Kanter, 1983, p. 215). Within 4 years, the Office of Civil Rights had asked over 500 school districts to develop a Lau plan for their language minority population based on the Lau Remedies.

Expectations for district mediation of language proficiency were further clarified in **Castañeda v. Pickard (1981)**. In this case, the Supreme Court set an important standard for determining whether school districts were taking appropriate action to address the linguistic needs of ELLs. The Court developed the following three-pronged test:

1. Is the school system "pursuing a program informed by an educational theory recognized as sound by some experts in the field or, at least, deemed a legitimate experimental strategy?"

2. Are the programs used by the school system "reasonably calculated to implement effectively the educational theory adopted by the school?"

3. Does the program "produce results indicating that the language barriers confronting students are actually being overcome?"

Using *Castañeda* as the standard, the courts have since upheld ESL and other English-only programs as legitimate ways of meeting the needs of ELLs, and the Office of Civil Rights has eased its prescriptive guidelines for bilingual education to include a broader range of programs. Since the 1980s, bilingual education has therefore received little legislative or legal support over other options that aim to meet the needs of bilingual learners (Gándara, et al., 2004). *Castañeda* continues to play an important role particularly as courts today consider the relationship between standards 2 and 3.

In June 2009, the Supreme Court voted 4–5 to send a case filed in Arizona in 1992, **Flores v. Arizona,** back to the state legislature. At issue in the initial case was whether the Arizona school system invested sufficient funds in the education of ELLs, with respect to educational outcomes. The Court ruling has now raised the question whether the current system of structured English immersion (4 hours prescribed instruction) is sufficient and effective.

One final court case that directly affects ELLs is **Plyer v. Doe (1982).** This court case does not deal with language programs but with the question of the right of children of undocumented immigrants to access schooling in the United States. The court concluded that these children have a right to be educated, arguing that not doing so "imposes a lifetime hardship on a discrete class of children not accountable for their disabling status."

Toward a Monolingual USA?
The Modern English-Only Movement

Starting with Hawai'ian senator S. I. Hayakawa's proposal to make English the official language of the United States in 1981, the past 3 decades have witnessed a modern Americanization movement. Multiple policies have been passed that limit the role of languages other than English in federal and state government agencies and the work place by eliminating bilingual services such as bilingual ballots and bilingual education (Crawford, 2000; Dicker, 2003; Woolard, 1989). In defense of their proposals, English-only supporters build on the popular image of the United States as a nation of immigrants who have succeeded economically by learning English and leaving their ethnic roots behind (Schmidt, 2000). They stress the need for one shared language for efficient government and communication and warn of the threatened status of English because of a perceived lack of motivation of the "new" immigrants to learn English (Wiley & Lukes, 1996). Bilingual services will keep immigrants and their children in ethnic ghettos, the argument goes, preventing them from accessing and participating in mainstream society and institutions.

By 2003, twenty-three states had declared English the official language of the state and constitutional amendments to achieve the same goal at the federal level continue to be proposed. Hawai'ian is officially bilingual, and four states (Washington, Oregon, New Mexico, and Rhode Island) have **English-plus resolutions**, affirming the value of bilingualism, English plus another language (Crawford, 2003). Since 2003, four more states have declared English the official language (Alaska, Arizona, Idaho, Kansas), making a total of 27 states (Figure 6.5).

The emphasis on monolingual (English-only) policies and assimilation has continued in the 21st century with the 2001 reauthorization of the Elementary and Secondary Education Act (the No Child Left Behind Act) and the passage of several state antibilingual education initiatives. These policies recall those enacted during the 1920s, when, as now, the country was suffering economically and the numbers of immigrants was increasing.

NO CHILD LEFT BEHIND ACT

The **No Child Left Behind Act (NCLB)** dismantled Title VII as it had been known for 32 years (Crawford, 2004a,b; Evans & Hornberger, 2005). The

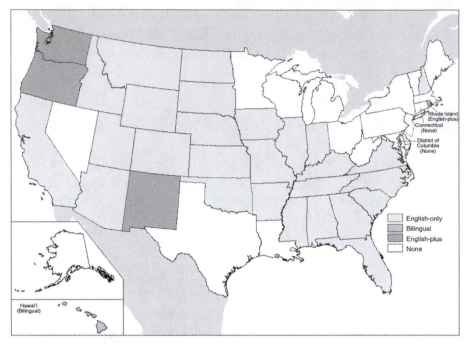

Figure 6.5 State language legislation

new legislation allocates funds for native language maintenance efforts for indigenous language speakers (Native Americans, Alaskans, Hawai'ians). While bilingual education is not prohibited under the law, funds are no longer allocated under NCLB to support this type of program for ELLs.

NCLB represents a significant change in federal educational policy in general. The ambitious goal of the act is to ensure that all children will meet grade level expectations by 2014. Increased accountability through standardized testing has become one of the main strategies to accomplish this goal. Schools and districts are held accountable for demonstrating that various subgroups (identified by race or ethnicity, special education status, and ELL status) make **adequate yearly progress (AYP)** toward reaching the 100% proficient goal. The law specifies that all students should be included in statewide testing (participation rates), initially with a focus on reading and math but with the addition of science in 2007. To help districts reach this goal, the legislation has made significant funds available for schools to implement compensatory programs in reading and math during the school day and as after-school programs.

NCLB has specific provisions for ELLs. Although initially all ELLs had to take the mandated state test in reading and math, this provision was amended to exempt ELLs from taking the reading test for 1 year, and they do have to take the math test in their first year in U.S. schools. Unfortunately, school districts' test participation rates are not calculated with this exemption in mind. To meet their participation targets, many districts therefore feel obliged to administer the test to ELLs in order to maintain participation rates. States also must formulate **annual measurable achievement objectives (AMAOs)** for ELLs. Each state has been required to develop English language proficiency standards and administer an English language proficiency test that is aligned with those standards. States subsequently had to set targets for the percentage of students making progress on this test (AMAO 1) and the percentage of students classified as "proficient" on this test (AMAO 2). Finally, schools are required to monitor students who have been exited from their language program for 2 years (the so-called former ELLs).

Under NCLB much more attention is paid to ELLs and their academic and language progress. Their inclusion as a specific subgroup for meeting AYP has significantly increased the visibility of ELLs in school and school districts. However, while the notion of high expectations and holding schools accountable for the learning of all students are worthy, NCLB has been challenged in its implementation at the state and local levels. Many scholars have pointed out that NCLB has instituted an unfair and punitive testing regime that has been particularly hard on ELLs. For these students, the use of inappropriate and invalid assessments for high-stakes purposes has been a major concern (Abedi, 2004; Menken, 2006). Since ELLs are still learning English, achievement tests developed for and normed on native speakers become a language test rather than reliable and valid measures of academic learning.

NCLB and its requirements for meeting AYP for all subgroups (including ELLs) has also had a significant impact on course offerings (Menken, 2008). Black (2006) reports a shift away from bilingual to English-only policies in one Texas school with a strong bilingual education program in response to observed lower scores of the English language learner population. Pressure to "ready" the students for the English test more quickly came at the cost of bilingual instruction. Moreover, a broader narrative emerged that blamed students' bilingualism (i.e., instructional time spent in Spanish) for low scores on the standardized test (in English). Under pressure to assess in English and through standardized tests, linguistic and cultural diversity were no longer viewed as productive resources in the school. A similar movement away from bilingual approaches has been noted in California, where access to bilingual education has been greatly restricted for bilingual children (Gándara, 2000; García & Curry-Rodriguez, 2000; Linton, 2007).

In addition to shifting away from a bilingual approach to an English-only approach to teaching, districts have also reported a narrowing of the curriculum. The measurement of progress through standardized tests in English that are heavily dependent on reading skills has led to an increased emphasis on basic reading skills in schools across the United States (Harper, de Jong, & Platt, 2008). In many schools, separate reading "blocks" have been organized to teach the discrete skills that are covered on the reading achievement test, frequently at the cost of higher-order thinking, higher-level reading comprehension skills, and access to authentic texts. Moreover, students are expected to master the same skills at the same time as prescribed by strict pacing guides and reinforced by the administration of specific assessments (Gutierrez, 2001; Harper, et al., 2008; Wright & Choi, 2006). In addition to operating on a narrow definition of what literacy is, the homogeneity of approaches and expectations for reading development leave little room for addressing differences in second language and literacy development and issues of culture for bilingual learners.

ENGLISH-ONLY BALLOT INITIATIVES

Recent attacks on bilingual approaches to educating ELLs began in 1997 in California, when the politician and millionaire Ron Unz authored a ballot initiative (Proposition 227) to replace bilingual programs with an English-only approach to instructing ELLs. Unz's purpose was to gather enough signatures among registered voters that his measure could circumvent the legislature and be decided by popular referendum. On June 2, 1998, Proposition 227 was approved by nearly a two-to-one margin (for the complete text, see http:catesol.org/unztext.html). Since then, the same political strategy has been used to pass similar mandates in two other states: Proposition 203 in Arizona in 2000 and Question 2 in Massachusetts in 2002; both passed with a two-thirds majority. With Amendment 31 in Colorado on the ballot, voters were able to defeat an attempt to mandate English-only there (Escamilla, Shannon, Carlos, & García, 2003). Oregon defeated a referendum in 2008, Measure 58, that would have abolished bilingual education in that state.

The three ballot initiatives that passed are framed within homogenizing discourses that stress that monolingualism in English is a prerequisite for national unity, that the position of English as a national language is threatened (particularly by Spanish), and that lack of English language proficiency is the cause of school failure for language minority students (Crawford, 1998, 2003; Galindo, 1997; Macedo, Dendrinos, & Gounari, 2003; Wright, 2005). These initiatives are almost identical in language with even more strict guidelines in Arizona and Massachusetts.

The preamble to the original California law establishes the primacy of English as the legitimate form of communication, declaring, "The English language is the common public language of the United States of America. . . . [It] is also the leading world language for science, technology, and international business, thereby being the language of economic opportunity." The superiority of English is further reinforced in the section dealing with program accountability, which requires districts to document annual progress in

English only. Learning in and through other languages is not validated as legitimate acquired knowledge and skills.

Each of the three state laws mandates that an English-only program placement (that is, sheltered English immersion) be the default placement for all ELLs. After 30 days of an English-only placement and only under specific conditions can parents request a waiver from this mandate to have their child be placed in an alternative program, such as bilingual education. Students older than 10 years, students who are already fluent in English, and students under the age of 10 with special needs are eligible for such waivers. The waiver process requires a personal visit to the school by a child's legal guardian, and annual renewal of the waiver. Massachusetts and Arizona also require a 250-word justification that cannot be related to the students' linguistic needs (i.e., English proficiency level) and the statement will be placed in the student's personal folder. The cumbersome waiver process and the potential for rejection of the waiver by superintendents greatly undermine parents' ability to obtain waivers as well as the willingness of districts to establish the complex process of initiating and tracking students whose parents want bilingual education.[1]

The monolingual intent of the laws can further be seen by constraints on the use of students' native languages. In the sheltered or structured English immersion classroom, only limited use can be made of the native language (Section 2) and all instructional materials to teach content or literacy must be in English. The recommendation that districts place students from different language backgrounds together in the same classroom further discourages and seeks to limit the use of languages other than English by students and teachers. A final key component of the laws is the expectation that ELL participation in their specialized program is "not to exceed one year." There is an assumption that ELLs can acquire sufficient English in the course of 1 year of specialized instruction. Thus, limiting program participation further underscores the push to an English-only, mainstream classroom in an as short a time as possible.

Maintaining Pluralist Approaches

While English-only and assimilationist policies dominate in the United States today, other discourses are being heard. As McCarty (2003) points

---

[1]In fact, in California, many districts have failed to develop a waiver process or communicate to parents that this option is available to them (Gándara et al., 2006). Case studies of individual schools have documented that parents are either misinformed or hindered by barriers to access to relevant and accurate information (García & Curry-Rodriguez, 2000; Maxwell-Jolly, 2000; Monzó, 2005).

out, despite homogenizing times, language revitalization and maintenance efforts that take place around the world show a continued desire for and recognition of the importance of diversity and language and cultural maintenance. Through the Indigenous Languages Act (1990) and the most recent Declaration of Indigenous Language Rights (2008), indigenous language speakers have formal, legal support for native language maintenance. Limited federal funding for indigenous language instruction under Title VII of NCLB has continued. A wide range of efforts to support indigenous language speakers' innovative efforts at language revitalization and language maintenance in the United States are on-going. McCarty (2003) describes several indigenous bilingual programs for Navajo (Arizona), Keres (New Mexico), and Hawai'ian Creole (Hawai'i). Some of these programs have been in existence since the late 1960s, such as the Rough Rock Community School (Francis & Reyner, 2002; Dick & McCarthy, 1997; McCarty, 1994; McCarty, 1998, 2003). Today this successful bilingual program is run completely by Navajo people from the community. The curriculum has locally relevant themes and offers formal language instruction in Navajo. The program's effectiveness has been important to help community members revalue their own language, "to resist and recast images of Navajo as 'second best.' This is a necessary reassertion of indigenous language rights" (McCarty, 2003, p. 36).

Another trend has been the growth of two-way immersion programs since the late 1980s. As additive bilingual programs promoting bilingualism and biliteracy for language minority and language majority language speakers, these programs also resist the monolingual hegemony of English. The positive outcomes that have consistently been associated with well-implemented two-way immersion programs have made them a serious alternative to English-only programs for teaching bilingual learners (Howard, Sugarman, & Christian, 2003; Krashen, 2004; Lindholm-Leary, 2001).

Finally, it is important to mention the increased attention to heritage language teaching (Kondo-Brown, 2005; Peyton, Lewelling, & Winke, 2001; Peyton, Ranard, & McGinnis, 2001; Valdés, Fishman, Chavez, & William, 2006). Most heritage language classes that are offered through formal schooling involve classes for college students, although high schools are increasingly offering classes for native speakers of the language (such as Spanish for Spanish speakers) (Roca & Colombi, 2003). In most cases, however, heritage language maintenance efforts for school-age children are community-based and hence fall outside the realm of federal or state educational policies. The growth in the number and range of heritage language programs or community-based language schools (including in Chinese, Japanese, and Korean) illustrates the value and the importance that parents and ethnic communities continue to place on native language and cultural maintenance, despite pressures to assimilate (Cho, Shin, & Krashen, 2004; Crawford, 1999).

Multiple Discourses in U.S. Language in Education Policy

A historical view of how linguistic diversity has been treated in the United States illustrates that it has been seen as a problem and as a right, as well as a resource (Ruiz, 1984). This view puts some persistent misconceptions about immigrants, assimilation, and bilingualism in perspective. For example, the use of native languages for schooling has been around for a long time. The myth that immigrants assimilated easily and quickly in the 1920s must be adjusted to take into consideration the difference between workforce demands and opportunities then and those we see today and actual school performance of different immigrant groups. Dropping out of school in the 1920s had less of an impact than it does today, because social mobility then was controlled less by formal schooling.

Policies are also not necessarily the same for different language groups. Looking back, policies toward slaves (and now toward AAVE) have been consistently assimilationist, reinforcing the hegemony of standard English. Policies toward indigenous languages have swung from overt coercive assimilationist to permissive bilingual approaches to the right to revitalize and maintain these languages (which is supported by international agreements). While immigrant languages were treated with more tolerance in the early years of nation-building, the symbolism of the 1900s Americanization movement that was able to link speaking English and assimilation with being an American (and fulfilling the American Dream) continues to shape policies toward immigrant languages (Olneck, 1989).

Although (some variant of) both discourses have been present throughout the history of the United States, the dominant role of English has never been questioned. Dicker (2003) observes, "What emerges . . . is a kind of multilayered time line: English is a constant presence throughout, existing with other languages that appear and sometimes die out in different parts of the country at various points along the time line" (p. 47). Alba, Logan, Lutz, and Stults (2002) conclude that the viability of bilingualism, not English ability, should be the main concern in the study of language maintenance and shift (Chapter 3). The history of language policy in the United States illustrates that the main question is not about the status of English but what roles, position, and status are given to languages other than English as part of the U.S. imagined community.

CHAPTER 6
Discussion & Activities

Critical Issues

1. How do the changes in the Bilingual Education Act (including No Child Left Behind) reflect the dominant discourses at the time?
2. A common argument is that bilingual education is a recently implemented experiment. In what ways could this claim be both true and false?
3. Which arguments by proponents of the modern-day English-only movement or by those who support English-only ballot initiatives such as Proposition 227 do you find the easiest and which the most difficult to counter?

Application & Reflection

4. Who is included and who is excluded in the imagined community when the United States is portrayed exclusively as a "nation of immigrants" who voluntarily chose to come here for new freedoms?
5. What are the pros and cons of declaring English the official language of the United States at this point in American history?
6. Select one state in the United States and research its language legislation (the constitution and official provisions for language in education policy). Compare your notes with others: how do states differ in their approaches? (Select another country, if you are interested in national policies in contexts other than the United States.)

Recommended Readings

Crawford, J. (2004b). *Educating English learners: Language diversity in the classroom* (5th ed.). Culver City: Bilingual Education Services.

> *Crawford's language policy Web site (http://www.languagepolicy.net/) books continue to be some of the best resources on language policy in the United States. In this book, Crawford provides an overview of language policies and education from colonial times to the present.*

Menken, K. (2008). *English learners left behind: Standardized testing as language policy.* Clevedon: Multilingual Matters.

> *This book provides a comprehensive analysis of No Child Left Behind legislation and how it has affected schools with English language learners.*

It illustrates how the legislation is a de facto language policy with important implications for the quality of schooling ELLs receive.

Rickford, J. R. (1999). *African American Vernacular English: Features, evolution, educational implications.* Malden: Blackwell.

This book provides a good introduction and overview of the linguistic features of African American Vernacular English and its role in schools.

Schmidt, R. S. (2000). *Language policies and identity politics in the United States.* Philadelphia: Temple University Press.

This book lays out how assimilationist and pluralist discourses have shaped the politics of language in the United States.

Program Models and Outcomes

GUIDING QUESTIONS

- *How long does it take English language learners to learn English and have access to the mainstream classroom?*
- *How do advocacy-oriented studies frame schooling for English language learners?*
- *How have effective school studies shifted the focus of the schooling for bilingual learners?*
- *What features characterize effective programs for multilingual children?*

KEY TERMS

reclassification	advocacy-based program evaluations
white space	effective school studies

A prevailing question in the schooling of bilingual learners is what language should be used for instructional purposes. In contrast to the support for multilingual development for majority language speakers (elite bilingualism), language education for minority language speakers has been much more controversial. For the latter group, and particularly for immigrants, concerns about their learning the societal language and assimilating to dominant social norms have tended to overshadow the potential of their developing multilingualism. As a result, the focus in schooling for minority language speakers has been on their learning the societal language quickly, and little attention has been paid to how they can achieve multilingual competence (including biliteracy). This focus has had important implications for how programs for language minority students are evaluated. The purpose of this chapter is to illustrate how program evaluation design affects how we define the purpose and content of language minority schooling, using the effectiveness debate in the United States as an example.

The Quest for the Perfect Model

Controversy over the bilingual approaches to teaching bilingual learners who have been identified as in need of language education services (i.e., English language learners[1]) that were initiated through the Bilingual Education Act and state laws led to close monitoring of programs. With the increased U.S. federal and state government funding came a demand for demonstrating bilingual program effectiveness that was driven by an overriding concern for rapid development of English language proficiency.

PROGRAM EVALUATION STUDIES

The majority of the large-scale evaluation studies and individual program evaluations that were completed in response to the demand for accountability took place as part of evaluation requirements of Title VII of the Elementary and Secondary Education Act, also known as the Bilingual Education Act (for overviews of these earlier studies see August & Hakuta, 1997; Crawford, 1997). Later, individual studies were analyzed collectively using meta-analytical research methods to compare outcomes from bilingual programs to those from English-only programs (Francis, Lesaux, & August, 2006; Genesee, Lindholm-Leary, Saunders, & Christian, 2005; Greene, 1998; Krashen & McField, 2005; Willig, 1985).

The program evaluations asked which program model, defined as bilingual or English-only, taught English faster or better. To address this question, the studies compared students in a bilingual program and an English as a Second language or other type of English-only program on a specific outcome measure in English, typically within the first 3 years of program implementation. Observed differences in student outcomes were subsequently explained in terms of language of instruction (i.e., bilingual or monolingual). In addition to English proficiency outcomes, another indicator of English language acquisition was length of program participation, that is, how long the student had been in the program before they were exited from the program. Program exit, or **reclassification**, refers to the point at which a district decides that a student is no longer in need of services and is placed without additional supports or accommodations in a mainstream classroom.

---

[1]In this chapter we use the term English language learner (ELL) because the program effectiveness debate involves programs specifically designed for this group of students. ELLs are a subgroup of bilingual learners.

A major criticism that has accompanied these studies is their methodological flaws (August & Hakuta, 1997). The individual, small-scale program evaluations especially have been heavily criticized because they typically did not control for important student background variables (such as social class, parental education, or initial proficiency in English and the native language) and other important contextual variables (program quality, teacher preparation) that may also have affected student outcomes (Gándara, Rumberger, Maxwell-Jolly, & Callahan, 2003).

Furthermore, the use of "bilingual" and "English-only" as program labels to classify different programs was assumed unproblematic and sufficient to distinguish among models. But their use causes confusion about which programs were under consideration and what type of bilingual or ESL programs were more effective than others (Collier, 1992; Thomas & Collier, 1997). Greene (1997), for example, notes that Rossell and Baker (1996) in their influential article on the ineffectiveness of bilingual instruction classified Canadian immersion programs under monolingual immersion models and, based on the positive outcomes of these programs, concluded that English-only immersion would be the preferable model for ELLs. However, Canadian immersion programs are in fact bilingual programs (see Chapter 5). Also, clustering diverse programs under the umbrella terms *bilingual* or *English-only* does not differentiate among the different program models and their potential outcomes. The label *bilingual education* can cover a program with 50% in the native language and 50% in English for 5 years as well as a program where the native language is used only in the initial year of the program.

When examining the outcomes of program evaluations, it is therefore important to understand exactly what kind of program is being evaluated and how comparisons between programs are achieved. Besides asking questions about the choice of medium of instruction, evaluations must ask about program goals, relevant target group characteristics, the actual distribution of languages across the curriculum at each grade level, and indicators of quality of implementation (e.g., teacher qualifications, available materials).

THE "HOW LONG" QUESTION

The debate about effectiveness has also resulted in a concern about length of program participation. Two strong assumptions that have guided this dimension of program outcomes are that (1) the shorter a student is in a bilingual or ESL program, the better the program model, and (2) the more students exit in a given year, the better the program model. Both of these assumptions must be critically examined.

Length of Program Participation

Length of program participation refers to how many years a student remains in an ESL or bilingual program before he or she is exited. The central question is, how long does it take an ELL to become proficient enough in English that he or she can fully participate in a mainstream classroom? The answer given in the English-only ballot initiatives (Proposition 227, Proposition 203, and Question 2) is that for most students 1 year should be sufficient. Looking at well-educated Russian-speaking immigrants in Israel, Levin, and Shohamy (2008) note that it took 7 to 9 years or even longer for students to reach comparative levels of achievement in math and literacy.

The discrepancy between these two conclusions can be partially explained by differences in how "language proficiency" is interpreted. Increasingly it has become clear that the way we use language in schools is quite different from how it is used in other contexts, with unique linguistic features that students have to learn (Bailey, 2007; Schleppegrell, 2004). The language of school includes the academic languages and literacies needed to learn effectively in and about the content areas (science, math, social studies, English language arts).

Those who argue for a longer English acquisition period expect ELLs to negotiate complex concepts and engage in critical thinking orally as well as through reading and writing in specific school contexts and at age-appropriate levels. Acquiring this level of language competence will take longer than developing enough competence to have simple conversations with peers. This is especially true for older students who need to negotiate complex content primarily through their second language with few of the nonlinguistic supports one might find in early childhood and elementary-level classrooms. While other factors, such as motivation, self-awareness, and opportunity, also play a role, the idea that the younger the second language learner, the better is partially true because the linguistic expectations we have for a 5-year-old in a kindergarten classroom are quite different from those for a 7th grader, who must competently participate in a 7th grade science class.

Acquiring the appropriate discourses of school may take 7 to 9 years in part because second language learners are reaching for a moving target. While ELLs are developing their English skills to engage in school tasks, their native English-speaking peers continue to move ahead, developing school-related language and literacy skills grade by grade. For every 1 year of learning growth of a native English speaker, a second language learner has to make more than 1 year growth over time to eventually reach the same level of performance (Cummins, 2000). While this finding does not imply that students must be segregated from their peers for 7 to 9 years, it does stress the importance of continued scaffolding of their social and academic language development.

Exit or Reclassification Rates

Reflecting the second assumption about the issue of how long, Gersten and Woodward (1995) state that a "critical indicator of the success of any bilingual instruction program for language minority students is the rate at which students leave specialized classes for second language learners and enter mainstream classes" (p. 227). Until the No Child Left Behind Act was passed, there was little consistency in the criteria or assessments used to determine exit or reclassification. States and districts within a state (and even schools within districts) used widely different cut-off scores and assessment instruments, making it difficult to compare programs at the school, district, or state level (Linquanti, 2001). A district with a low exit cut-off score may have a higher exit rate than a district with a more challenging cut-off score. Thus, comparing their exit rates would reveal nothing about program quality. Although this variation in practices is changing under the requirements of No Child Left Behind (NCLB), the 2001 reauthorization of the Elementary and Secondary Education Act, there remains a long tradition of different expectations for deciding when a student is "ready."

The assumption that higher exit rates reflect a more effective program is also problematic and, although few studies have addressed this issue, it lacks empirical support (Gándara & Merino, 1993; Linquanti, 2001). For one thing, this interpretation of the relationship between exit rates and program effectiveness does not take into account differences in program quality and student population, regardless of the program model. A well-funded bilingual program with qualified teachers is likely to have different outcomes than the same bilingual program model with fewer materials and less qualified teachers. Such "input" factors must be taken into account when considering program outcomes (Gándara, et al., 2003). Similarly, student characteristics are also likely to affect reclassification. An ESL program that enrolls mostly intermediate ELLs may be better positioned to reclassify students sooner than an ESL or bilingual program that works with beginners and newcomers. Older ELLs with strong literacy and schooling background in their native language have more linguistic and educational resources to build on and may need less time in an ESL or bilingual program than those with interrupted schooling and low levels of native language literacy.

Finally, program evaluations that have focused on exit rates have failed to ask a perhaps even more important question: Does a quick exit imply long-term academic school success, when controlling for student background and program variables? Indirect evidence against this "quick-exit" assumption comes from studies showing that ELLs in long-term bilingual programs are successful academically, including two-way immersion programs (Howard, Sugarman, & Christian, 2003; Krashen, 2004; Lindholm-Leary, 2001; Thomas & Collier, 2002) and maintenance bilingual education programs (e.g., Collier, 1992; Holm & Holm, 1990; J. Ramirez, Yuen, Ramey, & Pasta, 1990). Ramirez (1998) found that former ELLs performed better than English speakers on standardized tests in the San Francisco school district and reports that these students had, on average, attended a bilingual program for 4 to 5 years.

Long-term attendance in a high-quality, additive bilingual program results in more positive long-term outcomes (Thomas & Collier, 1997, 2002). Thus, long program attendance does not necessarily impede academic success. The question is one of program quality (see also Parrish, Perez, Merickel, & Linquanti, 2006).

Exit rates have gained renewed prominence with the passage of NCLB, under which districts are required to set targets for the percentage of students showing progress in English proficiency development (annual measurable achievement objective 1 [AMAO 1]) and for the percentage of ELLs expected to reach "proficiency" in English every year (AMAO 2). AMAO 2 is often equated with readiness to exit. However, the language of Title III of NCLB actually does not explicitly state this link, and "proficiency" in English does not necessarily mean that the student is no longer in need of specialized services. When Title III does discuss exited students, it is in the context of their being monitored for 2 years. The use of a single score on a language proficiency test for determining whether students can be exited is problematic. First, the link between a "proficient" score and subsequent academic achievement would need to be better understood. Second, there is need for multiple data sources for determining reclassification, including teacher judgment and academic performance (as measured, e.g., by an achievement test). Finally, responding to AMOA 2 results also requires districts to keep in mind that reclassification and exiting is a process rather than a fixed time that indicates whether a student is in or out of a program (Gándara & Merino, 1993; Lucas & Wagner, 1999). Helping students transition and providing them with continued appropriate support in the mainstream classroom is key to their continued success (de Jong, 2004a).

Program Evaluations and Outcomes

The interpretation of program evaluation results has been controversial. Some of the large-scale studies of program evaluation are critical of bilingual education (Danoff, 1978); others are supportive (J. Ramirez, et al., 1990; Thomas & Collier, 2002; United States General Accounting Office, 1987). Tallying the results of individual program evaluations, some reviewers claim that English-only programs are better (Baker & de Kanter, 1981; Rossell & Baker, 1996; Rossell & Ross, 1986), while other reviewers have concluded that bilingual education is more effective (Zappert & Cruz, 1977). The outcomes of these studies tend to reflect the ideological position of the research groups and the extent to which they value bilingualism as an outcome. Rossell & Ross (1986) concluded that studies that showed no differences between an ESL and a bilingual program meant no effect for bilingual education (a negative outcome). Zappert & Cruz (1977), on the other hand, counted the same outcome as positive. They reasoned that in the bilingual program, students developed English and native language skills, whereas the ESL program was able to teach only English. In one study bilingualism was valued as a program outcome, in the other only English proficiency counted.

Using meta-analysis, a statistical method that allows researchers to combine the results from multiple studies and determine effect sizes, several scholars have re-analyzed the data of these studies. A consistent finding that has emerged from this review of statistically more robust and scientifically sophisticated studies is that participation in bilingual education has small but significant positive effects over monolingual instruction for student achievement in English (Francis, et al., 2006; Genesee, et al., 2005; Krashen & McField, 2005). Similar results have been observed internationally, resulting in a consistent pattern of successful outcomes of bilingual education in the native language and in the societal language across a wide range of contexts (Benson, 2005a, 2005b; Cummins, 1999; Dutcher, 2003).

Limits of the Effectiveness Debate

The debate on program models and its underlying assumptions reflects different views of schooling of ELLs and continues to influence priorities in today's research. The focus and design of the program evaluations limit the scope and focus of language minority students' schooling, and they tend to reinforce an emphasis on separate programs as solutions to solving the "language problem." Furthermore, as program evaluations focus on outcomes (outputs), they rarely provide insights into what makes a program successful (inputs and processes).

DEFINING DESIRED OUTCOMES

Program evaluations maintain a definition of (most) desired outcomes through their choices of what they measure. Even a cursory look shows that in their design and analysis, past studies focused almost exclusively on (English) language outcomes. In one meta-analysis (Willig, 1985), 73% of the program outcomes included were related to language. Since "English proficiency" had to be easily measured on a large scale, most evaluation studies relied on standardized achievement tests in English (oral language proficiency, reading comprehension). Typically, these kinds of assessment focus on discrete language skills in isolation because these skills are much easier to measure than holistic language use. In a subtle way, then, a three-part narrowing of the focus of ELL schooling emerged and continues to be visible in today's debates: from language/literacy to English language/literacy, and then from

English language/literacy to discrete English language skills on a norm-referenced test.

Besides restricting desired outcomes to English proficiency, program evaluations further narrowed the scope of desired outcomes for English language learners by excluding from their purview other evaluation questions, such as "how well" students performed in the programs included in the study. Most evaluations were so focused on demonstrating the superiority of one model over the other that they often overlooked actual achievement. Gersten & Woodward (1995), in their comparison of an English immersion program that included a native language component with an English-only immersion program, found that by 7th grade students were scoring at the 15th percentile in vocabulary and the 21st percentile in total reading in the program with native language support and 16th and 24th percentile, respectively, in the English-only program. Although Gersten and Woodward interpret these results in favor of the English-only program, they point out that the more important question is, Why weren't students well prepared for grade-level reading expectations in either program?

Considering ELL performance in relationship to expected grade level performance allows researchers to consider whether programs close the gap for ELLs. Hakuta (2001) points out that this approach focuses our attention on the **white space** between actual performance and desired performance at a particular grade level for a given group of students (see Figure 7.1). The example from Gersten and Woodward stresses how important it is to consider

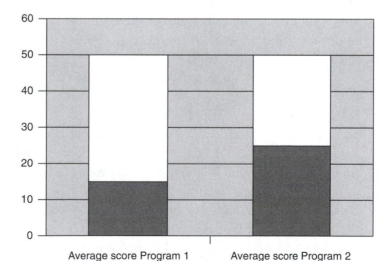

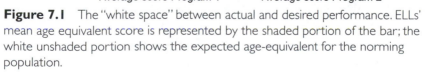

Figure 7.1 The "white space" between actual and desired performance. ELLs' mean age equivalent score is represented by the shaded portion of the bar; the white unshaded portion shows the expected age-equivalent for the norming population.

this white space and not merely whether students score higher or lower in particular programs.

The narrow definition of educational outcomes has received renewed emphasis and strength in the accountability systems mandated under NCLB. Standardized test scores of reading in English have become the standard for schools to show the growth and achievement of their students in reading, including English language learners (Hornberger & Evans, 2005). Student performance thus continues to be narrowly defined in this framework. Not surprisingly, the old evaluation paradigm also continues to be prominent in educational policy.

A number of studies have documented the impact of the restrictive language policies on program options, classroom practice, student achievement, and learning opportunities (Gándara & Hopkins, 2010; Parrish et al., 2006). These studies, undertaken in Arizona, California, and Massachusetts, have identified several areas of impact. First, bilingual program options have been significantly reduced because of changes in district policy and because fewer teachers are choosing to become bilingual teachers (Gándara, 2000; Gándara, Maxwell-Jolly, & Driscoll, 2005). Second, initial increases in standardized test scores (in English) after the passage of Proposition 227 have not been sustained in most districts. In each of the three states, the academic achievement gap between ELL and non-ELL performance has not decreased. In fact, increased drop-out rates and referral to special education have been noted as important negative effects of the laws (Gándara & Hopkins, 2010). Finally, reclassification rates have not markedly increased since 1998 (they were about 7% in 1997 and about 10% in 2005–2006). Most ELLs are reclassified after 3 to 4 years rather than the predicted 1 year (Grissom, 2004), though some have reported program attendance as long as 8 to10 years in the California public school system (Hill, 2004).

Recent reviews are thus still very concerned with the comparison of performance of ELLs in English-only and in bilingual education programs (e.g., Francis, et al., 2006; Rolstad, Mahoney, & Glass, 2005). In a recent newspaper article, MacDonald (2009) once more sets up the traditional dichotomy, arguing that bilingual advocates were wrong and that the English-only measures under Proposition 227 have worked. Despite her support for Proposition 227, she does have to conclude that "Hispanics' low academic achievement, high drop-out rates, and gang involvement—live on," illustrating the limits of the debate about language of instruction.

The evaluation designs and the effectiveness debate made acceptable the idea that English language proficiency is the only legitimate focus of schooling for bilingual learners. The current focus on school accountability as measured by English reading skills reinforces this narrow definition. Other desirable outcomes are excluded from the conversation, such as academic content learning and the development of critical thinking skills, native language proficiency, and positive sociocultural identity (Brisk, 2006). Broader educational goals become elusive for linguistically and culturally diverse students under a double standard of expectations (Cummins, 2007).

PROGRAMMATIC THINKING

Another question the effectiveness studies excluded was how well ELLs performed after they exited their specialized program. Program evaluations typically considered students' performance on English tests while they are still attending a specialized (bilingual or English-only) program, often within the first 3 years of the program and with a focus on lower grades (K–2). Although the use of exit rates as a program effectiveness measure considers ELL performance at a later point in their program, student performance beyond the program is still outside their purview. The long-term academic achievement of ELLs who went through a specialized program and were subsequently placed full time in the mainstream without specialized support is not of interest.

By narrowly focusing on the performance of ELLs still in a bilingual or English-only program, the effectiveness debate has ignored the actual goal of the programs: the majority of programs for ELLs (whether bilingual or ESL) aim to prepare ELLs to successfully participate in the mainstream classroom. To determine program effectiveness, it would make sense to consider long-term academic achievement after a student has been placed in the mainstream classroom.

One result of not assessing the performance of former (exited) ELLs is that the responsibility for ELLs' school success and for negotiating linguistic and cultural diversity is left to the specialized language programs and their teachers. The general education environment and mainstream teachers are excluded from the definition of who is responsible for providing effective instruction for ELLs. The effective model studies reinforce the idea that the "language problem" of ELLs will be taken care of in a separate program by ESL or bilingual teachers, undermining the development of a shared responsibility for the learning of all students.

FOCUS ON OUTPUT

Most program evaluations compared outcomes on tests to determine which program was better. But because they were not concerned with input or process factors, the studies often provided little detail about the program itself. Except for the programwide choice of language of instruction, the studies do not detail actual language distribution at the classroom or grade level, or effective strategies for teaching. Program factors such as teacher preparation, access to books, and class size were not included in these studies; nor did the studies consider possible variation in outcomes depending on student population.

Even when concluding that one program seemed to result in higher test scores than another program, these studies could not illuminate the practices that supported positive outcomes or resulted in negative outcomes. Because they set out primarily to prove or disprove that bilingual or English-only education works, August and Hakuta (1997) refer to these studies as **"advocacy-based" program evaluations**. They do not aim to increase our understanding of the educational, linguistic, cognitive, or other processes that may help explain the success or failure of a particular program model in reaching certain outcomes. The program evaluations and the debate that has followed them have been limited, therefore, in their contributions to our understanding of educational processes that support bilingual learners in their academic journey.

From Outcomes to Features

In the 1980s, research on program effectiveness shifted away from outcomes to the processes that could help explain the positive outcomes of effective schools or programs. Rather than comparing programs on their outcomes, the **effective school studies** sought to document the school-based processes that positively contributed to school success. This line of research reinforced the idea that schools can make a difference in student outcomes if they organize themselves around the key features or characteristics that emerged from the studies (Edmonds, 1979; Purkey & Smith, 1983). Even though they may not control the social and economic backgrounds of their students, schools do decide how to structure their learning environments for them and they can do this in more or less effective ways for diverse student populations. Unlike in previous studies, the attention in the effective school studies was on the practices that characterized an effective program or school. Often using a nomination process or a range of outcome indicators of success, researchers would identify effective schools, programs, or teachers and then describe in detail what characterized the practices in these classrooms or schools.

FEATURES OF EFFECTIVE BILINGUAL PROGRAMS AND SCHOOLS

Many effective bilingual education studies have focused on case studies of elementary schools (Carter & Chatfield, 1986; Christian & Genesee, 2001; Gold, 2006; Howard & Sugarman, 2007; Johnson & Swain, 1997), although more attention is being paid to secondary schools (Center for District and School Development, 2004; Henze & Lucas, 1993; Lucas, 1993; Lucas, Henze, & Donato, 1990; Short & Boyson, 2004; Short & Fitzsimmons, 2007).

Despite examining quite different contexts, the studies have identified a relatively consistent set of features that characterize effective approaches to bilingual education (Brisk, 2006; García, 1988; Gonzales, Huerta-Macías, & Tinajero, 1998; Howard, Sugarman, Christian, Lindholm-Leary, & Rogers, 2007; Mace-Matluck, 1990; Miramontes, Nadeau, & Commins, 1997). A brief summary follows.

At the school level, studies stress the importance of a whole-school approach that takes into consideration issues of linguistic and cultural diversity. Studies identify the following key elements of a whole-school approach:

- Building a strong knowledge base about bilingualism, second language acquisition, and minority schooling across the school, not limited to a special bilingual or ESL program

- Ensuring strong and knowledgeable leadership

- Sharing responsibility for reaching sociocultural, linguistic, and academic goals for all learners in the school

- Establishing a sense of community, within the school as well as with the home and wider community

A study by Lucas, Henze, and Donato (1990) was one of the first to examine successful practices at the secondary level. Their study included six high schools and describes the schoolwide practices that distinguished these high schools in their approach to working with their multilingual populations. One of the key factors was a schoolwide commitment to biliteracy and multiculturalism that was expressed by their taking such measures as hiring bilingual staff, communicating high expectations for minority pupils, offering advanced classes in the minority language, and providing counseling services that encouraged pupils to go to college. The authors conclude:

> This study strongly suggests that the diversity among students cannot simply be ignored. While the schools recognized the importance of integrating language-minority students with mainstream students and providing equally challenging instruction for all students, they did not try to minimize differences among mainstream and Latino students or among Latino students themselves. Approaches to schooling that value linguistic and cultural diversity and that promote cultural pluralism were welcomed and explored whenever possible. . . . Students' languages and cultures were incorporated into school programs as part of the efforts to create a context in which all students felt valuable and capable of academic success. (p. 338)

At the program level, quality of program implementation plays a key role. Although the selection of a program model is an important step in organizing a bilingual curriculum, its effectiveness is directly related to the quality of the actual practices that occur at each grade level. A high-quality program includes features such as:

- Sufficient material resources in both languages to implement the program (e.g., textbooks)

- A highly qualified bilingual staff proficient in the language or languages of instruction and knowledgeable about bilingualism, second language acquisition, and their implications for teaching

- Clear program articulation, that is, curricular grade level expectations and language use expectations for both languages are made explicit and provide a continuous experience for students for language and cognitive development

- Teacher collaboration (within and across languages)

Howard and Sugarman (2007) present case studies of four effective two-way immersion programs. They found that what set these programs apart was, above all, a commitment to ongoing learning and to the exchange of ideas and the promotion of higher order thinking (intellectualism). They also identified a culture of equity and leadership as factors that guided curriculum planning, the use of the two languages in the program, and consensus building.

At the classroom level, effective teachers engage in practices that provide an optimal learning environment for bilingual learners. In this research, teachers also:

- Maintain high expectations; they do not use limited English proficiency as an excuse for lowering standards

- Use current approaches to teaching that building on students' native and second language resources

- Implement a curriculum that reflects and builds on students' cultural experiences

- Use culturally and linguistically responsive instructional practices

Critical autobiographies are a good example of culturally responsive practices that allow students to examine events in their lives that affect them as bilingual individuals (Brisk, Burgos, & Hamerla, 2004; Brisk & Harrington, 2000). In this project-based approach to teaching, students describe their lives as bilingual-bicultural learners and connect their life stories to social, political, economic, cultural, and linguistic events through discussion and the reading of a wide range of fiction and nonfiction books. Critical autobiographies allow students to explore their own identities, and they provide an authentic context for language and literacy development.

SHIFTING THE DEBATE

The effective schools studies reframe the discussion about program effectiveness in important ways. The studies typically included more diverse indicators of success than just English language proficiency to identify effective schools or teachers. Among these indicators were school attendance, drop-out and graduation rates, and academic achievement. The studies broadened the purpose of schooling for ELLs, moving away from treating language of instruction as the main explanatory variable for ELL school success. Previous studies had been primarily quantitative, product (outcome-oriented) studies. By using qualitative research methods to reveal processes (classroom observations, interviews), the effective school studies presented a more holistic picture of effectiveness than the previous, product-oriented studies. The presence of multiple effective program and school features made it clear that effective schools are complex sites and that a range of input factors and features contribute to positive educational outcomes for ELLs.

These studies also highlight that quality of implementation is as important as the choice of medium of instruction for student outcomes. A poorly implemented program will likely have poor results, regardless of language of instruction. This is not to say that language of instruction does not matter. When programs choose bilingual competence as their outcome for all or some of their students, careful decisions about medium of instruction must be made in order to reach the desired linguistic outcomes. What the effective school studies emphasize, however, is that merely choosing a program design (e.g., two-way immersion) will not guarantee positive outcomes—schools must also pay close attention to the quality of program implementation. A two-way immersion program with poorly prepared teachers and minimal program articulation is less likely to have its desired impact than the same program model with well-prepared teachers and clear curriculum expectations. One shortcoming from some of the effective program research is that, while they provide an important snapshot of effective practices, they did not often document how a program arrived at successful practices. (Brisk, 2006, chap. 7, is a notable exception.) Another criticism has been that the effective school studies did not pay sufficient attention to objectively defined outcomes, relying too much on nominations without checking actual achievement patterns. To help us understand the relationship between inputs (contextual variables and school-based processes) and specific yet broadly conceived outcomes, future effectiveness research will need to include a combination of quantitative and qualitative methods.

Reframing the Effectiveness Debate

It is important to understand whether a particular approach for educating language minority students works. How outcomes and measures are defined reflect our priorities for language minority schooling. The advocacy-based evaluation studies and its accompanying model-driven debate limited the desired outcomes for ELLs to English language skills and the scope of their schooling to a (short-term) specialized program. Their evaluation questions centered on identifying the best model for any second language learner to learn English quickly without paying attention to contextual factors, student variation, and the academic language proficiency that is needed to succeed in school. Once a program was declared superior, little was known about the processes that contributed to program success. The program evaluations typically did not provide sufficient information to guide multilingual practices at the school, program, or classroom level. Furthermore, their focus on programs in isolation may discourage a whole-school approach to the schooling of bilingual learners.

A broader definition of outcomes emerged as part of the effective school movement. The effective school studies have helped educators better determine what school, program, and classroom conditions facilitate learning for bilingual children. These studies show that rather than simply the choice of medium of instruction (program model choice), a complex set of variables mediates the schooling experiences for bilingual children. This multiplicity of input and process factors also need to be taken into consideration when evaluating schooling approaches and educational outcomes for bilingual learners. As María Estela Brisk (2006), a long-term bilingual advocate and scholar, concludes, "For too long, advocates and educators have focused on finding the ideal way to teach English. The real choice is between compensatory and quality education" (2006, p. 14).

CHAPTER 7
Discussion & Activities

Critical Issues

1. McGroarty (1997) notes, "The sheer numbers of evaluation studies demonstrate not only the use of program evaluation as a political tool, but also of differing perspectives of what constitutes success in bilingual programs" (p. 77). Illustrate McGroarty's point with examples from this chapter.

2. How did the effective school studies shift the effectiveness debate? What are some key differences with the product-oriented program evaluations? What are strengths and drawbacks of each type of evaluation study?

Application and Reflection

3. Select a district with ELLs or look at your own district and determine how ELLs are identified, what program options are available to them, and how reclassification (exit) is determined. The chart below may help you collect the information.

	What tests/ assessments are used? In what language?	Who makes decisions?	What criteria are used?	Comments and questions
Identification				
Classification				
Program option				
Reclassification/exit				

4. Consider the extent that your own context reflects the three areas that have emerged from the effective school studies (whole-school approaches, program quality, and pedagogy). Select two or three indicators listed in the chapter and analyze how your school, program,

or classroom already aligns with these elements of effective practices for diverse learners. Where is there lack of alignment? How might you change practices that do not yet align?

Level of analysis	2–3 Effective school indicators listed in chapter	Examples of practices that align	Examples of practices that do not align
Whole-school approach			
Program quality			
Classroom practices			

Recommended Readings

Genesee, F., Lindholm-Leary, K. J., Saunders, G., & Christian, D. (2006). *Educating English language learners: A synthesis of research evidence.* Cambridge: Cambridge University Press.

> *This book pulls together what we know about second language and literacy development for school-age children and the implications for schools, including program development.*

Goldenberg, C. (2008, Summer). Teaching English language learners: What the research does—and does not—say. *American Educator*, 8–23, 43–44.

> *This article provides a balanced and comprehensive overview of the areas of research that have informed schooling for minority language learners.*

Howard, E. R., Sugarman, J., & Christian, D. (2003). *Trends in two-way immersion education: A review of the research.* Report 63. Baltimore: Center for Research on the Education of Students Placed At Risk.

> *This report focuses on the academic, language and literacy, and cross-cultural outcomes of two-way immersion programs. An on-going bibliography can be found on the Center for Applied Linguistics Web site at http://www.cal.org/twi/*

Principles for Multilingual Schools

GUIDING QUESTIONS

- *Why is a principled approach to practice necessary and important?*
- *What is the Principle of Educational Equity and why is it a core principle?*
- *What are the main ideas behind the Principles of Affirming Identities, Promoting Additive Bi/Multilingualism, and Structuring for Integration?*
- *How can educators analyze their policies and practices through the lenses of these four principles?*

KEY TERMS

Principle of Educational Equity	Principle of Affirming Identities
bias	Principle of Promoting Additive
disproportionality	Bi/Multilingualism
linguistic bias	integration
cultural bias	Principle of Structuring for
test bias	Integration

The research on program models and effective school features discussed in previous chapters provides important guidance on how to structure schooling for bilingual learners. While these studies make an important contribution, their results tend to be limited in their ability to help educators make decisions. Program evaluations, for example, typically provide insufficient detail to understand why a program works well or not. However, these studies, combined with theoretical frameworks, can be useful in considering by which principles educators can organize their policies and practices. This chapter introduces four organizing principles to guide such educational decision-making at the local level and to inform language policy in schools and classrooms.

Language Policy, Local Practice

Language policy processes are multilayered and socially constructed by individuals involved in policy implementation. While state or national policies regarding medium of instruction may result in certain program designs, how these program models find their way into practice is not a linear process but one that is influenced by how individuals at the district, school, and classroom level interpret the law or policy within their own context. The choice of program model, which language or languages to use for instruction, and how languages are to be distributed across the curriculum will depend on goals, target populations, local understandings about multilingual development in schools, available resources, anticipated language, culture, and academic learning outcomes in each context as well as on national, state, and local policies.

For example, students' different proficiency levels may influence the amount of time allocated to teach language, the subjects taught in each language, and the choice of the language or languages of initial literacy instruction. The European schools primarily enroll the children of civil servants who are expected to return to their home country. These schools begin with the students' native languages and then strategically build up to more and more academic instruction in the second language and then the third language. This program design is shaped by understandings about bilingual development in schools, program goals, and the specific context in which the European schools have developed.

When Miami Dade County in Florida expanded its bilingual programs in the 1960s after the success of Coral Way Elementary, school officials adjusted both the extent to which the two groups of students were taught together and the amount of time spent in each language according to students' English and Spanish proficiency levels as well as their beliefs about bilingual development in schools. Central Beach Elementary enrolled a more English-proficient Spanish-speaking population and also had more native English speakers than Coral Way Elementary. In response, the principal and the staff developed a model that integrated all students for core curriculum instruction in English (240 minutes) and Spanish (45 minutes), with additional Spanish or English as a second language classes for each language group separately (45 minutes). Yet another model was developed at Southside Elementary School, which decided to provide integrated instruction in Spanish and in English (50:50). Students were separated only for one block of language classes (Spanish as a second language for the English speakers and Spanish for Spanish speakers for the Spanish speakers) (Mackey & Beebe, 1977). While both schools chose program models that included the core features of bilingualism and integration, the details of implementation were responsive to the specific school contexts.

The same process of adaptation and accommodation to local conditions emerges as a program model is being implemented. The choice of a program model guides educators through a set of decisions about curriculum and language distribution. However, specific parameters may need adjustment each year, in response, for example, to curricular reform or significant demographic changes. A drop in enrollment or the sudden influx of a brand new group of students the school has not dealt with before will affect what it can or needs to do. If one student cohort at a certain grade level happens to have more students with disabilities or more newcomer immigrant students, the program may need to reconsider how special education services or bilingual/ English as a second language services are distributed or integrated within the model. Curricular changes, such as a mandate to implement a math or reading program or a regime of standardized testing, may also affect how a program model is implemented.

At the classroom level, teachers make daily decisions about language and language uses in relation to their students and their instructional goals. They make adjustments based on on-going assessments of their students' learning. Reflecting on their lessons, teachers may decide to increase opportunities for students to interact with one another by using more cooperative learning. They may notice that students need to ask more critical thinking questions. Or, seeing that their newcomers missed out on much of the content, they may draw on some native language resources to better assist them.

A choice for a particular pathway to multilingualism is therefore always embedded within the local context and must be flexible enough to respond to changes in that context. School responses to student diversity require setting academic, language/literacy, and sociocultural goals for the target populations. Educators then match the program model and classroom practices to these goals, adjusting for contextual variables such as student background characteristics, educator and community beliefs, and actual patterns of language use (Brisk, 2006; Fortune & Tedick, 2008; Freeman, 2004).

Four Principles for Language Policy in Education

Neither the choice of program model nor the implementation of effective program features is a straightforward affair once we consider the local context and the decisions educators must make every day. The need for flexibility and responsiveness does not imply randomly designed approaches to schooling in diverse settings. Decision making that is not grounded in a coherent

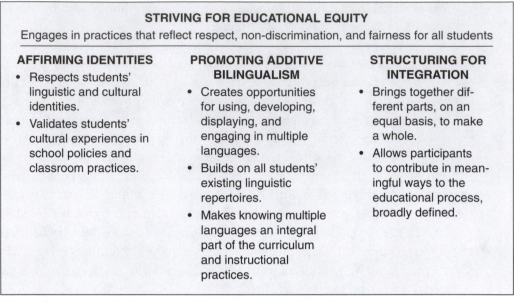

Figure 8.1   Four principles for decision making in multilingual schools

vision can easily fragment the schooling experiences for students, send mixed messages about students' languages and cultures, and fail to provide students with the necessary opportunities for consistent and continuous cognitive, social, and linguistic growth. Responding to external pressures or changing circumstances may result in practices that are not aligned with what we know about effective schooling for multilingual learners. To avoid these outcomes, educators' policies and actions need to be embedded within a principled approach against which locally contextualized and daily decisions can be assessed.

The first of the four principles that can guide decision making involves striving for educational equity, and it is an overarching principle. The other three principles, embedded within this core principle, more directly address linguistic and cultural diversity by affirming identities, promoting additive bi/multilingualism, and structuring for integration. Together, these principles can be used to reflect on, assess, and shape policies and practices. They can guide decisions at the district, school, program, and classroom levels involving, for example, curriculum and materials, instructional approaches, assessment practices, resource allocation, and parental and community involvement. Figure 8.1 presents an overview of the four principles. Although these principles can be applied to any policy level, this chapter and the following three chapters pay particular attention to district/school, program, and classroom-level decision-making.

Striving for Educational Equity

Educators who apply the *Principle of Educational Equity* create school environments where each individual feels valued and respected. They work together to ensure that formal and informal language policies and practices at the school, program, and classroom levels fairly represent the diversity in the school and do not discriminate systematically against certain groups of students.

In its broadest sense, equity affirms the equal moral value of all human beings and promotes respect for human rights. The Universal Declaration of Human Rights begins by recognizing "the inherent dignity and . . . the equal and inalienable rights of all members of the human family" and recognizing that this moral value "is the foundation of freedom, justice and peace in the world" (http://www.hrweb.org/legal/udhr.html). Articles 1, 2, and 16 of the declaration are particularly relevant for those working in schools (Figure 8.2).

Article 1

All human beings are born free and equal in dignity and rights. They are endowed with reason and conscience and should act towards one another in a spirit of brotherhood.

Article 2

Everyone is entitled to all the rights and freedoms set forth in this Declaration, without distinction of any kind, such as race, colour, sex, language, religion, political or other opinion, national or social origin, property, birth or other status.

Furthermore, no distinction shall be made on the basis of the political, jurisdictional or international status of the country or territory to which a person belongs, whether it be independent, trust, non-self-governing or under any other limitation of sovereignty.

Article 16

1. Everyone has the right to education. Education shall be free, at least in the elementary and fundamental stages. Elementary education shall be compulsory. Technical and professional education shall be made generally available and higher education shall be equally accessible to all on the basis of merit.

2. Education shall be directed to the full development of the human personality and to the strengthening of respect for human rights and fundamental freedoms. It shall promote understanding, tolerance and friendship among all nations, racial or religious groups, and shall further the activities of the United Nations for the maintenance of peace.

3. Parents have a prior right to choose the kind of education that shall be given to their children.

Figure 8.2   Articles 1, 2, and 16 of the Universal Declaration of Human Rights

THE IMPORTANCE OF THE PRINCIPLE OF EDUCATIONAL EQUITY

The **Principle of Educational Equity** is grounded in the fundamental respect of individuals for who they are. This attitude will be reflected in the interactions between and among the adults and children who come together in the school environment from different linguistic and cultural backgrounds (Miramontes & Commins, 2005). For bilingual learners, the equity principle turns our attention to how policies and practices reflect respect for their linguistic and cultural diversity and how they are treated as bilingual and bicultural individuals.

Policies of nondiscrimination along with awareness of and actions taken to counter the unequal treatment of students are central to the Principle of Educational Equity. Article 2 of the Universal Declaration of Human Rights states, "Everyone is entitled to all the rights and freedoms set forth in this Declaration, without distinction of any kind, such as race, colour, sex, language, religion, political or other opinion, national or social origin, property, birth or other status." The U.S. Constitution also stresses equal treatment of each person under the law. The Equal Protection Clause of the 14th Amendment, which was ratified in 1868, declares, "No state shall . . . deny to any person within its jurisdiction the equal protection of the laws." Since then, the Civil Rights Act of 1964 and the 1974 Equal Educational Opportunity Act, as well as other legislation, have further reinforced the importance of nondiscrimination in diverse settings (see Chapter 6).

"EDUCATIONAL EQUITY" AS A LENS FOR POLICY AND PRACTICE

The Principle of Educational Equity draws educators' attention to the twin values of respect and fairness (nondiscrimination). Respect is reflected in how administrators, teachers, students, and community members interact and treat one another, whether informally in the hallway or formally in meetings or in the classroom. Respect for cultural differences and multilingualism means that linguistic and cultural diversity are understood to make positive contributions to the school environment and as a resource for student learning and academic achievement. Applying the Principle of Educational Equity implies an awareness of possible sources of **bias** that may result in the unfair treatment of certain groups of students at the district, school, program, or classroom level and the realization that the same treatment does not necessarily imply equitable treatment.

Bias is typically formulated in terms of giving certain groups of students an advantage that is unfair or disproportionate. At the system level (district/school/program), equity issues are often considered in terms of equal access to services, programs, or other resources. **Disproportionality** occurs when the percentage of students assigned to a particular program is significantly higher or lower than the percentage of their enrollment in the school system. A well-known example is the tendency for minority students (particularly African Americans and bilingual learners) to be overrepresented in learning disability classes and underrepresented in programs labeled "gifted and talented." (Artiles, Rueda, Salazar, & Higareda, 2008; Skiba et al., 2008)

In the classroom, how teachers interact with their students and the expectations they communicate through these interactions may also reflect bias. When teachers tend to ask higher order thinking questions of one group (e.g., fluent English speakers) and lower order questions to another group (e.g., ELLs), their classrooms fail to provide the same range of learning opportunities for all students. Unequal treatment of students in the classroom by race, gender, ethnicity, or language proficiency is, unfortunately, still common. Studies in diverse classrooms illustrate that these inequities are reflected in a range of classroom practices, including differences in the number of opportunities for students to talk and participate and in the kind of feedback students receive from the teacher.

Bias also occurs in assessment when the tests used make unfair assumptions about the background knowledge of the students. **Linguistic bias** occurs when the items use unnecessarily difficult and familiar words in the item or responses. Test items are said to have a **cultural bias** when they assume background knowledge that is embedded in specific cultural experiences. For example, the prompt 'Write about what you would do on a snow day' assumes experience with snow and knowing that a snow day implies not going to school. For many newcomers, lack of familiarity with standardized test and how you fill them out can be another source of bias (**test bias**).

When inequities are identified, the Principle of Educational Equity calls for systemic changes to address those inequities. For example, a district may experience a significant increase in bilingual learner special education referrals in conjunction with an influx of students with limited proficiency in the school language. Educators who apply the equity principle will ask whether there may be bias in the referral process against second language learners (Klingner & Harry, 2006). They will critically examine why students are being referred and what tests are used to make decisions about students and their possible disabilities. Through their inquiries, they may find that mainstream teachers have interpreted normal second language and literacy development as signs of a language or cognitive delay. These educators may question whether what is happening in the mainstream classroom reflects an optimal language learning environment for bilingual learners. They may realize that their assessment tools for determining whether a student has a disability have been developed and normed for native speakers, making them invalid for use with second language learners. This application of the equity principle can uncover policies and practices that would lead to instructional and assessment biases, unfairly favoring native or fluent speakers of the school language.

Instead of blaming the students' lack of English proficiency, their bilingualism, or the absence of what teachers might consider "school-relevant" home literacy practices, these educators would consider how the system can respond more equitably to the linguistic and cultural diversity that now characterizes the school. They may decide to follow several possible avenues for action, such as changing the learning environment in the mainstream classroom, adapting the content of the test and how it is used, engaging in a more culturally and linguistically sensitive referral processes, providing professional development for teachers, and actively recruiting bilingual special education teachers (Artiles & Ortiz, 2002; Baca & Cervantes, 2003; Hamayan, Marler, Sanchez-Lopez, & Damico, 2007; Laing & Kamhi, 2003; Martin, 2009).

Recognizing unfair or biased practices is not always easy. It requires a commitment to equity and a careful examination of a wide range of data sources to reveal discriminatory patterns and advocate for change toward a more just system. It also requires an understanding that providing the same (equal) services does not necessarily provide equitable (fair) access. As the Court in *Lau v. Nichols* pointed out, a student who is not yet proficient in English will not benefit in the same way as a fluent English speaker from the same (English) instruction with the same (English) textbooks. A teacher who believes that doing the *same* for native English speakers and ELLs can systematically disadvantage the latter group of students.

By asking about how schools and classrooms, through their policies and daily practices and interactions, include or exclude certain students from access to curriculum or particular programs and by inquiring whether and how policies and practices may reflect bias toward certain groups of students, the Principle of Educational Equity avoids the assumption that the problem lies with students and their families. It rejects a deficit stance to the diverse linguistic and cultural experiences, knowledge, and skills that students bring to school.

The sections below provide a description of each of the three principles that follow from the core principle of educational equity, along with a brief discussion of its relevance and importance.

Affirming Identities

Educators who apply the *Principle of Affirming Identities* validate diverse cultural experiences in their school policies and classroom practices. They purposefully create spaces for diverse student voices.

Keeping equity in mind, the **Principle of Affirming Identities** examines how school policies and practices reflect respect for and affirm students' and teachers' diversity of linguistic and cultural experiences and beliefs. Central to the Principle of Affirming Identities are the interrelated issues of legitimization (how linguistic and cultural diversity is given a visible and valued place in the school) and representation (how different languages and cultures are represented).

THE IMPORTANCE OF THE PRINCIPLE OF AFFIRMING IDENTITIES

The extent to which school policies and practices reflect this principle is important in supporting students' social, linguistic, and academic development (see Chapter 2). The Principle of Affirming Identities is derived from the basic learning principle that engagement in and motivation for learning is facilitated when students feel validated for and can build on what they know. When students' developing sense of self is affirmed and extended through their interactions with teachers, they are more likely to apply themselves academically and participate actively in instruction (Cummins, 2001, p. 2). Affirming identities and providing spaces for identity negotiation in positive ways is fundamental to the academic success of culturally diverse students.

In contrast, negating the linguistic and cultural resources that students bring to school renders multilingual students invisible and inaudible. Not being valued for who they are may lead to students' believing that their academic effort does not count. In response, they may withdraw from the learning process altogether through nonparticipation. Or they may act out, engaging in behaviors of resistance that are not aligned with the school's expectations of "good" students (Fordham, 1988; Ogbu & Simons, 1998). When teachers and other students reinforce this negative image through their own behaviors and interactions, they may initiate and perpetuate a cycle of failure that for many students could end with alienation, low achievement, and dropping out (Deyhle, 1995; McCarty, Romero, & Zepeda, 2006).

"AFFIRMING IDENTITIES" AS A LENS FOR POLICY AND PRACTICE

The Principle of Affirming Identities encourages educators to ask how their policies and practices represent and value cultural and linguistic diversity. This principle can be applied at all policy levels (district, school, classroom) and areas of educational decision-making, such as curriculum and assessment. At the school level, educators can ask themselves whether and how their schoolwide initiatives (mission statement, school plans, textbook adoption, parent involvement activities) include and represent different languages and cultures and experiences. Administrators may ask whether and how their programs value cross-cultural differences and promote the development of positive social relationships among students from different racial, cultural, and class backgrounds. Applying this principle at the classroom level, teachers could examine whether and how their students have opportunities to represent and explore multiple identities and how their practices include their students' lived experiences in meaningful ways.

The Principle of Affirming Identities helps educators ensure that cultural differences in experiences in and outside school do not become a source of bias but are tapped into as a resource for learning. This principle avoids a "color-blind" approach that many teachers believe allows them to remain neutral and objective in their practices. Unfortunately, these teachers' assumption that the same is equitable for all does not recognize that their classrooms are already governed by certain cultural norms, ranging from accepted conventions around classroom participation behavior (e.g., raise your hand, one person speaks at the time) to notions about what counts as parent involvement. These norms will already be familiar to and taken for granted by some students and their families, most likely those who are members of the dominant, middle class culture and who are fluent standard English speakers (Varenne & McDermott, 1995). Recall Heath's (1983b) study of different literacy practices in African American and white families and how the schools valued those practices that matched those of the middle-class white community and failed to acknowledge and expand on the literacy practices of the low-income African American and white children. Students who differ from and may be unfamiliar with these assumed school norms can be at a disadvantage in "color blind" classrooms, if such a classroom means less meaningful interactions with the teacher or access to the curriculum.

Promoting Additive Bi/Multilingualism

Educators who apply the *Principle of Promoting Additive Bi/ Multilingualism* view language minority students' native language or languages as resources for teaching and learning. They make languages other than the standard school language visible and work to increase their status. They intentionally create opportunities for using, developing, displaying, and engaging with multiple languages.

The **Principle of Promoting Additive Bi/Multilingualism** examines school policies and practices from an additive bilingual perspective. Additive bilingual or multilingual contexts show respect for all of the languages or varieties in students' linguistic repertoires. These contexts encourage students to build on and extend the linguistic resources they bring with them to school. In these environments, students' home and school languages and literacies are understood as integrally related, and they are drawn on and used as resources for teaching and learning. Multilingualism is understood as a dynamic, recursive, developmental process, and is seen as an asset for the individual, group, and society. This additive bilingual perspective can be contrasted with the subtractive bilingual view that dominates in mainstream societies.

THE IMPORTANCE OF THE PRINCIPLE OF ADDITIVE BI/MULTILINGUALISM

The arguments for the importance of developing multilingual repertoires are discussed extensively in Chapters 2 and 3. As outlined in these chapters, bilingualism and biliteracy development have been linked with higher future aspirations, better mental health and family relations, better social integration, more cognitive benefits, and higher academic achievement. It is also noted that bilingual skills and biliteracy will not easily develop in dominant-language environments without parent, community, and school support and opportunities for authentic use.

Failure to build on students' linguistic resources also takes away a crucial tool for learning and transfer of previously developed skills for bilingual students. Often bilingual learners, particularly those who are in the beginning phases of learning the school language, are taught at an instructional level that is well below their actual cognitive abilities simply because they are not yet fluent in the school language. An absence of access to native language peers, personnel, and materials, often combined with poor second language teaching, greatly undermines bilingual learners' access to high-quality schooling. Finally, the failure to positively acknowledge students' linguistic expertise in schools affects multiple aspects of a bilingual student's learning experience in school. The intricate link between language and identity makes denying a space to students' native languages akin to silencing their voices and narrowing their identity options (cf., the Principle of Affirming Identities).

"ADDITIVE BI/MULTILINGUALISM" AS A LENS FOR POLICY AND PRACTICE

The Principle of Promoting Additive Bi/Multilingualism considers how multiple languages (and language varieties) and multiliteracies are made visible in the school and how they are used as resources for learning. Like the Principle of Affirming Identities, this principle needs to be applied to all areas of educational decision-making, including programs, curriculum, pedagogy, and assessment.

At the school level, educators can ask themselves how access to the school is provided to those who speak languages other than standard English.

This access might include materials as well as personnel. Administrators may ask what program model would best fit an additive bilingual mission within their context and whether their policies and practices align with their goals. If a two-way immersion is not a realistic option, they might consider what resources districts and schools can pool to provide access to languages other than English. Applying this principle at the classroom level, teachers could examine how they and their students create and find opportunities to use languages other than the school language for teaching and learning. They can reflect on whether and how they explicitly and consistently communicate the value of knowing more than just English to their students and their families.

The Principle of Promoting Additive Bi/Multilingualism stresses a language-as-resource orientation when working in linguistically and culturally diverse settings (Ruiz, 1984; see also Chapter 5). This principle insists on taking an additive stance regardless of context. While in many contexts a formal bilingual education program can be implemented to support students' development of bilingual repertoires, this is not true for all settings, particularly those with multilingual populations. Even when a full-fledged bilingual program is not possible, the Principle of Promoting Additive Bi/Multilingualism means that educators will still seek ways to create additive bilingual environment through other means, such as by offering heritage language classes or using bilingual teaching strategies (Cenoz, 2009; de Jong & Freeman, 2010).

Structuring for Integration

Educators who apply the *Principle of Structuring for Integration* establish inclusive policies and practices that encourage equal-status relationships among and participation by different constituencies. They take linguistic and cultural diversity and the implications for effective practices as their starting point for decision making.

In its broadest sense, **integration** refers to the process of bringing together different parts, on an equal basis, to make a whole (Brisk, 1991). The **Principle of Structuring for Integration** looks at how a school's various components (students, parents, teachers, as well as programs and activities) connect, relate, and interact with each other and how these relations reflect equal status among those involved. El-Haj (2006) refers to this integration process as one of "substantive inclusion" or "the capacity to participate fully [in the school community] and to contribute meaningfully to all its activities" (p.3).[1] Integration is a two-way process. Changes and accommodations are made for the benefit of all students based on the linguistic and cultural resources and identities of all students.

THE IMPORTANCE OF THE PRINCIPLE OF STRUCTURING FOR INTEGRATION

Collier (1995, p. 14) notes that to "break the cycle" of their being "perceived as remedial," special classes must be a "permanent, desired, integral part of the curriculum." Carter and Chatfield (1986) studied the interdependence between the quality of a language minority program and the rest of the school. They collected qualitative and quantitative data on an elementary school in California, Lauderbach, which had a bilingual program. The researchers point out that the relationship between the bilingual program and school organization was complex and not linear. The projects implemented in the bilingual program affected the entire school and the effectiveness of the entire school influenced the policies at the bilingual program level. Carter and Chatfield conclude, "Lauderbach is an effective school with an effective bilingual program. The bilingual program is not a separate part of the school but rather participates in, partakes of, and contributes to the positive student and educational climate outcomes" (p. 226).

Integration is also important at the student level. Student integration through small group work (cooperative learning structures) can contribute to the development of positive intergroup relationships between language minority students and language majority students, helping to break down stereotypes and develop positive attitudes among the students toward both languages and language groups (Cohen & Lotan, 1997; Slavin, 1985). In integrated classrooms, students' opportunities for language practice can be extended in ways that are often difficult to achieve in a setting with only second language learners.

Policies that do not take an integrated approach result in ineffective and unfair practices for bilingual learners. For example, the accountability system under No Child Left Behind initially did not include a specific provision for accountability for ELLs. A separate policy was formulated and added in a separate memorandum at a later date. But because the accountability system was not revised at the time, the current system continues to use invalid assessments and timelines as indicators of achievement for this group

---

[1]*Integration* is used here because the terms *inclusion* and *mainstreaming* have historically been associated with processes that, intentionally or unintentionally, are concerned with "fixing" the child in order to fit him or her into an existing structure (i.e., the standard curriculum classroom).

of students. The federal policy makers failed to consider the impact of linguistic and cultural diversity in designing a fair accountability system for all students, particularly bilingual learners. When certain groups are excluded from equal participation (e.g., minority parents, second language teachers), their voices and expertise cannot be used to inform policies and practices. The absence of a systemic integration of programs often translates into a lack of equal access to human and material resources, which undermines program quality for bilingual learners. Finally, the negative impact of minority student segregation on educational outcomes in the United States has been well-documented. While this is a vastly complex issue, minority student segregation in the United States is typically accompanied by less access to good teachers, lower expectations, and inadequate resources (Orfield, 2009; Rumberger & Gándara, 2004).

"STRUCTURING FOR INTEGRATION" AS A LENS FOR POLICY AND PRACTICE

The Principle of Structuring for Integration challenges educators to consider how all the different elements of the school come together. Like the two preceding principles, this principle affects all policy levels and areas of educational decision-making, including program integration, curricular and pedagogical integration, and assessment practices.

At the school level, the Principle of Structuring for Integration considers how the school organization, policies, and practices are developed with all learners and constituents in mind and with input from the different constituents that make up a school (parents, students, teachers, paraprofessionals, support personnel, the principal, and so on). When there are different programs within a school, this principle raises awareness of the extent to which these programs are integrated within the school culture. In the classroom, the principle asks teachers to critically consider whether students from different linguistic and cultural backgrounds have equal opportunities to meaningfully participate in the class and engage with the curriculum.

The Principle of Structuring for Integration stresses that integration is a process of building equal-status relationships among participants and is not simply a matter of placing them in the same space. It avoids adopting two policies that have largely failed linguistically and culturally diverse students. On one hand, it counters the discourse of the superiority of assimilation, which ignores linguistic and cultural differences by valuing the dominant language and cultural frames. On the other hand, it rejects imposed segregation, which stresses differences to such an extent that it effectively places multilingual students outside the mainstream and prevents them from having access to the resources they need to succeed. Instead, like the other principles, this principle aims to transform the system itself to ensure that what we consider "mainstream" practices are indeed inclusive and participatory.

Putting It All Together

The four principles are intended to engage educators in principled practices for their students that are flexible and contextually appropriate. To achieve effective schooling for diverse learners, they must be applied at all levels of educational decision-making. The challenge for schools is balancing the four principles together to achieve educational equity for all students, including multilingual learners. A two-way immersion program that promotes bilingualism and biliteracy (additive bilingualism), engages in culturally responsive classroom practices (affirming identities), and ensures minority and majority parent participation in program events (integration) will still fall short on the educational equity principle if the assessment system considers only achievement in the majority language. A social studies textbook that was selected because it is available in multiple languages (additive bilingualism) and is distributed evenly across all programs (educational equity) may, however, stereotype cultural or racial groups or take only one perspective on events. Such a choice may reflect a selection committee that did not pay sufficient attention to the affirming identities principle, perhaps because it did not include representation by all minority populations in the schools and wider community (integration principle).

The four principles are interdependent and, in an ideal school, policies and practices are aligned with each one. Achieving this ideal will be an ongoing challenge and target for educators. Applying the four principles requires a continuous process of reflection and action. The next three chapters consider the three principles separately within the core principle of educational equity in more detail, offering examples of the kinds of things educators (administrators and teachers and also researchers) can look for to answer the questions posed in this chapter.

CHAPTER 8
Discussion & Activities

Critical Issues

1. How is the "principled" approach described in this chapter different from the "model" thinking that has characterized many language-in-education policies (see discussion in Chapter 7)?

2. Create a brief presentation for school or district administrators that describes each principle discussed in this chapter, explains its importance for effective schooling for bilingual learners, and gives at least one example of a policy or practice that reflects the principle. You can use the table below to organize your ideas.

Principle	What does it mean?	Why is it important?	Examples
Educational Equity			
Affirming Identities			
Promoting Additive Bi/Multilingualism			
Structuring for Integration			

Reflection and Analysis

3. In the discussion of the Principle of Educational Equity the issue of disproportionality was raised. Do patterns of over- or underrepresentation exist for certain groups of students in your own context, for example, in terms of access to certain academic and nonacademic programs (e.g., after-school programs, advanced placement classes, gifted and talented classes) or special education placement or patterns of academic achievement or parent involvement? If they exist, what explanations are given for these patterns?

Recommended Readings

Brisk, M. E. (2006). *Bilingual education: From compensatory to quality education* (2nd ed.). Mahwah: Lawrence Erlbaum.

> Brisk rejects the view that bilingual education is compensatory, arguing instead that it needs to be conceptualized as quality education. Citing research on effective bilingual schools, in this book she discusses implications for curriculum, pedagogy, assessment, and home-school relationships.

El-Haj, A. R. T. (2006). *Elusive justice: Wrestling with difference and educational equity in everyday practice.* New York: Routledge.

> This book presents two case studies to illustrate how teachers respond to diversity in school. The author illustrates how definitions of the meaning and importance of certain differences (e.g., race, gender) take shape and, in turn, affect the kinds of learning environments that we create.

García, O. (2008). *Bilingual education in the 21st century: A global perspective.* Malden: Wiley-Blackwell.

> This book sees bilingualism and bilingual education as dynamic processes. The author argues for and gives extensive examples of pluralistic approaches to schooling for emergent bilinguals.

Affirming Identities in Multilingual Schools

GUIDING QUESTIONS

- In what ways can classroom interaction patterns reflect, represent, and create opportunities for diversity in cultural and linguistic identities?
- In what ways do curriculum, material, and assessment choices reflect and create spaces for certain identity options?
- How does the Principle of Affirming Identities negotiate sometimes conflicting realities between home, community, and school?

KEY TERMS

banking model of teaching	funds of knowledge
initiation-response-evaluation (IRE)	

Educators who apply the *Principle of Affirming Identities* validate diverse cultural experiences in their school policies and classroom practices. They purposefully create spaces for diverse student voices.

From the moment they step into school, bilingual children face multiple challenges to their linguistic and cultural identities as they negotiate different languages, notions of schooling and literacy, and cultural practices. Teachers play an important role in mediating this process to ensure successful and meaningful participation in school for their students. The Principle of Affirming Identities highlights the importance of constructing linguistic and cultural differences as positive contributors to the teaching and learning process and of avoiding a deficit approach that devalues these differences. This chapter focuses on how teachers can create spaces in their classroom that affirm the linguistic and cultural diversity of their students and how their students' different cultural experiences can be validated and used to inform teaching.

Role Definitions and Affirming Identities

Applying the Principle of Affirming Identities involves finding ways to tap into the cultural and linguistic resources that children bring to school and creating opportunities for them to display their knowledge and skills, which may be different from those traditionally found in schools, those prescribed by the national, state, or district curriculum, or those presented in their textbooks. National content standards and state curriculum frameworks do not always acknowledge cultural and linguistic diversity in explicit or affirmative ways (Sleeter & Stillman, 2005), and textbooks, supplementary materials, fiction and nonfiction trade books do not always represent (and may even misrepresent or stereotype) their students' cultures or experiences.

Pavlenko (2005) conducted a content analysis of English materials used for teaching adult ESL classes in the 1920s. She reports that women's identities, if included, were constructed primarily around their roles as wives and mothers. Yet, during those years, many women held jobs outside the home. This (lived) identity was excluded from the textbooks. As a result, the textbooks reinforced a certain, accepted identity for women that was based on the expectation that women belong in the home. And because they excluded women other than those in the home, these textbooks did not encourage conversations about such issues as working conditions and balancing work and family life. At that time, an approach that called for teaching "by the book" would have failed to affirm women's multiple identities.

Looking at children's books about the experiences of Latino children and families, Chappell and Faltis (2007) identified multiple, conflicting cultural models, including those that stress bilingual practices (e.g., code-switching) and those that communicate the desirability of monolingual practices. Another theme they identified was acceptance of American assimilation, along with a simplified, harmonious representation of the journey to assimilation (p. 260). Bilingual/bicultural identities were given little space in these books. Moreover, by presenting the process of assimilation as nonproblematic, the books failed to acknowledge that this process can in fact be wrought with real conflict, pain, and tensions as a result of different expectations at home, among peers, in the community, at school, and in the larger society. In a study of Chinese parents and their children, Qin (2006) found that the parents and children experienced difficulties communicating with each other. They were unable to bridge the cultural divide between them not only because of language differences but also because of the different ways each had been socialized as first and second generation immigrants. The choice of materials that teachers make thus affects the identity options that are open, marginalized, or left closed (Gay, 2000; Igoa, 1995; Nieto & Bode, 2008). Their materials send important messages to students about what is valued and important.

Engaging in culturally affirmative practices requires spaces where students' voices can be heard and their experiences can be validated. Teachers can create such spaces through their selection of textbooks and materials. Another important component is the roles teachers and students are expected to play in the classroom and what each contributes to the construction of knowledge in the classroom. The sections that follow examine teacher and student role definitions as one way of thinking about how linguistic and cultural diversity finds its way into the classroom. The first section looks at how certain roles are allocated through teacher-student interaction and the second section considers how teachers can include student experiences in their curriculum.

STRUCTURING LEARNER IDENTITIES THROUGH INTERACTION

Through their interactions with students, teachers indicate what they consider appropriate norms for behavior in the classroom. They may (verbally and nonverbally) reward students who are working quietly by themselves or those who contribute creative ideas about a certain topic. They may disapprove of students who call out their answers or students who do not help their peers with an assignment. These cultural norms also reflect teachers' role definitions, that is, what they view as the expected behavior assigned or ascribed to their role as teacher and the student's role as learner.

Cummins (1986, 2001) provides a useful framework for looking at role definitions. He distinguishes between collaborative and coercive orientations or role definitions in classrooms. A collaborative approach sees participants (teachers and students) as actively contributing to the learning process. Teachers' roles are described in terms of their being facilitators of learning who scaffold a collaborative process of knowledge construction. Students are viewed as producers and contributors of knowledge as well. Collaborative classrooms are organized around processes that encourage exploration and teacher-student and student-student interaction around the content. Students' contributions to the knowledge base constructed in the classroom are integral to the teaching and learning process. This knowledge base is jointly constructed using the linguistic and cultural resources available in the classroom.

In noncollaborative classrooms, roles are structured differently. In these classrooms the teacher's role is that of the transmitter or conveyer of a predetermined and circumscribed body of knowledge. (This process is also referred to as a transmission or a **banking model of teaching**.) The teacher is the only or primary source of legitimate knowledge (the expert), who is in charge of the learning process for all students (who are novices). Students' roles are that of receivers of knowledge. Cummins refers to these role definitions as coercive because teachers neglect students' linguistic and cultural experiences and require them to conform to a dominant language and culture mold.

De Mejia (1999) illustrates how the use of code-switching during storybook reading in a second language can change student participation and hence how students are positioned in their role as learners. She found that the Spanish-speaking students who were limited in English were effectively excluded from an active learning role in an English-medium preschool. While the teacher controlled the language input in English to make the reading as comprehensible as possible, the exclusive use of English led to teacher-dominated talk with little engagement with the content of the story. When the teacher decided to include Spanish, in addition to English, students were able to contribute their ideas and actively participate in constructing meaning from the story. In De Mejia's example, the teacher not only valued the students' native language as a language of learning (increasing its status); she also shifted the students' roles from nonparticipants to active learners and co-constructors of knowledge.

A different interaction pattern is traditionally found in the noncollaborative classroom, which often features a recitation script. This script involves an interactional sequence, referred to as an **initiation-response-evaluation (IRE)**, in which the teacher asks a question, the student responds, and the teacher provides feedback. IRE places the teacher in the expert and leader role. Gutierrez and Larson (1994) argue that a preponderance of recitation in a classroom encourages a construction of students' learner identities as passive receptors. They give the following example of such teacher-managed discourse. The teacher solicits answers to the question "What is special about mammals?" and the following discussion ensues:

> T = teacher; A = Ana; D = Diego; Ss = Various unknown students;
> [. . .] = omitted from original transcript.

T: We're mammals . . . too . . . okay . . . what's special about all mammals then [. . .] Ana . . . now tell us

A: They all have hair

T: Yes . . . so it's going to have hair . . . and what else about rhinoceros . . . what about all mammals . . . they all have hair . . . Ana . . . and there was another thing you guys should

> have learned from the mammal friends the other day . . . they all have hair and they all have something else . . . Diego

D: They have live babies

T: They all have live babies . . . good job . . . they have live babies . . . they don't come from what Diego . . . Diego they don't come out of what

SS: Eggs

T: They don't come out of eggs . . . great . . . [. . .]. (p. 28)

In this segment, the teacher is clearly in charge. She calls on each student to take a turn to respond, and after the evaluation ("good job"), she moves on to the next question and the next student. Students are expected to give the (one) correct answer. The focus is on affirming an already existing, agreed-upon body of knowledge. Students are not invited to comment on each other's responses, the teacher does not follow-up with other questions to include other students' insights or experiences, and she does not probe for more information. She is interested in seeing whether the students can correctly recite the information from the text. One way that teachers can position students as active contributors is therefore by asking more open-ended or divergent questions (i.e., multiple answers are possible) and by inviting students to comment on and build on what their peers have said. The following transcript illustrates a very different classroom dynamic. In this instance, the teacher, Ms. Hudson, begins the discussion by inviting students to explain how they calculated differences in height. Gabriela, Roberto, Jose, and Maria each provide an explanation to the class. Ms. Hudson acknowledges their contributions with a simple OK and then asks another student to present his or her thinking. After the four students have presented their explanations, Ms. Hudson continues:

MS. HUDSON: Can someone tell me how Roberto's and Maria's methods are alike?

CARLOS: They both took away from the little guy

MS. HUDSON: Anything else?

JAZMIN: They both had to open a 10 because there wasn't 7 1s to take away. So Roberto took his 7 from that 10 stick. He took 7 and left 3. And Maria took a 10 from the 6 10s and wrote it with the 1s and then took the 7 to leave 3.

MS. HUDSON: So, they were both thinking kind of alike but wrote it in different ways?

STUDENTS: Yes. (Cazden, 2001, p. 50)

In this lesson, students take on a more active role as learners and teachers. During the discussion, Ms. Hudson does not simply evaluate answers; she invites more comments and other responses to her questions (note her response to Carlos). In this classroom, students' contributions are valued and diverse student responses are possible and encouraged. Notice also the increased critical thinking and language use this particular whole-class classroom participation structure invites. Here the teacher uses her questions not simply to evaluate predefined knowledge. Instead, she extends and builds on students' responses and involves them in constructing knowledge.

VALIDATING STUDENTS' KNOWLEDGE: CURRICULUM PLANNING AND ASSESSMENT

Role definitions also become visible when considering how teachers include or exclude students' personal cultural experiences, knowledge, and skills in their curriculum and subsequently what and how they assess learning.

Curriculum Planning

Consistent with a collaborative role definition and shared knowledge construction is getting to know your students and finding ways to bring this knowledge into their curriculum. One approach that has set out to achieve this goal and validate the diverse knowledge and skills students bring from their home and their communities builds on students' **funds of knowledge** (González & Amanti, 1997; González, et al., 1995; Moll, 1992; Moll, Amanti, Neff, & Gonzalez, 1992; Moll & Gonzalez, 1996; Velez-Ibanez & Greenberg, 1992). The notion of funds of knowledge refers to the knowledge and skills children acquire at home and in the community. A unique part of the approach is that teachers go into their students' homes to learn about how other people make sense of their everyday lives (González, Andrade, Civil, & Moll, 2001). Teachers document the knowledge and skills students develop at home and in the community and try to use and validate these in their classroom. Teachers who participated in the 2001 study by González and colleagues commented on their ability to make more meaningful connections between content and their students' lives to enhance access to the curriculum. They became aware of their own previous deficit thinking and learned to focus on identifying what students do know rather than what they do not know in terms of the school's definition of knowledge and forms of language.

When teachers invite students to share what they know and consider their personal experiences in their planning, they are able to validate students' daily experiences and interests. Such validation is not limited to home- or community-based knowledge but extends into the students' experiences in school. Vasquez (2004) describes a kindergarten classroom where the teacher engaged her students in an authentic learning project. The students had become aware of the fact that one of their friends was vegetarian and could not participate in the lunch menu. Prompted by the unfairness of the situation, the teachers and students explored alternative menus and petitioned the principal for a different lunch menu. Thus, the teacher, whose actions were grounded in the children's lived experiences, integrated content (science, social studies) and literacy development in a meaningful way with authentic learning purposes.

In a transmission-oriented model there is an assumed body of knowledge to be taught to students. In the classroom, this translates to the teacher's selecting the topics that can be talked about and how these topics can be discussed. The topic may of course sometimes be dictated from the outside by curriculum guidelines and mandates. The exclusion of other ways of knowing becomes particularly visible in indigenous and colonial settings because of the distinct differences between formal national curriculum and local knowledge (Reagan, 2005; Semali, 1999). A teacher in Bolivia commented to her indigenous students:

> You should learn to earn money sitting as I do here, instead of doing dirty labour and having a hard time like your parents do as peasants, because of their ignorance, and because they don't read or write. Otherwise you will stay as slaves as you are now at home like indios. (Regalsky & Laurie, 2007, p. 240)

Bolivian indigenous agricultural practices reflect a deep knowledge of climate, soils, seeds, and growing cycles and support of a complex exchange of human labor and other energy sources between households. Rather than valuing this complex knowledge and using it as a resource for teaching, however, the teacher overtly disqualifies it, and in her interactions with her students, she positions it as irrelevant in school and for life (Regalsky & Laurie, 2007). Despite recent efforts to "indigenize" the curriculum (documenting such knowledge as fishing techniques in East Africa and how herbs and plants are used among the Maasai of Keny and Tanzania), the exclusion and devaluation of community-based local knowledge in favor of westernized knowledge continues to be the norm in classrooms in modern societies today.

What is important for our discussion is that in the process of simply transmitting knowledge, students' voices and personal narratives are easily ignored and devalued (Cazden, 2001), limiting their identity spaces. Gutierrez and Larson (1994, p. 32) give the example of a student, Agnes, who tells the story of a man who has killed several children in the name of Satan. Her lived experience sparks a lively discussion in the class. Her peers are very interested and ask questions about what is happening. The teacher's response to Agnes's story, however, is to downplay and devalue her experience, labeling the story as fantasy ("It's a story that has been passed down . . . sort of like a folktale and a fairy tale") and questioning its validity ("My guess would be that it's really not based on a lot of truth"). She also contrasts Agnes's narrative with formal school knowledge by giving a brief lecture on the definition and characteristics of folktales.

Assessing Content

Efforts to validate students' cultural experiences should extend to assessment of their work. Portfolio assessment, for example, allows students to demonstrate the progress they have made using their knowledge and skills, including their native language, through a variety of projects. It encourages them to reflect on their learning and set personal goals (Stefanakis, 2002, 2004). Portfolio assessments also create possibilities for students to explore different learner identities and affirm their diverse linguistic and cultural resources as tools for learning. They are collaborative and democratic: teacher and student negotiate instructional goals and means, and ways of demonstrating knowledge (Shohamy, 2001). In contrast, the assessment of a student's work on a paper-and-pencil test that has fixed and predictable answers is of less value because such tests allow for little variation in content and manner of responding. They are unlikely to tap into the experiences, knowledge, and skills bilingual students may have developed through different avenues and languages.

Affirming students' linguistic learning identities calls for a more holistic approach, which allows multilingual students to demonstrate their knowledge through multiple languages and not just through the societal language, whenever appropriate (see Chapter 3). When interpreting test results, teachers consider the entirety of students' linguistic repertoire, not just the skills developed in the standard language. They also acknowledge that language norms may be different in different languages and that these cultural differences need to be taken into consideration when assessing student progress.

When teachers choose to rely primarily on English-only, standardized assessments rather than creating spaces for different knowledge displays, they risk misrepresenting the knowledge and skills that bilingual students have and hence underestimating their academic performance. Affirming students' identities includes a focus on what they do know, not just the diagnosing of what they do not know.

Reflecting on the Principle of Affirming Identities in Practice

The preceding sections have examined educational practices that can support the implementation of the Principle of Affirming Identities. A common thread in these discussions is how diversity of viewing the world and knowledge about the world are represented in the school and how educators respond to this diversity in their daily interactions with students and the decisions they make related to role definitions, curriculum, and assessment. The following questions can help teachers reflect on their use of the affirming identities principle:

- *Curriculum decisions.* How do curricular topics/units build on and use students' cultural and linguistic knowledge and interests? How do materials include and reflect students' lived experiences and heritages? How do the curriculum and the materials reflect diversity in perspectives?

- *Pedagogical decisions.* How are students invited to participate and share what they know? Do activities permit different knowledge and skills to be used and constructed?

- *Classroom organization.* Does the IRE pattern dominate in the classroom? What kinds of questions do students and teachers ask?

- *Assessment decisions.* Do assessment tasks allow students to demonstrate what they know through a different means? Are assessments varied and authentic (e.g., portfolio assessments)?

These areas can be useful to researchers who wish to explore the Principle of Affirming Identities in practice.

This list, of course, is not exhaustive and other areas could easily be added. For example, the idea of shaping identities through interaction and the relative valuing of knowledge can be extended to the roles that are (allowed to be) enacted by other participants in the school. Principal-teacher interaction patterns may reflect a higher status for certain teachers. The extent to which teacher input on certain issues is valued and taken into consideration by principals may reflect particular role definitions as well. School personnel-parent interaction is another dimension where different role definitions can emerge. Minority parents are often positioned as not having the necessary or relevant knowledge to inform school practices (Black-ledge, 2000). In formal school meetings, such as parent-teacher conferences, they often become receivers of information about their child rather than collaborative partners in problem-solving. These power relations are most likely to occur with minority language parents when there is little awareness of how to effectively include translation to ensure full access to the information and meaningful participation in the meeting. Teachers can change these dynamics by asking parents to provide information and using that information as a valued source for problem-solving. In an intergenerational literacy project (Paratore, Melzi, & Krol-Sinclair, 1999), both teachers and parents brought information about a child's literacy practices and development to

TABLE 9.1	
The Principle of Affirming Identities at the Classroom Level	
Equity: Do my answers to these questions or inquiries apply to all my students and instruction in both languages?	
	Affirming Identities
Curriculum	How do my textbooks reflect my students' cultural backgrounds in nonstereotypical ways? If they do not, how can I mediate that lack?
	In what way do my themes consider the diversity in my students' background experiences?
	How do my activities invite multiple perspectives?
	In what way do my actions communicate high expectations to all my students?
Classroom interactions and activities	How I do encourage peer or small group collaboration in addition to whole group and individual work?
	In what ways do my assignments and tasks ask students to demonstrate and explore multiple perspectives or answers?
	In what ways do I invite students to share their background knowledge?
	In what ways do I create opportunities for students to raise questions and initiate topics of their interest?
	How do I structure my questions? Do my questions invite multiple possible answers and critical thinking?
Assessment	How do my assessments avoid linguistic and cultural bias?
	In what ways do I invite students to demonstrate their learning in multiple ways and through different assessment tasks?

the parent-teacher conference. This practice equalized the relationship between the parents and their child's teachers and positioned each individual as having expert and valued knowledge about the child.

Table 9.1 lists some of the questions teachers can ask to assess how their policies and practices align with this principle in their classrooms. These questions can also help researchers define their research agendas.

Policy to Practice: Challenges to Valuing Diverse Identities

The metaphor "to walk in both worlds" is often used to describe the goal of successful biculturalism and the desired outcome of efforts to affirm students' cultural identities. The following two sections illustrate the shortcomings of this metaphor. The first one warns against a too simplified interpretation of culture and identity within an affirmative framework; the second raises a question about whether schools are always the most appropriate site for including certain cultural practices.

WHOSE AND WHICH IDENTITIES?

In looking at the life-worlds of Central Yup-ik youngsters in Alaska, Henze and Vanett (1993) quickly realized that the two-world metaphor did not do justice to the complex linguistic and cultural worlds these youth had to negotiate. They had to reconsider what constituted bilingualism and biculturalism in the context of these Alaskan communities. First, they noted the diversity in proficiency: competence in both languages varied greatly from village to village. "Native language" reflected a continuum of skills rather than a fixed norm of standard language behaviors. Moreover, it appeared that at least three rather than two language varieties were used in the community: Yup'ik, standard English, and Village English. Village English, a variety of English with a strong Yup'ik grammatical structure, was used for daily communication and functioned as an important identity marker. Despite its prevalence in the community, Village English was not recognized in the schools, where it was dismissed as an inferior form of English. Similar patterns have also been found for other indigenized varieties of English, such as Nigerian English (Kirkpatrick, 2007; Mann, 2000).

García (2009) also questions traditional notions of bilingualism, pointing out that bilingual students in New York City come to school with skills in standard Spanish and English as well as nonstandard varieties of these languages and that these skills vary from student to student. Youth in a study by Zentella (1997) used three different varieties of Spanish (standard Puerto Rican Spanish, nonstandard Puerto Rican Spanish, English-dominant Spanish) and three of English (Puerto Rican English, African American Vernacular English, Hispanized English). She notes, "doing being bilingual" is not captured "by talking about Spanish and English as if they were monolithic codes" (p. 270).

Henze and Vanett (1993) also found that the Alaskan youth's different linguistic repertoires were accompanied by multiple-culture experiences that were at time in conflict with one another, including the world of the school (the "mainstream" dominant culture), popular culture through media, traditional cultural practices through interactions with elders, and contemporary Yup'ik culture. Similar experiences have been noted in other indigenous and urban communities as well, suggesting the danger of making a too simplified interpretation of linguistic and cultural identities (Asher, 2008; del Valle, 2000; Hadi-Tabassum, 2005; James & Woll, 2004; Louie, 2006; McKay & Wong, 1996).

Bosnian adolescents in the United Kingdom, for example, did not have as strong a Kosovan-Albanian identity as might be expected in a traditional model (Bash, 2005). Instead, the adolescents adopted cadences and vocabulary of Black English as their shared language based on the African American English they saw on television and the Internet, not on the surrounding "black" language varieties common in Great Britain (West Indian, Afro-Caribbean English). This language and identity choice serves a local purpose in that "it affords the group an identifiable common language, as well as the means to distinguish itself from other local groups" (p. 363). The study illustrates the complexity of the relationship between language choices and identities and the power of media to bring an international dimension to the experience of displacement (through migration).

Another example of the complex relationship between language and identity can be found in the world of the Deaf (Simms & Thumann, 2007). Deaf individuals construct different identities depending on whether their environments (including school) consider being d/Deaf as a physical handicap to be fixed or as a cultural marker. Skelton and Valentine (2003) present four interesting case studies of deaf youth in the United Kingdom, each with different perceptions of their deafness and their cultural identities. Even though each of these four students was deaf, they clearly negotiated different identities, and different aspects of their identities were salient in different domains and at different points in their lives.

Sophie saw her deafness as a handicap until she went to a school for the Deaf at the secondary level. At that point, she changed her perception of her deafness and became proud of her Deaf identity. Sean went through an oral education system and learned to lip read and use his voice to communicate. At 17 he attended a college for Deaf students and had to learn British sign language. Sean presented a hybrid and dynamic identity, because he could easily move between the hearing and the Deaf world and accepted the benefits from both educational systems. In contrast, Karl compared himself with the hearing world and felt negative about being deaf and using sign language. Finally, as an Asian (Pakistani), Muslim, and deaf adolescent, Bernice illustrates the multiplicity of identity and the complexity of the intersection of different worlds. She found herself less comfortable with white deaf people yet also excluded in her home (hearing) culture because her family did not sign. The importance of her religious identity led her to wish for a Muslim Deaf club.

These findings raise important questions about which identities schools are affirming. When limiting themselves to affirming their students' "two-languages-two-cultures," educators may fail to acknowledge that their students negotiate multiple (not just two), and often conflicting, worlds. The Principle of Affirming Identities reflects an understanding of identities as dynamic, changing according to different contexts, interconnected, and potentially hybrid. This principle also invites practitioners to find creative ways for student to express different aspects of their identities at school.

THE AMBIGUOUS ROLE OF SCHOOLS

While affirming cultural knowledge is an important aspect of respecting indigenous students' experiences, the sociopolitical context of indigenous schooling as well as deep differences between "western" ways of organizing the curriculum and indigenous ways of thinking may pose challenges to affirming identities within the context of formal schooling (Bishop, 2003; Harris, 1994; Henze & Vanett, 1993; Martinez, 2000; Morgan, 2005).

The history of oppression that has characterized many colonizing governments' relationship with indigenous populations puts government-run schools in an ambiguous position when it comes to promoting indigenous languages and culture. Unfortunately, discrepancies between policy and practice frequently occur in these schools. Despite stated policies in favor of bilingual or bicultural programs, it is not uncommon for schools to negate indigenous linguistic and cultural practices by hiring nonindigenous teachers who are not fluent in the indigenous language and are unfamiliar with the community's cultural practices (Henze & Vanett, 1993; Lipka, 1994). In considering the implementation of transitional bilingual education programs under the Title VII Bilingual Education Act, Ruiz (1984) found a similar discrepancy between a compliance and compensatory mentality and actual program quality and integrity.

In response to these discrepancies between policy and practice, some minority groups have expressed their preference for complete ownership and control over their children's education. The Navajo Rough Rock Community School is an example of a successful, community-based bilingual program with bilingual teachers from the community that is governed by community members (McCarthy, 2002). Bishop (2003) describes a school in New Zealand that organized itself around Maori, rather than majority, cultural values, such as community and respect for elders and the earth. He expresses his doubt that the same outcomes could be achieved in a government-run school because of core differences in assumptions about ways of being in the world.

The desire to take ownership of indigenous language and culture maintenance can also be related to practices that are considered sacred and therefore should to be taught only by particular individuals within the community. In some communities, the alphabetization of an oral language that is considered sacred is a controversial idea. Even though literacy development is strongly advocated in language revitalization research (Fishman, 2001), group members may resist giving over the power and control associated with the oral language (Cooper, 1989; Martinez, 2000). Real tensions may therefore arise between the school's discourses and the home or the community linguistic and cultural practices, and these tensions may not always best be overcome by insisting on bilingual or bicultural programs in school or by

including certain cultural practices in the curriculum (Freeman, Stairs, Corbierem, & Lazone, 1995; Harris, 1994; Martinez, 2000).

The link between schools and indigenous literacies and cultural practices needs extensive and open negotiations between school personnel,
parents, and community members to arrive at contextually sound culturally
affirmative practices (Lipka, 1994). What works and is appropriate in one
community may not work in another community. Different institutions (home,
community organization, schools) need to collaborate to examine how they
can include, reinforce, and complement each other's cultural and linguistic
practices.

Shifting Perspectives: The Language of Affirming Identities

The Principle of Affirming Identities draws our attention to how cultural
diversity and different ways of being, doing, and thinking are (re)presented
in the school and made visible as legitimate resources for teaching and learning. It challenges homogenizing trends to treat all students as having the
same linguistic and cultural experiences or educational needs (Sleeter &
Stillman, 2005). Schools play an important role in legitimizing what is valued and important. They validate certain knowledge by including it in the
curriculum and devaluing other kinds of ways of thinking and looking at the
world by excluding them. Values also become visible in the decisions that
are made about materials used for teaching, whether textbooks, trade books,
or other kinds of materials. Student identities are shaped by these decisions
and by the decisions teachers make in the classroom that are based on educators' definitions of what it means to be a teacher and a student.

The Principle of Affirming Identities also makes us sensitive to the
ambiguous position that schools may occupy as representatives of the dominant standard language and cultural practices. Recognition of these realities
requires educators and scholars to allow for complex relationships between
language and identity (as exemplified by the Bosnian students in the United
Kingdom) and for students' shifting identities over time and across contexts
(Fitts, 2006; Rampton, 2005).

Within the context of affirming identities, examining the process of validation and affirmation requires looking at individual students (case studies)
and their interactions with school and allowing them to give voice to their
experiences (e.g., Nieto, 1999; Rubinstein-Avila, 2007; Valdés, 2001). Moreover, questions about which languages/cultural practices and whose languages/
cultural practices, and hence which and whose identities are being affirmed and
empowered and which are merely tolerated or ignored and marginalized, need
to be explored and considered by policy makers, teachers, and researchers.

CHAPTER 9
Discussion & Activities

Critical Issues

1. Apply the idea of fractional and holistic views of bilingualism (described in Chapter 3) to our understanding of identity construction. What are some policy and practices that would align with a holistic view of identity? A fractional view?

2. The chapter applies the Principle of Affirming Identities to a particular policy level (the classroom) and three specific educational areas (curriculum, classroom interaction/activities, and assessments) (Table 9.1). Apply this lens to either a different policy level (state, district, school level) or a different educational practice (e.g., special education referrals, parent involvement, student promotion policies) and give examples of what practices could be implemented that would be aligned with this principle.

Application and Reflection

3. A major theme in this chapter is the importance of knowing your students to inform practice. What do you already know about your students' linguistic and cultural experiences? What strategies do you use to find out about them and their families? What else may you want to know? What are some barriers you are experiencing to getting to know your students?

4. Select a subject area (math, science, social studies). Does your required curriculum content (or textbook) reflect ways of knowing and viewing the world other than through the eyes of the dominant, western culture? If yes, in what ways? If no, how might you bring in different perspectives? In your evaluation, consider these questions:
   - Are diverse minority groups included in photos, pictures, or drawings? Who is included? Who is not?
   - Are references made to a diversity of perspectives in the text, for example, to different interpretations of events or different understandings of certain phenomena, different ways of doing things?
   - Do curriculum standards and lesson or unit objectives reflect multicultural perspectives?
   - Does the text reinforce or counter stereotypes about certain groups? Do the pictures?

5. Reflecting on your own teaching, consider the role of IRE patterns (recitation) in your classroom. (You can audio or videotape a segment of your class and analyze your question patterns.) How often do you use this pattern? What sort of questions do you ask (higher-order-, lower-order-thinking questions)? What do these patterns tell you about the role definitions that seem to operate in your classroom? If IRE dominates, how might you begin to shift to a more collaborative interactive pattern?

Recommended Readings

Moll, L. C., Amanti, C., Neff, D., & Gonzalez, N. (1992). Funds of knowledge for teaching: A qualitative approach to developing strategic connections between homes and classrooms. *Theory into Practice, 31*(132–141).

>   *This article shows teachers how to use students' "funds of knowledge" and explores the impact this approach can have on teaching and curriculum.*

Nieto, S. (1999). *The light in their eyes: Creating multicultural learning communities.* New York: Teachers College Press.

>   *This book gives voice to accounts by adolescent immigrants of their efforts to negotiate multiple languages and cultural worlds.*

Pavlenko, A., & Blackledge, A. (Eds.). (2004). *Negotiation of identities in multilingual contexts.* Clevedon: Multilingual Matters.

>   *This book provides a good overview of how theoretical notions of identity have changed from static to dynamic definitions. It considers the multiplicity of identities and identity construction with an emphasis on the complex relationship between language and identity.*

Reagan, T. (2005). *Non-western educational traditions: Indigenous approaches to educational thought and practice* (3rd ed.). Mahwah: Lawrence Erlbaum.

>   *This book discusses educational thought and practices in nonwestern contexts, including China and India and among indigenous populations in North America and the Roma (sometimes referred to as gypsies) in Eastern Europe. It also covers Islamic educational traditions.*

Promoting Additive Bi/Multilingualism

GUIDING QUESTIONS

- *How can educators engage in linguistic practices that reflect an additive bilingual stance in bilingual and monolingual settings?*

- *What are some challenges to reaching the goal of language status equalization?*

- *How does the policy of separating languages for instruction intersect with the principles of Promoting Additive Bilingualism and Affirming Identities?*

KEY TERMS

language status equalization
language compartmentalization

Educators who apply the *Principle of Promoting Additive Bi/Multilingualism* view language minority students' native language or languages as resources for teaching and learning. They make languages other than the standard school language visible and work to increase their status. They intentionally create opportunities for using, developing, displaying, and engaging with multiple languages.

This chapter offers illustrations of the kinds of practices that reflect the Principle of Promoting Additive Bi/Multilingualism. It also shows that maintaining a holistic, bilingual perspective can be challenging in the face of the monolingual societal forces that affect schools today.

Language Status and Additive Bi/Multilingualism

Educators seeking to implement the Principle of Promoting Additive Bi/Multilingualism are faced with the sociopolitical reality that inequalities exist regarding (speakers of) different languages and the treatment of linguistic diversity in the wider society. By default, the official or majority language takes up a dominant position in schools and is viewed and treated as a valuable, high-status language. Its central position in the school and its usage for teaching and learning are taken for granted. Speakers of minority languages, in contrast, typically have to struggle to find spaces in the school. Even informal use of the language (e.g., at lunch or recess) is not always viewed with approval.

The Principles of Educational Equity and Promoting Additive Bi/Multilingualism challenge schools to begin to address these inequalities by considering what their choice of programs, curriculum, materials, and assessment practices says about the value attached to different languages. They encourage educators to make choices that will increase the status of minority languages and their speakers in school rather than ignoring or marginalizing and devaluing the linguistic diversity and multilingual repertoires that children and their families bring to school. Using minority languages for high-status functions similar to those of the dominant language, or **language status equalization,** is therefore an important dimension of this principle. The sections that follow illustrate how decisions are made at the program and classroom levels related to increasing minority language status and explore how bilingual and monolingual teachers can engage in additive bilingual practices, even within multilingual or primarily dominant-language settings.

Increasing Language Status through Programmatic Decisions

An important decision in multilingual settings is the choice of the language or languages of instruction. Additive bilingual learning environments can be created formally by adopting an additive bilingual education model or through alternative approaches that take this principle in innovative directions in response to context.

IMPLEMENTING ADDITIVE BILINGUAL PROGRAMS

The choice of an additive language program is one of the most overt ways that a school can create additive bilingual learning environments that equally legitimize minority and majority languages. An important feature of these educational approaches (e.g., European schools, Canadian immersion programs, two-way immersion [TWI] programs) is that they teach the language while also teaching content through that language. Selecting an additive bilingual program model sends a strong message to students and parents about the value of the languages and can affirm the knowledge and experiences encoded in those languages. Educators must organize and articulate the learning environments for each of the languages to ensure the development of the desired language skills.

As they plan how to use the target languages, teachers can pay close attention to the status of the languages involved. With TWI programs, for example, they tackle the challenge of language status equalization at the program level through time allocation and choice of subject matter (Calderon & Minaya-Rowe, 2003; Howard & Christian, 2002; Howard & Sugarman, 2007; Soltero, 2004). They ensure that at least 50% or more of the instructional time is in the minority language and take care that academic subjects, not just nonacademic subjects, are taught through the minority language. The two languages are distributed evenly across grades, as in a 50:50 model, or, as in 90:10 models, are structured in favor of the minority language to counter the pervasive presence of English inside and outside school. In addition, TWI staff is aware of nonclassroom areas where linguistic inequities may appear, for example, in the language used for public announcements, library acquisitions, access to textbooks and supplementary materials, and the way the two languages are used outside the classroom. Figure 10.1 presents the

Program

- Both languages are equally valued throughout the program. Issues of language status are frequently discussed, and particular consideration is given to elevating the status of the minority language.
- All cultural groups are equally valued and are empowered to participate in and make decisions about all facets of the program, and the program has processes in place to ensure continuous cultural equity.

Curriculum

- There is an even divide between academic subjects and specials taught in each language. Language arts instruction is given in both languages and students are provided opportunities to develop academic language and cognitive skills in both languages. Students are made aware of linguistic diversity and language status issues as is developmentally appropriate.

Instruction

- Teachers and students work together to create a learning environment where all linguistic and cultural groups are equally valued and respected. Issues of linguistic and cultural equality are regularly discussed as is developmentally appropriate.

Figure 10.1   Equalizing language status. Source: Howard et al., 2007

- L1 as basis of instruction K–5 (decreases over time but is maintained K–12)
- L2 as subject (K–2)
- L2 as subject and medium of instruction for physical education and European hours (3–5)
- L2 as subject and medium of instruction for electives (6–7)
- L2 as medium of instruction for academic subjects (8–12)
- Introduction of compulsory L3 (grade 8)

Figure 10.2 European School model: Language distribution

broad goals for TWI programs related to issues of linguistic equity (Howard, Olague, & Rodgers, 2003).

The European schools take a similar approach, strategically building up to more and more academic instruction in the second language and then the third language. The design recognizes that, because of the limited access to the native language outside of school and the home, significant time must be spent in the native language to help the students, most of whom are children of foreign nationals, maintain their skills and develop content knowledge in preparation for their return to their home country. The European school model (Figure 10.2), like a 90:10 TWI model, begins with extensive instruction in the students' native language and a second language initially as a subject area. By 2nd or 3rd grade, the use of the second language as the medium of instruction extends to subjects that are less language dependent. Academically complex instruction in the second language is gradually increased until by 8th grade subjects such as science and history are taught in and through the second language. European identity development is supported through the common European hours.

In additive bilingual and multilingual education programs, language status equalization is often inherent in their design and finds its way formally into decisions about which language is used for which purpose for what amount of time. Sensitive to the dominance of the surrounding languages, additive bilingual programs often increase the amount of time in the minority languages in order to meet their goals of building and maintaining oral and literacy skills in minority languages, in addition to those in the majority language or languages.

ALTERNATE PATHWAYS TO MULTILINGUAL COMPETENCE

Additive bilingual education programs are highly context dependent. Implementing such a program requires access to a sufficient number of students from a similar language background, school and community (parent) willingness to support bilingualism and biliteracy development, qualified teachers, and access to sufficient material resources. These conditions, however, are not always present, and when school systems cannot select an additive bilingual model, creating additive bilingual environments becomes more challenging.

Although alternative approaches to developing multilingual competence may not always be described in terms of a particular program "model," in these approaches, minority languages and speakers of those languages are still viewed from a language-as-resource perspective and the value of bilingualism and biliteracy is communicated. One proposal for an innovative programmatic approach was noted by Freeman (2004) in Philadelphia. She describes a school plan for the implementation of a Spanish-English transitional bilingual education (TBE) program for ELLs, and a Spanish for Spanish speakers program for students placed in standard curriculum classrooms. When ELLs would exit the TBE program, they could continue some language and literacy development in their native language. Although ultimately the plan was not implemented, it reflects an innovative approach to bilingualism. A late-exit TBE program in Massachusetts offered students who exited the bilingual program in 5th grade the option of attending the middle school two-way immersion program or a language arts course for native speakers (de Jong, 2006). Innovative programming can combine subtractive models with other models to achieve an additive bilingual outcome.

Smith (2002) and Smith and Arnot-Hopffler (1998) describe how one school with a bilingual program extended the use of Spanish through a Spanish-medium after-school program, music and art classes taught in and through Spanish, and oral history projects with Spanish-dominant elders in the community. The use of Spanish was embedded in authentic tasks and drew on the community's linguistic and cultural funds of knowledge. This purposeful use of the Spanish language increased the status of the language as well as instructional time in the minority language.

Offering minority languages at the secondary level as a "foreign" language elective has been a more common strategy for continued minority language maintenance (Clyne, Isaakidi, Liem, & Hunt, 2004; Roca & Colombi, 2003). While less common languages often have to compete with more popular foreign languages, the inclusion of these languages is an important step in assigning formal status in the curriculum to minority languages and thus increasing their status. Chesterton, Seigler-Peters, Moran, and Piccioli (2004) describe efforts in Australia to increase language competence for students by implementing a grade 5–8 sequence of language classes. The Language Continuity Initiative involves nine languages, including Chinese, German, Indonesian, and Italian. Heritage language classes can also sometimes be formally linked with advanced placement classes or the International Baccalaureate program in an effort to legitimate these programs and offer more options for bilingual learners.

Community-based language schools also increasingly play an important role in bilingual proficiency development. Even though these programs take place outside of formal schooling, they provide access to instruction in the students' native languages and cultures. Sometimes also referred to as complementary schools, these settings provide a linguistic and cultural counterweight to predominantly English instruction in school (Conteh, Martin, & Robertson, 2007; Wei, 2006). These bilingual settings have become important sites for crossing linguistic and cultural borders. Links between formal schools and these community-run classes can support the development of multilingual repertoires and identities (Creese, Bhatt, Bhojani, & Martin, 2006; Martin, Bhatt, Bhojani, & Creese, 2006).

Alternate, program-like, systematically organized pathways to bi- or multilingualism are creative solutions in diverse contexts where the choice of an additive bilingual education model may not be imminent. They demonstrate the commitment of a district, school, or community to the value of bilingualism and biliteracy and their willingness to think "outside the box" to still engage in practices that reflect this value to the greatest extent possible in their particular context.

WHAT ABOUT SUBTRACTIVE PROGRAM ENVIRONMENTS?

The Principle of Promoting Additive Bi/Multilingualism takes on different forms in contexts where the societal language dominates because of the selection of a subtractive program model (without any language maintenance component), or when students and teachers come from many different linguistic and cultural backgrounds (multilingual schools). Aiming for equal status of the two (or more) languages is more difficult in subtractive bilingual or monolingual approaches because the higher status of and focus on learning English is inherent in its design.

The choice of TBE program does not imply a school environment that ignores the linguistic and cultural resources of students and parents. School staff can ensure that the school is a welcoming place for bilingual families by providing signage in multiple languages (e.g., welcome signs) and making sure that school communications and meetings are translated for parents (Gravelle, 1996). The administration at Carson Elementary School in Chicago, for example, ensured that the TBE program was fully integrated into the whole school (Education Alliance, 2000). They provided a multicultural learning environment for all students through curricular choices and school-wide activities. Though students' bilingual repertoires will be more limited, a TBE program does not have to take place in an assimilationist environment and devalue diversity. Embedding the TBE program in a broader context and approach that affirms students' linguistic and cultural identities throughout their school career can lead to educational practices that are more additive in nature rather than those that replace or displace students' languages and cultural experiences. At Carson Elementary, the three principles combined (i.e., affirming identities, additive bilingualism, and integration) provided a counter to the subtractive force of the TBE program.

Increasing Language Status in Non-Dual-Language Education Classrooms

Not all districts can implement extensive bilingual or multilingual programs. Sometimes this is an ideological decision, sometimes it results from a lack of resources. At other times, the student population is so diverse that it is impossible to cluster a sufficient number of students to establish a bilingual program. The Principle of Promoting Additive Bi/Multilingualism applies to these contexts as well. The sections that follow give some examples of how teachers can engage with this principle at the classroom level.

BILINGUAL TEACHERS IN SUBTRACTIVE ENVIRONMENTS

Even when bilingualism is not promoted through program-wide decisions, bilingual teachers can find ways to elevate the status of the minority language in their classrooms. In a case study of a bilingual teacher who proactively countered the hegemony of English in her classroom, Shannon (1995) notes that she maintained linguistic equity by ensuring similar quantity and quality of books in both languages, by using the minority language for similar social and academic purposes as English, and by insisting on high-demanding tasks in both languages.

Bilingual teachers can use bilingual teaching strategies to make instruction more comprehensible, engage students in cognitively challenging materials, and legitimize students' native languages as resources for learning. Freeman and Freeman (2000) recommend the *preview-view-review strategy* to teach complex content-area concepts to bilingual learners. Key concepts are introduced in the students' first language (preview), students work with those concepts in English (view), and then students review those concepts in their first language. The preview and review portions of the activity/ lesson/thematic unit could be facilitated by the bilingual teacher, teaching assistant, or tutor. Teachers can also structure the preview activities so that the bilingual learner works with a more competent bilingual peer to negotiate the meaning of that content area concept in his or her first language. The preview can be negotiated orally or it can draw on texts written in the native language; these native language texts might be commercially made, made by the teacher or student, or found on the Internet. For example, a unit on matter may first organize students into native language groups and elicit from students their experiences with liquids, solids, and gas in their native languages. During the view phase, the teacher can structure activities in which bilingual learners are integrated with English-speaking peers and use English to negotiate the meaning of the academic content that they were learning about in separate native language groups. In the unit on matter, the teacher may ask students to conduct experiments and write down their observations in English, using writing scaffolds for beginning writers. For the review phase, the teacher groups bilingual learners together again to reinforce and extend their learning in their native languages. In our example, the teacher could ask students to share their understandings of what matter is, the forms of matter, and how matter changes. Note that this strategic activity structure can simultaneously address the principles of affirming identities, promoting additive bi/multilingualism, and fostering integration. Both monolingual and bilingual teachers can use this approach in English-medium and bilingual education contexts.

Even in English-medium programs, the native language can be given a significant role. In a study of structured English immersion programs, Lucas and Katz (1994) found that creative use of the students' native languages contributed to program effectiveness. Students used their native languages to assist or tutor each other, to write, or to interact socially. Teachers used the native languages to check for comprehension, provide explanations, and interact socially with the students. Similar patterns have been noted in structured English immersion programs after the passage of English-only laws. Students' native languages were used to link to vocabulary and prior knowledge, to explain more abstract content to ensure access to grade-level appropriate content, to elicit student responses, and to build students' self-confidence (de Jong, 2008b; Manyak, 2002).

ADDITIVE BILINGUALISM IN MULTILINGUAL ENVIRONMENTS

Multilingual settings are becoming more and more common. New and more varied (im)migration patterns have resulted in even more linguistically and culturally diverse contexts. When teachers and students speak many different languages, the implementation of a bilingual program is generally not feasible. The societal language tends to become a lingua franca for communication, strengthening the dominant position of the language. In the absence of the formal support of a bilingual program design or large numbers of native language speakers, the goal of additive bilingualism can be challenging to reach. To counter the hegemonic role of English in these inherently more subtractive contexts, taking an additive bilingual stance becomes even more important. While monolingual teachers in particular may feel restricted in what they can do, especially with beginning language learners and parents, they can make several linguistic choices that value and affirm the language resources that students and parents bring to school.

To engage bilingual learners in a wide range of literacy activities that draw on the linguistic and cultural resources learners bring to school, Cummins recommends that teachers have students write dual language books or what he calls *identity texts*. He and his colleagues describe a multilingual literacies project implemented by monolingual English-speaking teachers working in linguistically and culturally diverse English-medium schools in Toronto (Cummins, et al., 2005; Cummins, Campoy, Ada, Winsler, & Bleiker, 2006). These teachers invited their students to write about topics that are aligned with the regular content-area instruction but written in English and their heritage language. Teachers organize students into same language groups (e.g., bilingual Urdu/English speakers in one group, bilingual Bengali/English speakers in another group), and students draw on each others' language and literacy strengths in English and their heritage language to write their books in two languages. Students publish their dual language books in a hard copy that becomes part of a multilingual library of student-made books for the school, and students publish their books on the Web. Publication on the Web facilitates students' development of computer literacies and allows the books to reach a wider audience.[1] Students also participated in multilingual language and literacy surveys and multilingual math activities (Schechter & Cummins, 2003). These activities reflect the staff's attitude that it is not sufficient to merely tolerate the presence of the students' native languages. They seek opportunities to make multilingualism visible in the curriculum and in the school and extend children's multilingual repertoires without the benefit of the presence of a bilingual program.

Finally, regardless of the setting, it is important for teachers to consider how they talk about bilingualism to their students and parents. Do they present it as an asset that is important to maintain and use as a resource or as interfering with learning English or confusing? Parents often look to school personnel for guidance on language use at home, and how teachers respond to these requests for information and assistance matters greatly. In a Canadian study, parents began to question the value of bilingualism as a result of their interactions with the school (Pacini-Ketchabaw, Bernhard, & Freire, 2001). One parent, Ms. Valenzuela, explained in Spanish:

> The teachers know that I speak Spanish with the children at home. One teacher told me that I had to speak English with them because they do not

---

[1]Go to http://thornwood.peelschools.org/Dual/ for detailed description of this process and examples of student-made dual language books in a variety of languages.

pronounce it properly. She also told me that my son needed to speak more English because of his poor pronunciation, and that I was not helping them by speaking Spanish at home.

When consulted, teachers can take the opportunity to affirm the importance of the native language for social and cognitive development. They can encourage literacy practices in the native languages and help create additive "bridges" between home and school (Soto, Smrekar, & Nekcovei, 1999), for example, by using dual language textbooks (Ernst-Slavit & Mulhern, 2003; D. Freeman & Freeman, 2000; Van Sluys & Reinier, 2006).

In multilingual settings, teachers can still advocate for native language tutors, acquire native language materials for their classroom, learn some basic phrases in their students' native languages, ask their students to share and teach their languages, and create opportunities for students to use their native languages with each other socially as well as for academic learning (Gravelle, 1996; Irujo, 2005). While the societal language will dominate multilingual classrooms, the use of the dominant language as a lingua franca does not have to imply a monolingual stance. School personnel have a wide range of choices available to them to validate minority languages as a resource for learning and affirming identities.

Reflecting on the Principle of Promoting Additive Bi/Multilingualism in Practice

Educators seeking to implement the Principle of Promoting Additive Bi/Multilingualism can use the following questions to reflect on their teaching practices.

- *Program structure.* Which language is used for what purposes and for how much time at each grade? What innovative programmatic approaches are implemented to support optimal multilingual competence development?

- *Curriculum decisions.* Are multilingual materials being used and displayed? Are the materials in both languages of high quality?

- *Pedagogical decisions.* Do teachers use bilingual teaching strategies? Are there meaningful opportunities for students to use their native languages as well as their second language? Does literacy instruction build on students' linguistic resources (e.g., identity texts)?

Note that these questions can also guide research. The list, of course, is not exhaustive and other areas could easily be added. For example, at the school level, educators can take a "linguistic inventory" of their school to see how languages are reflected in home-school communications, posters, flyers, and libraries, and in their classrooms. Following the holistic perspective on bilingualism that this principle represents, teachers can also examine their assessment tools to see whether their approach considers performance in the totality of the students' linguistic repertoires and not just in the majority language.

The Principle of Promoting Additive Bi/Multilingualism considers how educators' decisions promote the visibility, status, and treatment of languages other than the standard language within a school. It looks at what kinds of opportunities are created for using, developing, displaying, and engaging with multiple languages. It examines how knowing and being able to use multiple languages is displayed not as a hidden competence but as integral and visible part of the curriculum and instructional practices. Table 10.1 lists some of the questions teachers can ask to assess how their policies and practices align with this principle in their classrooms and implications for research.

TABLE 10.1	
The Principle of Promoting Additive Bilingualism at the Classroom Level	
Equity: Do my answers to these questions or inquiries apply to all my students and instruction in both languages?	
	Promoting Additive Bi/Multilingualism
Curriculum	How do I display and use materials in multiple languages, with particular attention to the languages of my students and the local community?
	How does the quality of the materials I use in the students' native languages compare to the quality of materials I use in the majority language?
	How does the quality of the curriculum in the minority language compare to the quality of the curriculum in the majority language?
	How do I address any discrepancies that I identify in the curriculum and materials that I use in my classroom?
Pedagogy & classroom interactions	How do I use bilingual teaching strategies (including multilingual identity texts)?
	How do I encourage students to use their bilingualism for learning?
	How are my instructional strategies for teaching in and through the minority and majority language "current" and sensitive to differences between the languages?
	How do I encourage students to use their native language?
	How do I communicate the value of bilingualism?
Assessment	How do I incorporate assessment in the native language?
	How do I consider my students' cognitive and language/literacy abilities in both languages together?

Educators make a wide range of decisions that can reflect an additive bilingual stance. Though some of these choices are more easily actualized in a school with an additive bilingual education model, many are within reach in multilingual contexts with a commitment to additive bilingual environments for all students.

Policy to Practice: Challenges to Language Status Equalization

The policy (goal of language equalization) to practice (achieving equal status) link is complex. On one hand, sociopolitical realities can interfere with even the best intentions. The power of English as the dominant language in U.S. society and its immediately perceived economic, educational, and political benefits is difficult to counter and requires constant vigilance about issues related to linguistic equity. On the other hand, policies implemented out of a commitment to linguistic equity may constrain other practices for bilingual learners. Both issues are discussed in the sections that follow.

(UN)EQUAL LANGUAGE STATUS ISSUES IN TWI PROGRAMS

TWI programs can elevate the status of the minority language more successfully than many other programs because of the way they align additive bilingual goals and program design (language allocation) for majority and minority language speakers. Especially when TWI involves the entire school (as opposed to a strand within the school), it is easier to establish bilingualism as the norm for the school. Even in committed TWI programs, however, the sociopolitical asymmetry that exists in U.S. society between English (high status position) and the minority language (low status position) re-emerges in TWI programs (Amrein & Peña, 2000; Freeman, 1998).

One area where discrepancies between intent (policy) and implementation (practice) have emerged is assessment. To achieve equal language status, teachers in TWI programs would ideally be engaged in similar assessments across the two languages. In reality, assessment in many TWI programs occurs in English but not as consistently in the minority language. Standardized achievement data to report to parents and legislators may be collected in English, whereas progress in the minority language is documented mostly through informal assessments. Such differences affect curriculum and instruction because they hold teachers accountable for learning in quite different ways. One teacher at Oyster Bilingual School in Washington, DC, one of the oldest TWI programs in the nation, commented, "A common complaint at Oyster is that the English teachers get stuck with all the paper work, and have to carry the curriculum load, while the Spanish teachers pretty much don't have to answer to anyone" (Freeman, 1998, p. 185).

The dominance of English assessment has been reinforced by the passage of the No Child Left Behind Act (Evans & Hornberger, 2005), as well as individual English-only state laws, such as Proposition 227 (Linton, 2007). For many TWI programs, the current accountability system with its severe penalties for not meeting certain annual achievement goals (as measured in English) presents a professional dilemma where assessment practices are not sensitive to patterns of second language development. In response to these pressures, administrators may be tempted to decrease instructional time in the minority language. Minority language instruction can also be undermined more subtly when after-school programming for the purpose of helping prepare or remediate for the mandated state test is provided only in English or when in-class test preparation may occur in English, regardless of the "planned" or intended language of instruction. Strong (and public) accountability for learning that occurs in English without parallel assessment and accountability structures in the minority language does not communicate equal value of what occurs in each language (Amrein & Peña, 2000).

The challenge of equal language status can also occur in the acquisition of material and human resources. Material resources such as books (fiction, nonfiction, reference materials) or instructional materials (software, teacher sample materials) are still published primarily in English, even though the availability of other-language resources has increased. Similarly, support personnel, such as Title I or Reading Recovery teachers, volunteer tutors, or special education teachers are more likely to be monolingual in English than bilingual. As a result, these services may be readily available in English but not in the minority language. This, in turn, affects instructional practices. TWI teachers in a well-established program commented that skill-based grouping for reading was possible in English but not in Spanish because of the lack of assessment tools and resource teachers, such as Title I and Reading Recovery teachers.

> [The students] take so many tests to see what their reading level in English is and based on that, they're grouped by ability. . . . But in Spanish, we don't have the results of any test that shows us where the kids are. . . . We don't have someone who will come in and take this group of kids based on their level. Basically, you just have the classroom teacher. (de Jong & Howard, 2009, p. 87)

These examples show how challenging it is to counter the dominance of English in U.S. society, even under the best of circumstances. Equalizing language status requires a high level of awareness about linguistic equity at the program, curriculum, and instructional levels and a proactive stance from staff to mediate between the sociopolitical realities and school practices.

LINGUISTIC COMPARTMENTALIZATION

A practice that has become almost axiomatic in bilingual education is the compartmentalization of languages, that is, keeping the languages of instruction separate (García, Skutnabb-Kangas, & Torres-Guzmán, 2006). In distinguishing "dual language programs" (additive bilingual education programs; see Chapter 5) from other bilingual approaches, such **language compartmentalization** is presented as a defining characteristic of these programs (in addition to the goal of bilingualism and biliteracy with a minimum of 50% instructional time in the minority language) (Howard, et al., 2003). In TWI programs, the two languages are kept separate by person, space, time, or curriculum (Hadi-Tabassum, 2005; Leung, 2006; Soltero, 2004). Foreign language classes for majority language speakers equally encourage the exclusive use of the target language for communication inside and outside the classroom (Cook, 2001; Macaro, 2001). Although there are several reasons for this recommendation, the sections that follow explore how the practice of maintaining separate linguistic environments may also undermine the creation of learning environments where bilingual skills are used and bilingual abilities are explored.

Creating Language Boundaries

Irujo (1998) notes that the recommendation to "stick" with one language "for sustained periods without translation or recourse to the alternative language" (p. 95) has been advocated for bilingual programs since the early 1970s. While the strong version (ban the native language) of the monolingual principle is perhaps too extreme, the weaker version (avoid and minimize the native language when teaching the second language) has been an accepted maxim in second/foreign language classroom since the 1880s (Cook, 2001). The expectation is that second/foreign language teachers will use a comprehensive set of second language teaching strategies to make their instruction comprehensible, avoid resorting to the native language, and encourage their students to use only the target language.

The monolingual principle is invoked for several reasons. It can be an attempt to replicate first (one) language acquisition processes where the child learns from receiving comprehensible input in the language and interacting with and through that language only (Krashen, 1985). In this framework, the use of the students' native language is seen as slowing down successful second language acquisition, limiting opportunities to be exposed to and use the target language for communicative purposes. Especially in foreign language teaching, learners generally have little access to the target language outside the classroom, so opportunities to use it within the classroom must be maximized (Macaro, 2001). While students' use of their native language may be tolerated (at least at the beginning levels), teachers are expected to avoid any code-switching. Mixed language input (and output) is seen as leading to an inability to function without mixing in either language.

Language compartmentalization is also advocated to protect the minority language against the encroachment of the dominant language. Without intervention, teacher and student language use in bilingual classrooms tends to privilege the dominant language. Observing a high school civics class, Milk (in a 1982 study cited in Milk, 1990) found that the only function for which Spanish was used equally often as English was elicitation, asking students to respond; in all other language functions English dominated. Studies across contexts have found that language use in bilingual settings favors the dominant language (Gurthie, 1984; Legarreta, 1977; Milk, 1990). If the goal of the program is to develop competence in two languages, these patterns of language use will undermine the development of competence in the minority language. Clear allocation of a separate time block and space for each language is one way to try to resist the hegemony of the dominant language.

A third argument focuses on translation in the classroom. The use of the native language when it means direct translation has uniformly been strongly discouraged. As Saville and Troike (1971) remind us, "when concepts are taught twice, children tend to 'tune out' the lessons in their second language; they learn not to listen, because they don't need to" (Saville & Troike, 1971, p. 27). Knowing that a translation is forthcoming may discourage second language learners from actively engaging with the language and can impede their second language development. To avoid this learning situation, teachers are discouraged from switching between languages during instruction.

Setting language boundaries is seen by some as a necessary condition for successful second language acquisition. Monolingual environments are more supportive of second language development, that is, they provide more opportunities to use the target language rather than relying on the native language. Especially in the context of dual language programs, such as TWI programs, separating the languages is also a way to protect minority language from the dominance of the societal language. It protects the use of the language by insisting on monolingual environments in both languages. By allocating specific and equal (or more) time to the minority language, TWI programs are able to value the minority language.

Diffusing Linguistic Borders

A strict language allocation or language separation policy is increasingly criticized for not reflecting the integrative nature of bilingual development (Cummins, 2008; Hadi-Tabassum, 2005). The native language plays an important role in second language learning as an efficient resource for communication, content learning, successful collaboration, and language/literacy development (Cook, 2001; Lin, 2006). It enhances the learning process, affirms students' identities and affiliations, and bridges different languages and cultures (Liang, 2006; Reyes, 2004). Using their entire linguistic repertoire, including code-switching or translanguaging, is natural for bilinguals and serves specific communicative functions.

Muller and Baetens Beardsmore (2004) provide an interesting multilingual vignette of the European hour in a European school in Belgium. In the early grades, the content of the European hour is mostly cultural (e.g., cooking). Instruction focuses on creating a comfortable and cooperative learning atmosphere where students work together toward specific goals. In their study, Muller and Baetens Beardsmore document how one teacher (a native speaker of French with competence in English and German) negotiated her interaction with her students who came from the Danish, Italian, Greek, English, and German streams within the school. Although the teacher's language (French) dominated, she acknowledged the various languages spoken by the students by inviting translations and using individual words in the other languages that students used. Both teacher and students asked for clarification or help to explain things in French (the target language) as well as the other languages. Code-switching was a communicative strategy that allowed everyone to use all linguistic resources available during the lesson.

Insisting on a strict separation of languages counters the children's multilingual realities as they negotiate their lives across and within linguistic and ethnic borders with their peers in school and outside (Dirim & Hieronymus, 2003; Rampton, 2005), as well as with adults through language brokering activities (Morales & Hanson, 2005; Orellana, Dorner, & Pulido, 2003). The practice also does not reflect the interrelatedness of the two language systems (Cummins, 1979; Genesee, Paradis, & Crago, 2003; Grosjean, 1989). Strict adherence to language compartmentalization has been criticized for returning to a more fractional view of bilingualism rather than taking a holistic view of bilingual development (Gumperz & Cook-Gumperz, 2005; Hadi-Tabassum, 2005). Keeping the two languages separate for instructional purposes is a highly artificial practice for bilingual individuals.

Reflecting on Language Alternation

If the goal of the program is the development of academic and social bilingualism, students need to engage with and have meaningful interactions with the linguistic repertoire they are expected to develop in both languages. Multilingual practices can enhance and accelerate this goal when students are encouraged to develop metalinguistic awareness about their languages and how language use varies according to topic and context (Cummins, 2008). Teaching for transfer includes writing bilingual books, exploring cognates, and connecting with sister classes that use both languages (Cummins, 2005). Another activity is to ask students to translate a poem from one language to the other. After they have given their translation, students then compare their translation to an official translation of the poem. Reflecting on the differences between the translations engenders a rich discussion about vocabulary choices and semantic relationships (see also Escamilla, Hopewell, Geisler, & Ruiz, 2007).

These insights suggest that a more thoughtful approach to language alternation in the classroom is needed. Research suggests that the role of code-switching may vary in keeping with the pedagogical focus. When access to content and accomplishing content-based tasks is the main focus, the use of multiple codes does not appear problematic and may better facilitate learning. Jacobson (1990) found that code-switching (not direct translation) aided math achievement for ELLs. Bilingual teachers can focus on communicating the content and "when addressing the whole class they switch at the level of concepts and not in the middle of the sentence" (Brisk, 1991, p. 119). Brisk gives the example of Helaine, one of the bilingual teachers, to illustrate this practice.

HELAINE: What are you measuring? *Teresa, que estás midiendo?*

TERESA: *Ángulos*

HELAINE: *Cuál son los dos ángulos?* Show me two angles.

Improved access to content learning through rich native language semantic explorations can aid in understanding subject matter discourse patterns and content in the second language (Liang, 2006). Milk (1990) argues, "when the primary goal . . . is academic content, including development of higher level concepts and completion of cognitively demanding tasks, prohibition of access to the native language becomes a highly debatable proposition."

When biliterate development is the focus, the exclusion of the other language as a resource for learning does not seem necessary or desirable. Emergent bilingual writers use linguistic resources from their native and second languages as they brainstorm, draft, and revise their writing products. For young writers, cross-linguistic transfer is a natural process that plays an important role in scaffolding output in the second language (Brisk, 2006; de la Luz Reyes & Halcon, 2001; Dworin, 2003; Gort, 2006; Huerta-Macías & Quintero, 1992; Peréz, 2004; Reyes & Azuara, 2008). One area where monolingually designed classroom environments appear important is in second language oral language development (Brisk, 2006). When the teacher uses one language consistently, students will have more oral input and opportunities for practice and will be better able to push their language output (Saunders & O'Brien, 2006; Swain, 1995).

If the goal of the program is the development of academic and social bilingualism, students must engage with and have meaningful interactions with the linguistic repertoire they are expected to develop in both languages. Multilingual practices do not hinder this development; in fact, they can enhance and accelerate it as students are encouraged to transfer what they know from their native language and develop metalinguistic awareness about their languages and how language use varies according to topic and situational context.

Shifting Perspectives: The Language of Additive Bi/Multilingualism

The Principle of Promoting Additive Bi/Multilingualism draws educators' attention to issues of language status and linguistic equity when working with bilingual learners. It reflects the combined efforts toward overtly legitimizing languages other than the dominant language as languages of communication, of teaching and learning, in addition to providing access to high quality instruction in the majority language. Organizing practices with the Principle of Promoting Additive Bi/Multilingualism in mind can be challenging in the face of the sociopolitical realities around a largely monolingually oriented society like that of the United States. Even in additive bilingual contexts such as TWI programs, leakage between policy and practice occurs. Protecting the use of the minority language within the boundaries of the school, program or classroom is therefore an important issue. At the same time, a strict policy of linguistic compartmentalization fails to affirm the holistic nature of bilingualism and the bilingual realities that children live in. Indeed, extreme separation, which may cause "students not to experience bilingualism" (Brisk, 2006, p. 143), runs counter to the interconnectedness of bilinguals' language systems and their experienced cultural and linguistic realities.

This chapter has emphasized that language status equalization is not merely a matter of the presence or the absence of those practices that achieve equal status between two or more languages. Rather, the Principle of Promoting Additive Bi/Multilingualism is better framed as a process and an outcome to continually strive for. The Principle of Promoting Additive Bi/Multilingualism therefore challenges scholars to better understand how multilingual repertoires can be developed for different populations and under different conditions (Cziko, 1992).

Providing equitable access to high quality instruction and multilingual competence development requires a range of opportunities. Programmatic decisions or the decision for teachers or students to use multiple languages within one classroom or lesson need to be considered with respect to specific program and instructional goals. The multilingual practices of the European common hour, for example, were congruent with the teacher's focus on communication and building positive intergroup relations. The principle stresses that, within a holistic, additive bilingual approach, asking whether bilingual strategies should be used does not make much sense. Rather we need to better understand when and what kind of alternating languages or translanguaging practices will be beneficial for which students and for what purposes, such as identity affirmation, content learning, literacy development, and oral language development (Ustunel & Seedhouse, 2005). Within the context of promoting additive bi/multilingualism, then, questions about when, how, and under what conditions do teachers use both languages in order to support bilingual (or multilingual) development alongside with content development need to be explored by policy makers, teachers, and researchers (Lin, 2006, p. 292).

CHAPTER 10
Discussion & Activities

Critical Issues

1. Table 10.1 presents some indicators of the Principle of Promoting Additive Bi/Multilingualism for the classroom level. Besides doing a linguistic inventory as mentioned in the chapter, what might you look for when applying the lens of this principle at the *school* level? What about the *district* level?

2. The monolingual principle has dominated much of foreign and second language teaching. What has been your own policy with regard to your language use and that of your students? Where do you insist on monolingualism and where are you more flexible about the use of multiple languages? What is your rationale?

Application and Reflection

3. One question educators must ask themselves is, Whose language or languages are valued in our school? Look at your own school or visit a school with ELLs or nonstandard English speakers and make an inventory of the "linguistic and cultural landscape" of the school.
   - Find out the distribution of the students' languages spoken at home for all students, not just ELLs. Ask how many school personnel are bilingual and what their function is in the school.
   - Where are languages other than standard English displayed? Which languages are displayed? Where are they heard? Does the school send any formal communications (parent letters, report cards, notices of events) in languages other than English? Who is responsible for translating these notices?
   - Visit the school library and ask about books or audiovisual materials in languages other than English. What is their policy? Where are the books and materials located and displayed? How many books are there and in which languages? What kinds of books are they (fiction, nonfiction) and who do they target (early childhood, upper elementary, adults)?
   - If there are bilingual or multilingual materials, are they comparable in quality (and quantity) to materials in English? How are they displayed?
   - Does the district or school make an effort to hire and retain bilingual teachers and support personnel, such as social workers or school psychologists?

- Visit a classroom. What evidence do you see of the multilingual and multicultural population on the walls, in the classroom library, in textbooks?
4. Consider Table 10.1 and Figure 10.1. In what ways does your classroom or school already meet the goal of language status equalization? What could you do to align your practices more closely with these goals?
5. Do you see or hear your students code-switch in their oral language or their writing? What purpose does this serve for them as a tool for learning and building relationships? As a teacher, how do you or could you tap into these bilingual skills? (If it is difficult to observe your students, interview them about their bilingual practices.)

Recommended Readings

Cazden, C. B. (2001). *Classroom discourse: The language of teaching and learning.* Portsmouth: Heinemann.

> *This book examines the role of language in the classroom and how teachers and students shape learning through language. It also illustrates how these discourses are culturally bound and the implications for research and practice.*

Heller, M., & Martin-Jones, M. (Eds.). (2000). *Voices of authority: Education and linguistic difference.* Westport: Ablex.

> *This book shows how language status differences and access to effective schooling intersect. Examples from international contexts (ranging from the United Kingdom to Botswana) illustrate the power of language decisions in the classroom.*

Lin, A. (2006). Beyond linguistic purism in language-in-education policy and practice: Exploring bilingual pedagogies in a Hong Kong science classroom. *Language and Education, 20*(4), 287–305.

> *This article offers a compelling argument for changing research paradigms when looking at multiple language use in the classroom. The author's research reframes the question from whether to when code-switching is used and examines how code-switching supports learning.*

Structuring for Integration

GUIDING QUESTIONS

- *What are the benefits of homogeneous and heterogeneous grouping by language or ethnicity?*
- *What is the difference between integration and assimilation?*
- *What factors may undermine the linguistic benefits of integrating native and non-native speakers? How can teachers mediate these patterns?*

KEY TERMS

educational segregation
linguistic equity

> Educators who apply the *Principle of Structuring for Integration* establish inclusive policies and practices that encourage equal-status relationships among and participation by different constituencies. They take linguistic and cultural diversity and the implications for effective practices as their starting point for decision making.

The Principle of Structuring for Integration emphasizes issues of equal status and participation within a context of affirming identities and additive bi/ multilingualism to inform policies and practices. Providing such equitable learning environments for all students when students, teachers, and the school community come from linguistically and culturally diverse backgrounds is not easy. This chapter focuses on the challenge of creating equitable learning environments when integrating minority and majority language speakers.

Integration, Segregation, and Assimilation

In discussions of bilingual learners, integration relates to two other often-used concepts: segregation and assimilation. To understand the tensions that may emerge when implementing the Principle of Structuring for Integration, it is important to understand how segregation and assimilation have shaped classroom practices for bilingual learners in quite different ways.

THE COST OF SEGREGATION

Much of the schooling of bilingual learners (and its research base) has largely taken place outside what has been considered "the mainstream." During the 1920s through the 1950s, separate schools were created for various groups, such as Mexican American and Native American students (Donato & Garcia, 1992; Donato, Mechaca, & Valencia, 1991; Gonzales, 1990). Later, schools resorted to the implementation of separate programs within schools, including ESL and bilingual programs. By the 1970s, specialized programming was the most common remedy to meet civil rights requirements after *Lau v. Nichols* (1974). Federal and state legislation and policies and bilingual education advocates did not ignore the issue of students' **educational segregation**, i.e.,clustering a particular group of students in designated programs or schools. Sustained segregation in a bilingual or ESL program was to be avoided. Some educators warned that separate bilingual programs would result in bilingual tracking and thus exclude bilingual students "from vital resources, services, and life experiences essential to children's ultimate survival in a competitive society" (Melendez, 1981; cited in Castellanos, 1983, p. 147).

Rather than considering more integrated program models, educators focused on limiting program participation to a certain period (e.g., 3 years) to avoid long-term segregation and emphasized a rapid exit from the program into the standard curriculum classroom. This "in-or-out" approach (Gándara & Merino, 1993) mirrored other programs that were embraced during this period in response to the increased diversity in public schools, such as separate special education resource rooms, compensatory programs for students struggling in reading or math, and tracking students in separate classes based on their academic abilities (Fass, 1989; Minow, 1985).[1]

In the absence of an integrated approach, most bilingual (and many ESL

---

[1]Establishing separate programs for only ELLs was further reinforced by funding formulas and program evaluations. Federal or state funding for bilingual or ESL programs was not allocated to include fluent English speakers in the program, thus reducing a district's incentive to implement more integrated programs. The American Institute of Research heavily criticized bilingual program directors for allowing bilingual students who had been classified as proficient in English to continue to participate in the program (Danoff, 1978).

programs) have largely operated at the periphery of their schools, generally with limited resources (Olsen, 1997; Valdés, 2001). Research on this issue is limited; few studies have taken a program-within-a-school approach, although anecdotal evidence abounds with reports by bilingual and ESL teachers about teaching in closets or being relegated to the basement or separate buildings (Nieto, 2002). This kind of program marginalization had significant consequences. Being marginalized negatively affected program quality (fewer resources, discrepancies between bilingual and general education curriculum and pedagogy) and the status of bilingual/ESL teachers whose expertise was not valued and whose voices were silenced (de Jong, 1996; Lemberger, 1997; Valenzuela, 1999). One bilingual program teacher summarized her experiences as follows:

> People looked upon my class as a remedial class. It was just a temporary something to fill in until these kids knew enough English. There was no respect for what we were doing or why . . . [and] the students are treated like second class citizens and don't really belong. . . . Little things would give those messages, a performance would be happening for second grade classes and only regular second grade classes would get the announcement and not the TBE second grade classes. Things like that. Second grade would plan a fieldtrip that didn't include the TBE classes, things like that. I mean, it was constant messages saying you don't count, you're not really second grade. It was just constantly those messages, you don't count, you're not up to par, you're not one of us. To me and to the kids. (de Jong, 1996, p. 55)

This kind of program shaped the schooling experiences of the students who remained socially and academically isolated from the rest of the school and were treated as outsiders.

Unless bilingual education is conceptualized as an integrated model, it will, by definition, separate bilingual learners from nonbilingual program students. When separate programs are accompanied by a remedial and compensatory view and implemented with insufficient human and material resources, the homogeneous grouping can easily lead to marginalization, tracking bilingual learners into low-quality programs or courses (Olsen, 1997). The existence of integrated models and schools where the bilingual program is fully integrated does show that the choice of bilingual program does necessarily mean marginalization. However, the history of bilingual education has demonstrated that most such programs lead to isolation, fragmentation, and stigmatization. Because of this history, (language) minority student segregation is considered detrimental for bilingual learners and seen as diametrically opposed to the more inclusive classroom. Segregation can come at a high cost if the group is treated inequitably or their program is assigned a low-status position with access to fewer resources than other programs.

THE COST OF ASSIMILATION

Some have argued that the best solution for language minority schooling is therefore to place bilingual learners in the standard curriculum classroom and educate them alongside native English speakers. Such linguistically heterogeneous settings carry important benefits. As outlined in Chapters 3 and 8, majority and minority language student integration can support the building of positive cross-cultural relationships and overcome stereotypes and negative attitudes toward members of other groups. Bringing native and non-native speakers of a language together can also extend opportunities for language use and meaningful second language learning. Native speakers are important language models who can scaffold language learning for their second language learning peers, and their presence encourages authentic communicative language use (Christian, 1996; Howard, Sugarman, Christian, Lindholm-Leary, & Rogers, 2007; Lantolf, 2000). Moreover, placing ELLs in the standard curriculum classroom can ensure better access to the regular curriculum content.

Standard curriculum classroom placement avoids the physical segregation of bilingual learners and has the potential of providing effective second language learning environments. For such placement to be integrative and equitable, however, it cannot occur without significant changes to the mainstream classroom setting. Early on in the history of ELL schooling, Cárdenas warned, "the placement of a child in a strange and alien cultural, linguistic, or economic instructional setting is no less an injustice or a barrier to learning than his placement in a segregated setting (p. 62; cited in González, 1979, p. 26).

Teachers must change their practices in order to avoid inequities resulting from standard curriculum placement. Early studies in multi-ethnic and linguistically diverse classrooms noted that, without such changes, the following interaction patterns emerge: fewer student initiations, fewer turns given to students, less (positive) teacher feedback, and less engagement in extended conversations for language minority students than for fluent majority language speakers, even when the minority students were fluent in the dominant, societal language (Biggs & Edwards, 1991; Cazden, 1990; Laosa, 1978; Losey, 1995). When lack of proficiency in the language of instruction is added to the mix, further disadvantages may arise. Those still in the process of learning the dominant language lose out when mainstream teachers do not (or do not know how to) make the accommodations necessary to meet their linguistic and cultural needs (Harper & de Jong, 2004).

Unfortunately, relatively few standard curriculum teachers have received any formal professional development related to ELLs (Menken & Antunez, 2001) and are not prepared to work with these students (Gándara, Maxwell-

Jolly, & Driscoll, 2005; Short, 2002a; Walker, Shafer, & Iiams, 2004). As a result, ELLs often find themselves in a classroom with inappropriate (low) expectations or without the language support they need (Harklau, 1999; Harper & Platt, 1998; Schinke-Llano, 1983; Verplaetse, 2000). Verplaetse (2000) documented secondary content teachers' tendency to avoid asking questions of beginning ELLs, reducing their classroom participation and opportunities to use the language. Although significantly more attention is currently paid to general teacher preparation for bilingual learners (Brisk, 2008; Fillmore & Snow, 2002; Lucas & Grinberg, 2008), most classrooms continue to fall short as learning environments for linguistically and culturally diverse students. Without efforts by teachers to facilitate the process of integration with attention to issues of equal status and access, they will continue to do so.

FINDING THE BALANCE: TOWARD INTEGRATION

While the marginalization that has accompanied student segregation clearly comes at a high cost, grouping bilingual learners together can support their cognitive, sociocultural, and linguistic development. If students share a native language, they can more easily draw on native language resources as well as their second language skills for academic and language/literacy development (Anton & DiCamilla, 1999). Grouping them together can provide learning opportunities that placement with fluent speakers of the second language may not allow for. Varonis and Gass (1984) found active meaning negotiation in the second language and extended language use in the interactions among second language learners. They speculate that "shared incompetence" as second language learners may actually lower the anxiety to perform (and be compared to native speakers), leading to more willingness to take risks, ask for clarification, and negotiate the meaning of what the other person has said. Bilingual students often participate more in their bilingual or ESL classroom than in their standard curriculum setting. Flanigan (1988) found that the bilingual student she observed was more verbal and appeared more confident in the ESL classroom. Davidson (1997) describes a bilingual high school student who "often falls silent in integrated settings, not speaking unless spoken to" (p. 28). Being with other bilingual learners appears to be an advantage for the students. Grouping students from the same ethnic and linguistic background can also support the development of stronger (bi)cultural identities (Andersson, 1971; Faltis, 1994). Finally, specialized programs with trained staff can provide targeted support for second language development, a culturally sensitive curriculum, comprehensible content instruction at the students' cognitive and academic level, and more cultural sensitivity from bilingual and bicultural teachers. These teachers can more easily establish meaningful links between home and school.

Separate grouping clearly has some advantages. The early TWI programs recognized the strength of instructional separation in response to differences in student language proficiency levels. When Miami Dade County, Florida, expanded their TWI programs in the 1960s following the success of Coral Way Elementary, school officials varied the amount of time the two groups were taught together (integration) and the amount of time each student spent in each language, in response to his or her English and Spanish speaking abilities. Coral Way Elementary itself initially separated Cuban Spanish speakers and Anglo English speakers for instruction in English and Spanish until 3rd grade for all academic subjects (though not for specials such as art and music). From 4th grade up, students were integrated for all subjects.

The Principle of Structuring for Integration reminds us that grouping bilingual learners homogeneously by language is not an either/or proposition. Careful grouping can benefit bilingual learners by providing a culturally and linguistically responsive learning environment where their learning can be scaffolded and challenged appropriately. The Principle of Structuring for Integration recognizes that neither segregation (with marginalization) nor simple placement of bilingual learners in a mainstream classroom without attention to their specific linguistic and cultural needs will provide an equitable learning environment. Each grouping configuration (homogeneous and heterogeneous) has important linguistic, sociocultural, and academic advantages when done purposefully and thoughtfully.

Segregation and assimilation maintain the same status hierarchy between language majority and language minority students. The differential program status in separate programming adds to the negative impact of segregation by marginalizing students and their learning (Carter & Chatfield, 1986). In assimilative classroom settings, the status hierarchy is maintained by the unequal treatment of language minority students and their linguistic and cultural resources. Without changes, these students are expected to make the adjustments to a classroom that remains organized around dominant cultural and linguistic practices.

The Principle of Structuring for Integration mediates between these two propositions by stressing the importance of equal status relations. When applying this principle, educators balance the benefits of giving specialized attention to linguistic and cultural issues and having a common vision for all learners while avoiding the marginalization of multilingual learners in the classroom and the school community.

Reflecting on the Principle of Structuring for Integration in Practice

The preceding discussion has highlighted some conditions for effectively implementing the Principle of Structuring for Integration by building on the benefits of both homogeneous and heterogeneous groupings and avoiding the pitfalls associated with segregation and assimilation. Educators seeking to implement this principle can reflect on the following questions:

- *School organization*. How are multiple programs, their staff, and their students included into whole school decision-making? How are transitions from one program to another facilitated?

- *Program structure*. How do programs include meaningful opportunities for interaction with teachers and students from other programs?

- *Curriculum decisions*. How is there consistency among grade levels and programs in curriculum content and equal access to materials and other resources to teach? Is the curriculum sufficiently challenging in each program?

- *Pedagogical decisions*. How do all teachers across programs in the school use strategies that acknowledge the strengths and needs of culturally and linguistically diverse students? Do all teachers have the preparation to be able to accomplish this (professional development)?

- *Classroom organization*. How is peer interaction facilitated? Do all students have equal opportunities to participate in small groups as well as in whole class instruction?

Table 11.1 presents some of the questions teachers can ask to assess how their policies and practices align with this principle in their classroom. These questions can also help researchers define their research agendas.

Policy to Practice: Challenges to Student Integration

The presence of native and non-native speakers can be exploited effectively when students are put to work on cooperative learning activities (Cohen, Lotan, Scarloss, & Arellano, 1999; Jacob, Rottenberg, Patrick, & Wheeler, 1996; McGroarty, 1989). This kind of integration typically takes place in a dominant-language setting. In non-TWI integrated bilingual education models, the majority language is the primary instructional language during the integrated time, although bilingual practices (such as bilingual vocabulary

TABLE 11.1		

The Principle of Structuring for Integration at the Classroom Level

Equity: Do my answers to these questions or inquiries apply to all programs, teachers, and students?

	Structuring for Integration
Curriculum	How is my curriculum coordinated with teachers in other programs and grade levels?
	How do I plan and collaborate with other teachers?
	Do different programs have equal access to resources (support personnel, books, equipment)?
Pedagogy & classroom interaction	How do I provide opportunities for peer interaction to build relationships, for language development, and for academic learning?
	How do I make sure that all my students are able to participate meaningfully in whole group and small group configurations?
	How do I make sure that my interactions with my students are equitable according to linguistic background and other variables?
Assessment	How do my assessments reflect a comprehensive definition of outcomes for bilingual learners?
	How do our assessments for bilingual learners compare to our assessments for monolingual learners? Are they equally valid, reliable, and appropriate?
	How are results reported and explained to parents and other constituents?

lists and bilingual worksheets) and grouping of bilingual and non-bilingual students can be used to mediate this monolingual bias (de Jong, 2006). In these kinds of settings, roles and goals are typically unidirectional: the language minority student is the non-native speaker (novice) and the language majority student is the native speaker (expert), and the primary outcome is to use and learn the dominant language.[2]

TWI programs are unique in that they strive to capitalize on the potential of native/non-native speaker integration in the context of an additive bilingual program. Both minority and majority language speakers take on novice and expert roles across the two languages in the program. With their additive bilingual focus, their sensitivity to language status issues, and their

[2]In some "foreign" language classrooms the opposite can occur: a native minority language speaker (e.g., Spanish heritage language speaker) can take on the role of "expert," particularly in oral language use (Blyth, 2003).

explicit commitment to student integration, TWI settings are therefore optimal settings to explore the integration principle.

As more ethnographic research is conducted in TWI programs and classrooms, it has become clear that realizing this potential of integration consistently for all students can be challenging, particularly when the minority language is the language of instruction. As with efforts at language status equalization, sociopolitical realities affect the process of integration. The following sections consider how the linguistic benefits of integration are realized across languages for all students in the TWI program (de Jong & Howard, 2009), and highlight the importance of different acquisition contexts for the two languages in the program.

DIFFERENTIAL ACQUISITION CONTEXTS IN TWI PROGRAMS

TWI programs must meet a dual agenda: a mostly foreign language learning agenda for native English speakers and a second language development agenda for minority language speakers (Valdés, 1997).[3] Despite the many pedagogical similarities between (elementary) foreign and second language teaching, the social and political contexts differs significantly. As a high-status language, English is much more pervasive inside and outside the school environment than the minority language. Thus, while minority language speakers may have access to their native language at home, majority language speakers may have little access to the minority language once they leave the school. One consequence of this sociopolitical reality is that minority students' oral second language skills (in English) develop more rapidly than those of majority students in the minority language (Edelsky & Hudelson, 1978; Montague & Meza-Zaragosa, 1999). Minority language speakers make an early shift to English dominance, while native English speakers in TWI programs continue to be clearly dominant in English (Howard, Christian, & Genesee, 2004).

As a result of these differentiated growth patterns in second language proficiency, minority language TWI teachers are much more likely to teach students with a wide range of oral proficiency and literacy levels, from a beginning non-native speaker to a fluent native speaker. This pattern will lessen but persist across grade levels. In English, the gap between native speakers and second language learners is smaller and is closed more quickly orally and in basic literacy skills (de Jong, 2004b). Negotiating these different

---

[3]The notion of "native speaker" is problematic in TWI programs where students speaking a wide range of English language varieties and minority language varieties are enrolled and where a student's status as a "native speaker" may indeed change as he or she becomes more bilingual (e.g., Fitts, 2006). However, for clarity of discussion here, the more static labels of native/non-native speakers are maintained.

proficiency levels, particularly in the minority language, is a challenging task for teachers.

TEACHER ACCOMMODATIONS DURING INTEGRATION

It is unavoidable that TWI teachers must make modifications to stretch instruction to include all learners. Especially when the language of instruction is the minority language, they have to use a wide range of strategies to ensure comprehensibility for all students and equal student participation. These linguistic modifications, while necessary to provide a meaningful immersion experience, may lead to differences in curriculum expectations, limited opportunities for extended language use for native minority language speakers, and less exposure to rich and complex teacher language.

Observing identical routines in a kindergarten and a 6th grade classroom in Spanish and English, Freeman (1998) found more emphasis on academic skill building in English than in Spanish because of the differences in students' second language abilities. Her description of the kindergarten opening routine is telling. Referring to the information provided on the board ("Today is ———", "We have ——— girls", etc.), she notes:

> In the English activity, the format includes full sentences on each line. In the Spanish activity, only the first line is a complete sentence; the other lines include only nouns and articles. We see here a first example of skills discrepancies between English and Spanish with more skills required in English. (p. 198)

Freeman explains:

> The concern at the kindergarten level is on listening comprehension. The students need to understand Spanish in context and understand the relationship between the Spanish and English components that they will be exposed to for the next few years. Since the students all have a stronger English base, there can be more of an emphasis on skills acquisition at this stage in English. (p. 200)

In a study that considered English/Gaelic immersion programs that enrolled Irish-speaking and English-speaking students, teachers also emphasized comprehension skills over production skills to accommodate the second language learners. In fact, they stated that it was "fairer to treat all the children the same" than to separate them out (Hickey, 2001, p. 466). Nonverbal responses were also encouraged by a 3rd grade teacher who used total physical response to scaffold her second language learners for a story retelling task (Takahashi-Breines, 2002).

The teacher's own language use may also be accommodated to such an extent that the overall input to the class will not sufficiently stretch the linguistic or cognitive capabilities of the native speakers of the minority language. Lindholm-Leary (2001) found that instruction in the minority language, Spanish, was characterized by simple verb forms (present tense) and simple utterance complexity (one to two words or short sentences). In another study, involving eleven K–5 TWI teachers, she observed that, of all the questions asked, 63% were lower-order questions. Lindholm-Leary concludes:

> This type of learning environment is less than optimal for developing oral language skills or higher levels of academic and cognitive skills. Students rarely had opportunities to actually produce language with the teacher and, when they did, the language they produced was limited to short, simplistic, factual-recall responses. (p. 139)

Other studies have also indicated less rich teacher input, teacher-student interaction, questioning, and lesson pacing as a result of accommodating for the presence of (beginning) second language learners in TWI classrooms (Howard, Sugarman, & Christian, 2003; Montague & Meza-Zaragosa, 1999; Takahashi-Breines, 2002). One is left wondering to what extent native minority language speakers are appropriately challenged in their social and academic language use during these lessons.

While these curricular and pedagogical accommodations seem appropriate for beginning second language learners, their positive impact on the native speakers and their learning is less evident. The latter students have fewer opportunities to use their oral language (and literacy) skills for grade-level appropriate content learning and literacy development. Hickey (2001) observes, "While providing an opportunity for [foreign language] learners to interact with native-speaker peers, [integration] provides a challenge to educators to support and enrich the [native language] language skills of the native speakers in a situation of language contact" (p. 444). Matching teacher talk and instructional activities to the proficiency level of the second language learner is important; however, the impact of such modifications on the language and literacy needs of native minority language speakers must also be analyzed (Valdés, 1997).

STUDENTS' LANGUAGE USE DURING INTEGRATION

A central idea in TWI is that second language learners have access to peers and teachers as native language models. In TWI programs, Lindholm-Leary (2001) points out, "there is always a native speaker of each language to serve as a good language model. Therefore, there should be more opportunities for students to produce longer and more complex utterances in their second language" (p. 139). Research on group work in native language and second language classrooms confirms that students often use more complex and more extensive language when engaged in cooperative learning (Jacob, et al., 1996; Kagan, 1986; McGroarty, 1989). At first glance, heterogeneous grouping and cooperative learning structures makes sense in the integrated TWI class-room. When a small group includes native speakers, additional opportunities for extending the (second) language can be created in natural ways. Pairing native and non-native speakers during integrated times to take advantage of the presence of peer language models is a core strategy in TWI classrooms. The expectation is that this process will be the same in both languages and bi-directional, that is, the native English speaker models for the minority language speaker in English and the roles are switched in the minority language.

Because of differences in acquisition contexts, however, this expecta-tion generally does not hold true in multilingual contexts across languages. Whereas the native minority language speakers are frequently already bilin-guals to some extent, native English speakers are typically monolinguals at time of entry into the program (although they may speak different varieties of English). As noted earlier, the subsequent foreign and second language acquisition process does not occur at similar rates. The language learning context is therefore not the same when English is the language of instruction and when the minority language is the target language.

This asymmetric situation affects the quality of instruction in the mi-nority language more than that in English. Without a great deal of teacher scaffolding, native English speakers often do not have the oral proficiency to carry out their academic tasks exclusively in and through the minority language when working with their native minority-language-speaking peers, especially in the first couple of years in the program. This situation affects both the quality of interactions among students and language choice. How-ard and Loeb (1999), for example, found that, while conversation among students during Spanish writing was limited to single word translations and mechanics, discussions in English were frequently rich and focused on the writing content. Under these circumstances, native minority language speak-ers have fewer opportunities to use their oral language skills for grade-level appropriate content learning and literacy development. In a 1st grade TWI classroom, Anglo students were not able to engage in exploratory dialogue about the math content with their bilingual peers because of their limited productive skills (Angelova, Gunarwarneda, & Volk, 2006).

Another consequence of the greater bilingual skills of the minority lan-guage speakers is that English becomes an important resource for bridging the communication gap. In a study of a middle school TWI program, McCollum (1999) observed, "Classes with open structures such as science were charac-terized by high levels of English usage because they afforded students many opportunities to socialize and cultivate peer group relationships" (p. 129). Although TWI students will consistently use the target language with their teacher (Oller & Eilers, 2002; Potowski, 2004), they tend to switch to English with peers, especially during group work. When working together on academic tasks or for social interactions, students will select the language of most efficient communication, English. Pierce (2000) provides an example from a 3rd grade Spanish-English TWI classroom. She describes how a native Spanish speaker discussed a math problem completely in Spanish with his native-English-speaking partner, only to receive a response of noncomprehension. Rather than rephrasing the math problem in Spanish in more comprehensible language, the native Spanish speaker proceeded with a translation in English. When asked later why he did not explain it again in Spanish, the student responded that it was easier to do it in English. In other words, English becomes the "default" language of choice as soon as the obligation to use Spanish disappears.

The choice in favor of English can also be a matter of its recognized higher societal status and students' identity choices. Griego-Jones (1994) found that kindergartners in a TWI program chose English as the language of communication to discuss their writings, even when they were clearly not fluent in that language. They saw "Spanish as acceptable to use, but seemed to view it as a vehicle they leaned on as they worked to become more proficient [in English]" (p. 4). Language choice and status issues may become more and more important as students grow older. Potowksi (2004, 2006) also found that 5th grade students' language choices reflected identity choices and a recognition of English as the language with higher status.

The switch to English, while natural, has significant implications for how language learning opportunities are distributed across the two languages and the ways in which both groups of students are expert role models for each other. First, it restricts language minority students' opportunities to act as the native language model during group work (though they may scaffold in English). Moreover, these students may not have equal opportunities to use their native language for the rich academic and social use suggested by the literature on the advantages of group work. Similarly, reliance on English during Spanish instruction also limits opportunities for native English speakers to use the minority language in a wider range of language functions across settings with peers and with the teacher, further hindering their second language development (Carrigo, 2000; Edelsky & Hudelson, 1982; Griego-Jones, 1994; Howard & Christian, 1997).

THE TENSIONS OF INTEGRATION

The benefits of integration in TWI settings have been noted by several researchers. Students translate individual words (Pierce, 2000) and explain syntax and word usage to each other (for an overview, see Howard, Sugarman, & Christian, 2003). Integrated settings also offer multiple opportunities for scaffolding during literacy events (Rubinstein-Avila, 2003). However,

- Increase minority language status outside the classroom, e.g., through before- and after-school enrichment programs, early childhood programs, visuals.
- Increase minority language status inside the classroom, e.g., through increased instructional time in the minority language, high expectations for work in the minority language, use of the minority language for similar purposes as the majority language (especially in bilingual classrooms with one teacher).
- Monitor quality of teacher and student talk in the minority language, e.g., through questioning techniques that encourage more extended language use.
- Create language enrichment opportunities through flexible grouping by native or second language competencies.
- Use bilingual strategies when integrating bilingual and nonbilingual students.
- Provide adequate social and academic language scaffolding, e.g., through language structures or "chunks" (especially important in TWI).
- Ensure expert roles for minority language students in a variety of contexts and tasks.

Figure 11.1   Strategies for integration with equity

integration and equity stand in a complex relationship to one another. Equal learning opportunities and access to language models are not automatically equally distributed in general, and across the two languages and the speakers of those languages in bilingual contexts in particular.

The example of TWI illustrates the challenge of equitable learning environment across languages for different groups of students when native and non-native speakers are integrated. Particularly during instruction in the minority language, negotiation of the multiple proficiency levels is challenging. When students are predominantly grouped heterogeneously by language, the integrated setting may not provide an optimally challenging learning environment for native minority language speakers in their language use and exposure to rich, academic language. Figure 11.1 presents additional strategies to promote **linguistic equity**, or the striving for a more equal distribution of instruction, services, and use of languages in the program.

Linguistically heterogeneous settings require teachers to mediate the benefits of integration for second language learning and its potential drawbacks for native language and literacy development in the minority language. Tatum (1997), examining African American students in a largely desegregated school, argues that offering both integrated and nonintegrated time is important in order to provide students with different identity spaces. Two 5th grade teachers in a two-way immersion program wanted to separate native

Spanish and native English speakers for Spanish language arts instruction to better meet the goal of bilingualism and biliteracy for all their students. The native English speakers needed more formal basic grammar instruction in Spanish to solidify structures to which they had been exposed since kindergarten. The Spanish speakers, in contrast, needed to build advanced vocabulary and literacy skills. The 5th grade teachers proposed to divide the students for 2 hours a week for Spanish language arts. This practice ran counter to the level of student integration this program model calls for, for most or all of the school day. However, the teachers had weighed the advantages and disadvantages of student integration against the linguistic needs of their students. They knew that if they integrated the students, the Spanish speakers would not be challenged enough. The administration agreed and that particular year, the native English speakers received Spanish as a second language instruction with a focus on grammar in context, and the native Spanish speakers worked with challenging literature in Spanish. The following year, when the gap between the two groups was not as great, the teachers went back to full integration (de Jong, 2002). Note that in this case, the purpose of grouping by language group was to provide enrichment for the minority students, not remedial work, and thus it did not involve the establishment of a "lower track" for minority students. The use of flexible cooperative learning groupings that are based on native or second language proficiency becomes a key strategy in creating equitable integrated TWI and non-TWI classrooms.

Shifting Perspectives: The Language of Integration

Historically, the segregation (marginalization)/inclusion (assimilation) dichotomy has developed as an either/or solution to increased linguistic and cultural diversity. The integration principle emphases an and-and (equal status) approach that effectively responds to student differences without stigmatizing these differences (Minow, 1985). To avoid the pitfalls of segregation and assimilation, it is important to pay close attention to status issues. Integrating students from diverse background involves a negotiation process from all participants with respect for the linguistic and cultural resources that each student brings to the classroom community. The social, academic, and linguistic benefits of student integration will be more equitably realized for all students when teachers view integration as a process and are aware that their classroom must become a setting where "students learn and interact in groups with students from other races and cultures. It requires equal educational opportunities, equal group status, and cross-racial contact" (Meier & Stewart, 1991, p. 20).

From an integration perspective, asking whether to segregate bilingual learners in separate programs or place them in assimilation-oriented mainstream classroom settings is not very productive—both settings have benefits and drawbacks. What the examples in this chapter show is that the integration of native and non-native speakers in the classroom cannot become an axiom that is implemented without regard to context and instructional goals. Grouping native speakers with non-native speakers may not always optimally support learning for all students. In-depth academic concept development may be more beneficial in the students' native language whereas reviewing and practice could be done in the second language to support the development of the latter (see, e.g., the preview-view-review strategy discussed in Chapter 10). Meaningful interaction among students from different ethnic and linguistic backgrounds may better support sociocultural goals; yet, as Tatum's (1997) study shows, separating them may allow teachers to address cross-cultural issues specific to a particular group.

Within the context of the Principle of Structuring for Integration, the discussion of homogeneous and heterogeneous grouping is thus reframed as an "and-and" proposition. Rather than asking whether to segregate or assimilate, the principle asks policy makers, educators, and researchers to examine which grouping will be most effective and equitable in meeting linguistic, sociocultural, and academic goals (Commins, 2008). More broadly, the Principle of Structuring for Integration asks how certain groupings and configurations in the school (including those that involve the implementation of separate programs, the organization of parent activities, or the configuration of teacher teams for curriculum development) need to be structured to achieve equal participation and equitable outcomes.

CHAPTER 11
Discussion & Activities

Critical Issues

1. How is the idea of integration different from both segregation and assimilation? What does it have in common with these approaches to the schooling of bilingual learners?

2. Table 11.1 provides examples of the principle of integration at the classroom level. Apply this principle to your context at the school or program level. The following questions might help:
   - Where is the expertise base for teaching bilingual learners? (Who has done professional development in this area?) How is this expertise shared formally (at staff meetings, workshops, etc.) and informally?
   - Do schoolwide policies and activities take bilingual children into account, e.g., translation at meetings, bilingual home-school communications, performances that reflect the interest and cultural experiences of the bilingual students, information for guest speakers or artists who address the whole school on how to make their presentation more comprehensible?
   - Hiring practices: How many teachers and support personnel (school psychologists, social workers) are bilingual? How many of those are not teaching in a bilingual/ESL specialized program? Does your school make a conscious effort to attract bilingual and teachers who share the linguistic and cultural backgrounds of the students in the school?
   - Do formal (i.e., institutionalized, not dependent on the initiative of the individual teacher) collaborative relationships exist between bilingual/ESL teachers and mainstream teachers? What are the kinds of activities teachers collaborate on? If co-teaching occurs, do both teachers teach together or does one teacher typically take the lead?

Application and Reflection

3. Looking at your own context, what kind of participation do you observe of newcomers or beginning ELLs in the classroom? If there is a separate ESL program, are there differences between their participation in that classroom and the mainstream classroom? What strategies are used to facilitate their integration into the classroom?

4. What are some barriers that allow for effective integration in your context? What makes schoolwide engagement challenging? What

hinders teacher collaboration across programs? What conditions make for less optimal opportunities for student interaction at the classroom level?

Recommended Readings

Cohen, E. G., & Lotan, R. A. (1997). *Working for equity in heterogeneous classrooms: Sociological theory in practice.* New York: Teachers College Press.
> *Cohen's research has focused on how status issues affect group work in racially and culturally diverse settings. In this book, she presents her theory of complex instruction and shows how teachers can mediate these status issues to reach equity in their classrooms.*

García, O., Skutnabb-Kangas, T., & Torres-Guzmán, M. (2006). *Imagining multilingual schools: Language in education and glocalization.* Clevedon: Multilingual Matters.
> *This book poses key questions about policy and implementation in multilingual settings, looking at such issues as language development and identity and integration and segregation of language minority children among indigenous language speakers in the Americas and minority language speakers in Spain, France, India, and Botswana.*

Howard, E. R., & Sugarman, J. (2007). *Realizing the vision of two-way immersion: Fostering effective programs and classrooms.* Washington: Center for Applied Linguistics and Delta Systems.
> *This book presents the key features of successful two-way immersion programs in four schools. These features include teacher collaboration, the purposeful integration of the program in the school, and alignment of curriculum and pedagogical principles.*

Moving Forward

GUIDING QUESTIONS

- *How can we characterize the language of assimilationist and pluralist discourses?*
- *Why is there a need for more than one pathway to advocacy for pluralist policies and practices?*
- *How can the four principles help to frame pluralist agendas?*

As contact among speakers of different languages around the world continues due to (im)migration, transnational migration, and technological advances, policy makers, educators, and researchers need to understand how to provide high quality schooling options in linguistically and culturally diverse contexts. This chapter summarizes the main themes of this book and concludes by calling for a dual advocacy approach, one that finds ways to articulate and define language policy and practices from a bilingual (pluralist) perspective while tackling the inconsistencies in the assumptions underlying assimilationist-informed actions.

Discourses and Language Decisions in School

Throughout the book teachers have been positioned as language decision makers in their classroom and their schools. Through their daily decisions about language and language use, teachers help shape students' linguistic and cultural identities as well as their academic and language and literacy development. Through their choice of medium of instruction, of literacy activities, of curriculum, and of assessment tools as well as in the ways they structure student participation and interaction, teachers explicitly and implicitly value certain linguistic and cultural practices.

Teachers do not make language decisions in a vacuum. Federal, national, state, and local policies direct language choices and possibilities at the school and classroom levels. A school may decide to implement a Chinese-English two-way immersion program or may be required to implement a particular math curriculum adopted and mandated by the district. Educational policies such as No Child Left Behind and Proposition 227 that value and count only outcomes in English become de facto language policies as educators adapt their linguistic practices and make curricular changes to align with these policies (Menken, 2008; Shohamy, 2006). Thus, while teachers have considerable agency as they make their language decisions on the local level, these broader structures expand and constrain the language options teachers can explore.

As educators formulate educational policies, conduct research, and engage in a wide range of schooling practices, their actions reflect specific ways of viewing the role of linguistic and cultural diversity in the world and in a particular society or community. These different ways of viewing diversity can be broadly identified as pluralist and assimilationist discourses. Pluralist and assimilationist discourses are best conceived as different orientations toward linguistic and cultural diversity rather than as each other's opposite. They are ultimately concerned with distinctly different set of questions, reflect different views of bilingualism and diversity, and value different educational outcomes (see Table 12.1).

Pluralist perspectives begin with the recognition that linguistic and cultural diversity is an integral part of modern life that can be mobilized to unify and problem solve. The imagined community of the pluralist has many elements coming together, some remaining distinct, others connecting to create new and unique spaces. Pluralist discourses reflect multiplicities, not dichotomies, and recognize that there are important advantages for the individual, the community, and society in developing multilingual repertoires, including cognitive, educational, cultural, and economic benefits. Pluralist discourses attempt to break through the double standard that would limit these benefits to only certain (dominant) identities and groups in society. Policies within pluralist discourses stress creative, collaborative approaches to developing multilingual competence for all students, from all language groups. Pluralist-oriented educators have a holistic understanding of what it means to become bilingual and biliterate. They engage in practices that are committed to educational equity and reflect a culturally and linguistically additive approach that systemically integrates linguistic and cultural diversity into all that they do. Chapters 8 through 11 describe this approach as enacting the Principles of Affirming Identities, Promoting Additive Bi/Multilingualism, and Structuring for Integration within a framework of an educational equity.

Assimilationist discourses focus on standardizing diverse elements to a

TABLE 12.1

Pluralist and Assimilationist Discourses

	Pluralist/multilingual discourse	Assimilationist/monolingual discourse
Guiding question	How can we employ linguistic diversity in solving social, environmental, and technological problems?	How can we achieve greater efficiencies through the reduction and streamlining of diversity?
Orientation toward linguistic and cultural diversity	Additive view; linguistic and cultural diversity as positive forces to be built upon and used • Diversity is the norm • Multilingualism supports cross-linguistic and intercultural communication • Cognitive, educational, cultural, political, and economic benefits of multilingualism should be available to all	Dis/replacement (subtractive) view; linguistic and cultural diversity needs to be limited • Monolingualism is the norm • One language is needed to support effective communication, efficiency, and national unity
View of bilinguals and bilingualism	Bilingualism from a holistic perspective: • Bilingual with one developing bilingual linguistic repertoire • Focus on language use in sociocultural, political context • Assessment across two languages, combining skills • Unitary system where transfer occurs Literacy and language as sociocultural practices (ideological) • Diversity of approaches; rejects one-size-fits-all • Constructivist model of learning and teaching	Bilingualism from a fractional perspective: • Bilingual with two discrete monolingual repertoires • Focus on language system as autonomous code • Assessment in one language, separate skills • Container system where language interference occurs Literacy and language as autonomous systems (neutral) • Standardization of approaches • Transmission model of teaching and learning
Preferred program models	Additive bilingual programs with the goal of supporting bilingual competence	Monolingual programs or bilingual programs with the goal of teaching societal language
Policy to practice	Focus on equity through affirming identities, additive bilingualism, and integration	Focus on the same educational experiences through assimilation, instruction in the societal language, and inclusion or segregation

common norm for the sake of efficiency and national identity. A common, national language is crucial to maintaining political and social cohesion. In the assimilationist imagined community (too many) linguistic and cultural differences will conflict with a nation's ability to maintain a peaceful unity. Mastery of the societal language is presented as a necessary condition of becoming part of the political, economic, and cultural mainstream. Finding the most efficient way to teach the societal language to minority language speakers therefore takes a central position in educational practice. While at times tolerant of linguistic and cultural differences, teachers stress the socialization into mainstream linguistic and cultural practices in school represented by practices that tend to emphasize a common core of knowledge and skills, native-speaker standard language norms, and dominant cultural values.

Pluralist and assimilationist discourses conceptualize policy problems in distinctly different ways and hence seek different solutions. As seen in Chapters 4 and 6, elements of both discourses can be identified in policies and practices from different times and contexts. Now, globalization has given new impetus to both discourses. On one hand, we see policies that reflect (a return to) more traditionally defined imagined communities that stress homogeneity and a one-to-one relationship between language and identity. On the other hand, we see increased awareness of and valuing of the heterogeneity of linguistic and cultural experiences and identities.

Because the distinctions between assimilationist and pluralist discourses touch on such central issues, tensions between those who represent or work within these discursive frames will continue to exist and find their way into educational debates. Differences in their views of diversity, of language and bilingualism, and of how schools should be structured result in a continuous negotiation of the meaning of fundamental questions about who belongs to a community (national as well as classroom communities) and who has access to what kind of schooling.

The Need for Dual Pathways to Advocacy

How can educators contribute to shifting discourses? From an equity perspective, understanding and valuing the diversity of students' and families' linguistic and cultural practices and experiences and using this diversity for organizing schools and classrooms is key to providing multilingual learners with equal access to high-quality schooling. An important challenge for educators of multilingual learners who must operate within an assimilationist-oriented environment is therefore how to create spaces for more pluralist discourses.

One strategy has been to engage with those in power or those supporting assimilationist discourses and try to convince them that taking on a pluralist discourse perspective is the "better" way. The extensive public debate on the various English-only ballot initiatives or the discussions about No Child Left Behind illustrate how different groups express their support or opposition to the laws. While the arguments from both sides differ, the definition of the problem remains the same.

In the debate on Question 2 in Massachusetts, for example, supporters of bilingual education found themselves responding primarily to their opponents' definition of the problem (lack of English language proficiency) and their solution (1 year of an English-only program). Although supporters of bilingual education provided different interpretations of the role of English proficiency, they did little to question the premise that the lack of such proficiency is the main problem to be solved. In fact, many opponents of the proposition stressed that "everybody agreed" that the purpose of the schooling of ELLs is to teach them English. The main difference was in what path to take to English proficiency (monolingual or bilingual). Supporters of bilingual education also stressed the difference between social and academic language proficiency to counter the call for only 1 year of program participation. References to the benefits and importance of developing multilingual repertoires for the individual and society, as well as discussions about broader educational outcomes (for example, content learning or high school graduation), remained largely outside of the debate (Macedo, Dendrinos, & Gounari, 2003). English monolingual discourse, with its narrow focus on what language to use as medium of instruction, prevailed in the debate.

The Massachusetts example suggests that positioning pluralist discourses as a mirror (opposite) of assimilationist discourses can in fact render multilingual discourse frames invisible. The dominance of assimilationist discourses in society easily leads to the adoption of assimilationist definitions of problems and solutions as the primary policy frame, even by those whose views are more pluralistic in nature. While this may affect language choices (in the Massachusetts case the legitimization of monolingual or bilingual instructional models), it does little to change the underlying discourses about linguistic and cultural diversity in schools (Luke, McHoul, & Mey, 1990). This phenomenon raises an important question: how can we shift policies and practices from monolingual to multilingual approaches and perspectives? Below I argue that such a shift needs to acknowledge the differences in ideological orientations toward linguistic and cultural diversity that distinguish these discourses. To develop and maintain scholarship, policies, and practices from a multilingual, pluralist perspective, the vocabulary and the definition of problems and solutions need to be generated from within pluralist discourses. Shifting toward pluralist language policy discourses and advocacy may therefore need two pathways for advocacy.

ENGAGING WITH DOMINANT DISCOURSES

The first pathway could focus on uncovering discontinuities within assimilationist discourses. Within this approach, the bilingual versus English-only debate could, for example, be rephrased in terms of how different English-only programs reach long-term social, language, and academic goals for linguistically and culturally diverse students. When the comparison with bilingual education is excluded from the policy discourse, this question calls for careful analysis of the strengths and weaknesses of English-only policies and their positive and negative impact on student learning. The recent discussion by MacDonald (2009) about the impact of Proposition 227 is a good example of a focus on the failure of bilingual education with little discussion of the similar lack of impact of the English-only practices on long-term achievement indicators that matter, such as drop-out rates, high school graduation, college attendance, and unemployment. The misleading focus on bilingual education and achievement at lower grade levels fails to hold the English-only policy accountable for its purported claim that it will effectively and efficiently prepare bilingual learners for the 21st century.

Researchers thus can make an important contribution by moving beyond the dichotomy that has characterized too much of the effectiveness debate. Allowing the framing of the current effectiveness debate to continue to be one between bilingual and English-only programs (i.e., reinforcing the oppositional relationship between pluralist and assimilationist discourses) avoids closer examination of such issues. In contrast, engaging in the analysis of data that would highlight key features of effective practices in English-medium schools could provide different insights about what schools can do to support ELLs and educational attainment. Linking these discussions to short-term and long-term educational outcomes (language, literacy, content, and sociocultural development) can more meaningfully inform policy and practice. Indeed, a discussion of these issues is likely to support practices that reflect a more pluralistic stance (Delpit & Dowdy, 2002; Gay, 2000; Gersten & Baker, 2000; Lucas & Katz, 1994).

FRAMING PLURALIST DISCOURSES

Simply engaging thoughtfully with assimilationist frames will be insufficient, however, to accomplish a shift to more pluralist discourses. A second pathway for advocacy must be to articulate a multilingual discourse "in its own right," with its own agenda. Such pluralist discourses have been described in this book as those taking a holistic and context-sensitive approach to linguistic and cultural diversity in schools. Pluralist discourses are holistic because they view bi/multilingual systems as interconnected, integrated, and creative rather than as the simple addition of two or more discrete, monolingual systems. They are context-sensitive because they recognize that multilingual practices are always embedded within localized and broader sociopolitical contexts.

For multilingual discourses to find their way into policy and practice, educators need to formulate policies and identify practices and conditions for multilingual students' success that are informed by scholarship that takes a multilingual and bilingual perspective (Castek, et al., 2005). Examining practice from a pluralist perspective, in turn, informs and influences our theoretical understandings of linguistic and cultural diversity in school (August & Hakuta, 1997). The four principles defined in Chapter 8—the Principles of Educational Equity, Affirming Identities, Promoting Additive Bi/Multilingualism, and Structuring for Integration—can be applied separately as analytical lenses for reflection on scholarship, policies, and practices, but they also must be considered together to create equitable, optimal learning environments for all students.

The Four Principles and Pluralistic Discourses: Policies, Practices, and Research

The four principles can be used to systematically frame a holistic, context-sensitive, pluralist agenda. The Principle of Educational Equity puts the question of fairness and nondiscrimination at the forefront of educational decision-making, whether it be formal policies, daily classroom practices, or research agendas. This overarching principle embraces the three other principles as it asks whether actions that may be aligned with each principle are applied equitably for all learners, and whether policies may have disproportionate effects on certain individuals or groups of students. This principle insists that educators respond to inequities by looking for systemic solutions rather than blaming students and their families. The Principle of Educational Equity requires that researchers identify research questions that allow inequities to become visible at all policy levels and engage in data collection and use analytical methods that help reveal these patterns. This approach may include critically examining the definition of school outcomes, for example, by expanding the definition of outcomes to include outcomes other than those officially sanctioned by the government, such as the definition of dropout (highlighting the experiences of underrepresented groups such as migrants and refugees and older students with limited former schooling), or conducting classroom-based research that considers opportunities to learn for different groups of students.

Within the Principle of Affirming Identities educators validate diverse cultural experiences in their school policies and classroom practices. This principle shifts the perspective away from static one-language-one-culture notions to a dynamic understanding of multiple identities, and it stresses the need to provide spaces for diverse voices. Policies and practices that are aligned with this principle include the use of curricula and materials that reflect different perspectives and represent different cultural groups in all of their diversity. Educators create collaborative classrooms where students are viewed as active co-constructors of knowledge and meaningful contributors to the learning process. Research can critically analyze cultural and linguistic representations of different focal identities, and document how spaces for multiple identities are created. A wide range of research methods can be used, including stories, narrative inquiry, case studies, and other analytical approaches (qualitative and quantitative) to give voice to those traditionally silenced (Smith, 1999).

The Principle of Promoting Additive Bi/Multilingualism treats language minority students' home languages as resources for teaching and learning. Languages other than the standard school language are made visible in the school. In applying this principle, educators collaborate to create opportunities for using, developing, displaying, and engaging with all of the languages in students' linguistic repertoires. Employing this principle changes subtractive bilingual learning environments to those where linguistic equity (language status equalization) is the goal. The Principle of Promoting Additive Bi/Multilingualism rejects the notion of linguistic compartmentalization in favor of an understanding of functional hybrid language practices that are the norm in multilingual environments. This principle invites us to explore bilingualism and biliteracy development as holistic phenomena that can be examined in their own right, and not in a simple relationship to native-speaker norms.

Policies that are grounded in this perspective focus on providing learners with opportunities to develop multilingual repertoires across contexts. Practices may include the implementation of additive bilingual program models or collaboration between schools and complementary community-based language schools. Educators use assessments that consider student performance in and across languages and engage in bilingually oriented teaching strategies. They weigh how their multilingual practices contribute to academic outcomes for specific target groups, including content learning and oral language and literacy development. In addition to examining multilingual practices and linking them to pedagogical outcomes, researchers investigate how multilingualism can be developed under different conditions with different target populations, critically examining how language proficiency is defined and assessed in different contexts and for different purposes. Experts in authentic assessment and evaluation contribute to the development of fair assessments that reflect a bilingual perspective, and accountability systems that take bilingual development into consideration. At its core, research grounded in this principle makes bi/multilingualism and bi/multiliteracy development its point of departure, rather than first or second language development, and considers bi- and multidirectional influences among languages and bilingual phenomena, such as transfer and translanguaging, as dynamic expressions of "doing bilingual." Exploring these phenomena will require researchers to look at language-in-use across different contexts using analytical tools such as surveys, ethnography, or discourse analysis.

The centrality of contextualizing practice also implies that studies of language-in-education policies must move beyond the textual analysis of formal government documents to include localized interpretations and implementation of policies. Policy impact studies need to include but also look further than the level of program models to examine how practices at the school and classroom levels are shaped by policies, as well as how educators adapt and change policies to accommodate their own context. Interpretive studies can thus augment more quantitatively oriented studies in a mixed method approach that will contribute to our developing understanding of the complexity of language policy processes.

The Principle of Structuring for Integration draws attention to the whole school and how the different parts fit together to benefit the whole (school) community. It focuses on the establishment of inclusive policies and practices that encourage equal-status relationships among different constituencies. Educators take linguistic and cultural diversity and the implications for effective practices as their starting point for decision making. This principle encourages a shift away from standardized homogenizing programs and classrooms with monolingual norms that characterize our understanding of the academic mainstream under assimilationist discourses. Applying this principle means that "mainstream" programs and classrooms become integrated, heterogeneous learning environments in which multilingualism, multiculturalism, and equal access for linguistically and culturally diverse populations are the norm.

Policies and practices that align with the Principle of Structuring for Integration take a whole-school perspective on the education of diverse learners, as reflected in curriculum, pedagogy, and assessment practices, as well as the distribution of expertise related to multilingualism and multilingual education, teacher collaboration, and program integration. Research from an integrative perspective investigates and documents issues of representation, organizational features of language minority schooling, and how specialized programs are positioned within a school. At the classroom level, a critical examination is made of classroom participation patterns, grouping patterns, and language, literacy, content, and scoiocultural outcomes.

Table 12.2 illustrates how the four principles reflect a pluralist discourse centered around four key concepts: fairness, multiplicity, linguistic equity, and equal status. Using these concepts, the principles reframe the educational debate by asking a different set of questions for practice and research, thus shifting the focus of policies, practice, and scholarship. Rather than assuming the system is fair for all and that any shortcomings are to blame on external (i.e., student, home) factors, the principles examine whether a school system's own policies and practices may have discriminatory impact on certain groups. They inquire whose identities are represented and provide space for marginalized voices to be heard and their perspectives affirmed. The principles ask whether and how linguistic and cultural diversity is treated in daily interactions between teachers and students and how it is reflected in curriculum, pedagogy, and assessment practices. They explore how opportunities for bilingualism and biliteracy development can be optimized in a particular school context and student population, and how cultural similarities and differences can function as powerful resources for teaching and learning.

The four principles guide professional efforts to construct policies, instructional practices, and research from a pluralist (dynamic, holistic, multilingual, sociocultural) perspective and they are interconnected. When professionals attend to all of these principles, they can reinforce one another. Lack of attention to one of the principles can lead to new inequities. Using and building on students' linguistic resources is a practice that reinforces the Principle of Additive Bi/Multilingualism as well as the Principle of Affirming Identities. Without these two principles, the Principle of Structuring for Integration easily turns into an assimilationist approach where linguistic and cultural differences are ignored or where cultural and linguistic differences are constructed as deficits. Similarly, without the Principle of Structuring for Integration, policies and practices may be aligned with the other two principles but they are visible only in the margins and fail to impact the broader school environment, for example, in an isolated bilingual classroom with little follow-up when students leave the classroom (de Jong, 1996, 2006; Shannon, 1995). Educational equity calls for a careful balancing of the demands that each of these principles places on policy makers at all decision-making levels, including teachers. Rather than allowing the pluralist agenda to be defined in response to the priorities of assimilationist discourses, engaging in scholarship, policy, and practice that is informed by a pluralist (bilingual, multilingual) perspective is another pathway to advocacy. Both advocacy pathways, disrupting assimilationist discourses and articulating pluralist discourses, are important to the effort to create the necessary political and educational spaces for alternative educational discourses about multilingualism and cultural diversity.

TABLE 12.2			
Shifting Perspectives: Pluralist Discourses			
	Pluralist perspectives	**Guiding question**	**Policies and practices**
Principle of Educational Equity	Same does not imply equitable; equal access	How do policies, practices, and research include and affect different groups of students?	*Key words:* Fairness, nondiscrimination *Practices:* The Principles of • Affirming Identities • Promoting Additive Bi/Multilingualism • Structuring for Integration
Principle of Affirming Identities	Multiple, socially constructed	How do educators (including administrators, teachers, and scholars) give voice to those who have traditionally been marginalized or excluded? How do our policies, teaching practices, and scholarship reflect and validate learners' diverse cultural experiences?	*Key word:* Multiplicity *Practices:* Funds of knowledge; culturally and linguistically responsive teaching; authentic learning and assessment
Principle of Promoting Additive Bi/Multilingualism	Multilingual language practices; holistic view of bilingualism (dynamic, developmental)	What conditions support bi/multilingual and bi/multiliteracy development for different groups of students in diverse contexts?	*Key word:* Linguistic equity *Practices:* Additive bilingual programs; bilingual teaching approaches
Principle of Structuring for Integration	Equal-status integration at school, program, classroom levels	How are the various organizational elements organized to meet bilingual/biliteracy, academic, and sociocultural goals for different groups of students?	*Key word:* Equal status *Practices:* Whole-school approaches; collaboration; flexible student grouping

Moving Toward Bi/Multilingual Discourses

Moving toward pluralist discourses requires action at all policy levels. Passing formal laws or regulations at the state and federal levels is not enough. Educators must critically examine their own policies and practices if they are to move toward more equitable practices. Through their daily actions, educators, policy makers, and researchers can engage in small and large acts of advocacy that create openings for pluralist discourses and encourage pluralist practices for multilingual learners. As argued throughout this book, these actions and decisions matter greatly in shaping the experiences of multilingual children and their participation in school.

CHAPTER 12
Discussion & Activities

Critical Issues

1. Identify other examples of the first pathway for advocacy than the one provided in the text. What are some other questions that can be raised to challenge the assimilationist discourses on their own terms?
2. Revisit your list of actions from Chapter 1. Consider your role as a teacher, school or district administrator, researcher and the kinds of language decisions you engage in. Identify additional language and literacy policies and practices relative to to your role(s)?

Application and Reflection

3. Throughout this text, you have analyzed your own context from the perspective of each principle separately. Now consider the four principles together. Select one or two educational areas (e.g., curriculum, assessment) and reflect on the extent to which all four principles apply. If you are a graduate student or a scholar, consider the extent to which all four principles apply in the research that you are reading and the research agendas that are pursued at your institution.

Recommended Readings

Cenoz, J. (2009). *Towards multilingual education: Basque educational research from an international perspective*. Clevedon: Multilingual Matters.
> *In this book, Cenoz proposes to replace the traditional descriptions of multilingual programs with a "continua of multilingual education." Using Basque schools in Spain, where schools use Basque, Spanish, and English for instruction, as an example, she illustrates how the idea of continua can better capture the contextualized nature of multilingual education.*

Crawford, J. (2008). *Advocating for English learners: Selected essays*. Clevedon: Multilingual Matters.
> *These essays present recent arguments and policies about language and languages in the United States. The author calls for collective advocacy to help change the discourse about linguistic diversity.*

Torres-Guzmán, M. E., & Gómez, J. (2009). *Global perspectives on multilingualism: Unity in diversity.* New York: Teachers College Press.
> *Drawing on case studies from around the world, this book stresses the importance of preserving linguistic diversity and offers new paradigms for talking about and engaging in multilingual practices.*

Glossary

academic language proficiency. Language features and functions associated with formal schooling, including the language for learning subject matter.

acquisition planning. Language policy activities aimed at increasing the number of speakers of a particular language or their fluency.

additive bilingualism. Bilingual acquisition context in which learning a second language does not imply the replacement of the first language but is added onto first language repertoires.

adequate yearly progress (AYP). Target of the percentage of students expected to score proficient on state test (part of No Child Left Behind legislation).

advocacy. Organized efforts and actions to create a just, decent society.

advocacy-based program evaluations. Program evaluations that set out to prove that one program model is better than the other.

Amendment 31. Colorado ballot initiative defeated by voters in 2001 that would have made English-only the default program for ELLs in the state.

Americanization movement. Efforts that focused on helping immigrants learn English and become "American" in cultural practice; the emphasis was on assimilation.

anglocentricity. View that English and British culture is superior to non-English languages and cultures.

Annual Measurable Achievement Objectives (AMAO). Annual targets related to the number of ELLs making progress on a language proficiency test, for ELLs being proficient on the language proficiency test, and the percentage of ELLs meeting annual yearly progress.

appropriation. The adoption of a concept or behavior with a local interpretation

assimilation. Process of giving up nondominant languages and cultural practices to increasingly exclusive participation in dominant linguistic and cultural practices.

assimilationist discourses. Ways of thinking and talking about the world that views (too much) linguistic and cultural diversity as a hindrance to sociocultural, economic, and political development.

balanced bilingual. Term often used to describe someone equally fluent in two languages (at the level of an educated person) (synonyms include ambilingual, equilingual, maximal bilingual, symmetrical bilingual).

banking model of teaching. View of teaching that stresses the expert role of a teacher in transmitting a body of knowledge to students.

bias. Tendency toward a particular ideology, result, or preference. When applied to tests, it implies that the test systematically advantages or disadvantages a particular group of students on a particular criterion not considered relevant for outcomes, such as race or gender.

Bilingual Education Act. Title VII of the Elementary and Secondary Education Act funding bilingual education at the federal level between 1968 and 2000.

bilingual learner. Children who are acquiring two or more languages at home and at school (also: emergent bilingual).

bilingualism. Competence in two languages developed by individual speakers (also: bilinguality)

Brown v. Board of Education. 1954 Supreme Court ruling that segregation (of African Americans) is unconstitutional, declaring that "separate educational facilities are inherently unequal."

Canadian immersion programs. Bilingual programs for majority language speakers in which initial instruction is in the second language and the first language is introduced later.

Castañeda v. Pickard. 1982 Supreme Court ruling that developed a three-pronged test to determine "appropriate action" to meet the needs of ELLs: expert base, resource allocation, and program outcomes.

circumstantial bilingualism. Acquisition context where becoming bilingual is not a choice but a necessity for survival (synonyms include folk bilingualism).

Civil Rights Act (1974). Provides for nondiscrimination in public spaces, including schools.

code-switching. The use of two grammatical systems within the same linguistic. exchange; can occur within a phrase or sentence (intrasentential code-switching) and across phrases or sentences (intersentential code-switching); serves multiple functions in bilingual or multilingual conversation or text.

cognates. Words from two languages that have similar sounds and meanings.

common underlying proficiency (CUP). Developed by Jim Cummins; a model that stresses the interrelatedness of the two language systems of bilinguals in the brain (also think-tank model).

communicative competence. Ability to use language appopriately, according to context.

community-based language schools. Classes in the minority language organized by the ethnic minority community. (also: complementary schools).

continua of biliteracy model. Framework developed by Nancy Hornberger to capture bilingual proficiency (oral-written; receptive-productive) as it is influenced by medium, context, and content.

corpus planning. Language policy activities that focus on the language system itself, e.g., alphabetization.

cultural bias. Occurs when test item assume background knowledge that is embedded in specific cultural experiences.

diglossia. The relatively stable distribution of two languages or varieties of the same language within a particular community for different purposes or functions.

disproportionality. Occurs when the percentage of students assigned to a particular program is significantly higher or lower than the percentage of their enrollment in the school system.

doublets. Words that bilinguals know in both languages.

educational segregation. Involves the clustering of students based on a criterion (race, language proficiency) at the program or school level.

effective school studies. Studies that try to identify the common features that characterize schools identified as effective schools for diverse learners.

elective bilingualism. Acquisition context in which becoming bilingual is a choice rather than a necessity (also elite bilingualism; voluntary bilingualism).

Elementary and Secondary Education Act (ESEA). Federal law passed in 1965 to regulate funds to states and districts for elementary and secondary schools.

English as an additional language (EAL) students. Term for students who speak languages other than English at home (term used particularly in the United Kingdom) (also emergent bilinguals, bilingual learners, limited English proficient)

English language learner (ELL). A student who speaks a language other than English and who isare still in the process of acquiring English.

English-plus resolutions. State resolutions affirming the value of competence in English and another language.

ethnolinguistic vitality. Indicator of the chances for language maintenance and minority language use within a community based on status, demographic factors, and institutional support.

Europe's Framework Strategy for Multilingualism. Policy formulated by the European Union that aims for multilingual competence for its members (native language, English, and one other language).

European School model. Additive multilingual education programs designed primarily for children of foreign nationals.

expanded circle. The outermost of the three concentric circles conceived by Braj Kachru (1985) to describe the level of English use within a country; in the expanded circle English is primarily a foreign language for its inhabitants.

Flores v. Arizona. On-going court case in Arizona about the funding of education for ELLs.

fractional view of bilingualism. Considers bilinguals as two monolinguals in one with a focus on discrete language skills.

funds of knowledge. Children's knowledge and skills that they have developed in their homes and the community.

globalization. Process that involves the increasing interconnectedness of economic, political, and cultural economies worldwide.

glocalization. Customization of goods that are sold worldwide to local market conditions and characteristics.

hegemony. Influence exerted by a dominant group; occurs with respect to language and culture when subordinate groups freely accept a dominant group's negative views about them and their language as "true" and natural.

heritage language classes. Language classes for heritage language speakers, individuals from a minority language background with varying levels of competence and cultural identification in the minority language.

holistic view of bilingualism. Considers the two languages of a bilingual person as part of an integrated whole; a bilingual person should not be seen as two monolinguals in one.

identity. The way one constructs one's relationship with the world and others; sense of self.

imagined community. Term used by Benedict Anderson to indicate that national identities are constructed phenomena. In the absence of daily contact with eachs, individuals have to imagine the other members of the community, who they are, what they do, how they think. These assumptions about cultural and linguistic practices, values, beliefs become part of who is considered part of the community.

initiation-response-evaluation (IRE). Recitation script in which the teacher initiates a question, the student replies, and the the teachers evaluates the correctness of the student's response.

inner circle. The innermost of the three concentric circles conceived by Braj Kachru (1985) to describe the level of English use within a country; in the inner circle English is the native language for the great majority of inhabitants.

integration. Process of bringing together different parts, on an equal basis, to make a whole.

integrated bilingual education models. Bilingual education models that integrate speakers of the dominant language and minority language speakers.

integrated transitional bilingual education. Model of transitional bilingual education (TBE) in which minority language students share instructional time with students placed in a mainstream classroom in an effort to overcome the negative impact of segregating the minority language students while they are becoming familiar with the new language and culture.

interdependence hypothesis. Developed by Jim Cummins; states that proficiency in the second language is related to proficiency in the native language. See also common underlying proficiency (CUP).

intergenerational language transmission. Language acquisition context where children acquire their native language from their parents.

IQ test. Designed to measure an assumed intelligence quotient, believed to be innate (also called general intelligence factor or the g factor).

language attrition. Loss of specific language skills of an individual speaker.

language brokering. The practice of children translating for his or her parents or other adults in the community to help them gain access to services or information.

language compartmentalization. Strategy that stresses that the two languages of instruction be kept separate by the teacher in a bilingual teaching context.

language domains. Spheres of activity defined by specific times, settings, and role relationships.

language dominance. The language in which a bilingual child is assessed as most proficient; used for program placement and special education referral testing.

language ideology. Commonsense notions about language, language acquisition, and language use.

language policy. Formal and informal decisions about language use; includes laws, regulations, and statutes, as well as practices.

language revitalization. Efforts at increasing the number of (fluent) speakers of an endangered language.

language shift. Increased use of the dominant language over the use of a minority language.

language status equalization. Efforts to make the status of and access to the minority language more like that of the majority language.

language transfer. Bi-directional process of using knowledge about one language for learning another language.

language-as-problem orientation. View of language diversity as the cause of social problems or underachievement of minority language speakers.

language-as-resource orientation. Approach to language policy that views linguistic diversity as a source of expertise that contributes to political, economic, and cultural goals.

language-as-right orientation. Language policy orientation that stresses the right not to be discriminated against because of language and the right to use and develop one's native language.

Lau Remedies. Guidelines developed by the Office of Civil Rights to implement the 1974 *Lau v. Nichols* Supreme Court decision; retracted in the 1980s.

Lau v. Nichols. 1974 Supreme Court case involving 1,700 Chinese students in San Francisco; the Court ruled that without accommodations there cannot be equal access for students who do not speak English, even if they are given the same resources as English speakers.

limited English proficient (LEP) students. Term for students who speak a language other than English and who have limited ability in listening, speaking, reading, or writing ability in English (also emergent bilinguals, bilingual learners, English as an Additional Language speakers)

lingua franca. Language used among speakers who do not share a native language.

linguistic bias. Occurs when test items use unnecessarily difficult and familiar words in the item or responses.

linguistic ecology. Study of language within the context of linguistic and cultural diversity and biodiversity.

linguistic equity. See also language status equalization.

linguistic human rights movement. Views the use of the native language (including through formal schooling) as a human right; engages in efforts to recognize the right to use native languages in public domains (such as schools).

linguistic imperialism. Term developed by Robert Phillipson to describe the processes by which the English language is used to maintain inequalities among different groups in society.

linguistic instrumentalism. Motivation to learn, use, or develop a language for economic or political ends (contrast: symbolic reasons).

mainstream multilingual and bilingual models. Additive bilingual programs for majority language speakers.

maintenance bilingual program. Additive bilingual program for minority language speakers.

meta-analysis. Quantitative research methodology that allows researchers to find effect sizes across different studies.

metalinguistic awareness. Ability to think and talk about language and language systems.

meta-narratives. National discourses that define national identities (who belongs).

Meyer v. Nebraska. 1954 Supreme Court case involving a parochial school teacher accused of teaching the Bible in German to an elementary-age student. The Court ruled that the state does not have a compelling interest to forbid the teaching of languages other than English in school.

minority or dominated languages. Language used by language groups who are politically and socially placed in a minority situation (status).

moribund languages. Languages that are no longer used by children.

multilingualism. Development of linguistic repertoires in more than two languages.

Native American Languages Act (1990). Granted Native Americans the right to use and teach their own languages in schools.

native language. The language (or languages) a child grows up speaking.

nativism. Belief that foreigners and all things "foreign" are inferior to what is considered native to the country.

newcomer program. Programs developed at the secondary level, particularly for students with limited schooling or literacy in their native language.

No Child Left Behind Act (NCLB). The 2001 reauthorization of the Elementary and Secondary Education Act with an emphasis on accountability to ensure that all students meet grade level expectations by 2014.

official language. Language that has been declared in the constitution the language of a nation or other political unit.

orientalism. Approach that advocated the use of local languages for instruction in colonial nations while insisting on western-based curriculum.

outer circle. The middle of the three concentric circles conceived by Braj Kachru (1985) to describe the level of English use within a country; in the outer circle, English is used as a second language by most inhabitants of a country but it is the dominant language used for government, schooling, and so forth, as a result of British or American colonialism.

pluralist discourses. Ways of thinking and talking about the world that consider linguistic and cultural diversity as a resource for sociocultural, political, and economic development.

portfolio assessment. Assessment of a student's learning through the longitudinal collection and analysis of student work related to specific learning objectives.

preview-view-review strategy. Bilingual teaching strategy that uses the native langauge for preview and review, and the second language for concept reinforcement and language development (view).

Principle of Affirming Identities. Stresses the importance of validating and making visible cultural diversity.

Principle of Educational Equity. Stresses nondiscriminatory practices and the equal value of every human being.

Principle of Promoting Additive Bi/Multilingualism. Stresses the importance of developing multilingual repertoires.

Principle of Structuring for Integration. Focuses on equal access to meaningful participation at the classroom, program, and school level.

Proposition 227. State legislation making English-only placement the default placement for ELLs in California (1998). Bilingual option can be pursued only through a separate waiver process.

Proposition 203. 2000 English-only ballot initiative in Arizona, similar to Proposition 227 and Question 2.

pull factors. Positive factors about a country or community that draw people to move and settle there.

pull-out second language classes. Classes taught by specialist second language teachers who take students out of the standard curriculum classroom for a portion of the day.

push factors. Negative factors in their home community or country that drive people to migrate push-in second language model. Monolingual model in which a specialist second language teacher works in the classroom with the standard curriculum teacher, keeping ELLs with their fluent English-speaking peers.

Question 2. Referendum passed in Massachusetts in 2002 to change the state's 30-year-old transitional bilingual education law, making English-only the default program for ELLs in the state. (Legislators subsequently exempted two-way immersion from the waiver requirements.)

reclassification. Categorization of ELLs as "proficient"; typically implies leaving (exiting) specialized language support.

recitation script. Interaction between teachers and students characterized by teacher-dominated talk that follows an Initiation-Response-Evaluation pattern.

regional minority languages. Languages typically with a long history of linguistic, cultural, and political traditions in a particular, circumscribed geographical area.

reluctant bilingual discourse. A transitional bilingual discourse that uses students' native languages to facilitate assimilation.

second language. A language learned at a later stage than the native language.

self-contained second language programs. Full-time programs for minority language speakers to teach content and the dominant language.

semilingualism. Pejorative term to describe what is considered limited skills in two languages.

separate underlying proficiency (SUP). Developed by Cummins; refers to the separateness of the two language systems of bilinguals, best represented by a container view of two separate systems competing for cognitive space.

sheltered English instruction. See specially designed academic instruction in English (SDAIE).

simultaneous biliteracy development. Development of reading and writing skills in two languages at the same time.

simultaneous language acquisition. Acquisition of two languages at the same time, generally before the age of 3 (also bilingual acquisition).

singlets. Words that bilinguals know in only one of their two languages.

social language proficiency. Language features and functions associated with interpersonal communication.

social networks. Set of relationships with others across different domains that affect which language and language features are used.

societal or dominant language. Language used for communication in the public domain (media, government, educational institutions).

SOCRATES. European university faculty and student exchange program.

specially designed academic instruction in English (SDAIE). Instruction that is adapted for second language learners by the use of visuals, hands-on learning, and other strategies that make instruction in the second language more comprehensible.

standard language ideology. View that the standard language variety (and its speakers) is (naturally) superior to other varieties of the language.

status planning. Language policy activities that focus on elevating the status of a particular language by extending the domains where it is used.

steamer classes. 1-year classes for immigrants during the 1920s estabished in New York and Boston.

structured English immersion. Mandated English-only option under Proposition 227, Proposition 203, and Question 2, defined primarily as an English language development program, though some states have interpreted it to include content instruction as well.

subtractive bilingualism. Acquisition of a second language that occurs at the expense of maintaining and developing the first language.

successive language acquisition. Acquisiton of a second language after first language acquistion (after age 3).

test bias. Occurs as a result lack of familiarity with (standardized) tests and to fill them out.

threatened languages. Languages that a decreasing number of children are learning.

threshold hypothesis. Theoretical hypothesis put forth by Cummins claiming that there may be a minimum level of bilingualism necessary in order to observe positive cognitive effects and avoid negative effects.

time-on-task argument. The more time spend in the second language, the better the language will be learned, with the implication that time spend in the native language detracts from second language acquisition.

transitional bilingual education (TBE). Subtractive bilingual education model for minority language speakers in which the native language is used only temporarily as a bridge to learning the societal language.

translanguaging. Dynamic view of code-switching that focuses on how code-switching is used for different communicative purposes and meaning making.

transnationalism. The phenomenon of back and forth movement between the home country and other countries, supporting identification with multiple national identities two-way immersion (TWI). Integrated model of additive bilingual education for native majority and native minority language speakers.

vernacular languages. Languages used for daily communication among people in a particular community.

voluntary bilingualism. Acquisition context in which becoming bilingual is a choice rather than a necessity (also elective bilingualism; elite bilingualism).

waiver process. In English-only ballot initiatives, the steps necessary to secure permission to offer bilingual options to some students.

white space. Term used by Kenji Hakuta to indicate the difference between actual and expected grade level performance.

world Englishes. Multiple varieties of English that have developed globally as a result of language contact between English and other languages.

References

Abedi, J. (2004). The No Child Left Behind Act and English language learners: Assessment and accountability issues. *Educational Researcher, 33*(1), 4–14.

Adams, D. W. (1995). *Education for distinction: American Indians and the boarding school experience, 1975–1928.* Lawrence: University Press of Kansas.

Adams, D. W. (1995). *Education for distinction: American Indians and the boarding school experience 1975–1928.* Lawrence: University Press of Kansas.

Afendras, E. A., Miller, S., Aogain, E. M., Bamgbose, A., Kachru, Y., Saleemi, A. P., et al. (1995). On "new/non-native" Englishes: A gamelan. *Journal of Pragmatics, 24,* 295–321.

Alba, R. (2005). Bilingualism persists, but English still dominates. Retrieved January 9, 2007, from http://migrationinformation.com/Feature/print.cfm?ID=282

Alba, R., Logan, J., Lutz, A., & Stults, B. (2002). Only English by the third generation? Loss and preservation of the mother tongue among the grandchildren of contemporary immigrants. *Demography, 39*(3), 467–484.

Allen, B. M. (2002). ASL-English bilingual classroom: The families' perspectives. *Bilingual Research Journal, 26,* 1–20.

Allington, R. (2002). *Big brother and the National Reading Curriculum: How ideology trumped evidence.* Portsmouth: Heinemann.

Amaral, O. M. (2001). Parents' decisions about bilingual programs models. *Bilingual Research Journal, 25*(1&2), 1–23.

Amrein, A., & Peña, R. A. (2000). Asymmetry in dual language practices: Assessing imbalance in a program promoting equality. *Education Policy Analysis Archives, 8*(8). Available at http://epaa.asu.edu/ojs/article/view/399

Anderson, B. (1991). *Imagined communities. Reflections on the origin and spread of nationalism.* (2nd ed.). New York: Verso.

Andersson, T. (1971). Bilingual education: The American experience. *Modern Language Journal, 55*(7), 427–440.

Angelova, M., Gunarwarneda, D., & Volk, D. (2006). Peer teaching and learning: Co-constructing language in a dual language first grade. *Language and Education, 20*(3), 173–190.

Anton, M., & DiCamilla, F. (1999). Socio-cognitive functions of L1 collaborative interaction in the L2 classroom. *Modern Language Journal, 83*(2), 233–247.

Appel, R., & Muysken, P. (2005). *Language contact and bilingualism.* Amsterdam: Amsterdam University Press.

Aronin, L. (2005). Theoretical perspectives of trilingual education. *International Journal of the Sociology of Language, 171,* 7–22.

Artiles, A. J., & Ortiz, A. A. (Eds.). (2002). *English language learners with special education needs.* Washington, DC, and McHenry, IL: Center for Applied Linguistics and Delta Systems.

Artiles, A. J., Rueda, R., Salazar, J. J., & Higareda, I. (2008). Within-group diversity in minority disproportionate representation: English language learners in urban school districts. *Exceptional Children, 71*(3), 283–300.

Asher, N. (2008). Listening to hyphenated Americans: Hybrid identities of youth from immigrant families. *Theory into Practice, 47,* 12–19.

August, D., Carlo, M. S., Dressler, C., & Snow, C. E. (2005). The critical role of vocabulary development for English language learners. *Learning Disabilities Research & Practice, 20*(1), 50–57.

August, D., & Hakuta, K. (1997). *Improving schooling for language-minority children: A research agenda.* Washington, DC: National Academic Press.

August, D., & Shanahan, T. (2006). *Developing literacy in second-language learners: Report of the national literacy panel on language-minority children and youth.* Mahwah: Lawrence Erlbaum.

Azurmendi, M. J., Bachoc, E., & Zabaleta, F. (2001). Reversing language shift: The case of Basque. In J. A. Fishman (Ed.), *Can threatened languages be saved? Reversing language shift, revisited: A 21st century perspective* (pp. 234–259). Clevedon: Multilingual Matters.

Baca, L. M., & Cervantes, H. Y. (2003). *The bilingual special education interface* (4th ed.). Upper Saddle River, NJ: Merrill Prentice Hall.

Bacchi, C. (2000). Policy as discourse: What does it mean? Where does it get us? *Discourse: Studies in the Cultural Politics of Education, 21*(1), 45–57.

Baetens Beardsmore, H. (1995). The European school experience in multilingual education. In T. Skutnabb-Kangas (Ed.), *Multilingualism for all* (pp. 21–68). Lisse, NL: Swets and Zeitlinger.

Bailey, A. (2007). *The language demands of school: Putting academic English to the test.* New Haven: Yale University Press.

Bailey, B. (2007). heteroglossia and boundaries. In M. Heller (Ed.), *Bilingualism: A social approach* (pp. 257–276). New York: Palgrave.

Baker, C. (2006). *Foundations of bilingual education and bilingualism* (4th ed.). Clevedon, UK: Multilingual Matters.

Baker, K., & de Kanter, A. (1983). *Bilingual education.* Lexington: D. C. Heath.

Baker, K. A., & de Kanter, A. A. (1981). *Effectiveness of bilingual education: Review of the literature.* Washington, DC: U.S. Department of Education, Office of Planning, Budget and Evaluation.

Bamgbose, A. (1998). Torn between the norms: Innovations in world Englishes. *World Englishes, 17*(1), 1–14.

Bamgbose, A. (2001). World Englishes and globalisation. *World Englishes, 20*(3), 357–363.

Bamgbose, A. (2003). A recurring decimal: English in language policy and planning. *World Englishes, 22*(4), 419–431.

Bangura, A. K., & Muo, M. C. (2001). *United States Congress and bilingual education.* New York: Peter Lang.

Barkhuizen, G. P. (2002). Language-in-education policy: Students' perceptions of the status and role of Xhosa and English. *System, 30*, 499–515.

Baron, Dennis. (n.d.) Spanish abuse. http://www.english.illinois.edu/-people-/faculty/debaron/essays/spanish.htm

Bash, L. (2005). Identity, boundary, and schooling: Perspectives on the experiences and perceptions of refugee children. *Intercultural Education, 16*(4), 351–366.

Bayley, R., & Schecter, S. R. (2003). *Language socialization in bilingual and multilingual societies.* Tonawanda, NY: Multilingual Matters.

Bayley, R., Schecter, S. R., & Torres-Ayala, B. (1996). Strategies for bilingual maintenance: Case studies of Mexican-origin families in Texas. *Linguistics and Education, 8*, 389–408.

Beacco, J.-C., & Byram, M. (2003). *Guide for the development of language education policies in Europe.* Strasbourg, LU: Council of Europe.

Bearse, C. A., & de Jong, E. (2008). Cultural and linguistic investment: Adolescents in a secondary two-way immersion program. *Equity & Excellence in Education, 41*(3), 325–340.

Benson, C. (2005a). Bilingual schooling as educational development: From experimentation to implementation. In J. Cohen, K. McAlister, K. Rolstad, & J. MacSwan (Eds.), *Proceedings of the 4th International Symposium on Bilingualism.* Somerville, MA: Cascadilla Press.

Benson, C. (2005b). *Girls, educational equity, and mother tongue-based teaching.* Bangkok: UNESCO.

Benton, R., & Benton, N. (2001). RLS in Aotearoa/New Zealand 1989–1999. In J. A. Fishman (Ed.), *Can threatened languages be saved? Reversing language shift, revisited: A 21st century perspective* (pp. 423–450). Clevedon: Multilingual Matters.

Berg, E. C., Hult, F. M., & King, K. A. (2001). Shaping the climate for language shift? English in Sweden's elite domains. *World Englishes, 20*(3), 305–319.

Berlin, I. (1980). Time, space, and the evolution of Afro-American society on British mainland North America. *American Historical Review, 85*(1), 44–78.

Berrol, S. C. (1982). Public schools and immigrants: The New York City experience. In R. J. Weiss (Ed.) *American education and the European immigrant: 1840–1940* (pp. 31–43). Urbana: University of Illinois Press.

Berrol, S. C. (1995). *Growing up American: Immigrant children in America; Then and Now.* New York: Twayne.

Berry, J. W. (2005). Acculturation: Living successfully in two cultures. *International Journal of Intercultural Relations, 29*, 697–712.

Berry, J. W., Phinney, J. S., Sam, D., & Vedder, P. (2006). Immigrant youth: Acculturation, identity, and adaptation. *Applied Psychology: An International Review, 55*(3), 303–332.

Bialystok, E. (2001). *Bilingualism in development: Language, literacy, & cognition.* Cambridge: Cambridge University Press.

Bialystok, E. (2009). Bilingualism; The good, the bad, and the indifferent. *Bilingualism: Language and Cognition, 12*(1), 3–11.

Bialystok, E., Craik, F. I. M., & Freedman, M. (2007). Bilingualism as a protection against the onset of symptoms of dementia. *Neuropsychologia, 45*, 459–464.

Bialystok, E., Craik, F. I. M., Klein, R., & Viswanathan, M. (2004). Bilingualism aging, and cognitive control: Evidence from the Simon task. *Journal of Experimental Psychology: Learning, Memory, and Cognition, 34*, 859–873.

Biggs, A. P., & Edwards, V. (1991). "I treat them all the same": Teacher-pupil talk in multiethnic classrooms. *Language and Education, 5*(3), 161–176.

Birch, B. M. (2007). *English L2 reading: Getting to the bottom* (2nd ed.). Mahwah, NJ: Lawrence Erlbaum.

Bishop, R. (2003). Changing power relations in education: Kaupapa Maori messages for "mainstream" education in Aotearoa/New Zealand [1]. *Comparative Education, 39*(2), 221–238.

Bjorklund, S. (2005). Toward trilingual education in Vaasa/Vasa, Finland. *International Journal of the Sociology of Language, 171*, 23–40.

Black, W. R. (2006). Constructing accountability performance for English language learner students: An unfinished journey toward language minority rights. *Educational Policy, 20*(1), 197–224.

Blackledge, A. (2000). *Literacy, power, and social justice.* Stoke-on-Trent: Trentham Books.

Bloomfield, L. (1933). *Language.* New York: Holt.

Blyth, C. (Ed.). (2003). *The sociolinguistics of foreign-language classrooms.* Boston: Heinle & Heinle.

Bourhis, R. Y. (2000). Acculturation, language maintenance, and language shift. In J. Klatter-Folmer & P. Van Avermaet (Eds.), *Theories on maintenance and loss of minority languages: Towards a more integrated explanatory framework* (pp. 5–37). New York: Waxmann Muenster.

Boyd, S., & Huss, L. (Eds.). (2001). *Managing multilingualism in a European nation-state.* Clevedon, UK: Multilingual Matters.

Boyson, B. A., & Short, D. J. (2003). *Secondary school newcomer programs in the United States.* Santa Cruz, CA: Center for Research on Education, Diversity & Excellence.

Brisk, M. E. (1981). Language policies in American education. *Journal of Education, 63*(1), 3–15.

Brisk, M. E. (1991). Toward multilingual and multicultural mainstream education. *Journal of Education, 173*(2), 114–129.

Brisk, M. E. (2006). *Bilingual education: From compensatory to quality education* (2nd ed.). Mahwah, NJ: Lawrence Erlbaum.

Brisk, M. E. (Ed.). (2008). *Language, culture, and community in teacher education.* Mahwah, NJ: Lawrence Erlbaum.

Brisk, M. E.; Burgos, A., & Hamerla, S. R. (2004). *Situational context of education: A window into the world of bilingual learners.* Mahwah, NJ: Lawrence Erlbaum.

Brisk, M. E., & Harrington, M. (2000). *Literacy and bilingualism: A handbook for all teachers.* Mahwah, NJ: Lawrence Erlbaum.

Brock-Utne, B. (2001a). Education for all: in whose language? *Oxford Review of Education, 27*(1), 115–134.

Brock-Utne, B. (2001b). The growth of English for academic communication in the Nordic countries. *International Review of Education, 47*(3&4), 221–233.

Brock-Utne, B. (2007). Learning through a familiar language versus learning through a foreign language - A look into some secondary school classrooms in Tanzania. *International Journal of Educational Development, 27*, 487–498.

Brown, H. D. (2006). *Principles of language teaching and learning.* Englewood Cliffs, NJ : Prentice Hall.

Brown v. Board of Education of Topeka, 347 U.S. 483 (1954).

Brumberg, S. B. (1986). *Going to America, going to school: The Jewish immigrant public school encounter in turn-of-the-century New York City.* New York: Praeger.

Brutt-Griffler, J. (2002). *World English: A study of its development.* Clevedon, UK: Multilingual Matters.

Brutt-Griffler, J., & Samimy, K. K. (2001). Transcending the nativeness paradigm. *World Englishes, 20*(1), 99–106.

Buriel, R., Perez, W., De Ment, T. L., Chavez, D. V., & Moran, V. R. (1998). The relationship of language brokering to academic performance, biculturalism, and self-efficacy among Latino adolescents. *Hispanic Journal of Behavioral Sciences, 20*(3), 283–297.

Burnaby, B., & Reyhner, J. (Eds.). (2002). *Indigenous languages across the community.* Seventh Annual Stabilizing Indigenous Languages Symposium, Toronto, May 11–14, 2000. Flagstaff: Northern Arizona University.

Calderon, M., & Minaya-Rowe, L. (2003). *Designing and implementing two-way bilingual programs: A step-by-step guide for administrators, teachers, and parents.* Thousand Oaks: Corwin Press.

Canagarajah, A. S. (1999). *Resisting linguistic imperialism in English teaching.* Oxford: Oxford University Press.

Canagarajah, A. S. (2000). Negotiating identities through English: Strategies from the periphery. In T. Ricento (Ed.), *Ideology, politics, and language policies: Focus on English* (pp. 121–132). Philadelphia: John Benjamins.

Carlo, M., August, D., Mclaughlin, B., Snow, C. E., Dressler, C., Lippman, D., et al. (2004). Closing the gap: Addressing the vocabulary needs of English-language learners in bilingual and mainstream classrooms. *Reading Research Quarterly, 39*(2), 188–215.

Carrigo, D. L. (2000). *Just how much English are they using? Teacher and student language distribution patterns between Spanish and English in upper grade, two-way immersion Spanish classes.* Unpublished doctoral dissertation, Harvard University.

Carter, T. P., & Chatfield, M. (1986). Effective schools for language minority students. *American Journal of Education, 97*, 200–233.

Castañeda v. Pickard, 648 F.2d 989 (1981).

Castek, J., Lev, J. D., Coiro, J., Gort, M., Henry, L., & Lima, C. (2005). *Developing new literacies among multilingual learners in the elementary grades.* University of Connecticut.

Castellanos, D. (1983). *The best of two worlds: Bilingual-bicultural education in the U.S.* Trenton: New Jersey State Department of Education.

Cazabon, M., Nicoladis, E., & Lambert, W. E. (1998). *Becoming bilingual in the Amigos two-way immersion program.* Santa Cruz, CA: National Center for Research on Cultural Diversity and Second Language Learning.

Cazden, C. B. (1990). Differential treatment in New Zealand: Reflections on research in minority education. *Teaching and Teacher Education, 6*(4), 291–303.

Cazden, C. B. (2001). *Classroom discourse: The language of teaching and learning.* Portsmouth: Heinemann.

Cazden, C. B., John, V. P., & Hymes, D. (1972). *Functions of language in the classroom.* New York: Teachers College Press.

Cenoz, J. (2003). The additive effect of bilingualism on third language acquisition: A review. *International Journal of Bilingualism, 7*(1), 71–87.

Cenoz, J. (2005). English in bilingual programs in the Basque country. *International Journal of the Sociology of Language, 171*, 41–56.

Cenoz, J. (2009) *Towards multilingual education. Basque educational research from an international perspective.* Clevedon, UK: Multilingual Matters.

Cenoz, J., & Hoffman, C. (2003). Acquiring a third language: What role does bilingualism play? *International Journal of Bilingualism, 7*(1), 1–5.

Cenoz, J., & Valencia, J. F. (1994). Additive trilingualism: Evidence from the Basque country. *Applied Psycholinguistics, 15*, 195–207.

Chan-Tibergien, J. (2006). Cultural diversity as resistance to neoliberal globalization: The emergence of a global movement and convention. *Review of Education, 52*, 89–105.

Chappell, S., & Faltis, C. (2007). Spanglish, bilingualism, culture, and identity in Latino children's literature. *Children's Literature in Education, 38*, 253–262.

Chen, S.-C. (2006). Simultaneous promotion of indigenisation and internationalisation: New language-in-education policy in Taiwan. *Language and Education, 20*(4), 322–337.

Chesterton, P., Steigler-Peters, S., Moran, W., & Piccioli, M. T. (2004). Developing sustainable language learning pathways: An Australian perspective. *Language, Culture, and Curriculum, 17*(1), 48–57.

Cho, G., Shin, F., & Krashen, S. (2004). What do we know about heritage languages? What do we need to learn about them? *Multicultural Education, 11*(4), 23–26.

Christian, D. (1996). Two-way immersion education: Students learning through two languages. *Modern Language Journal, 80*(1), 66–76.

Christian, D., & Genesee, F. (Eds.). (2001). *Bilingual education.* Alexandria, VA: TESOL.

Christian, D., Montone, C. L., Lindholm, K. J., & Carranza, I. (1997). *Profiles in two-way immersion education*. Washington, DC, and McHenry, IL: Center for Applied Linguistics and Delta Systems.

Christofides, L. N., & Swidinsky, R. (1994). Wage determination by gender and visible minority status: Evidence from the 1989 LMAS. *Canadian Public Policy, 20*(1), 34–51.

Clyne, M., Isaakidi, T., Liem, I., & Hunt, R. (2004). Developing and sharing community language resources through secondary school programmes. *International Journal of Bilingual Education and Bilingualism, 7*(4), 255–278.

Clyne, M. G. (1997). Some of the things trilinguals do. *International Journal of bilingualism, 1*(2), 96–116.

Coady, M., & O'Laoire, M. (2002). Mismatches in language policy and practice in education: The case of Gaelscoileanna in the Republic of Ireland. *Language Policy, 1*, 143–158.

Cohen, D., de la Vega, R., & Watson, G. (2001). *Advocacy for Social Justice: A Global Action and Reflection Guide*. West Hartford: Kumarian Press.

Cohen, E. G., & Lotan, R. A. (1997). *Working for equity in heterogeneous classrooms: Sociological theory in practice*. New York: Teachers College Press.

Cohen, E. G., Lotan, R. A., Scarloss, B. A., & Arellano, A. R. (1999). Complex instruction: Equity in cooperative learning classrooms. *Theory into Practice, 38*(2), 80–86.

Collier, P., Honohan, P., & Moene, K. (2001). Implications of ethnic diversity. *Economic Policy, 16*(32), 129–166.

Collier, V. P. (1989). How long? A synthesis of research on academic achievement in a second language. *TESOL Quarterly, 23*(3), 509–531.

Collier, V. P. (1992). A synthesis of studies examining long-term language minority student data on academic achievement. *Bilingual Research Journal, 16*(1&2), 187–212.

Collier, V. P. (1995). *Promoting academic success for ESL students*. Woodside, NY: Bastos Books.

Commins, N. L. (1989). Language and affect: Bilingual children at home and at school. *Language Arts, 66*, 29–43.

Commins, N. L. (2008, November 14). Design, delivery, and equity: The inextricable links. Paper presented at the La Cosecha, Santa Fe, NM.

Commission of the European Communities (2005). *A new framework strategy for multilingualism: Communication from the Commission to the Council, the European parliament, the European economic and social committee, and the committee of the regions*. Retrieved June 15, 2009, from http://ec.europa.edu/education/policies/lang/doc/com596_en.pdf

Conklin, N. F., & Lourie, M. A. (1983). *A host of tongues: Language communities in the United States*. New York: Free Press.

Constantino, R., & Lavadenz, M. (1993). Newcomer schools: First impressions. *Peabody Journal of Education, 69*(1), 82–101.

Conteh, J., Martin, P., & Robertson, L. (2007). *Multilingual learning stories from schools and communities in Britain*. Sterling, UK: Trentham Books.

Cook, V. (1999). Going beyond the native speaker in language teaching. *TESOL Quarterly, 33*(2), 185–209.

Cook, V. (2001). Using the first language in the classroom. *Canadian Modern Language Review, 57*(3), 402–423.

Cook, V. (Ed.). (2003). *Effects of the second language on the first*. Clevedon, UK: Multilingual Matters.

Cooper, R. L. (1989). *Language planning and social change*. Cambridge: Cambridge University Press.

Corson, D. (1999). *Language policy in schools: A resource for teachers and administrators*. Mahwah: Lawrence Erlbaum.

Corson, D. (2001). *Language diversity and education*. Mahwah: Lawrence Erlbaum.

Cortino, J., de la Garza, R., & Pinto, P. (2007, February). *No entiendo: The effects of bilingualism on Hispanic earnings*. ISERP working paper 07-03. http://iserp.columbia.edu/files/iserp/2007_03.pdf

Craig, B. A. (1996). Parental attitudes toward bilingualism in a local two-way immersion program. *Bilingual Research Journal, 20*(3&4), 383–410.

Crawford, J. (1992). *Language loyalties: A source book on the official English controversy* (4th ed.). Chicago: University of Chicago Press.

Crawford, J. (1997). *Best evidence: Research foundations of the Bilingual Education Act*. Washington, DC: National Clearinghouse for Bilingual Education.

Crawford, J. (1998). *The bilingual education story: Why can't the news media get it right?* Paper presented to the National Association of Hispanic Journalists, June 26. Retrieved August, 25, 2005, from http://ourworld.compuserve.com/homepage/jcrawford/NAHJ.htm

Crawford, J. (1999). *Bilingual education: History, politics, theory, and practice.* (4th ed.). Los Angeles: Bilingual Educational Services.

Crawford, J. (2000). *At war with diversity*. Clevedon, UK: Multilingual Matters.

Crawford, J. (2004a). *No Child Left Behind: Misguided approach to school accountability for English language learners*. Paper presented at Forum on Ideas to Improve the NCLB Accountability Provisions for Students with Disabilities and English Language Learners, sponsored by the Center on Education Policy, Washington, DC, September 14, 2004. Retrieved June 10, 2008, from http://users.rcn.com/crawj/langpol.misguided.pdf

Crawford, J. (2004b). *Educating English learners: Language diversity in the classroom* (5th ed.). Culver City, CA: Bilingual Education Services.

Crawford, J. (2008). *Advocating for English language learners: Selected essays*. Clevedon, UK: Multilingual Matters.

Creese, A., Bhatt, A., Bhojani, N., & Martin, P. (2006). Multicultural, heritage, and learner identities in complementary schools. *Language and Education, 20*(1), 23–43.

Cuevas, G. J. (2005). Teaching mathematics to English language learners: Perspectives for effective instruction. In A. G. Huerta-Maciá (Ed.), *Working with English language learners: Perspectives and practice* (pp. 69–86). Dubuque, IA: Kendall/Hunt.

Cummins, J. (1979). Linguistic interdependency and the educational development of bilingual children. *Review of Educational Research, 49*, 222–251.

Cummins, J. (1981). Empirical and theoretical underpinnings of bilingual education. *Journal of Education, 63*(1), 16–29.

Cummins, J. (1986). Empowering language minority students. *Harvard Educational Review, 15*, 18–36.

Cummins, J. (1999). The ethics of doublethink: Language rights and the bilingual education debate. *TESOL Journal, 8* (3), 13–17.

Cummins, J. (2000). *Language, power, and pedagogy: Bilingual children in the crossfire*. Clevedon, UK: Multilingual Matters.

Cummins, J. (2001). *Negotiating identities: Education for empowerment in a diverse society* (2nd ed.). Los Angeles: California Association for Bilingual Education.

Cummins, J. (2005). A proposal for action: Strategies for recognizing heritage language competence as a learning resource within the mainstream classroom. *Modern Language Journal, 89*(4), 585–592.

Cummins, J. (2007). Pedagogies for the poor? Realigning reading instruction for low income students with scientifically based reading research. *Educational Researcher, 36*(9), 564–572.

Cummins, J. (2008). Teaching for transfer: Challenging the two solitudes assumption in bilingual education. In N. H. Hornberger (Ed.), *Encyclopedia of Language and Education* (2nd ed.).Volume 5, pp. 65–76). New York: Springer.

Cummins, J., Bismilla, V., Chow, P., Giampapa, F., Cohen, S., Leoni, L., et al. (2005). Affirming identity in multicultural classrooms. *Educational Leadership, 63*(1), 38–43.

Cummins, J., Campoy, I. F., Ada, A. F., Winsler, A., & Bleiker, C. (2006). Identity texts and literacy development among preschool English learners: Enhancing learning opportunities for children at risk for learning disabilities. *Teachers College Record, 11*, 2380–2405.

Cziko, G. A. (1992, March). The evaluation of bilingual education: From necessity to probability to possibility. *Educational Researcher, 21*(2), 10–15.

Daniels, R. (1990). *Coming to America: A history of immigration and ethnicity in American life*. New York: HarperCollins.

Danoff, M. N. (1978). *Evaluation of the impact of the ESEA Title VII Spanish/English bilingual education program: Overview of study and findings*. Palo Alto, CA: American Institutes for Research. (ERIC Document Reproduction Service No. ED154 634)

Datta, M. (2000). My story: An introduction. In M. Datta (Ed.), *Bilinguality and biliteracy: Principles and practice* (pp. 1–13). New York: Continuum.

Davidson, A. L. (1997). Marbella Sanchez: On marginalization and silencing In M. Seller & L. Weis (Eds.), *Beyond black and white: New faces and voices in U.S. schools* (pp. 15–44). Albany: State University of New York Press.

Davies, A. (1989). Is international English an interlanguage? *TESOL Quarterly, 23*(3), 447–467.

De Houwer, A. (1990). *The acquisition of two languages from birth: A case study*. New York: Cambridge University Press.

De Houwer, A. (2004). Trilingual input and children's language use in trilingual families in Flanders. In C. Hoffman & J. Ytsma (Eds.), *Trilingualism in the individual, family, and society* (pp. 118–138). Clevedon, UK: Multilingual Matters.

De Houwer, A. (2007). Parental input patterns and children's bilingual use. *Applied Psycholinguistics, 28*, 411–424.

de Jong, E.J. (1996). *Integrating language minority education in elementary schools*. Unpublished doctoral dissertation, Boston University.

de Jong, E.J. (2002). Effective bilingual education: From theory to academic achievement in a two-way bilingual program. *Bilingual Research Journal, 26*(1), 65–84.

de Jong, E.J. (2004a). After exit: Academic achievement patterns of former English language learners. *Education Policy Analysis Archives, 12*(50). Available at http://epaa.asu.edu/epaa/v12n50/

de Jong, E.J. (2004b). L2 proficiency development in a two-way and developmental bilingual program. *NABE Journal of Research and Practice, 2*(1), 77–108.

de Jong, E.J. (2006). Integrated bilingual education: An alternative approach. *Bilingual Research Journal, 30*(1), 23–44.

de Jong, E.J. (2008a). Bilingual Education. In Salkind, N. (ed) *Encyclopedia of Educational Psychology* (pp. 97–103). Thousand Oaks: Sage publications.

de Jong, E.J. (2008b). Contextualizing policy appropriation: Teachers' perspectives, local responses, and English-only ballot initiatives. *Urban Review, 40*(4), 350–370.

de Jong, E.J., & Freeman, R. (2010). Bilingual approaches. C. Leung and A. Creese (Eds.), *English as an Additional Language: Approaches to teaching linguistic minority students*, (pp.108–122). London: SAGE.

de Jong, E.J., Gort, M., & Cobb, C. D. (2005). Bilingual education within the context of English-only policies: Three districts' responses to Question 2 in Massachusetts. *Educational Policy, 19*(4), 595–620.

de Jong, E.J., & Howard, E. R. (2009). Integration in two-way immersion education: Equalising linguistic benefits for all students. *International Journal of Bilingual Education and Bilingualism, 12*(1), 81–99.

de la Luz Reyes, M. (1992). Challenging venerable assumptions: Literacy instruction for linguistically different students. *Harvard Educational Review, 62*(427–446).

de la Luz Reyes, M. (2001). Unleashing possibilities: Biliteracy in the primary grades. In M. de la Luz Reyes & J. J. Halcon (Eds.), *The best for our children: Critical perspectives on literacy for Latino students* (pp. 96–121). New York: Teachers College Press.

de la Luz Reyes, M., & Halcon, J. J. (2001). *The best of our children: Critical perspectives on literacy for Latino students.* New York: Teachers College Press.

De Mejia, A. M. (1999). Bilingual storytelling: Code switching, discourse control, and learning opportunities. *TESOL Journal, 7* (6), 4–10.

De Mejia, A. M. (2002). *Power, prestige, and bilingualism: International perspectives on elite bilingual education.* Bristol: Multilingual Matters.

de Varennes, F. (1996). *Language, minorities, and human rights.* The Hague: Martinus Nijhoff.

de Varennes, F. (2004). The right to education and minority language. Retrieved July 26, 2006, from http://www.eumap.org/journal/features/2004/minority_education/edminlang/

del Valle, J. (2000). Monoglossic policies for a heteroglossic culture: Misinterpreted multilingualism in modern Galicia. *Language & Communication, 20,* 105–132.

Delpit, L. (1995). *Other people's children: Cultural conflict in the classroom.* New York: New Press.

Delpit, L., & Dowdy, J. K. (2002). *The skin that we speak: Thoughts on language and culture in the classroom.* New York: New Press.

Deuchar, M., & Quay, S. (2000). *Bilingual acquisition: Theoretical implications of a case study.* Oxford: Oxford University Press.

Dewey, M. (2007). English as a lingua franca and globalization: An interconnected perspective. *International Journal of Applied Linguistics, 17*(3), 323–352.

Deyhle, D. (1995). Navajo youth and Anglo racism: Cultural integrity and resistance. *Harvard Educational Review, 65*(3), 403–445.

Diaz, R. M., & Klingler, C. (2001). Towards an explanatory model of the interaction between bilingualism and cognitive development. In E. Bialystok (Ed.), *Language processing in bilingual children* (pp. 167–192). Cambridge: Cambridge University Press.

Dick, G. and McCarty, T. (1997) Reclaiming Navajo: language renewal in an American Indian community school. In N. Hornberger (Ed.) *Indigenous literacies in the Americas: Language planning from the bottom up* (pp. 69–94). Berlin and New York: Mouton de Gruyter.

Dicker, S. J. (2003). *Languages in America: A pluralist view* (2nd ed.). Clevedon, UK: Multilingual Matters.

Dijkstra, T., & van Hell, J. G. (2004). Testing the language mode hypothesis using trilinguals. *International Journal of Bilingual Education and Bilingualism, 6*(1), 2–16.

Dirim, I., & Hieronymus, A. (2003). Cultural orientation and language use among multilingual youth groups: "For me it is like we all speak one language." *Journal of Multilingual and Multicultural Development, 24*(1&2), 42–55.

Dolson, D. P. (1985). Bilingualism and scholastic performance: The literature revisited. *NABE Journal, 10*(1), 1–35.

Donato, R., & Garcia, H. (1992). Language segregation in desegregated schools: A question of equity. *Equity and Excellence, 25*(2–4), 94–99.

Donato, R., Mechaca, M., & Valencia, R. R. (1991). Segregation, desegregation, and integration of Chicano students: Problems and prospects. In R. R. Valencia (Ed.), *Chicano school failure and success: Research and policy agendas for the 1990s* (pp. 27–63). London: Falmer Press.

Dorian, N.C. (1981). *Language death. The life cycle of a Scottish Gaelic dialect,* Philadelphia: University of Pennsylvania Press.

Dronkers, J. (1993). The causes of growth of English education in the Netherlands: Class or internationalisation? *European Journal of Education, 28*(3), 295–307.

Dutcher, N. (2003). *The promise and perils of mother tongue education.* Bangkok: UNESCO Bangkok.

Dworin, J. E. (2003). Insights into biliteracy development: Toward a bidirectional theory of bilingual pedagogy. *Journal of Hispanic Higher Education, 2*(2), 171–186.

Earle, C. (1992). Pioneers of providence: The Anglo-American experience, 1492–1792. *Annals of the Association of American Geographers, 82*(3), 478–499.

Easterly, W., & Ross, L. (1997). Africa's growth tragedy: Policies and ethnic divisions. *Quarterly Journal of Economics, 112*(4), 1203–1250.

Edelsky, C. (1986). *Writing a bilingual program: Habia una vez.* Norwood, NJ: Ablex.

Edelsky, C., & Hudelson, S. (1978). Acquiring a second language when you are not the underdog. In S. D. Krashen & R. C. Scarcella (Eds.), *Issues in second language research* (pp. 36–42). Rowley, MA: Newbury House.

Edelsky, C., & Hudelson, S. (1982). The acquisition (?) of Spanish as a second language. In F. Barkin, E. A. Brandt, & J. Ornstein-Galicia (Eds.), *Bilingualism and language contact: Spanish, English, and Native American languages* (pp. 203–227). New York: Teachers College Press.

Edelsky, C., Hudelson, S., Flores, B., Barkin, F., Altwerger, B., & Jilbert, K. (1982). Semilingualism and language deficit. *Applied Linguistics, 4*(1), 1–22.

Edmonds, R. R. (1979). Effective schools for the urban poor. *Educational Leadership, 37*(1), 15–27.

Education Alliance. (2000). *Rachel Carson Elementary, transitional bilingual education.* Northeast and Islands Regional Educational Laboratory, Brown University. Available at http://www.alliance.brown.edu/pubs/pos/rachelcarson.html

Edwards, J. (1994). *Multilingualism.* London: Penguin.

Edwards, J. (2001). The ecology of language revival. *Current Issues in Language Planning, 2*(2&3), 231–241.

El-Haj, A. R. T. (2006). *Elusive justice: Wrestling with difference and educational equity in everyday practice.* New York: Routledge.

Ernst-Slavit, G., & Mulhern, M. (2003, September). Bilingual books: Promoting literacy and biliteracy in the second-language and mainstream classroom. *Reading Online*, 1–13.

Escamilla, K. (2000). *Bilingual means two: Assessment issues, early literacy, and Spanish-speaking children.* Paper presented at A Research Symposium on High Standards in Reading for Students from Diverse Language Groups: Research, Practice, and Policy, Washington, DC.

Escamilla, K. (2006). Semilinguism applied to the literacy behaviors of Spanish-speaking emerging bilinguals: Biliteracy or emerging biliteracy. *Teachers College Record, 108*(11), 2329–2353.

Escamilla, K., Chavez, L., & Vigil, P. (2005). Rethinking the "gap": High-stakes testing and Spanish-speaking students in Colorado. *Journal of Teacher Education, 56*(2), 132–144.

Escamilla, K., & Coady, M. (2001). Assessing the writing of Spanish-speaking students. In S. R. Hurley & J. V. Tinajero (Eds.), *Literacy assessment of second language learners* (pp. 43–63). Boston: Allyn and Bacon.

Escamilla, K., & Hopewell, S. (2007). *The role of code-switching in the written expression of early elementary simultaneous bilinguals.* Paper presented at the Annual Meeting of American Educational Research Association, Chicago.

Escamilla, K., Hopewell, S., Geisler, D., & Ruiz, O. (2007). *Transitions to biliteracy: beyond Spanish and English.* Paper presented at the Annual Meeting of American Educational Research Association, Chicago.

Escamilla, K., Shannon, S. M., Carlos, S., & Garcia, J. (2003). Breaking the code: Colorado's defeat of the anti-bilingual education initiative (Amendment 31). *Bilingual Research Journal, 27*(3), 357–382.

Estes, J. (1999). *How many indigenous American languages are spoken in the United States? By how many speakers?* Washington, DC: National Clearinghouse for Bilingual Education.

Eurobarometer (2005). *Europeans and languages.* Brussels: European Commission.

Evans, B. A., & Hornberger, N. H. (2005). No Child Left Behind: Repealing and unpeeling federal language education policy in the United States. *Language Policy, 4*, 87–106.

Faingold, E. D. (2004a). *Multilingualism from infancy to adolescence: Noam's experience.* Greenwich: Information Age.

Faingold, E. D. (2004b). Language rights and language justice in the constitutions of the world. *Language Problems and Language Planning, 28*(1), 11–24.

Faltis, C. J. (1994). Doing the right thing: Developing a program for immigrant and bilingual secondary students. In R. Rodriguez (Ed.), *Compendium of readings in bilingual education: Issues and practices* (pp. 39–47). San Antonio: Texas Association for Bilingual Education.

Fantini, A. (1985). *Language acquisition of a bilingual child: A sociolinguistic perspective (to age ten).* San Diego: College-Hill Press.

Fass, P. (1989). *Outside/in: Minorities and the transformation of American education.* Oxford: Oxford University Press.

Fearon, J.D., & Laitin, D.D. (1996). Explaining interethnic cooperation. *The American Political Science Review, 90*(4), 715–735.

Fearon, J.D., & Laitin, D.D. (2003). Ethnicity, insurgency, and civil war. *The American Political Science Review, 97* (1), 75–90.

Ferguson, C. (2003). Diglossia. In C. B. Paulston & G. R. Tucker (Eds.), *Sociolinguistics: The essential readings* (pp. 345–358). Malden: Blackwell.

Ferguson, G. (2006). *Language planning and education.* Edinburgh: Edinburgh University Press.

Fillmore, L. W. (1991a). Second-language learning in children: A model of language learning in social context. In E. Bialystok (Ed.), *Language processing in bilingual children* (pp. 49–69). Cambridge: Cambridge University Press.

Fillmore, L. W. (1991b). When learning a second language means losing the first. *Early Childhood Research Quarterly, 6*, 323–346.

Fillmore, L. W. (2000). Loss of family languages: Should educators be concerned? *Theory into Practice, 39*(4), 203–210.

Fillmore, L. W., & Snow, C. E. (2002). What teachers need to know about language. In C. T. Adger, C. E. Snow, & D. Christian (Eds.), *What teachers need to know about language* (pp. 7–53). Washington, DC: Center for Applied Linguistics.

Fish, M. S., & Brooks, R. S. (2004). Does diversity hurt democracy? *Journal of Democracy, 15*(1), 154–166.

Fishman, J. A. (1966). Some contrasts between linguistically homogeneous and linguistically heterogeneous polities. *Sociological Inquiry, 36*, 146–158.

Fishman, J. A. (1972). *The sociology of language: an interdisciplinary social science approach to language in society.* Rowley: Newbury House.

Fishman, J. A. (Ed.). (2001). *Can threatened languages be saved?* Clevedon, UK: Multilingual Matters.

Fishman, J. A. (2003). Bilingualism with and without diglossia: Diglossia with and without bilingualism. In C. B. Paulston & G. R. Tucker (Eds.), *Sociolinguistics: The essential readings* (pp. 359–368). Malden, MA: Blackwell.

Fitts, S. (2006). Reconstructing the status quo: Linguistic interaction in a dual-language school. *Bilingual Research Journal, 29*(2), 337–365.

Flanigan, B. (1988). Second language acquisition in the elementary schools: The negotiation of meaning by native-speaking and nonnative-speaking peers *Bilingual Review/La Revista Bilingue, 14*(3), 25–40.

Flores v. Arizona, 516 F.3d 1140 (2008).

Fogleman, A. (1998). From slaves, convicts, and servants to free passengers: The transformation of immigration in the era of the American Revolution. *Journal of American History 85*(1), 43–76.

Fordham, S. (1988). Racelessness as a factor in Black students' school success: Pragmatic strategy or pyrrhic victory? *Harvard Educational Review, 58*(1), 54–84.

Fortune, W. T., & Tedick, J. (2008). *Pathways to multilingualism: Evolving perspectives on immersion education.* Clevedon: Multilingual Matters.

Fradd, S., & Boswell, T. (1996). Spanish as an economic resource in metropolitan Miami. *Bilingual Research Journal, 20*(2), 283–337.

Francis, D., Lesaux, N., & August, D. (2006). Language of instruction. In D. August & T. Shanahan (Eds.), *Developing literacy in second-language children* (pp. 365–413). Mahwah, NJ: Lawrence Erlbaum.

Francis, N., & Reyhner, J. (2002). *Language and literacy teaching for indigenous education: A bilingual approach.* Clevedon: Multilingual Matters.

Freeman, R. (1998). *Bilingual education and social change.* Clevedon: Multilingual Matters.

Freeman, D. E., & Freeman, Y. S. (2000). *Teaching reading in multilingual classrooms.* Portsmouth, NH: Heinemann.

Freeman, D. E., & Freeman, Y. S. (2001). *Between worlds: Access to second language acquisition* (2nd ed.). Portsmouth: Heinemann.

Freeman, K., Stairs, A., Corbierem, E., & Lazone, D. (1995). Ojibway, Mohawk, and Inuktitut alive and well? Issues of identity, ownership, and change. *Bilingual Research Journal, 19*(1), 39–69.

Freeman, R. (1998). *Bilingual education and social change.* Clevedon, UK: Multilingual Matters.

Freeman, R. (2004). *Building on community bilingualism.* Philadelphia: Caslon.

Friedlander, M. (1991). *The Newcomer Program: Helping immigrant students succeed in U.S. schools.* Washington, DC: National Clearinghouse for Bilingual Education.

Gajo, L. (2007). Linguistic knowledge and subject knowledge: How does bilingualism contribute to subject development? *International Journal of Bilingual Education and Bilingualism, 10*(5), 563–581.

Gal, S. (1979). *Language shift. Social determinants of linguistic change in bilingual Austria.* New York: Academic Press.

Galindo, R. (1997). Language wars: The ideological dimensions of the debates on bilingual education. *Bilingual Research Journal, 21*(2&3), 103–141.

Gándara, P. (2000). In the aftermath of the storm: English learners in the post-227 era. *Bilingual Research Journal, 24*(1&2), 1–13.

Gándara, P., & Hopkins, M. (Eds.). (2010). *Forbidden language: English learners and restrictive language policies.* New York: Teachers College Press.

Gándara, P., Maxwell-Jolly, J., & Driscoll, A. (2005). *Listening to teachers of English language learners: A survey of California teachers' challenges, experiences, and professional development needs.* Center for the Future of Teaching and Learning, Santa Cruz.

Gándara, P., Maxwell-Jolly, J, Garcia, E. Asato, J., Gutierrez, K., Stritikus, T. & Curry, J. (2000). *The initial impact of Proposition 227 on the instruction of English learners.* Davis: University of California. Linguistic Minority Institute. Education Policy Center.

Gándara, P., & Merino, B. J. (1993). Measuring the outcomes of LEP programs: Test scores, exit rates, and other mythological data. *Educational Evaluation and Policy Analysis, 15*(3), 320–338.

Gándara, P., Moran, R., & García, E. E. (2004). Legacy of Brown: Lau and language policy in the United States. *Review of Research in Education, 28*, 27–46.

Gándara, P., Rumberger, R. W., Maxwell-Jolly, J., & Callahan, R. (2003). English learners in California schools: Unequal resources, unequal outcomes. *Education Policy Analysis Archives, 11* (36).

García, E. E. (1988). Attributes of effective schools for language minority students. *Education and Urban Society, 83*(4), 387–398.

García, E. E., & Cuellar, D. (2006). Who are these linguistically and culturally diverse students? *Teachers College Record, 108*(11), 2220–2246.

García, E. E., & Curry-Rodriguez, J. E. (2000). The education of limited English proficient students in California schools: An assessment of the influence of Proposition 227 in selected districts and schools. *Bilingual Research Journal, 24*(1&2), 15–36.

García, O. (2008). *Bilingual education in the 21st century: A global perspective.* Malden, MA: Wiley-Blackwell.

García, O. (2009). Education, multilingualism, and translanguaging in the 21st century. In T. Skutnabb-Kangas, R. Phillipson, A. K. Mohanty, & M. Panda (Eds.), *Social justice through multilingual education* (pp. 140–158). Bristol: Multilingual Matters.

García, O., Skutnabb-Kangas, T., & Torres-Guzmán, M. (2006). *Imagining multilingual schools: Language in education and glocalization* Clevedon: Multilingual Matters.

Garret, P. B. (2007). Language socialization and the (re)production of bilingual subjectivities. In M. Heller (Ed.), *Bilingualism: A social approach* (pp. 233–257). New York: Palgrave.

Gass, S. M., & Selinker, L. (2008). *Second language acquisition: An introductory course* (3rd ed.). New York: Routledge.

Gay, G. (2000). *Culturally responsive teaching: Theory, research, and practice.* New York: Teachers College Press.

Genesee, F. (1999). *Program alternatives for linguistically diverse students.* Santa Cruz: Center for Research on Education, Diversity & Excellence.

Genesee, F. (2004). What do we know about bilingual education for majority language students? In T. K. Bhatia & W. Ritchie (Eds.), *Handbook of bilingualism and multiculturalism* (pp. 547–576). Malden: Blackwell.

Genesee, F., Lindholm-Leary, K. J., Saunders, W.M., & Christian, D. (2006). *Educating English language learners: A synthesis of research evidence.* Cambridge: Cambridge University Press.

Genesee, F., Lindholm-Leary, K. J., Saunders, W.M., & Christian, D. (2005). English language learners in U.S. schools: An overview of research. *Journal of Education for Students Placed at Risk, 10*(4), 363–385.

Genesee, F., Paradis, J., & Crago, M. B. (2003). *Dual language development and disorders: A handbook on bilingualism and second language learning*. Baltimore: Paul H. Brooks.

Gersten, R., & Baker, S. (2000). What we know about effective instructional practices for English-language learners. *Exceptional Children*, 6(4), 454–470.

Gersten, R., & Woodward, J. (1995). A longitudinal study of transitional and immersion bilingual education programs in one district. *Elementary School Journal*, 95(3), 223–239.

Getz, L. M. (1997). *Schools of their own: The education of Hispanos in New Mexico, 1850–1940*. Albuquerque: University of New Mexico Press.

Giacchino-Baker, R., & Piller, B. (2006). Parental motivation, attitudes, support, and commitment in a Southern Californian two-way immersion program. *Journal of Latinos and Education*, 5(1), 5–28.

Gibbons, P. (2002). *Scaffolding language, scaffolding learning*. Portsmouth, NH: Heinemann.

Glass, T. E. (1988). Federal policy in Native American education, 1925–1985. *Journal of Educational Policy*, 3(2), 105–121.

Glenn, C. L. (with de Jong, E.J.). (1996). *Educating immigrant children: Schools and language minorities in twelve nations*. New York: Garland.

Golash-Boza, T. (2005). Assessing the advantages of bilingualism for the children of immigrants. *International Migration Review*, 39(3), 721–753.

Gold, N. (2006). *Successful bilingual schools: Six effective programs in California*. San Diego, CA: San Diego County Office of Education.

Goldenberg, C. (2008). Teaching English language learners: What the research does—and does not—say. *American Educator*, 8–23, 43–44.

Goldstein, T. (2003). Contemporary bilingual life at a Canadian high school: Choices, risks, tensions, and dilemmas. *Sociology of Education*, 76, 247–264.

Gonzales, G. (1990). *Chicano education in the era of segregation*. Cranbury: Associated University Press.

Gonzales, M. L., Huerta-Macías, A., & Tinajero, J. V. (Eds.). (1998). *Educating Latino students: A guide to successful practice*. Lancaster: Technomic.

González, J. M. (1979). *Bilingual education in the integrated school: Some social and pedagogical factors*. Rosslyn, VA: NCBE.

González, N., & Amanti, C. (1997). Teaching anthropological methods to teachers: The transformation of knowledge. In C. Kottak, J. White, R. Furlow & P. Rice (Eds.), *The teaching of anthropology: Problems, issues, and decisions* (pp. 353–359). Mountain View, CA: Mayfield.

González, N., Andrade, R., Civil, M., & Moll, L. C. (2001). Bridging funds of distributed knowledge: Creating zones of practices in mathematics. *Journal of Education for Students Placed At Risk*, 6(1&2), 115–132.

González, N., Moll, L. C., Tenery, M. F., Rivera, A., Rendon, P., Gonzales, R., et al. (1995). Funds of knowledge for teaching in Latino households. *Urban Education*, 29, 444–471.

Gonzalez, R. D. (2001). Lessons from colonial language policies. In R.D. Gonzalez (Ed.) *Language ideologies: Critical perspectives on the official English movement* (pp. 195–219). Urbana, IL: National Council of Teachers of English.

Gort, M. (2006). Strategic codeswitching, interliteracy, and other phenomena of emergent bilingual writing: Lessons from first grade dual language classrooms. *Journal of Early Childhood Literacy*, 6(3), 323–354.

Gort, M. (2008). "You give me idea!": Collaborative strides toward bilingualism, biliteracy, and cross-cultural understanding in a two-way partial immersion program. *Multicultural Perspectives*, 10(4), 192–200.

Gort, M., de Jong, E. J., & Cobb, C. D. (2008). Seeing through a bilingual lens: Structural and ideological contexts of structured English immersion in three Massachusetts districts. *Journal of Educational Research and Policy Studies*, 8(2), 41–67.

Gorter, D. (2005). Three languages of instruction in Fryslan. *International Journal of the Sociology of Language*, 171, 57–73.

Grabe, W., & Stoller, F. L. (2002). *Teaching and researching reading*. London: Longman.

Graddol, D. (2006). *English Next*. London: British Council.

Gravelle, M. (1996). *Supporting bilingual learners in school*. Stoke-on-Trent: Trentham Books.

Greene, J. P. (1997). A meta-analysis of the Rossell and Baker review of bilingual education research. *Bilingual Research Journal*, 21(2&3), 103–122.

Greene, J. P. (1998). *A meta-analysis of the effectiveness of bilingual education*. Austin, TX: Thomas Rivera Policy Institute.

Gregory, E. (1998). Siblings as mediators of literacy in linguistic minority communities. *Language and Education*, 12(1), 33–55.

Griego-Jones, T. (1994). Assessing students' perceptions of biliteracy in a two-way bilingual classroom. *Journal of Educational Issues of Language Minority Students*, 13(Spring), 79–93.

Grin, F., & Vaillancourt, F. (1997). The economics of multilingualism: Overview and analytical framework. *Annual Review of Applied Linguistics*, 17, 43–65.

Grissom, J. B. (2004). Reclassification of English learners. *Education Policy Analysis Archives*, 12 (36). Retrieved August 2, 2004, from http://epaa .asu.edu/epaa/v12n36

Grosjean, F. (1982). *Life with two languages: An introduction to bilingualism*. Cambridge, MA: Harvard University Press.

Grosjean, F. (1989). Neurolinguists, beware! The bilingual is not two monolinguals in one person. *Brain and Language*, 36, 3–15.

Grosjean, F. (1998). Studying bilinguals: Methodological and conceptual issues. *Bilingualism: Language and Cognition*, 50, 131–149.

Gumperz, J., & Cook-Gumperz, J. (2005). Making space for bilingual communicative practice. *Intercultural Pragmatics*, 2(1), 1–23.

Gurthie, L. F. (1984). Contrast in teachers' language use in a Chinese-English bilingual classroom. In J. Handscombe, R. A. Orem, & B. P. Taylor

(Eds.), *On TESOL '83: The question of control.* (pp. 39–52). Washington, DC: TESOL.

Gutierrez, K. (2001). Smoke and mirrors: Language policy and educational reform. In J. Larson (Ed.), *Literacy as snake oil* (pp. 111–122). New York: Peter Lang.

Gutierrez, K., & Larson, J. (1994). Language borders: Recitation as hegemonic discourse. *International Journal of Educational Reform, 3*(1), 22–36.

Hadi-Tabassum, S. (2005). *Language, space and power: A critical look at bilingual education.* Clevedon: Multilingual Matters.

Hakuta, K. (1996). *Mirror of language.* New York: Basic Books.

Hakuta, K. (2001). *Key policy milestones and directions in the education of English language learners.* Prepared for the Rockefeller Foundation Symposium Leveraging Change: An Emerging Framework for Educational Equity, April 5, 2001, Washington, DC. Retrieved September 16, 2010 from http://www.stanford.edu/~hakuta/www/docs/rockefeller/

Hakuta, K., Butler, Y. G., & Witt, D. (2000). *How long does it take English learners to attain proficiency?* Santa Ana: University of California, Linguistic Minority Research Institute.

Hakuta, K., & D'Andrea, D. (1991). Some properties of bilingual maintenance and loss in Mexican background high-school students. *Applied Linguistics, 13*(1), 72–99.

Hale, K. (1992). Language endangerment and the human value of linguistic diversity. *Language, 68*(1), 35–42.

Hall, J. K., Cheng, A., & Carlson, M. T. (2006). Reconceptualizing multicompetence as a theory of language knowledge. *Applied Linguistics, 27*(2), 220–240.

Hamayan, E., Marler, B., Sanchez-Lopez, C., & Damico, J. (2007). *Special education considerations for English language learners: Delivering a continuum of services.* Philadelphia: Caslon.

Hamers, J. F., & Blanc, M. H. A. (2000). *Bilinguality and bilingualism* (2nd ed.). Cambridge: Cambridge University Press.

Handlin, O. (1982). Education and the European immigrant, 1820–1920. In B. J. Weiss (Ed.), *American education and the European immigrant: 1840–1940* (pp. 3–16). Urbana: University of Illinois Press.

Harklau, L. (1999). The ESL learning environment in secondary school. In C. Faltis & P. Wolfe (Eds.), *So much to say: Adolescents, bilingualism, and ESL in the secondary school* (pp. 42–60). New York: Teachers College Press.

Harper, C. A., & de Jong, E. (2004). Misconceptions about teaching ELLs. *Journal of Adolescent & Adult Literacy, 48*(2), 152–162.

Harper, C. A., de Jong, E., & Platt, E. J. (2008). Marginalizing English as a second language teacher expertise: The exclusionary consequence of *No Child Left Behind. Language Policy, 7,* 267–284.

Harper, C. A., & Platt, E. J. (1998). Full inclusion for secondary school ESOL students: Some concerns from Florida. *TESOL Journal, 7*(5), 30–36.

Harris, S. (1994). "Soft" and "hard" domain theory for bicultural education for indigenous groups. *Peabody Journal of Education, 69*(2), 140–153.

Hartmann, E. G. (1967). *The movement to Americanize the immigrant.* New York: AMS Press.

Hause, J. (2003). English as a lingua franca: A threat to multilingualism. *Journal of Sociolinguistics, 7*(4), 556–578.

Havighurst, R. J. (1978, March). Indian education since 1960. *Annals of the American Academy of Political and Social Sciences, 436,* 13–26.

Heath, S. B. (1977). A national language academy? Debate in the new nation. *Linguistics, 189,* 9–43.

Heath, S. B. (1982). What no bedtime story means: Narrative skills at home and school. *Language and Society, 11*(1), 49–76.

Heath, S. B. (1983a, May/June). Language policies. *Society,* 56–73.

Heath, S. B. (1983b). *Ways with words: Language, life and work in communities and classrooms.* Cambridge: Cambridge University Press.

Heller, M., & Martin-Jones, M. (Eds.). (2000). *Voices of authority: Education and linguistic difference.* Westport: Ablex.

Henze, R. C., & Lucas, T. (1993). Shaping instruction to promote the success of language minority students: An analysis of four high school classes. *Peabody Journal of Education, 63*(1), 54–81.

Henze, R. C., & Vanett, L. (1993). To walk in two worlds—or more? Challenging a common metaphor of native education. *Anthropology and Education Quarterly, 24*(2), 116–134.

Herdina, P., & Jessner, U. (2002). *A dynamic model of multilingualism: Perspectives of change in psycholinguistics.* Clevedon: Multilingual Matters.

Hickey, T. (2001). Mixing beginners and native speakers in minority language immersion: Who is immersing whom? *Canadian Modern Language Review, 57*(3), 443–474.

Higham, J. (1998). *Strangers in the land: Patterns of American nativism, 1860–1925* (4th ed.). New Brunswick, NJ: Rutgers University Press.

Hill, E. G. (2004). *A look at the progress of English language learners.* Sacramento: Legislative Analysts' Office.

Hill, H. C. (1991). The Americanization movement. *American Journal of Sociology. 24*(6), 609–642.

Hinton, L. (1994). *Flutes of fire: Essays on California Indian languages.* Berkeley: Heyday Books.

Hinton, L. (2001). Involuntary language loss among immigrants: Asian-American linguistic autobiographies. In J. E. Alatis & A.-H. Tan (Eds.), *Language in our time: Bilingual education and Official English, Ebonics and standard English, immigration and the Unz initiative* (pp. 203–252). Washington, D.C.: Georgetown University Press.

Hinton, L. (2003). Language revitalization. *Annual Review of Applied Linguistics, 23,* 44–57.

Hinton, L., & Hale, K. (Eds.). (2001). *The green book of language revitalization in practice.* San Diego: Academic Press.

Hoffman, C. (1998). Luxembourg and the European schools. In J. Cenoz & F. Genesee (Eds.), *Beyond bilingualism: Multilingualism and multilingual education* (pp. 143–174). Clevedon: Multilingual Matters.

Hoffman, C. (2001). Towards a description of trilingual competence. *International Journal of Bilingualism, 5*(1), 1–17.

Hoffman, E. (1989). *Lost in translation: A life in a new language.* New York: Penguin.

Holm, A., & Holm, W. (1990, March). Rock Point, A Navajo way to go to school: A valediction. *Annals of the American Association of Political Science Studies, 508,* 170–184.

Hornberger, N. H. (1989). Continua of biliteracy. *Review of Educational Research, 59*(3), 271–296.

Hornberger, N. H. (1998). Language policy, language education, language rights: Indigenous, immigrant, and international perspectives. *Language in Society, 27,* 439–458.

Hornberger, N. H., & Evans, B. (2005). No Child Left Behind: Repealing and unpeeling federal language education policy in the United States. *Language Policy, 4,* 87–106.

Hornberger, N. H., & Lopez, L. E. (1998). Policy, possibility, and paradox: Indigenous multi-lingualism and education in Peru and Bolivia. In J. Cenoz & F. Genesee (Eds.), *Beyond bilingualism: Multilingualism and multilingual education* (pp. 206–242). Clevedon: Multilingual Matters.

Hornberger, N. H., & Skilton-Sylvester, E. (2000). Revisiting the continua of biliteracy: International and critical perspectives. *Language and Education, 14*(2), 96–122.

Horner, K., & Weber, J. J. (2008). The language situation in Luxembourg. *Current Issues in Language Planning, 9*(1), 69–128.

Howard, E. R., & Christian, D. (1997). The development of bilingualism and biliteracy in two-way immersion students. Paper presented at the Annual Meeting of the American Educational Research Association, Chicago.

Howard, E. R., & Christian, D. (2002). *Two-way immersion 101: Designing and implementing a two-way immersion program at the elementary level.* Santa Cruz, CA, and Washington, DC: Center for Research on Education, Diversity & Excellence and Center for Applied Linguistics.

Howard, E. R., Christian, D., & Genesee, F. (2004). *The development of bilingualism and biliteracy from grades 3 to 5: A summary of findings from the CAL/CREDE study of two-way immersion education.* Santa Cruz, CA, and Washington, DC: Center for Research on Education, Diversity & Excellence and Center for Applied Linguistics.

Howard, E. R., & Loeb, M. I. (1999). "Como se dice windsurfing?" Talking about writing in two-way immersion classrooms. Paper presented at the Annual Statewide Conference for Teachers of Linguistically and Culturally Diverse Students.

Howard, E. R., Olague, N., & Rodgers, D. (2003). *The dual language program planner: A guide for designing and implementing dual language programs.* Santa Cruz, CA, and Washington DC: Center for Applied Linguistics and Center for Research on Education, Diversity & Excellence.

Howard, E. R., & Sugarman, J. (2007). *Realizing the vision of two-way immersion: Fostering effective programs and classrooms.* Washington: Center for Applied Linguistics and Delta Systems.

Howard, E. R., Sugarman, J., & Christian, D. (2003). *Trends in two-way immersion education: A review of the research.* Report 63. Baltimore: Center for Research on the Education of Students Placed At Risk.

Howard, E. R., Sugarman, J., Christian, D., Lindholm-Leary, K. J., & Rogers, D. (2007). *Guiding principles for dual language education* (2nd ed.). Washington, DC: Center for Applied Linguistics.

Hudelson, S. (1984). Kan yu ret an rayt in Ingles: Children becoming literate in English as a second language. *TESOL Quarterly, 18,* 221–238.

Hudelson, S. (1987). The role of native language literacy in the education of language minority children. *Language Arts, 64,* 827–841.

Huerta-Macías, A., & Quintero, E. (1992). Code-switching, bilingualism, and biliteracy: A case study. *Bilingual Research Journal, 16*(3–4), 69–90.

Hunt, G. (2007). Failure to thrive? The community language strand of the additive bilingual project at an Eastern Cape Community School, South Africa. *Journal of Research in Reading, 30*(1), 80–96.

Hurtado, A., & Vega, L. (2004). Shift happens: Spanish and English transmission between parents and their children. *Journal of Social Issues, 60,* 137–155.

Huss, L., Grima Camilleri, A., & King, K. (2003). *Transcending monolingualism: Linguistic revitalisation in education.* Lisse, NL: Swets and Zeitlinger.

Igoa, C. (1995). *The inner world of the immigrant child.* Mahwah, NJ: Lawrence Erlbaum.

Internet World Stats. (2009). Internet World Users by Language: Top 10 languages. http://www.internetworldstats.com/stats7.htm

Irujo, S. (1998). *Teaching bilingual children: Beliefs and behaviors.* Boston: Heinle & Heinle.

Irujo, S. (2005). Promoting native language and culture in English-only programs. Retrieved June 12, 2009, from http://www.coursecrafters.com/ELL-Outlook/2005/may_jun/ELLOutlookITIArticle3.htm

Jacob, E., Rottenberg, L., Patrick, S., & Wheeler, E. (1996). Cooperative learning: Context and opportunities for acquiring academic English. *TESOL Quarterly, 30*(2), 253–280.

Jacobson, R. (1990). Allocating two languages as a key feature of a bilingual methodology. In R. Jacobson & C. Faltis (Eds.), *Language distribution issues in bilingual schooling* (pp. 3–17). Philadelphia, PA: Multilingual Matters.

James, M., & Woll, B. (2004). Black Deaf or Deaf Black? Being Black and Deaf in Britain. In A. Pavlenko & A. Blackledge (Eds.), *Negotiation of identities in multilingual contexts* (pp. 125–161). Clevedon, UK: Multilingual Matters.

Jimenez, R. T., Garcia, G. E., & Pearson, D. (1995). Three children, two languages, and strategic reading: Case studies in bilingual/monolingual reading. *American Educational Research Journal, 32*(1), 67–97.

Jisa, M. (2000). Language mixing in the weak language: Evidence from two children. *Journal of Pragmatics, 32*, 1363–1386.

Johnson, R. K., & Swain, M. (Eds.). (1997). *Immersion education: International perspectives.* Cambridge: Cambridge University Press.

Jones, S., & McEwen, M. (2000). A conceptual model of multiple dimensions of identity. *Journal of College Development, 41*(4), 405–415.

Jordan, C. (1995). Creating cultures of schooling: Historical and conceptual background of the KEEP/Rough Rock collaboration. *Bilingual Research Journal, 19*(1), 83–100.

Kachru, B. B. (1985). Standards, codification, and sociolinguistic realism: The English language in the outer circle. In R. Quirk & H. G. Widdowson (Eds.), *English in the world: Teaching and learning the language and literatures* (pp. 11–30). Cambridge: Cambridge University Press.

Kachru, B. B., Kachru, Y., & Nelson, C. (2006). *The handbook of world Englishes.* New York: Wiley-Blackwell.

Kagan, S. (1986). Cooperative learning and sociocultural factors in schooling. In C. F. Leyba (Ed.), *Beyond language: Social and sociocultural factors in schooling language minority students* (pp. 231–298). Los Angeles: Evaluation, Dissemination, and Assessment Center, California State University.

Kenner, C. (2004). *Becoming biliterate: Young children learning different writing systems.* Stoke on Trent: Trentham Books.

King, K. (2004). Language policy and local planning in South America: New directions for enrichment bilingual education in the Andes. *International Journal of Bilingual Education and Bilingualism, 7*(5), 334–347.

King, K., & Benson, C. (2004). Indigenous language education in Bolivia and Ecuador: Contexts, changes, and challenges. In J. W. Tollefson & A. B. M. Tsui (Eds.), *Medium of instruction policies: Which agenda? Whose agenda?* (pp. 241–263). Mahwah, NJ: Lawrence Erlbaum.

King, K., Schilling-Estes, N., Fogle, L., Lou, J. J., & Soukup, B. (Eds.). (2008). *Sustaining linguistic diversity: Endangered and minority languages and language varieties.* Washington, DC: Georgetown University Press.

Kirkpatrick, A. (2007). *World Englishes: Implications for international communication and English language teaching.* Cambridge: Cambridge University Press.

Klingner, J. K., & Harry, B. (2006). The special education referral and decision-making process for English language learners: Child study team meetings and placement conferences. *Teachers College Record, 108*(11), 2247–2281.

Kloss, H. (1998). *The American bilingual tradition.* Washington, DC, and McHenry, IL: Center for Applied Linguistics and Delta Systems.

Knell, E., Siegel, L. S., Qiang, H., Miao, P., Yanping, C., Lin, Z., et al. (2007). Early English immersion and literacy in Xi'an, China. *Modern Language Journal, 91*(3), 395–417.

Kondo-Brown, K. (2005). Differences in language skills: Heritage language learners. *Modern Language Journal, 89*(4), 563–581.

Krashen, S. D. (1985). *The input hypothesis: Issues and implications.* London: Longman.

Krashen, S. D. (2004). The acquisition of academic English by children in two-way programs: What does the research say? Paper presented at the Annual Meeting of the National Association for Bilingual Education, Albuquerque. Retrieved June 15, 2009, from http://www.sdkrashen.com/articles/the_2-way_issue/all.html

Krashen, S. D., & Terrell, D. (1983). *The natural approach: Language acquisition in the classroom.* Hayward, CA: Alemany Press.

Krashen, S. D., & McField, G. (2005). What works? Reviewing the latest evidence on bilingual education. *Language Learner, 34*, 7–10.

Krauss, M. (1992). The world's languages in crisis. *Language, 68*(1), 4–24.

Kymlicka, W., & Patten, A. (2003). Language rights and political theory. *Annual Review of Applied Linguistics, 23*, 3–21.

LaFromboise, T. D., Coleman, H., & Gerton, J. (1993). Psychological impact of biculturalism: Evidence and theory. *Psychological Bulletin, 114,* 395–412.

Laing, S. P., & Kamhi, A. (2003). Alternative assessment of language and literacy in culturally and linguistically diverse populations. *Language, Speech, and Hearing Services in Schools, 34,* 44–55.

Lambert, W. E. (1977). The effects of bilingualism on the individual: Cognitive and sociocultural consequences. In P. A. Hornby (Ed.), *Bilingualism: Psychological, social, and educational implications* (pp. 15–27). New York: Academic Press.

Lambert, W. E., & Cazabon, M. (1994). *Students' views of the Amigos program.* Santa Cruz, CA: National Center for Research on Cultural Diversity and Second Language Learning.

Lambert, W. E., & Taylor, D. M. (1996). Language in the lives of ethnic minorities: Cuban American families in Miami. *Applied Linguistics, 17*(4), 477–500.

Lane, H. (2005). Ethnicity, ethics, and the Deaf-World. *Journal of Deaf Studies and Deaf Education, 10*(3), 291–310.

Lantolf, J. P. (2000). *Sociocultural theory and second language learning.* Oxford: Oxford University Press.

Lao, C. (2004). Parent's attitudes toward Chinese-English bilingual education and Chinese-language use. *Bilingual Research Journal, 28*(1), 99–117.

Laosa, L. M. (1978). Inequality in the classroom: Observational research on teacher-student interactions. *Aztlan, 8*(283), 51–67.

Lasagabaster, D. (2001). Bilingualism, immersion programmes and language learning in the Basque country. *Journal of Multilingual and Multicultural Development, 1*(2), 401–425.

LaSasso, C., & Lollis, J. (2003). Survey of residential and day schools for deaf students in the United States that identify themselves as bilingual-bicultural programs. *Journal of Deaf Studies and Deaf Education, 8*(1), 79–91.

Lau v. Nichols, 414 U.S. 563 (1974).

Lee, P. (1996). Cognitive development in bilingual children: A case for bilingual instruction in early childhood education. *Bilingual Research Journal, 20*(2&3), 499–522.

Leeman, J. (2004). Racializing language: A history of linguistic ideologies in the U.S. census. *Journal of Language and Politics, 3*(3), 507–534.

Legarreta, D. (1977). Language choice in bilingual classrooms. *TESOL Quarterly, 11*(1), 9–16.

Leman, J. (1990). Multilingualism as norm, monolingualism as exception: The Foyer model in Brussels. In M. Byram & J. Leman (Eds.), *Bicultural and trilingual education* (pp. 7–29). Clevedon: Multilingual Matters.

Lemberger, N. (1997). *Bilingual education: Teachers' narratives*. Mahwah: Lawrence Erlbaum.

Leopold, W. (1939). *Speech development of a bilingual child: A linguist's record. Vol. I. Vocabulary growth in the first two years*, Evanston, IL: Northwestern University Press.

Leu, J.D., Castek, J., Coiro, J., Gort, M., Henry, L., & Lima, C. (2005). *Developing new literacies among multilingual learners in the elementary grades.* Retrieved September 6, 2010 from http://www.ucop.edu/elltech/leupaper010605.pdf.

Leung, C. (2006). Language and content in bilingual education. *Linguistics and Education, 16*, 238–252.

Leung, C., Harris, R., & Rampton, B. (1997). The idealised native speaker, reified ethnicities, and classroom realities. *TESOL Quarterly, 31*(3), 543–560.

Levin, T., & Shohamy, E. (2008). Achievement of immigrant students in mathematics and academic Hebrew in Israeli school: A large-scale evaluation study. *Studies in Educational Evaluation 34*(1), 1–14.

Lewis, M. P. (Ed.) (2009). *Ethnologue: Languages of the World.* (16th Ed.). Dallas, TX.: *SIL International.* Online version: http://ethnologue.com.

Li, D. (1998). "It's always more difficult than you plan and imagine:" Teachers' perceived difficulties in introducing the communicative approach in South Korea. *TESOL Quarterly, 32*(4), 677.

Li, G. (2006). Biliteracy and trilingual practices in the home context: Case studies of Chinese-Canadian children. *Journal of Early Childhood Literacy, 6*(3), 355–381.

Lian, B., & Oneal, J. R. (1997). Cultural diversity and economic development: A cross-national study of 98 countries, 1960–1985. *Economic Development and Cultural Change, 46*(1), 61–77.

Liang, X. (2006). Identity and language functions: High school Chinese immigrant students' code-switching dilemmas in ESL classes. *Journal of Language, Identity, and Education, 5*(2), 143–167.

Lightbown, P. M., & Spada, N. (2009). *How languages are learned* (3rd ed.). Oxford: Oxford University Press.

Lin, A. (2006). Beyond linguistic purism in language-in-education policy and practice: Exploring bilingual pedagogies in a Hong Kong science classroom. *Language and Education, 20*(4), 287–305.

Lindholm-Leary, K. J. (2001). *Dual language education.* Clevedon: Multilingual Matters.

Lindholm, K. J. (1987). *Directory of two-way bilingual programs: Two-way bilingual education for language minority and language majority students.* Los Angeles: University of California Center for Language Education and Research.

Linquanti, R. (2001). *The redesignation dilemma: Challenges and choices in fostering meaningful accountability for English learners.* Sacramento, CA: West Ed/Linguistic Minority Research Institute.

Linton, A. (2004). A critical mass model of bilingualism among U.S.-born Hispanics. *Social Forces, 83*(1), 279–314.

Linton, A. (2007). Spanish-English immersion in the wake of California Proposition 227: Five cases. *Intercultural Education, 18*(2), 111–128.

Lipka, J. (1994). Language, power, and pedagogy: Whose school is it? *Peabody Journal of Education, 69*(2), 71–93.

Lippi-Green, R. (1997). *English with an accent: Language, ideology, and discrimination in the United States.* New York: Routledge.

Ljosland, R. (2007). English in Norwegian academia: A step toward diglossia? *World Englishes, 26*(4), 395–410.

Lo Bianco, J. (2005). Globalisation and national communities of communication. *Language Problems and Language Planning, 29*(2), 109–133.

Losey, K. M. (1995). Mexican American students and classrooms interaction: An overview and critique. *Review of Educational Research, 65*(3), 283–318.

Louie, V. (2006). Growing up in transnational worlds: Identities among second -generation Chinese and Dominicans. *Identities: Global Studies in Culture and Power, 13*, 363–394.

Lucas, T. (1993). Secondary schooling for students becoming bilingual. In B. M. Arias & U. Casanova (Eds.), *Bilingual education: Politics, practice, research* (pp. 113–143). Chicago: University of Chicago Press.

Lucas, T., & Grinberg, J. (2008). Responding to the linguistic reality of mainstream classrooms: Preparing all teachers to teach English language learners. In M. Cochran-Smith, S. Feiman-Nemser, & D. J. McIntyre (Eds.), *Handbook of research on teacher education: Enduring questions in changing contexts* (3rd ed., pp. 606–636). New York: Routledge.

Lucas, T., Henze, R. C., & Donato, R. (1990). Promoting the success of Latino language minority students: An exploratory study of six high schools. *Harvard Educational Review, 60*(3), 315–340.

Lucas, T., & Katz, A. (1994). Reframing the debate: The roles of native languages in English-only programs for language minority students. *TESOL Quarterly, 28* (3), 537–561.

Lucas, T., & Wagner, S. (1999). Facilitating secondary English language learners' transition into the mainstream. *TESOL Journal*, 8 (4): 6–13

Luke, A., McHoul, A. W., & Mey, J. L. (1990). On the limits of language planning: Class, State, and Power. In R. B. J. Baldauf & A. Luke (Eds.) *Language planning and education in Australasia and the South Pacific* (pp. 25–44). Clevedon: Multilingual Matters.

Lyons, J. J. (1990, March). The past and future directions of federal bilingual-education policy. *Annals of the American Academy of Political and Social Sciences*, 508, 66–80.

Macaro, E. (2001). Analysing student teachers' codeswitching in foreign language classrooms: Theories and decision making. *Modern Language Journal*, 85(4), 531–548.

MacDonald, H. (2009). The bilingual ban that worked. *City Journal*, 19(4). Retrieved September 19, 2010 from http://www.city-journal.org/2009/19_4_bilingual-education.html.

Mace-Matluck, B. J. (1990). The effective schools movement: Implications for Title VII and bilingual education projects. In L. M. Malavé (Ed.), *Annual Conference Journal NABE '88–'89* (pp. 83–95). Washington, DC: NABE.

Macedo, D., Dendrinos, B., & Gounari, P. (2003). *The hegemony of English*. Boulder, CO: Paradigm.

Mackey, A. (2007). *Conversational interaction in second language acquisition. A series of empirical studies.* Oxford: Oxford University Press.

Mackey, W., & Beebe, V. N. (1977). *Bilingual schools for a bicultural community: Miami's adaptation to the Cuban refugees*. Rowley, MA: Newbury House.

MacSwan, J., Rolstad, K., & Glass, G. V. (2002). Do some school-age children have no language? Some problems of construct validity in the Pre-Las Español. *Bilingual Research Journal*, 26(2), 213–238.

Maffi, L. (Ed.). (2001). *On biocultural diversity: Linking language, knowledge, and the environment*. Washington, DC: Smithsonian Institution Press.

Maneva, B. (2004). "Maman, je suis polyglotte": A case study of multilingual language acquisition from 0 to 5 years. *International Journal of Multilingualism*, 1(2), 109–122.

Mann, C. C. (2000). Reviewing ethnolinguistic vitality: The case of Anglo-Nigerian pidgin. *Journal of Sociolinguistics*, 4(3), 458–474.

Manyak, P. C. (2002). "Welcome to salon 110": The consequences of hybrid literacy practices in a primary-grade English immersion class. *Bilingual Research Journal*, 26(2), 213–234.

Marshall, J. (2004). *Language change and sociolinguistics: Rethinking social networks*. New York: Palgrave Macmillan.

Martí, F., Ortega, P., Idiazabal, I., Barreña, A., Juaristi, P., Junyent, C., et. al. (2005). *Words and worlds: World languages review*. Clevedon, UK: Multilingual Matters.

Martin, D. (2009). *Language disabilities in cultural and linguistic diversity*. Bristol, UK: Multilingual Matters.

Martin Jones, M., & Jones, K. (2000). Multilingual literacies. In M. Martin Jones & K. Jones (Eds.), *Multilingual literacies* (pp. 1–16). Philadelphia: John Benjamins.

Martin, P., Bhatt, A., Bhojani, N., & Creese, A. (2006). Managing bilingual interactions in a Gujarati complementary school in Leicester. *Language and Education*, 20(1), 5–22.

Martinez, R. B. (2000). Language and tribal sovereignty: Whose language is it anyway? *Theory into Practice*, 39(4), 211–219.

Martínez-Roldán, C. M., & Sayer, P. (2006). Reading through linguistic borderlands: Latino students' transactions with narrative text. *Journal of Early Childhood Literacy*, 6(3), 293–322.

Matsinhe, S. F. (2005). The language situation in Mozambique: Current developments and prospects. In B. Brock-Utne & R. K. Hopson (Eds.), *Languages of instruction for African emancipation: Focus on postcolonial contexts and considerations* (pp. 119–146). Cape Town: Centre for Advanced Studies of African Society.

May, S. (2000). Uncommon languages: The challenges and possibilities of minority language rights. *Journal of Multilingual and Multicultural Development*, 21(5), 366–385.

May, S. (2002). Maori-medium education in Aotearoa/New Zealand. In J. W. Tollefson & A. B. M. Tsui (Eds.), *Medium of instruction policies: Which agenda? Whose agenda?* (pp. 21–42). Mahwah, NJ: Lawrence Erlbaum.

May, S., & Aikman, S. (2003). Indigenous education: addressing current issues and developments. *Comparative Education*, 39(2), 139–145.

McCarty, T. L. (1993). Federal language policy and American Indian education. *Bilingual Research Journal*, 17(1&2), 13–34.

McCarty, T. L. (1994). Bilingual education policy and the empowerment of American Indian communities (1). *Journal of Educational Issues of Language Minority Students*, 14, 23–42.

McCarty, T. L. (1998). Schooling, resistance and American Indian languages. *International Journal of the Sociology of Language*, 132, 27–41.

McCarty, T. L. (2002). *A place to be Navajo: Rough Rock and the struggle for self-determination in indigenous schooling*. Mahwah: Lawrence Erlbaum.

McCarty, T. L. (2003). Revitalizing indigenous languages in homogenizing times. *Comparative Education*, 39(2), 147–163.

McCarty, T. L., Romero, M. E., & Zepeda, O. (2006). Reclaiming the gift: Indigenous youth counter-narratives on native language loss and revitalization. *American Indian Quarterly*, 30(1&2), 28–48.

McCollum, P. (1999). Learning to value English: Cultural capital in a two-way bilingual program. *Bilingual Research Journal*, 23(2&3), 113–134.

McGroarty, M. (1989). The benefits of cooperative learning arrangements in second language. *NABE Journal*, 13(2), 127–143.

McGroarty, M. (1997). Language policy in the USA: National values, local loyalties, pragmatic pressures. In W. Eggington & H. Wren (Eds.), *Language policy: Dominant English, pluralist challenges.* (pp. 67–90). Philadelphia: John Benjamins.

McKay, S. L. (2003). Toward an appropriate EIL pedagogy: Re-examining common ELT assumptions. *International Journal of Applied Linguistics, 13*(1), 1–22.

McKay, S. L., & Wong, S.-L. C. (1996). Multiple discourses, multiple identities: Investment and agency in second-language learning among Chinese adolescent immigrant students. *Harvard Educational Review, 66*(3), 577–608.

McLaughlin, B. (1984). *Second language acquisition in childhood: Vol. 1. Preschool children.* Mahwah, NJ: Lawrence Erlbaum.

McLaughlin, F. (1995). Haalpular identity as response to Wolofization. *African Languages and Cultures, 8*(2), 153–168.

McQuillan, J., & Tse, L. (1995). Child language brokering in linguistic minority communities: Effects on cultural interaction, cognition, and literacy. *Language and Education, 9*(3), 195–215.

Meier, K., & Stewart, J. (1991). *The politics of Hispanic education.* Albany: SUNY Press.

Meisel, J. M. (2007). The weaker language in early child bilingualism: Acquiring a first language as a second language? *Applied Psycholinguistics, 28,* 495–514.

Menken, K. (2006). Teaching to the test: How No Child Left Behind impacts language policy, curriculum, and instruction for English language learners. *Bilingual Research Journal, 30*(2), 521–546.

Menken, K. (2008). *English learners left behind: Standardized testing as language policy.* Clevedon: Multilingual Matters.

Menken, K., & Antunez, B. (2001). *An overview of the preparation and certification of teachers working with limited English proficient LEP students.* Washington, DC: National Clearinghouse for Bilingual Education.

Menyuk, P., & Brisk, M. E. (2005). *Language development and education. Children with varying language experience.* New York, NY: Palgrave.

Meyer v. Nebraska, 324 F. 3d 655 (1923).

Milk, R. D. (1990). Integrating language and content: Implications for language distribution in bilingual classrooms. In R. Jacobson & C. Faltis (Eds.), *Language distribution issues in bilingual schooling* (pp. 32–44). Bristol: Multilingual Matters.

Milroy, J., & Milroy, L. (1999). *Authority in language: Investigating standard English* (3rd ed.). London: Routledge.

Milroy, L. (2001). Bridging the micro-macro gap: Social change, social networks, and bilingual repertoires. In J. Klatter-Folmer & P. Van Avermaet (Eds.), *Theories on language maintenance and loss of minority languages: Towards a more integrated explanatory framework* (pp. 39–64). New York: Waxmann Muenster.

Minow, M. (1985). Learning to live with the dilemma of difference: Bilingual and special education. *Law and Contemporary Problems, 48*(2), 157–211.

Miramontes, O. B., & Commins, N. (2005). *Linguistic diversity and teaching.* Mahwah, NJ: Lawrence Erlbaum.

Miramontes, O. B., Nadeau, A., & Commins, N. (1997). *Restructuring schools for linguistic diversity: Linking decision-making to effective programs.* New York: Teachers College Press.

Mitchell, R., & Miles, F. (2004). *Second language learning theories* (2nd ed.). London: Arnold.

Moll, L. C. (1992). Bilingual classrooms and community analysis: Some recent trends. *Educational Researcher, 21*(2), 20–24.

Moll, L. C., Amanti, C., Neff, D., & Gonzalez, N. (1992). Funds of knowledge for teaching: A qualitative approach to developing strategic connections between homes and classrooms. *Theory into Practice, 31*(132–141).

Moll, L. C., & Dworin, J. E. (1996). Biliteracy developments in classrooms: Social dynamics and cultural possibilities. In D. Hicks (Ed.), *Discourse, learning, and schooling.* Cambridge: Cambridge University Press.

Moll, L. C., & Gonzalez, N. (1996). Teachers as social scientists: Learning about culture from household research. In P. M. Hall (Ed.), *Race, ethnicity, and multiculturalism: Missouri Symposium on Research and Educational Policy* (Vol. I, pp. 89–114). New York: Garland.

Montague, N. S., & Meza-Zaragosa, E. (1999). Elicited response in the pre-kindergarten setting with a dual-language program: Good or bad idea? *Bilingual Research Journal, 23*(2–3), 289–296.

Morales, A., & Hanson, W. (2005). Language brokering: An integrative review of the literature. *Hispanic Journal of Behavioral Sciences, 27*(4), 471–503.

Morgan, W. J. (2005). Local knowledge and globalization: Are they compatible? In C. Cullingford & S. Gunn (Eds.), *Globalization, education, and culture shock* (pp. 35–74). Burlington: Ashgate.

Mufwene, S. S. (2002). Colonization, globalization, and the plight of "weak" languages. *Journal of Linguistics, 38,* 375–395.

Mufwene, S. S. (2003). *Globalisation and the myth of the killer languages: What's really going on?* Perspectives on Endangerment conference, Evangelische Akademie Tutzing, Germany, November 4–6. Retrieved September 16, 2010 from http://humanities.uchicago.edu/faculty/ mufwene/publications/globalization -killerLanguages.pdf

Mufwene, S. S. (2006a). *Language endangerment: An embarrassment for linguistics.* Paper presented at the 42nd meeting of the Chicago Linguistics Society.

Mufwene, S. S. (2006b). *Myths and globalization: What African demolinguistics reveals. Presentation,* University of British Columbia, September 15, University of Georgia.

Muhlhausler, P. (2000). Language planning and language ecology. *Current Issues in Language Planning, 1*(3), 306–367.

Muller, A., & Baetens Beardsmore, H. (2004). Multilingual interaction in plurilingual classes: European school practice. *International Journal of Bilingual Education and Bilingualism, 7*(1), 24–42.

Myers-Scotton, C. (2006a). How codeswitching as an available option empowers bilinguals. In M. Putz, J. A. Fishman, & J. Aertselaer (Eds.), *Along the routes of power: Explorations of empowerment through language* (pp. 73–87). New York: Mouton de Gruyter.

Myers-Scotton, C. (2006b). *Multiple voices: An introduction to bilingualism*. Malden, MA: Blackwell.

National Reading Panel. (2000). *Teaching children to read: An evidence-based assessment of the scientific research literature on reading and its implications for reading instruction, reports of the subgroups*. Rockville, MD: National Institute of Child Health and Human Development.

Nettle, D. (1998). Exploring global patterns of language diversity. *Journal of Anthropological Archeology, 17*, 354–374.

Nettle, D. (2000). Linguistic fragmentation and the wealth of nations: The Fishman-Pool hypothesis reexamined. *Economic Development and Cultural Change, 48*(2), 335–348.

Nettle, D., & Romaine, S. (2000). *Vanishing voices: The extinction of the world's languages*. New York: Oxford University Press.

Nieto, S. (1999). *The light in their eyes: Creating multicultural learning communities*. New York: Teachers College Press.

Nieto, S. (2002). *Language, culture, and teaching: Critical perspectives for a new century*. Mahwah, NJ: Lawrence Erlbaum.

Nieto, S., & Bode, P. (2008). *Affirming diversity* (5th ed.). Boston: Pearson.

Northwest Regional Education Laboratory & Center for District and School Development (2004). *English language learner (ELL) programs at the secondary level in relation to student performance*. Portland, Oregon: Author.

Norton, B. (1997). Language, identity, and the ownership of English. *TESOL Quarterly, 31*(3), 409–428.

Nunan, D. (2003). The impact of English as a global language on educational policies and practices in the Asian-pacific region. *TESOL Quarterly, 37*(4), 589–613.

O'Brien, K. B. (1961). Education, Americanization, and the Supreme Court: The 1920s. *American Quarterly, 13*(2), 161–171.

Odlin, T. (1989). *Language transfer: Cross-linguistic influence in language learning*. Cambridge: Cambridge University Press.

Ogbu, J., & Simons, H. (1998). Voluntary and involuntary minorities: A cultural-ecological theory of school performance with some implications for education. *Anthropology & Education Quarterly, 29*(2), 155–188.

Okano, K. (2006). The impact of immigrants on long-lasting minorities in Japanese schools: Globalisation from below. *Language and Education, 20*(4), 338–354.

Oller, D. K., & Eilers, R. E. (Eds.). (2002). *Language and literacy in bilingual children*. Clevedon: Multilingual Matters.

Oller, D. K., Pearson, B. Z., & Cobo-Lewis, A. B. (2007). Profile effects in early bilingual language and literacy. *Applied Psycholinguistics, 28*, 191–280.

Olneck, M. R. (1989). Americanization and the education of immigrants, 1900–1925: An analysis of symbolic action. *American Journal of Education, 97*(4), 398–423.

Olsen, L. (1997). *Made in America: Immigrant students in our public schools*. New York: New Press.

Orellana, M. F., Dorner, L., & Pulido, L. (2003). Accessing assets: Immigrant youth's work as family translators or "para-phrasers." *Social Problems, 50*(4), 505–524.

Orfield, G. (2009). *Reviving the goal of an integrated society: A 21st century challenge*. Los Angeles, CA: The Civil Rights Project/Proyecto Derechos Civiles at UCLA.

Osborne, A. B. (1996). Practice into theory into practice: Culturally relevant pedagogy for students we have marginalized and normalized. *Anthropology & Education Quarterly, 27*(3), 285–314.

Ovando, C. J., Collier, V., & Combs, M. C. (2003). *Bilingual and ESL classrooms: Teaching in multicultural contexts*. New York: McGraw Hill.

Pacini-Ketchabaw, V., Bernhard, J. K., & Freire, M. (2001). Struggling to preserve home language: The experiences of Latino students and families in the Canadian school system. *Bilingual Research Journal, 25*(1&2), 1–28.

Padilla, A. M. (2006). Bicultural social development. *Hispanic Journal of Behavioral Sciences, 28*(4), 467–497.

Paikeday, T. M. (1985). May I kill the native speaker? *TESOL Quarterly, 19*(2), 390–395.

Paratore, J. R., Melzi, G., & Krol-Sinclair, B. (1999). *What should we expect of family literacy? Experiences of Latino children whose parents participate in an intergenerational literacy project*. Newark: International Reading Association.

Parrish, T. B., Perez, M., Merickel, A., & Linquanti, R. (2006). *Effects of the implementation of Proposition 227 on the education of English language learners, K–12: Findings from a five-year Evaluation; Final Report*. San Francisco: American Institutes of Research/WestEd.

Patanaray-Ching, J., Kitt-Hinrichs, B., & Nguyen, V. (2006). Inquiring into a second language and the culture of school. *Language Arts, 83*(3), 248–257.

Paulston, C. B. (1994). *Linguistic minorities in multilingual settings*. Philadelphia: John Benjamins.

Pavlenko, A. (2005). "Ask each pupil about her methods of cleaning": Ideologies of language and gender in Americanization instruction. *International Journal of Bilingual Education and Bilingualism, 8*(4), 275–297.

Pavlenko, A., & Blackledge, A. (2004). Introduction: New theoretical approaches to the study of negotiation of identities in multilingual contexts. In A. Pavlenko & A. Blackledge (Eds.), *Negotiation of identities in multilingual contexts* (pp. 1–33). Clevedon, UK: Multilingual Matters.

Pawels, A. (2005). Maintaining the community language in Australia: Challenges and roles for families. *International Journal of Bilingual Education and Bilingualism, 8*(2/3), 124–131.

Pearson, B. Z., Fernandez, S., & Oller, D. K. (1995). Cross-language synonyms in the lexicon of bilingual infants: One language or two? *Journal of Child Language, 22*, 345–368.

Pearson, B. Z., Umbel, V. C., Andrews de Flores, P., & Cobo-Lewis, A. B. (1999). *Measuring cross-language vocabulary in childhood bilinguals at different stages of development*. Austin: Texas Research Symposium on Language Diversity.

Pease-Alvarez, L. (2002). Moving beyond linear trajectories of language shift and bilingual language socialization. *Hispanic Journal of Behavioral Sciences, 24*(2), 114–137.

Pennycook, A. (1994). *The cultural politics of English as an international language*. Essex: Pearson Education.

Pennycook, A. (1998). *English and the discourses of colonialism*. New York: Routledge.

Pennycook, A. (2001). Lessons from colonial language policies. In R. D. González (Ed.), *Language ideologies: Critical perspectives on the official English movement*. (Vol. 2, pp. 195–219). Urbana, IL: National Council of Teachers of English.

Pennycook, A. (2003). Global Englishes, Rip Slyme, and performativity. *Journal of Sociolinguistics, 7*(4), 513–533.

Pennycook, A. (2004). Language policy and the ecological turn. *Language Policy, 3*, 213–239.

Peregoy, S. F., & Boyle, O. F. (2008). *Reading, writing and learning in ESL. A resource book for teaching K-12 English learners* (5th ed.). Boston: Pearson.

Peréz, B. (1998). *Sociocultural context of language and literacy*. Mahwah, NJ: Lawrence Erlbaum.

Peréz, B. (2004). *Becoming biliterate: A study of two-way bilingual immersion education*. Mahwah, NJ: Lawrence Erlbaum.

Perlmann, J. (1990, March). Historical legacies: 1840–1920. *Annals of the American Academy of Political and Social Sciences, 508*, 27–37.

Peyton, J. K., Lewelling, V., W. , & Winke, P. (2001). Spanish for Spanish speakers: Developing dual language proficiency. Retrieved March 12, 2006, from http://www.cal.org/resources/digest/spanish_native.html

Peyton, J. K., Ranard, D., & McGinnis, S. (2001). *Heritage language in America: Preserving a national resource; Language in education—Theory and practice*. McHenry, IL: Delta Systems Company.

Phelan, P., Davidson, A. L., & Cao, H. T. (1991). Students' multiple worlds: Negotiating the boundaries of family, peer, and school cultures. *Anthropology & Education Quarterly, 22*, 225–250.

Philips, S. U. (1972). Participant structure and communicative competence: Warm Springs children in community and classroom. In C. B. Cazden, V. P. John, & D. Hymes (Eds.), *Functions of language in the classroom* (pp. 370–394). New York: Teachers College Press.

Phillipson, R. (1992). *Linguistic imperialism*. Oxford: Oxford University Press.

Phillipson, R. (1998). Globalizing English: Are linguistic human rights an alternative to linguistic imperialism? *Language Sciences, 20*(1), 101–112.

Phillipson, R. (2001). English for globalisation or for the world's people? *International Review of Education, 47*(3–4), 185–200.

Phillipson, R. (2003). *English only? Challenging language policy*. London: Routledge.

Phinney, J. S., & Ong, A. D. (2007). Conceptualizing and measurement of ethnic identity: Current status and future directions. *Journal of Counseling Psychology, 54*(3), 271–281.

Pierce, M. (2000). *Native/Non-native speaker collaboration in a two-way bilingual education class*. Unpublished doctoral dissertation, Boston University.

Pool, J. (1991). The official language problem. *American Political Science Review, 85*(2), 495–514.

Pop, V. (2009, September 25). English most studied language in EU schools. *EUObserver*. Retrieved September 16, 2010 from http://euobserver.com/851/28719

Portes, A., & Hao, L. (1998, October). E pluribus unum: Bilingualism and the loss of language in the second generation. *Sociology of Education, 71*, 269–294.

Portes, A., & Rumbaut, R. G. (2001). *Legacies: The story of the immigrant second generation*. Berkeley and Los Angeles: University of California Press.

Portes, A., & Schauffler, R. (1994). Language and the second generation: Bilingualism yesterday and today. *International Migration Review, 28*(4), 640–661.

Potowski, K. (2004). Student Spanish use and investment in a dual immersion classroom: Implications for second language acquisition and heritage language maintenance. *Modern Language Journal, 88*(1), 75–101.

Potowski, K. (2006). *Language and identity in a dual immersion school*. Clevedon: Multilingual Matters.

Purkey, S. C., & Smith, M. P. (1983). Effective schools: A review. *Elementary School Journal, 83*(4), 427–452.

Qin, D. B. (2006). "Our child doesn't talk to us anymore": Alienation in immigrant Chinese families. *Anthropology & Education Quarterly, 37*(2), 162–179.

Quay, S. (2001). Managing linguistic boundaries in early trilingual development. In J. Cenoz & F. Genesee (Eds.), *Trends in bilingual acquisition* (pp. 149–200). Philadelphia: John Benjamins.

Ramirez, J. D. (1998). *Performance of redesignated fluent-English-proficient students (R-FEPs)*. San Francisco: San Francisco Unified School District.

Ramirez, J. D., Yuen, S. D., Ramey, D. R., & Pasta, D. (1990). *Final report: Longitudinal study of immersion strategy, early-exit and late-exit transitional bilingual education programs for language-minority children*. San Mateo: Aguirre International.

Ramos, F. (2007). What do parents think about two-way bilingual education? An analysis of responses. *Journal of Latinos and Education, 6*(2), 139–150.

Rampton, B. (2005). *Crossing: Language and ethnicity among adolescents*. Manchester: St. Jerome.

Rappa, A. L., & Wee, L. (2006). *Language policy and modernity in Southeast Asia*. New York: Springer.

Read, A. W. (1937). Bilingualism in the Middle Colonies, 1725–1775. *American Speech, 12*(2), 93–99.

Reagan, T. (2002). Toward an "Archeology of Deafness": Etic and emic constructions of identity in conflict. *Journal of Language, Identity, and Education, 1*(1), 41–66.

Reagan, T. (2005). *Non-western educational traditions: Indigenous approaches to educational thought and practice* (3rd ed.). Mahwah: Lawrence Erlbaum.

Regalsky, P., & Laurie, N. (2007). "The school, whose place is this?" The deep structures of the hidden curriculum in indigenous education in Bolivia. *Comparative Education, 43*(2), 231–251.

Reyes, I. (2004). Functions of code switching in school children's conversations. *Bilingual Research Journal, 28*(1), 77–98.

Reyes, I., & Azuara, P. (2008). Emergent biliteracy in young Mexican immigrant children. *Reading Research Quarterly, 43*(4), 374–398.

Reyhner, J. (1993). American Indian language policy and school success. *Journal of Educational Issues of Language Minority Students, 12*(3), 35–59.

Reyhner, J., Cantoni, G., St. Clair, R. N., & Yazzie, E. P. (1999). *Revitalizing indigenous languages.* Fifth Annual Stabilizing Indigenous Languages Symposium, Louisville, KY, May 15–16, 1998. Flagstaff: Northern Arizona University.

Ricento, T. (2000). Historical and theoretical perspectives in language policy and planning. *Journal of Sociolinguistics, 4*(2), 196–213.

Ricento, T. (2003). The discursive construction of Americanism. *Discourse & Society, 14*(5), 611–637.

Ricento, T. (2005). Problems with the "language-as-resource" discourse in the promotion of heritage languages in the U.S.A. *Journal of Sociolinguistics, 9*(3), 348–368.

Ricento, T., & Hornberger, N. H. (1996). Unpeeling the onion: Language planning and policy and the ELT professional. *TESOL Quarterly, 30*, 401–427.

Rickford, J. (1996). Regional and social variation. In S. L. McKay & N. H. Hornberger (Eds.), *Sociolinguistics and language teaching* (pp. 151–194). New York: Cambridge University Press.

Rickford, J. R. (1999). *African American Vernacular English: Features, evolution, educational implications.* Malden, MA: Blackwell.

Rizvi, H. (2007). Native people score historic political victory. *Terraviva UN Journal, 15*, 1–2.

Robertson, R. (1995). Glocalization: Time-space and homogeneity-heterogeneity. In M. Featherstone, S. Lash, & R. Robertson (Eds.), *Global modernities* (pp. 25–44). London: Sage.

Roca, A., & Colombi, M. C. (2003). *Mi lengua: Spanish as a heritage language in the United States.* Washington, DC: George Washington University Press.

Rodriguez, R. (1982). *Hunger of memory: The education of Richard Rodriguez.* New York: Bantam Books.

Rolstad, K., Mahoney, K., & Glass, G. V. (2005). The big picture: A meta-analysis of program effectiveness research on English language learners. *Educational Policy, 19*(4), 572–594.

Romaine, S. (1995). *Bilingualism* (2nd ed.). Malden, MA: Blackwell.

Romaine, S. (2000). *Language in society: An introduction to sociolinguistics* (2nd ed.). Oxford: Oxford University Press.

Rossell, C. H., & Baker, K. (1996). The educational effectiveness of bilingual education. *Research in the Teaching of English, 30*(1), 7–74.

Rossell, C. H., & Ross, M. J. (1986). The social science evidence on bilingual education. *Journal of Law & Education, 15*(4), 385–419.

Rubinstein-Avila, E. (2003). Negotiating power and redefining literacy expertise: Buddy reading in a dual-immersion programme. *Journal of Research in Reading, 26*(1), 83–97.

Rubinstein-Avila, E. (2007). From the Dominican Republic to Drew High: What counts as literacy for Yanira Lara? *Reading Research Quarterly, 42*(4), 568–589.

Ruiz, R. (1984). Orientations in language planning. *NABE Journal, 7*(2), 15–34.

Rumbaut, R. G., Massey, D. S., & Bean, F. D. (2006). Linguistic life expectancies: Immigrant language retention in Southern California. *Population and Development Review, 32*(3), 447–460.

Rumberger, R. & Gándara, P. (2004). Seeking Equity in the Education of California's English Learners, *Teachers College Record, 106*, 2031–2055.

Russell, C. (2002). Language, violence, and Indian mis-education. *American Indian Culture and Research Journal, 26*(4), 97–112.

Sakai, S., & D'Angelo, J. F. (2005). A vision of World Englishes in the expanding circle. *World Englishes, 24*(3), 323–327.

Sánchez, M. T. (2006). *Teachers' experiences implementing English-only educational legislation.* Unpublished doctoral dissertation, Lynch School of Education, Boston College.

Sanz, C. (2000). Bilingual education enhances third language acquisition: Evidence from Catalonia. *Applied Psycholinguistics, 21*, 23–44.

Saunders, G. (1988). *Bilingual children: From birth to teens.* Philadelphia: Multilingual Matters.

Saunders, W., & O'Brien, G. (2006). Oral language. In F. Genesee, K. J. Lindholm-Leary, W. M. Saunders, & D. Christian (Eds.), *Educating English language learners: A synthesis of research evidence* (pp. 14–63). Cambridge: Cambridge University Press.

Saville, M. R., & Troike, R. (1971). *A handbook of bilingual education.* Washington, DC: Teachers of English to Speakers of Other Languages.

Schecter, S. R., & Bayley, R. (1997). Language socialization practices and cultural identity: Case studies of Mexican-descent families in California and Texas. *TESOL Quarterly, 31*(3), 513–541.

Schecter, S. R., & Bayley, R. (1998). Concurrence and complementarity: Mexican-background parents' decisions about language and schooling. *Journal for a Just and Caring Education, 4*(1), 47–64.

Schechter, S. R., & Cummins, J. (2003). *Multilingual education in practice: Using diversity as a resource.* Portsmouth: Heinemann.

Schinke-Llano, L. (1983). Foreigner talk in content classrooms. In H. W. Seliger & M. J. Long (Eds.), *Classroom-oriented research in second language acquisition* (pp. 146–168). Rowley, MA: Newbury House.

Schleppegrell, M. J. (2004). *The language of schooling: A functional linguistics perspective*. Mahwah, NJ: Lawrence Erlbaum.

Schlossman, S. L. (1983a). Is there an American tradition of bilingual education? German in the public elementary schools, 1840–1919. *American Journal of Education, 91*(2), 139–186.

Schlossman, S. L. (1983b). Self-evident remedy? George I. Sanchez, segregation, and enduring dilemmas in bilingual education. *Teachers College Record, 84*(4), 871–907.

Schmid, C. (2000). The politics of English only in the United States: Historical, social, and legal aspects. In R. D. Gonzalez (Ed.), *Language ideologies: Critical perspectives on the Official English movement* (Vol. 1, pp. 62–86). Urbana: National Council of Teachers of English.

Schmidt, R. S. (2000). *Language policies and identity politics in the United States*. Philadelphia: Temple University Press.

Schwarzer, D. (2001). *Noah's ark: One child's voyage into multiliteracy*. Portsmouth, NH: Heinemann.

Seidlhofer, B. (2004). Research perspectives on teaching English as a lingual franca. *Annual Review of Applied Linguistics, 24*, 209–239.

Semali, L. (1999). Community as classroom: Dilemmas of valuing African indigenous literacy in education. *International Review of Education, 45*(3&4), 305–319.

Serra, C. (2007). Assessing CLIL at primary school: A longitudinal study. *International Journal of Bilingual Education and Bilingualism, 10*(5), 582–602.

Shannon, S. M. (1995). The hegemony of English: A case study of one bilingual classroom as a site of resistance. *Linguistics and Education, 7*, 175–200.

Shin, S. J. (2005). *Developing in two languages*. Clevedon: Multilingual Matters.

Shohamy, E. (2001). Democratic assessment as an alternative. *Language Testing, 18*(4), 373–391.

Shohamy, E. (2006). *Language policy: Hidden agendas and new approaches*. New York: Routledge.

Short, D. J. (2002a). Language learning in sheltered social studies classes. *TESOL Journal, 11*(1), 18–24.

Short, D. J. (2002b). Newcomer programs: An educational alternative for secondary immigrant students. *Education and Urban Society, 34*(2), 173–198.

Short, D. J., & Boyson, B. A. (2003, December). Establishing an effective newcomer program. Retrieved June 15, 2009, from http://www.cal.org/resources/Digest/ 0312short.html

Short, D. J., & Boyson, B. A. (2004). *Creating access: Language and academic programs for secondary school newcomers*. Washington, DC, and McHenry, IL: Center for Applied Linguistics and Delta Systems.

Short, D. J., & Fitzsimmons, S. (2007). *Double the work: Challenges and solutions to acquiring language and academic literacy for adolescent English language learners*. New York: Alliance for Excellent Education.

Silverstein, M. (1996). Monoglot "standard" in America: Standardization and metaphors of linguistic hegemony. In D. Brenneis & R. K. S. Macaylay (Eds.), *The matrix of language: Contemporary linguistic anthropology* (pp. 284–306). Boulder: Westview.

Simms, L., & Thumann, H. (2007). In search of a new, linguistically and culturally sensitive paradigm in Deaf education. *American Annals of the Deaf, 152*(3), 302–311.

Skelton, T., & Valentine, G. (2003). "It feels like being Deaf is normal": An exploration into the complexities of defining D/deafness and young D/deaf people's identities. *Canadian Geographer, 47*(4), 451–466.

Skiba, R. J., Simmons, A. B., Ritter, S., Gibb, A. C., Rausch, M. K., Cuadrado, J., et al. (2008). Achieving equity in special education: History, status, and current challenges. *Exceptional Children, 74*(3), 264–288.

Skutnabb-Kangas, T. (2000). *Linguistic genocide in education or worldwide diversity and human rights?* Mahwah: Lawrence Erlbaum.

Skutnabb-Kangas, T. (2001). Linguistic human rights in education for language maintenance. In L. Maffi (Ed.), *On biocultural diversity: Linking language, knowledge, and the environment* (pp. 397–411). Washington, DC: Smithsonian Institution Press.

Skutnabb-Kangas, T. (2002). Marvelous human rights rhetoric and grim realities: Language rights in education. *Journal of Language, Identity, and Education, 1*(3), 179–205.

Skutnabb-Kangas, T., Maffi, L., & Harman, D. (2003). *Sharing a world of difference: The earth's linguistic, cultural, and biodiversity*. Paris: UNESCO, Terralingua, and World Wide Fund for Nature.

Slavin, R. E. (1985). Cooperative learning: Applying contact theory in desegregated schools. *Journal of Social Issues, 41*(3), 45–62.

Sleeter, C. E., & Stillman, J. (2005). Standardizing knowledge in a multicultural society. *Curriculum Inquiry, 35*(1), 27–46.

Slowinski, J. (1998). SOCRATES invades Central Europe. *Education Policy Analysis Archives, 6*(9). Available at http://epaa.asu.edu/epaa/v6n9.html

Smiler, K., & McKee, R. L. (2006). Perceptions of Maori deaf identity in New Zealand. *Journal of Deaf Studies and Deaf Education, 12*(1), 93–111.

Smith, L. H. (1999). *Decolonizing methodologies, Research and indigenous peoples*. London: Zedbooks.

Smith, P. (2002). Ni a pocha va a llegar: Minority language loss and dual language schooling in the U.S.–Mexico borderlands. *Southwest Journal of Linguistics, 21*(1), 165–183.

Smith, P., & Arnot-Hopffer, E. (1998). Exito bilingue: Promoting Spanish literacy in a dual language immersion program. *Bilingual Research Journal, 22*(2–4), 103–119.

Soltero, S. (2004). *Dual language teaching and learning in two languages.* New York: Pearson.

Sonntag, S. K., & Pool, J. (1987). Linguistic denial and linguistic self-denial: American ideologies of language. *Language Problems and Language Planning, 11*(1), 47–65.

Soto, L. D., Smrekar, J., L., & Nekcovei, D. L. (1999). *Preserving home languages and cultures in the classroom: Challenges and opportunities.* Washington, DC: National Clearinghouse for Bilingual Education.

Spener, D. (1988). Transitional bilingual education and the socialization of immigrants. *Harvard Educational Review, 58*(2), 133–153.

Spolsky, B. (2003). Reassessing Maori regeneration. *Language in Society, 32,* 553–578.

Spolsky, B. (2004). *Language policy.* Cambridge: Cambridge University Press.

Stairs, A. (1994). The cultural negotiation of indigenous education: Between microethnography and model-building. *Peabody Journal of Education, 69*(2), 154–171.

Stefanakis, E. H. (2002). *Multiple intelligences and portfolios: A window into the learner's mind.* Portsmouth: Heinemann.

Stefanakis, E. H. (2004). Assessing young immigrant students. In M. Sadowski (Ed.), *Teaching immigrant and second-language students: Strategies for success* (pp. 21–32). Cambridge: Harvard Education Press.

Stevens, G. (1999). A century of U.S. censuses and the language characteristics of immigrants. *Demography, 36*(3), 387–397.

Strong, M. (1995). A review of bilingual-bicultural programs for deaf children in North America. *American Annals of the Deaf, 122,* 84–94.

Stroud, C. (2001). African mother-tongue programmes and the politics of language: Linguistic citizenship versus linguistic human rights. *Journal of Multilingual and Multicultural Development, 22*(4), 339–355.

Stroud, C. (2003). Postmodernist perspectives on local languages: African mother-tongue education in times of globalisation. *International Journal of Bilingual Education and Bilingualism, 6*(1), 17–36.

Sutton, M., & Levinson, B. A. U. (2000). Introduction: Policy as/in practice; A sociocultural approach to the study of educational policy. In M. Sutton & B. A. U. Levinson (Eds.), *Policy as Practice: Toward a comparative sociocultural analysis of educational policy* (pp. 1–22). Westport: Ablex.

Swain, M. (1995). Three functions of output in second language learning. In G. Cook & B. Seidlhofer (Eds.), *Principles and practice in applied linguistics: Studies in honour of H. G. Woodson* (pp. 125–144). Oxford: Oxford University Press.

Szasz, M. C. (1983). American Indian education: Historical perspective. *Peabody Journal of Education, 61*(1), 109–112.

Takahashi-Breines, H. (2002). The role of teacher-talk in a dual-language immersion third grade classroom. *Bilingual Research Journal, 26*(2), 213–235.

Tatum, B. D. (1997). *Why are all the black kids sitting together in the cafeteria?" and other conversations about race.* New York: Basic Books.

Teitelbaum, H., & Hiller, R. J. (1977). Bilingual education: The legal mandate. *Harvard Educational Review, 47*(2), 128–170.

Thomas, W. P., & Collier, V. P. (1997). *School effectiveness for language minority students.* Washington, DC: National Clearinghouse for Bilingual Education.

Thomas, W. P., & Collier, V. P. (2002). *A national study of school effectiveness for language minority students' long-term academic achievement.* Santa Cruz, CA: Center for Research on Education, Diversity & Excellence.

Tollefson, J. W., & Tsui, A. B. M. (Eds.). (2004). *Medium of instruction policies: Which agendas? Whose agenda?* Mahwah, NJ: Lawrence Erlbaum.

Tong, F., Irby, B., Lara-Alecio, R., & Mathes, P. (2008). English and Spanish acquisition by Hispanic second graders in developmental bilingual programs. *Hispanic Journal of Behavioral Sciences, 30*(4), 500–529.

Tse, L. (1995). Language brokering among Latino adolescents: Prevalence, attitudes, and school performance. *Hispanic Journal of Behavioral Sciences, 17*(2), 180–193.

Tse, L. (2001). Resisting and reversing language shift: Heritage-language resilience among U.S. native biliterates. *Harvard Educational Review, 71*(4), 676–708.

Tseng, V., & Fuligni, A. J. (2000). Parent-adolescent language use and relationships among immigrant families with East-Asian, Filipino, and Latin American backgrounds. *Journal of Marriage and the Family, 62,* 465–476.

Tucker, J. T. (2006). *The ESL logjam: Waiting times for adult ESL classes and the impact on English learners.* Los Angeles: National Association of Latino Elected and Appointed Officials

UNESCO (United Nations Educational, Scientific, and Cultural Organization). (1953). *The use of the vernacular languages in education.* Monographs on Foundations of Education, No. 8. Paris: Author.

UNESCO. (1993). Index to *Red book on endangered languages: Northeast Asia.* Retrieved September 6, 2010 from. http://www.helsinki.fi/~tasalmin/nasia_index.html

UNESCO. (2003). *Education for a multilingual word.* Paris: Author.

United Nations. (2009). International migration report 2006: A global assessment. Available at http://www.un.org/esa/population/publications/2006_MigrationRep/report.htm

U.S. General Accounting Office. (1987). *Bilingual education: A new look at the research evidence.* Washington, DC: Author.

U.S. General Accountability Office (2009). *Comprehensive plan needed to address persistent foreign language shortfalls.* Washington, DC: Author.

Ustunel, E., & Seedhouse, P. (2005). Why that, in that language, right now? Code-switching and pedagogical focus. *International Journal of Applied Linguistics, 15*(3), 302–325.

Valadez, C., MacSwan, J., & Martinez, C. (2002). Toward a new view of low achieving bilinguals:

A study of linguistic competence in designated "semilinguals."*Bilingual Review, 25*(3), 238–248.

Valdés, G. (1997). Dual-language immersion programs: A cautionary note concerning the education of language-minority students. *Harvard Educational Review, 67*(3), 391–429.

Valdés, G. (2001). *Learning and not learning English.* New York: Teachers College Press.

Valdés, G. (2005). Bilingualism, heritage language learners, and SLA research: Opportunities lost or seized? *Modern Language Journal, 89*(3), 410–434.

Valdés, G., & Figueroa, R. A. (1996). *Bilingualism and testing: A special case of bias.* Norwood: Ablex.

Valdés, G., Fishman, J. A., Chavez, R., & William, P. (2006). *Developing minority language resources: The case of Spanish in California.* Clevedon, UK: Multilingual Matters.

Valenzuela, A. (1999). *Subtractive schooling: U.S.–Mexican youth and the politics of caring.* New York: State University of New York Press.

Van Parijs, P. (2000). The ground floor of the world: On the socio-economic consequences of linguistic globalisation. *International Political Science Research, 21*(2), 217–233.

Van Sluys, K., & Reinier, R. (2006). "Seeing the possibilities": Learning from, with, and about multilingual classrooms communities. *Language Arts, 83*(4), 321–331.

VanPatten, B. (2003). *From input to output: A teacher's guide to second language acquisition.* Boston: McGraw-Hill.

Varenne, H., & McDermott, R. (1995). Culture "as" disability. *Anthropology & Education Quarterly, 26*(3), 324–348.

Varonis, E., & Gass, S. (1984). Non-native/ non-native conversations: A model for negotiation of meaning. *Applied Linguistics, 6*(1), 71–90.

Vasquez, V. M. (2004). *Negotiating critical literacies with young children.* Mahwah: Lawrence Erlbaum.

Velez-Ibanez, C., & Greenberg, J. (1992). Formation and transformation of funds of knowledge among U.S. Mexican households. *Anthropology & Education Quarterly, 23*, 313–335.

Veltman, C. (1983). Anglicization in the United States: Language environment and language practice of American adolescents. *International Journal of the Sociology of Language, 44*, 99–114.

Verplaetse, L. S. (2000). How content teachers allocate turns to limited English proficient students. *Journal of Education, 182*(3), 19–35.

Volk, D., & de Acosta, M. (2001). Many different ladders, many ways to climb: Literacy events in the bilingual classrooms, homes, and community of three Puerto Rican kindergartners. *Journal of Early Childhood Literacy, 1*(2), 193–224.

Walby, S. (2000). Analyzing social inequality in the twenty-first century: Globalization and modernity restructure inequality. *Contemporary Sociology, 29*(6), 813–818.

Walker, A., Shafer, J., & Iiams, M. (2004). "Not in my classroom": Teacher attitudes towards English language learners in the mainstream classroom. *NABE Journal of Research and Practice, 2*(1), 130–160.

Walters, J. (2005). *Bilingualism: The sociopragmatic-psycholinguistic interface.* Mahwah: Lawrence Erlbaum.

Wannagat, U. (2007). Learning through L2–content and language integrated learning (CLIL) and English as medium of instruction (EMI). *International Journal of Bilingual Education and Bilingualism, 10*(5), 663–682.

Wee, L. (2005). Intra-language discrimination and linguistic human rights: The case of Singlish. *Applied Linguistics, 26*(1), 48–69.

Wei, L. (2000). Dimensions of bilingualism. In L. Wei (Ed.), *The bilingualism reader* (pp. 3–25). New York: Routledge.

Wei, L. (2006). Complementary schools, past, present and future. *Language and Education, 20*(1), 76–83.

Weisskirch, R. S. (2005). The relationship of language brokering to ethnic identity for Latino early adolescents. *Hispanic Journal of Behavioral Sciences, 27*(3), 286–299.

Whitemore, K. F., & Crowell, C. G. (2005). Bilingual education students reflect on their language education: Reinventing a classroom 10 years later. *Journal of Adolescent & Adult Literacy, 49*(4), 270–285.

Whitin, P., & Whitin, D. J. (2006). Making connections through math-related book pairs. *Teaching Children Mathematics, 13*(4), 196–202.

Wierzbicki, S. (2004). *Beyond the immigrant enclave network change and assimilation.* New York: LFB Scholarly Publishing

Wiese, A.-M., & García, E. E. (1998). The Bilingual Education Act: Language minority students and equal educational opportunity. *Bilingual Research Journal, 22*(1), 1–18.

Wiley, T. G. (1996). Languages and planning policies. In S. L. McKay & N. H. Hornberger (Eds.), *Sociolinguistics and language teaching* (pp. 103–148). New York: Cambridge University Press.

Wiley, T. G. (2000). Continuity and change in the function of language ideologies in the United States. In T. Ricento (Ed.), *Ideology, politics, and language policies: Focus on English* (pp. 67–85). Philadelphia: John Benjamins.

Wiley, T. G., & Lukes, M. (1996). English-only and standard English ideologies in the U.S. *TESOL Quarterly, 30*(3), 511–535.

Willig, A. C. (1985). A meta-analysis of selected studies on the effectiveness of bilingual education. *Review of Educational Research, 55*(3), 269–317.

Wodak, R., de Cillia, R., Reisigl, M., & Liebhart, K. (1999). *The discursive construction of national identity.* Edinburgh: Edinburgh University Press.

Woolard, K. A. (1989). Sentences in the language prison: The rhetorical structuring of an American language policy debate. *American Ethnologist, 16*(2), 268–278.

Woolard, K. A. (1998). Language ideology as a field of inquiry. In B. B. Schieffelin, K. A. Woolard, & P. V. Kroskrity (Eds.), *Language Ideologies: Practice and Theory* (pp. 3–47). New York: Oxford University Press.

Woolard, K. A., & Schieffelin, B. B. (1994). Language ideology. *Annual Review of Anthropology, 23*, 55–82.

Wright, S. (2004). *Language policy and language planning: From nationalism to globalisation.* New York: Palgrave MacMillan.

Wright, W. E. (2002). A catch-22 for language learners. *Educational Leadership, 64*(3), 22–27.

Wright, W. E. (2005). The political spectacle of Arizona's Proposition 203. *Educational Policy, 19*(5), 662–700.

Wright, W. E., & Choi, D. (2006). The impact of language and high-stakes testing policies on elementary school English language learners in Arizona. *Education Policy Analysis Archives, 14*(13). Available at http://epaa.asu.edu/ojs/article/view/84

Yang, J. (2005). English as a third language among China's ethnic minorities. *International Journal of Bilingual Education and Bilingualism, 8*(6), 552–567.

Yoo, S.-Y., & Lee, S. (2006). Mother brand English as an effective approach to teach English for young children as a foreign language in Korea. *Reading Improvement, 43*(4), 185–193.

Ytsma, J. (2001). Towards a typology of trilingual primary education. *International Journal of Bilingual Education and Bilingualism, 4*(1), 11–22.

Zappert, L. T., & Cruz, B. R. (1977). *Bilingual education: An appraisal of empirical research.* Berkeley: BAHIA Press.

Zentella, A. C. (1997). *Growing up bilingual.* Malden, MA: Blackwell.

Zhou, M. (1997). Growing up American: The challenge confronting immigrant children and children of immigrants. *Annual Review of Sociology, 23*, 63–95.

Index

Note: Page numbers followed by f refer to figures; page numbers followed by t refer to tables.